Sensation Drama, 1860–1880

Edinburgh Critical Editions of Nineteenth-Century Texts
Series Editor: Julian Wolfreys

Published titles

Richard Jefferies, After London; or Wild England
Edited by Mark Frost

Marie Corelli, A Romance of Two Worlds: A Novel
Edited by Andrew Radford

Sensation Drama, 1860–1880: An Anthology
Edited by Joanna Hofer-Robinson and Beth Palmer

Agriculture and the Land: Richard Jefferies' Essays and Letters
Edited by Rebecca Welshman

Maxwell Gray, The Silence of Dean Maitland: A Novel
Edited by Julian Wolfreys

Jane Porter, Thaddeus of Warsaw: A Novel
Edited by Thomas McLean and Ruth Knezevich

Forthcoming titles

William Barnes, Dialect Poems in The Dorset County Chronicle
Edited by Thomas Burton and Emma Mason

Geraldine Jewsbury, Critical Essays and Reviews (1849–1870)
Edited by Anne-Marie Beller

Hartley Coleridge, The Complete Poems
Edited by Nicola Healey

George Gissing, The Private Papers of Henry Ryecroft
Edited by Thomas Ue

Philip James Bailey, Festus: A Novel
Edited by Mischa Willett

William Morris on Socialism: Uncollected Essays
Edited by Florence Boos

Hubert Crackanthorpe, Wreckage: Seven Studies
Edited by David Malcolm

Visit the Edinburgh Critical Editions of Nineteenth-Century Texts
website at: edinburghuniversitypress.com/series/ecenct

Sensation Drama, 1860–1880

An Anthology

Edited by Joanna Hofer-Robinson
and Beth Palmer

EDINBURGH
University Press

Edinburgh University Press is one of the leading university presses in the UK.
We publish academic books and journals in our selected subject areas across the
humanities and social sciences, combining cutting-edge scholarship with high editorial
and production values to produce academic works of lasting importance. For more
information visit our website: edinburghuniversitypress.com

Edinburgh University Press Ltd
The Tun – Holyrood Road
12(2f) Jackson's Entry
Edinburgh EH8 8PJ

Typeset in 11/12.5 Baskerville and Times New Roman by
IDSUK (DataConnection) Ltd, and
printed and bound in Great Britain.

A CIP record for this book is available from the British Library

ISBN 978 1 4744 3953 4 (hardback)
ISBN 978 1 4744 3955 8 (webready PDF)
ISBN 978 1 4744 3956 5 (epub)

Contents

List of Illustrations

Grateful acknowledgement is made to the following sources for permission to reproduce material in this book that has been previously published elsewhere. Every effort has been made to trace copyright holders, but if any have been inadvertently overlooked, the publisher will be pleased to make the necessary arrangement at the first opportunity.

Acknowledgements

The advice of colleagues and the support of our friends and families have contributed significantly to our work on this anthology. Innumerable conversations, coffees and dinners have each played a part in bringing this project to completion; however, special thanks must be given to the following people: Oskar Cox Jensen, Michael Hofer-Robinson, Luke Holden, David Meyer, Kevin Murray and Kate Newey. Work on this collection has been carried out at the University of Surrey, University College Dublin and University College Cork, and we are grateful for the support and advice of colleagues at these institutions. The School of Literature and Languages, University of Surrey, has generously funded research assistance, research trips and imaging fees.

List of Archives

N.B. References to specific records are given in the notes.

Lord Chamberlain's Collection, British Library (London, UK)
Mander and Mitchenson Collection, University of Bristol (Bristol, UK)
Mary Braddon Archive, Canterbury Christchurch University
(Canterbury, UK)
Robert Lee Wolff Collection of Nineteenth Century Fiction, Harry
Ransom Center, The University of Texas at Austin (Austin, TX)
Theatre Collection, Houghton Library, Harvard (Cambridge, MA)
Pettingell Collection, Templeman Library, University of Kent
(Canterbury, UK)
V&A (Victoria and Albert Museum) Theatre and Performance
Archive (London, UK)

Glossary of Irish Words, as Anglicised in *The Colleen Bawn*

Translations provided by Dr Kevin Murray (University College Cork) unless otherwise stated.

Acushla < short form of Irish 'A chuisle mo chroí' (lit. 'o pulse of my heart') = **My heart's beloved!**

Agrah < 'a ghrá' = **My love! / My dear!**

Alanna < 'a leanbh' = **My child! / My darling!**

Aroon < 'a rún' = **My dear!**

Asthore < 'a stór' = **Darling!**

A suilish machree < 'A sholais mo chroí' = **O light of my heart!**

Avick < 'a mhic' = **My son! My lad!**

Avourneen < 'a mhuirnín' = **My darling! / My dear!**

Colleen Bawn < 'cailín bán' = **white or fair girl**

Colleen Ruaidh < 'cailín rua' = **red-haired girl**

Coppaleen < 'capaillín' = **little horse, pony**

Cruiskeen Lawn < 'crúsicín lán' (lit. 'a full little jug') = **a bumper (of liquor (often whiskey))**

Gore doutha = **without a doubt** (trans. Parkin (1987), p. 23)

Gramachree < 'ghrá mo chroí' = **O love of my heart!**

Machree < 'mo chroí' (lit. 'my heart') = **My darling!**

Mavourneen < 'mo mhuirnín' = **My darling! / My dear!**

Mulvather = **to perplex**

Shebeen < 'síbín' = **an unlicensed drinking house**

Spalpeen < 'spailpín' = **an agricultural labourer**

Thurra moa dhiol = **your soul to the devil** (Parkin (1987), p. 23)

Weerasthrue = **oh Mary, what sorrow!** (Parkin (1987), p. 23)

Whist = **Listen! / Be quiet!** (may derive from Irish *éist* 'listen!')

Worra = **broke, penniless**

Series Editor's Preface

The nineteenth century saw an unprecedented, prodigious production of literary texts. Many of these, often best-sellers or offering vital commentaries on cultural, political and philosophical issues of the period engendering debate, did not survive in print long into the twentieth century, regardless of putative quality, however measured. Edinburgh Critical Editions of Nineteenth-Century Texts seeks to bring back to the reading public and the scholarly eye works of undeniable importance during the time of their first publication and reception, which have, often unjustly, disappeared from print and readers' consciousness. Covering fiction, long and short, non-fiction prose and essays, and poetry, with comprehensive critical introductions and carefully chosen supporting appendices, germane to the text and the context of the volume, Edinburgh Critical Editions of Nineteenth-Century Texts provides definitive, annotated scholarly reprints.

Introduction

'Sensational gratifications', argues an anxious reviewer in the *St. James's Magazine* in 1862, are rushed after by an epicurean public in 'every species of entertainment'. Diverse performers, including tight-rope walkers, trapeze artists, novelists and dramatists, are alike discussed as caterers to an 'unwholesome taste'.[1] This reviewer was not alone in worrying over a new appetite for the artificial stimulation of the mind and body through plays, novels and other popular amusements. However, critics mustering against 'sensation', such as Margaret Oliphant writing anonymously in *Blackwood's Magazine*, found themselves ranged against influential supporters, including George Augustus Sala, Justin McCarthy and even G. H. Lewes, who were more enthusiastic about this contemporary phenomenon.[2] Scholars have, over the last thirty years or so, paid attention to sensation as a nexus for debates about public taste and morality in the 1860s. The vast majority of this work has focused on the sensation novel.[3] Early critical works, like Winifred Hughes's genre-defining monograph (1980), have been supplemented by more recent interventions approaching sensation fiction in relation to themes such as fashion, professionalism or imperialism.[4] Sensation fiction is now a frequently discussed topic in Victorian literary studies, and novels by Wilkie Collins and Mary Elizabeth Braddon are often found on undergraduate reading lists. Its dramatic counterpart has received less attention, even though it was just as contentious as sensation fiction. Indeed, the reviewer in the *St. James's Magazine* singles out 'dramatic representation' as the most pervasive form of sensation and feels 'obliged to record grave objections to such performances'.[5] Thought-provoking research has been undertaken on sensation drama and its audiences (Lynn Voskuil, Tiffany Watt-Smith), its relationship to modernity (Nicholas Daly) and to commodity culture (Kate Mattacks), and its positioning in terms of genre

---

1. Anon. (1862), pp. 340, 342.
2. Oliphant (1862), pp. 574–80; Sala (1868), pp. 449–58; McCarthy (1864), pp. 24–49; and Lewes (1863), pp. 132–44.
3. For valuable summaries of critical works in this field see Knight (2009) and Beller (2017).
4. See Choudhury (2016), Constantini (2015) and Banerjee (2014), respectively, for work on these topics.
5. Anon. (1862), p. 342.

(Caroline Radcliffe, Catriona Mills), gender (Sos Eltis, E. Ann Kaplan) and race (Ian Henderson, Katy Chiles, Sarah Meer). Yet, while famous figures such as Dion Boucicault and Wilkie Collins have been the focus of research, many of those writing for the stage remain relatively unknown and students of sensation drama face an uphill struggle in orienting themselves within a vast array of performance texts that are not always easily accessible. The project of this anthology is to provide access to scholarly editions of key sensation plays and to establish a critical framework to encourage further interest in this field. We aim to provide students and researchers with a starting point from which to undertake more detailed explorations of the genre by asking what was so different about the dramas produced in the 1860s and 1870s that caused contemporaries to note the arrival of a new style of drama.

While claiming sensation drama as a significant and distinct genre, this anthology also seeks to show how these plays fit into wider theatrical contexts. Both critics and advocates of sensation drew connections between sensation and melodrama in the 1860s. The *St. James's Magazine* asserts that sensation is a disreputable form by likening it to early nineteenth-century melodramas such as *Frankenstein* (1823). By contrast, an 1863 piece in the *London Review* sought to defend contemporary theatre from accusations of decay by tracing continuities of situations and style from Matthew Monk Lewis's gothic melodrama, *Castle Spectre* (1797), to contemporary sensational productions.[6] If there is a difference, the article suggests, then it is only that stage technologies are so much improved that modern plays are far more impressive and exciting. Nevertheless, a proliferation of commentary on the nature or 'philosophy' of sensation as a dramatic genre from the early 1860s on indicates that contemporaries registered a cultural shift in theatrical culture in this period, and that this change was crystallised by the sensation genre.[7] By 1864, the sensation drama was a distinct enough genre for Henry J. Byron to publish a volume of *Sensation Dramas for the Back-Drawing Room* giving amateur players the opportunity to act out – and send up – sensational tropes. Sensation drama can indeed be understood as a significant strand in a long and complex history of melodrama on stage, running from the eighteenth century right up to the contemporary moment, but it is also well worth exploring as a distinctive genre in its own right, an exploration we hope this anthology will facilitate.

Previous studies of sensation drama have generally focused on their trademark sensation scenes, the 'special effects-driven' climaxes

---

6. Anon. (1863), pp. 38–9, p. 38.
7. See the examples given above and many others, including: 'B' (1865), pp. 809–13; Mansel (1863), pp. 481–514; and Sala (1867), pp. 45–55.

enabled by significant advances in stage technologies in the mid-nineteenth century.[8] The dramas featured in this anthology are identifiably sensational because they feature impressive visual effects and stunts, such as a head-first dive to rescue the drowning heroine in *The Colleen Bawn* (1860), the last-minute rescue of a character tied to railway tracks as a locomotive approaches in *Under the Gaslight* (1867), and a spectacular avalanche in *The Missing Witness* (1874). These are the tip of the iceberg: sensation dramas staged all sorts of eye-popping scenes, from the eponymous heroine's acts of arson in William Suter's version of *Lady Audley's Secret* (1863) to a shipwreck at the Cape of Good Hope in T. W. Robertson's *For Love* (1867). These special effects were the primary attraction of sensation dramas, and – as the culmination of prolonged dramatic tension – were meant to set pulses racing and make hair stand on end. One reason why the critic writing in the *St. James's Magazine* is wary of sensation is because it addressed audiences' instincts rather than their intellect. The reviewer finds this troubling because such involuntary somatic responses cut across boundaries of class and education. Disparate audiences could be united by their felt reactions to sensation drama, even while the pricing of tickets meant that social classes typically remained physically segregated in the auditorium. But these effects did not just work on the body and bypass the mind or the emotions. Indeed, as Voskuil and others have argued, sensation paradoxically relied on the conscious cultivation of spontaneous feelings:

> Many spectators, after all, knew the plots on which a number of sensation plays were based, either from reading popular novels themselves or from talking them over on the streets. Others had read reviews of sensation plays in newspapers like the popular *Illustrated London News*. They knew how and what they were supposed to feel without relinquishing the sense of shock and spontaneity that was part of the experience of viewing sensation drama.[9]

Playgoers simultaneously recognised the theatricality of the special effects, and chose to suspend their disbelief in order to experience authentic thrills. Thus sensation scenes were much more than just showy effects calculated to shock audiences and boost ticket sales. They required sophisticated spectators, adept and active consumers of spectacle.

8. N. Daly (2009), p. 3.
9. Voskuil (2004), p. 85.

It was not just the shock value of these scenes that playgoers responded to; it was also often their verisimilitude. As Radcliffe argues, plays that stage extraordinary events frequently did so in realistic settings in order to 'place the receptor (audience) in the *same space* as the object viewed' and, in doing so, make what was 'out of bounds' accessible.[10] The 'out of bounds' might refer to a space the audience would not usually have access to, like a prison or courtroom, or it might refer to an event outside moral boundaries, like an on-stage murder or abduction. Either way, the verisimilitude of these scenes was supposed to reduce the perceived distance between the audience and the 'out of bounds'. Sensation scenes, then, curated a sense of immediacy – of direct contact between the audience and the action – which could provoke contradictory reactions of shock and pleasure simultaneously. The *Era* praised the attention to detail in F. B. Chatterton's 1874 revival of *Lost in London* at the Princess's Theatre (written by Watts Phillips and first staged in 1867). No 'continental theatre', the reviewer proudly asserts, 'ever produced such marvellous realism as the brougham which drives up to a villa in the Regent's park in this drama'.[11] Boucicault, the leading proponent of sensation drama, also used on-stage realism to engage audiences in his *Trial of Effie Deans* (1863), famous for its law court scene, and in *The Long Strike* (1866), his adaptation of *Mary Barton*, which featured what seemed to be a working telegraph office. Sensation scenes and the somatic responses they brought about could thus be created by mind-bogglingly *real* representations of the contemporary and quotidian, as much as by the extreme and more remotely plausible scenes of avalanches, shipwrecks and conflagrations.[12]

Some major sensation dramatists resented how important their sensation scenes became for reviewers and the public (even while they enjoyed significant financial returns) because this focus implied that their writing was not sophisticated, but merely formulated to facilitate a spectacular set piece. In a published letter '*To the Editor of the "Times"*' in 1862, for instance, Boucicault protested that *The Colleen Bawn*'s death-defying rescue scene was 'not introduced into the drama until it had been played for some time, and had achieved its popularity'.[13] Boucicault is not famous for his modesty. Nevertheless, he *is* an accomplished

10. Radcliffe (2009), p. 41.
11. Anon. (1874a), p. 11.
12. Although see N. Daly (2017), which suggests that fire was not actually a remote possibility in many nineteenth-century theatres.
13. Boucicault (1862), p. 203. Similarly, Augustin Daly's brother wrote that the effectiveness of *Under the Gaslight* (1867) to 'hold the spectator in breathless suspense [. . .] was wrought by moral agencies which were potent without the climax of the visible railroad train' that is the centrepiece of its sensation scene (J. F. Daly (1917), p. 75).

playwright: he engages with contemporary issues of gender, nation and race; his *dramatis personæ* challenge stock theatrical types; and his dialogue is laden with satirical quips. Whether his comments about *The Colleen Bawn*'s sensation scene have a basis in fact or not, then, if one takes his objection to the 'cant word "sensation"' seriously it is possible to look beyond these important special effects and perceive the recurrence of further tropes in sensation dramas which differentiate this genre of plays from earlier melodramas and later popular drama.

Firstly, sensation plays often refuse to give their audiences the same kind of resolution we usually find in melodrama, and the moral questions they pose are much less black and white. One reason for this is that the *dramatis personæ* do not necessarily adhere to stock types. For example, the heroine of Wilkie Collins's *The New Magdalen* (1873) is not a persecuted paragon of virtue, threatened by the machinations of a dastardly villain, but reveals both principled and designing characteristics. In this sense, Collins's play is distinct from earlier melodrama as well as the 'wicked woman' plays popular in the 1890s. Related to this moral complexity is the rejection of female passivity in favour of much more outspoken and vigorous female characters. In sensation plays, women rescue men (*Under the Gaslight*) or take decisive actions to alter the course of events, such as shooting threatening ruffians (*The Red Hand*, 1868) or engaging in a hand-to-hand struggle with a murderer (*The Missing Witness*). Mrs H. Young, or Melinda Young, forged a successful career writing for the East End theatres and specialised in morally ambiguous heroines, including the criminal protagonists of *Adèle d'Escars; or The Picklock of Paris* and *Eyes in the Dark* (both submitted to the censor in 1866 for staging at the Effingham Theatre). Sarah Lane, manager of the Britannia Theatre, gives us a similarly complex heroine in *Red Josephine* (1880, Britannia). Josephine is a gambler who commits a murderous act of vengeance for the man she loves yet the audience is directed to sympathise with her actions.[14] Sensation heroines sometimes reflect on their own agency, such as Anne Chute in *The Colleen Bawn*, who explicitly highlights her own autonomy by saying, 'I haven't a big brother to see after me – and self-protection is the first law of nature,' something a hand-wringing melodramatic heroine would never do.[15]

We also found a consistent interest in crime, mystery and violence. Abductions, shootings, stabbings, arson attacks, murders and attempted murders of all kinds feature repeatedly in sensation drama. At times, the over-accumulation of such incidents seems comic. A contemporary

14. However, see an interesting exploration of how far this attribution can be trusted in Davis (1999).
15. Boucicault, *The Colleen Bawn*, p. 124.

review of *The Red Hand* (1868) indicates that the sensational could quickly
tip into the ridiculous: 'Horrors are accumulated on horrors' head, without remorse, and the heroine is abducted four times – thrice in full sight
of the audience.'[16] However, sensation is not reducible to such extreme
events. In fact, the most successful and effective sensation dramas are
those which leave audiences with a troubling sense of irresolution, even
after the final curtain. For instance, extreme events are often interwoven
with a plot in which identities were faked, doubled or fraudulent in some
way. Illegitimate children feature with some frequency in sensation plots.
Towards the end of the Marryat and Young play, Miss Chester bravely
admits to her son that he is the 'bastard substitute for a dead child'.[17]
Although Rupert turns out to have been legitimate all along and the
family are reunited at the curtain drop, his uncertain status for much of
the play prompts an identity crisis from which much of the action ensues.
Mistaken identities are a key feature of sensation plays and both villains and heroes take on disguises that serve to highlight the contingency
of the audience's knowledge about any character seen on stage. Tom
Taylor's *Ticket of Leave Man* (1863) was influential in utilising disguise for
both its hero detective, Hawkshaw, and its criminal villain. Hawkshaw,
unwittingly talking to his masked nemesis, threatens: 'He has as many
outsides as he has aliases. You may identify him for a felon today, and
pull your hat off to him for a parson tomorrow. But I'll hunt him out
of all his skins.'[18] The removal of disguises as a dramatic *dénouement* is a
trope we see repeated in other sensation plays, like Suter's *Holly Bush Hall*
(1860), and which has a long afterlife on stage and screen.

Sensation scenes, stirring verisimilitude, daring women, emotional
extremes, violence, crime, fraud and mystery are potent ingredients.
Even Henry Morley, no admirer of sensation drama, admits that the
'strength of incident' to be found in such plays is impressive. Morley,
like many other contemporary critics, reserved his ire for the genre's
reliance 'on tricks of plot or stage effect' without a contextualising
development of story and character.[19] We suggest that such critics, in
concentrating only on their objections to clap-trap plots or unbeliev-
able characters, overlook the overall effect created by sensation plays.
It is certainly not easy to define and discuss audience affect, particularly at a historical distance. Even at the time, commentators found
sensation difficult to describe. The reviewer of *The Red Hand* eventually gives up trying to list precisely which features of the piece make it

16. Anon. (1868), pp. 752–62, pp. 752–3.
17. Marryat and Young, p. 301.
18. Taylor (1863), n.p.
19. Morley (1866), p. 367.

'ultra-sensational' and argues that this play is beyond description. The somatic response, or 'affective adhesive', simulated by sensation dramas was perhaps particularly difficult to pin down because it coexisted with the knowing management of those feelings by audiences.[20] This knowingness was shared by the sensation dramatists who self-consciously situated their work in the broader cultural contexts of sensation, and all the anxieties and excitements it stood for. *Miss Chester*, for example, self-consciously references sensational themes, while a character like Conn in Boucicault's *The Shaughraun* (1874) provides a comic and self-reflexive commentary on the play's sensational events.[21]

Although all of the plays presented in this anthology are linked by their engagement with one or more of the devices we have outlined above, we do not suggest that sensation drama can be defined purely by a set of tropes. In fact, the plays collected here suggest that sensation is a flexible, multi-layered genre, which picks up and discards its apparently typical characteristics to surprise and challenge the audience. It is a flexible but distinct form most popular from 1860 to 1880, and highly self-reflexive about its own performance codes and its status in the popular imaginary.

Sensational contexts

The place of sensation drama in the popular imaginary was undeniably linked to the sensation novel, a form popular during the same period which utilised many of the same tropes. Numerous sensation plays were adapted from the sensation novels of writers like Collins and Braddon. Andrew Maunder references fifty adaptations of Braddon's novels alone running during the later Victorian period in London and the provinces.[22] Helen C. Black, writing in 1893, tells us that 'at one time nine adaptations of [Marryat's] novels were running simultaneously in provincial theatres'.[23] Ellen Wood's *East Lynne* was both a best-selling novel and a perennial favourite of touring companies well into the twentieth century. Novels were not only a source of thrilling plotlines. Adaptation theorists have long since rejected fidelity criticism and favoured a view of adaptation as a process of creative dialogue between the adapter, their source and further cultural influences. Even as early as the 1870s,

---

20. Voskuil (2002), p. 245.
21. See p. 258 for references to bigamy and the deceased wife's sister controversy in *Miss Chester*.
22. Maunder (2013), p. 61.
23. Helen C. Black (1893), *Notable Women Authors of the Day*, Glasgow: David Bryce and Son, p. 90. Qtd in Newey (2005), p. 180.

however, sensation dramatists were acutely conscious of reciprocal pathways of intermedial exchange. Collins called the play and the novel 'Twin sisters', and thought carefully about how the demands of each genre necessitated the careful modulation of content across forms.[24] For example, as Janice Norwood has argued with respect to *The Woman in White* (1860), Collins purposefully redirected his dramatisations away from their fictive counterparts, both to create new suspense and to foil pirates.[25] While not wishing to underplay the importance of the links between sensation fiction and sensation plays, this anthology seeks to offer something of a corrective to prior critical reviews of sensation drama, which often privilege the novel by focusing on adaptations of well-known sensation fiction. Although the first play in this collection is an adaptation of Charles Reade's 1856 novel, *It Is Never Too Late to Mend*, this was itself adapted from Reade's play, *Gold* (1853), and so emphasises the messy interrelatedness of literary and dramatic representation in the period, rather than privileging one form above another.

As noted above, the other form with which sensation plays are often linked is melodrama. Originating in France as *mélo-drame* in the late eighteenth century, these plays accompanied by music first achieved popularity in Britain as part of the repertoire of illegitimate theatre performed in minor playhouses.[26] Yet, as the century progressed and the laws policing theatrical entertainments were revised, melodrama was widely popularised across patent and minor houses, and across the social classes. Described by Peter Brooks as a mode that 're-enacts the menace of evil and the eventual triumph of morality', it delivered a Manichean and polarised world view in which characters expressed 'basic psychic conditions' through heightened and hyperbolic speech and gesture.[27] Yet despite its typically black-and-white moral landscape, and its use of spectacular effects to stimulate audience excitement, Jacky Bratton (2003), Marc Brodie (2004) and Elaine Hadley (1995), among others, examine how melodrama became a forum for the negotiation and critique of social identities and political movements, such as the anti-Poor Law or temperance campaigns. Meanwhile, Caroline Radcliffe and Kate Newey each make cases for the 'metatheatrical awareness' of melodrama more broadly, considering the ways in which plays construct self-reflexive dialogues between the stage and the auditorium, or between a variety of media.[28] Sensation drama certainly echoes this 'metatheatrical awareness'

---

24. Wilkie Collins (1990 [1852]), p. xxxvii.
25. Norwood (2007), pp. 222–36. See also Pearson (2007) for a similar argument about Collins's adaptation of *The Moonstone*.
26. See Moody (2007), particularly 'The invention of illegitimate culture', pp. 10–47.
27. Brooks (1995 [1976]), pp. 15, 4.
28. Radcliffe (2009), pp. 38–52; Newey (1997), p. 85.

and it too could be used to express discontent around social problems such as alcohol abuse in Reade's *Drink* (1879) or female disempowerment in Marryat and Young's *Miss Chester*. Sensation plays coexisted with, rather than replaced, melodrama. Early nineteenth-century melodramas such as *The Miller and His Men* (1813) continued to be staged and printed in the second half of the century, and mid-century melodramas such as Boucicault's incredibly popular *The Corsican Brothers* (1852) or *The Relief of Lucknow* (1858) clearly feed into the sensation plays of the 1860s and beyond. Boucicault is typical of sensation dramatists in having straddled these overlapping categories – never quite letting go of melodrama, even while his later plays confront and challenge its formulaic plots, speech and characterisation. For instance, the domestic safety to which the melodrama usually returns its characters is disrupted by the many sensation plays that situate their unsettling plots in genteel domestic spaces, such as William Suter's adaptation of *Aurora Floyd* (1863). Simultaneously, however, these plays rely on audiences' recognition of the domestic trope in order to be effective.

It is conceivable that, as Michael Pisani argues, the most significant change between earlier melodramas and later sensation plays was that 'dramas of gritty realism – which had been "sensational" in their lurid effects since the 1830s in working-class playhouses like the Coburg or the Bowery – moved into theatres like the Princess's, Drury Lane, and even the Adelphi', so that 'the sordid and the prurient were to some degree legitimized, at least in middle-class consciousness'.[29] Melodrama certainly lacked respectability, even though, as Jane Moody (2007) argues, the circulation of actors and plots between the East and West Ends of London reveals its cross-class appeal. Certain critics may still have wished to deny the extent to which melodrama had an impact on Victorian theatrical cultures, but the cross-class phenomenon of sensation drama made continuing this claim untenable. Sensation dramas played to packed houses in the West End, and managers spent large sums of money to produce sensational special effects. Still, sensation was not merely gentrified melodrama. Indeed, our decision to include Hazlewood's, rather than Charles Reade's, adaptation of *Never Too Late to Mend* was made to emphasise the ongoing and fluid circulation of influence between East and West End theatres. It is both difficult to disentangle sensation from melodrama, and unproductive to claim that there was a definitive break. In Brooks's words, melodrama endured as an 'inescapable dimension of modern consciousness'.[30] However, there is value in understanding how sensation drama was conceived of as a

---

29. Pisani (2014), p. 170.
30. Brooks (1995 [1976]), p. vii. Elaine Hadley (1995) makes a similar argument.

distinct cultural phenomenon around 1860, which shifted the conditions of theatrical culture in the mid-Victorian period.

Theatrical conditions and cultures

While early melodramas staged fires and waterfalls to wow audiences,
by the 1860s technological changes in lighting (moving from oil to gas,
focusable limelight and, later, electricity), complex trap-work and stage
hydraulics, and new materials such as cheap metallic foils and more vivid
dyes for costumes, all expanded the possibilities for spectacle on stage in
the latter half of the nineteenth century.[31] An article in the *Era* in 1866
tells us that theatregoers 'are nightly calling into their presence the scenic artist, who has conjured up before them landscapes of surpassing
beauty or fairy palaces of dazzling grandeur' to applaud their work.[32]
William Beverley at Drury Lane, Frederick Fenton at the Victoria and his
brother Charles at the Strand are names mostly lost to us now, but 'viv-
idly impressed on the memory of the playgoer' of the 1860s and 1870s.[33]
This marks a significant change from earlier productions. Jerome K.
Jerome quips that 'the "entirely new and elaborate scenery" so minutely
described in the posters' was usually only the posturing of stage managers, at least 'at the minor theatres'.[34] However, the effectiveness of the
scenery in sensation dramas was genuine – even Henry Morley admits
that an impressive set can 'force' a success from unpromising material.[35]
Still, this sea-change in audience reception was not matched by a complete overhaul of stage technologies; just as melodrama continued to be
played alongside sensation plays, so new machinery coexisted with older
techniques. The beautiful blue gauze that created the startling effect of
shimmering water in *The Colleen Bawn* was made to ripple by the 'twenty
small men and boys underneath it' and the sound of the approaching
train in *Under the Gaslight* was brought about by both wind machines and
the off-stage thumping of hammers on iron boards.[36] Sensation plays
often still needed down-stage or carpenter's scenes, during which stage
hands working behind a drop could set up the complex staging required
for the next sensation scene. These scenes often used large 'practicables'
(three-dimensional stage fixtures on which actors could climb), such as
the ivy-covered tower in Boucicault's *The Shaughraun*. Shocking though

31. See Baugh (2005), pp. 324–5; Booth (1981), pp. 1–29, pp. 60–92.
32. Anon. (1866a), p. 4.
33. Ibid., p. 4.
34. Jerome (1891), p. 46.
35. Morley (1866), p. 258.
36. Pisani (2014), pp. 199, 170.

the effects were, therefore, behind-the-scenes personnel mediated the audience's perception of the new through a combination of established and novel means.

To ensure a return on the financial investment necessitated by the expensive sets and technologies of a sensation scene, managers had to be convinced that the play would maintain its popularity over a long run. Consequently, one effect of the genre's popularity was that the short, rapidly changing theatre programmes of the early nineteenth century changed to the longer runs that we still see in the West End today. This in turn helped to bring about what Joseph Donahue calls the 'demise of the old repertory company' but simultaneously offered the potential for more stable incomes for those actors lucky enough to be cast in long-running successes.[37] *The Colleen Bawn* broke records with its run of 230 performances over ten months in 1860–1, while *Peep o' Day* by E. E. Falconer ran for 346 consecutive nights between November 1861 and December 1862 at the Lyceum. Falconer played in both productions and must have felt that sensation drama was helping to make the usually peripatetic actor's life more comfortable, although many of his colleagues would still have found obtaining professional recognition and returns much more difficult.

In the 1860s, sensation dramatists also led the way in securing more favourable conditions for playwrights. Earlier in the nineteenth century, it was difficult for dramatists to make a living from playwrighting alone. Particularly in working-class theatres, such as those situated in London's East End, dramatists often received a flat fee of between £2 and £10 for each play, or they might be paid as little as 30 shillings a week as a 'house dramatist'.[38] The insatiable appetite for new drama kept up a constant demand for new work or pirated translations, and writers such as Andrew Halliday or J. R. Planché serviced that demand. C. H. Hazlewood is the most prolific of those working in the 1860s: 103 plays bearing his name were submitted to the Lord Chamberlain to be licensed between 1859 and 1869.[39] The fees paid to dramatists in West End theatres could be much higher, and Boucicault ensured even better returns when he pressured managers to adopt a new profit-sharing system in the 1860s. Boucicault's system derived from his experience of French and American theatres, 'in which author payments were reckoned on a scaled percentage of house receipts'.[40] Rather than accepting a flat rate

---

37. Donahue (2004), p. 254.
38. Stephens (1992), p. 66.
39. See Davis (1992) and Norwood (2014) on the Britannia and Hazlewood's significance as house dramatist to the theatre.
40. Stephens (1992), p. 54.

when he took *The Colleen Bawn* to London's Adelphi Theatre, Boucicault insisted on a contract which guaranteed him an equal share of the
play's takings as the manager. This agreement with Benjamin Webster
gave Boucicault an income of several hundred pounds per week during
The Colleen Bawn's run at the Adelphi, and the dramatist further boosted
his earnings by setting up two touring companies to play the drama
in the provinces at the same time, which added approximately £500
per week. Not all dramatists were able to follow Boucicault's example,
of course. Still, his business acumen and the popularity of sensation
drama significantly contributed to changing the position and potential
remuneration received by playwrights in the nineteenth century. Moreover, empowered by the unprecedented popularity of their dramas, and
the high salaries they could receive, sensation dramatists are significant
to changing theatrical cultures in ways that are borne out in legisla-
tive change, such as securing greater protection from copyright laws, for
which Boucicault, Reade and many others actively campaigned.[41]

Nevertheless, sensation writers also participated in the intertextual
ebb and flow of piracies, translations, adaptations and appropriations
that were constant features of nineteenth-century playbills.[42] Dramatists worked from various sources, including French plays (such
as Charles Young's 'free adaptation' of Édouard Romberg's *L'Infidèle*
(1884)), periodical fiction (Clara Cavendish's *The Woman of the World*
(1858) is advertised as 'adapted from *Reynold's Miscellany*') and journalism (Hazlewood's *The Casual Ward; or, A Night in the Workhouse* (1866)
is adapted from a piece of investigative journalism in the *Pall Mall
Gazette*).[43] In Britain, the 1842 Copyright Act had increased the dura-
tion of copyright for books and dramatic works to seven years after
the author's death, while in the United States an amendment to an
equivalent act in 1856 gave dramatists greater control over the rights to
perform and publish their work than they had hitherto enjoyed. However, enforcement was challenging, particularly because the misalign-
ment of international copyright laws meant dramatists could not claim
damages for unauthorised stagings or piracies of their works overseas.
Letters held in the Templeman Library's Boucicault Collection record
an infringement case that Boucicault brought against the manager of
the Theatre Royal Wolverhampton, John Delafield, in the early 1860s.

41. For example, Boucicault was involved in the campaign by dramatists to push through the
    amendment to the American 1831 Copyright Act in 1856 (Fawkes (2011 [1979]), p. 91).
42. See Norwood (2015), 'Adaptation and the Stage in the Nineteenth Century'. This special
    issue of *Nineteenth-Century Theatre & Film* contains several stimulating articles exploring
    this topic.
43. Plays were also adapted into other forms. Wilkie Collins's adaptation of his own play *The
    Red Vial* (1858) into the novel *Jezebel's Daughter* (1880) is just one example.

Henry Young's 'The Bride of Garryowen or The Colleen Bawn' premiered at this provincial theatre on 1 April 1861, and was later advertised under a different title to try to avoid an injunction ('Cushla ma Chree'). Boucicault was at a disadvantage because the play had first premiered in America, and in 1863 'the Vice-Chancellor dismissed the plaintiff's bill with costs, on the ground that by first representing *The Colleen Bawn* at New York he was not, upon the construction of the International Copyright Act, entitled to copyright in England'.[44] Though Boucicault's international career had helped him to secure a more stable income, it simultaneously hampered his efforts to claim creative ownership. Later Boucicault went so far as to rewrite earlier plays he had produced in America to make them 'original' – and so protected – in England, and ensured his dramas had copyright performances in England or Canada before they premiered in America.[45]

To add further difficulties, the legal situation failed to recognise the reciprocity between fictive and dramatic writing. One 'pirated Author and Composer' wrote to *The Times* complaining:

> as the law at present stands, any playwright who pleases may dramatize any novel he fancies without let or hindrance on the part of the author. [. . .] Any one has the same right as Mr. Boucicault to dramatize from the Irish novel [*The Collegians*] from which he took his play of Colleen Bawn, provided always [. . .] that they pirate direct from the Irish novel, and not from the work at second-hand of their co-partner in literary plunder.[46]

By the 1860s, well-known authors like Collins and Dickens had long agitated against unauthorised dramatisations of their works, for which they received no financial return.[47] Dickens famously counselled Ellen Wood that English law does not 'give you the power of preventing ANY stage adaptations of your book', although she was consoled by the fact that the pirated plays of *East Lynne* probably continued to push book sales for decades after publication.[48] Not all novelists or dramatists were as accepting as Wood. Charles Reade successfully launched

---

44. Templeman Library Special Collections, Boucicault Collection, UKC-CALB-BIO. F205506, 'Material relating to law suits/infringement of copyright in which Boucicault was involved'. Anon. (1864), 'Boucicault v. Delafield', *The Times*, 25 May, newspaper cutting.
45. Fawkes (2011 [1979]), p. 134.
46. Templeman Library Special Collections, Boucicault Collection, UKC-CALB-BIO. F205506, 'Material relating to law suits/infringement of copyright in which Boucicault was involved'. A pirated Author and Composer (1867), 'Authors v. Dramatic Authors. To the Editor of The Times', *The Times*, 19 Nov., newspaper cutting.
47. For more on this topic, see, for example, Bisla (2013).
48. Charles Dickens to Ellen Wood, '19 January 1866', in Dickens (1999), p. 146.

litigation against the publisher T. H. Lacy for printing Hazlewood's version of *Never Too Late to Mend*, and against Benjamin Oliver and his son George Conquest for staging an unauthorised adaptation of this work at the Grecian Theatre, London.[49] But, as *The Times*'s 'pirated Author and Composer' recognises, dramatists were no more deferential to each other than to the novelists they adapted, and also regularly sued each other for light-fingered dealings with respect to both their adaptations and original dramas. Delafield was not the only person against whom Boucicault launched proceedings for infringing the copyright of *The Colleen Bawn*, and Samuel Lane, the manager of London's Britannia Theatre, agreed to withdraw Hazlewood's 'Eily O'Connor' when threatened with an injunction.[50] Boucicault was himself successfully sued by Augustin Daly for appropriating the famous railway sensation scene from *Under the Gaslight* in *After Dark* (1868). Still, it is clear that a culture of unauthorised adaptation and appropriation remained a commonplace, even vital, part of sensation theatre. Daly's injunction did not stop the dramatists from working together when Boucicault was in New York in the mid-1870s.[51]

International perspectives

Morley and Boucicault each left written accounts which suggest that the term 'sensation drama' was coined in response to the hugely successful trend for spectacular effects in London's West End, which began with *The Colleen Bawn*. However, accepting Boucicault's argument that he 'was the means of bringing [the word "sensation"] into use' belies contemporary recognition of the genre's portability.[52] Firstly, in building on earlier melodramas, sensation plays evolved in dialogue with an already highly mobile repertoire. As we know, melodrama originated in France and achieved international popularity through practices of piracy, translation, adaptation and appropriation. The increased transcontinental mobility of actors, playwrights and ideas contributed to a context of international exchange, which intensified and shifted in the period when sensation drama evolved. By the 1860s, cultural dialogues were dialectic and encompassed multiple media. For example, in 1866, an adaptation of Wilkie Collins's *The Woman in White* by the famous German playwright Charlotte Birch-Pfeiffer was staged at theatres in Berlin and Vienna. Cities as far apart as Rotterdam and Melbourne also

49. See Meer (2015), pp. 22–38.
50. Davis (1992), p. 19.
51. J. F. Daly (1917), p. 77.
52. Boucicault (1862), p. 203.

enjoyed adaptations of the novel.[53] Augustin Daly's *Leah, The Forsaken*
(1862) was reviewed in *Harper's Weekly* as 'an English adaptation of a
German sensational drama'.[54] Meanwhile, Daly, Boucicault and Marryat all worked in both Britain and America, and Boucicault also spent
a significant amount of time in Australia, France and Ireland.

Henry Morley suggests that the transatlantic relationship is particularly important. Indeed, he bases his claim that Boucicault was responsible for coining the term 'sensation' for London's West End on the fact
that the dramatist had 'imported for us from the other side of the Atlantic, [the] "sensation" scene'.[55] Aside from *The Colleen Bawn*, another play
that Boucicault successfully exported from the United States to Europe
was *The Poor of New York* (1857). The play was staged across Britain in the
1860s, relocalised for different cities: *The Poor of Liverpool* (10 February
1864), *The Poor of Manchester* (18 March 1864), *The Poor of Birmingham*
(2 April 1864), *The Poor of Leeds* (16 May 1864), *The Streets of Glasgow*
(6 June 1864) and so on.[56] Moving in the same direction, Augustin Daly's
dramas were also widely staged at British theatres from the 1860s on,
after they premiered in America. In a letter written in 1878, Daly called
the actor-manager George Conquest 'one of the English robbers who
[has] despoiled me of my railroad scene, and one of the hundreds who
[has] played my *Gaslight*'.[57] Of course, these examples follow multiple
dramatisations of Harriet Beecher Stowe's novel *Uncle Tom's Cabin* (1852)
for European theatres, which also features a sensational escape scene
across an icy Mississippi River. However, unlike Boucicault's and Daly's
later sensation plays, the scripts deposited with the Lord Chamberlain
indicate that the adaptations of *Uncle Tom's Cabin* that were staged in
London theatres in the 1850s were largely written by local dramatists,
rather than international imports.[58] The shift in theatrical culture that
sensation represents is thus conceived through, and seen as a product
of, increased global mobility – just as the speed of modern travel itself
became a staple means of eliciting a sensational effect.

Both Morley's dismissive view of sensation as a 'now popular
Americanism introduced by Mr. Boucicault' and the fact that the
American reviewer for *Harper's Weekly* locates the origin of sensation
drama in Germany reinforces the fact that the genre retained risqué or
derogatory connotations, even though it was often played in high-end

---

53. Norwood (2009), p. 223.
54. J. F. Daly (1917), p. 49.
55. Morley (1866), p. 282.
56. N. Daly (2017), n.p.
57. J. F. Daly (1917), p. 275.
58. For example, by J. Courtney, Edward Fitzball, G. D. Pitt, William Brough, and Tom
    Taylor and Mark Lemon (all deposited in 1852).

theatres.[59] Sensation is repeatedly represented as a foreign import: a label which is supposed to account for its shocking content at the same time as it imaginatively disassociates the eager playgoing public from this highly popular genre. For, even though sensation drama's alleged place of origin shifts to accommodate each reviewer, it is resolutely positioned as a theatrical style 'Other' to the critic's 'national drama'. Of course, these assertions reveal snobbish attitudes to certain types of popular culture, as well as how drama was used to conceive of and convey ideas about national identities. It suggests, for instance, that the genre's promise to elicit somatic responses was perceived as a result of bringing foreign sensibilities uncomfortably into contact with the audience. Yet in pushing sensation into a liminal imaginative space, these contemporary critics simultaneously express the fluid mobility of the theatrical cultures from which the genre emerged.

Given the portability of sensation drama, it is paradoxical that its shocking effect depended on the apparent immediacy or verisimilitude of action and place. Boucicault recognised audiences' desires for immediacy in how he conceived of the special effects in his sensation scenes. *The Poor of New York* climaxes with the burning of a tenement in New York's Five Points, but Boucicault changed the play's cultural references and setting when he relocalised the drama for various cities. In *The Poor of Liverpool*, for instance, audiences saw 'elaborate recreations of such familiar city sights as the Adelphi Hotel [. . . and the] tenement in the Five Points was transformed for Liverpool audiences into 19½ Cherry Lane'.[60] A much-quoted letter by Boucicault records how he conceived the immediacy of the setting as a direct contributor to the audience's sense of excitement and suspense: 'I localize it for each town, and hit the public between the eyes; so they see nothing but fire.'[61] Thus Boucicault suggests that the power of the sensation scene to produce a thrilling effect is increased by directly relating the on-stage action to the lives of the playgoers themselves. In this, Boucicault built on techniques from 'local' dramas, which feature on the playbills for minor theatres in London from at least the 1830s. These dramas typically set criminal plots or extreme events in the theatre's immediate surroundings, and so titillated audiences by suggesting their close proximity to shocking on-stage action. Heidi Holder has argued that these specific locations provide pleasure by embedding the drama in 'a fully realised world, a visual realm that authenticates the

59. Morley (1866), p. 366.
60. N. Daly (2017), n.p.
61. Boucicault, Letter to Edward Stirling from the Royal Hotel, Glasgow, qtd in N. Daly (2017), n.p.

action on stage'.[62] For sensation dramas, however, evoking the local area often necessitated acts of cultural translation, of which audiences were aware, as when *Under the Gaslight* was relocalised for British audiences as 'Rail, River and Road' at the New East London Theatre in 1868.[63] Consequently, the simultaneously international and local perspective afforded by plays like these provided particularly potent 'sensational gratifications', in which the verisimilitude with which extreme events are presented excites an audience fully aware of their artifice.

Sensation after 1880

We chose the twenty years from 1860 as the chronological span of this anthology because those decades represent the high-water mark for sensation drama, during which the genre was extensively discussed by critics and commentators. However, our porous and flexible definition of sensation drama means that we can identify sensational elements in many cultural settings throughout the late nineteenth and early twentieth centuries. As we have seen, theatrical adaptations such as *Lady Audley's Secret* and *East Lynne* were regularly revived in the later part of the nineteenth century and into the twentieth. The reach of sensation went far beyond famous plays, though, and parodies helped to extend the impact of sensation and to prolong its life in the cultural imaginary. From its very inception, the genre and its tropes were mocked in burlesques such as Henry J. Byron's *Eighteen Hundred and Sixty Three; or, The Sensations of the Past Season, with a Shameful Revelation of 'Lady Someone's Secret'* (opened on Boxing Day 1863). Festive entertainments often drew on highly topical material to raise a laugh, and here Braddon's Lady Audley is given a comedic afterlife. Eliza Shurrock also wrote a domestic comedy in 1863 called *Brumley's Wife: Or, the Sensation Scene* (Princess's Theatre, Glasgow), in which a young wife is driven mad by her attempts to write a sensation play. W. S. Gilbert's comic operetta satirises *A Sensation Novel* in dramatic form and was staged with much hilarity at Thomas German Reed's Gallery of Illustration in 1871. Kate Mattacks has astutely argued that Watts Phillips's pastiche play, *The Woman in Mauve* (1865), is not just a parody, but a 'response to how the sensation genre had become cultural capital'.[64] The play not only parodied Collins's *The Woman in White*, but

---

62. Holder (2007), p. 106. Local dramas were played frequently at Sadler's Wells in the 1830s. These include Thomas Wilks's *The Red Crow* (1834), George Almar's *The Clerk of Clerkenwell* (1834) and *The Ruby Ring; or, The Murder at Sadler's Wells* (1840). For further details, see Hofer-Robinson (2018), pp. 73–8.
63. 'Rail, River and Road' is discussed in the notes for *Under the Gaslight*.
64. Mattacks (2016), p. 66.

it also drew on *Lady Audley's Secret* and Boucicault's *Arrah-na-Pogue* (1864) to highlight self-consciously the intertextual nature of sensation and the commodified status of its tropes.

Sensation remained significant in theatrical culture up to the end of the nineteenth century and into the twentieth, and not only as the target of mockery: for example, in the dramas of the Melville brothers. Walter Melville drew on sensation's use of morally complex female characters thrown into extreme scenarios in plays such as *The Worst Woman in London* (1899), which featured an ambitious and cross-dressing heroine. Sensation mixed with *fin de siècle* anxieties about the New Woman in these plays, and, more often than not, these 'bad' women were brought into line by the last act. The Melville brothers also looked back to earlier dramatists' use of sensation scenes to excite and provoke audiences. Frederick Melville's *Her Forbidden Marriage* (1903) follows the verisimilitude of key scenes in Halliday's *The Great City* (1867) and Watts Phillips's *Lost in London* (1867), but instead of bringing a carriage on stage, it has the bride and groom eloping in a real motor car. Theatre managers also continued to stage sensation scenes. The 'autumn dramas' at Drury Lane were where audiences flocked to see the biggest spectacles of this period. Cecil Raleigh's *The Price of Peace* played at Drury Lane from September to December 1900 and featured realistic renderings of the House of Commons and Westminster Abbey, as well as a collision staged between a yacht and a liner. *The Whip*, which Raleigh co-wrote with Henry Hamilton in 1909, made an even bigger splash with its train crash and live-action horse race staged on a moving treadmill.[65] *The Whip* was designed by one of the best-known scenic artists of the time, Bruce 'Sensation' Smith, whose innovative work in set design and engineering earned him plaudits from theatregoers.[66] Arthur Collins, the producer of this and many other Drury Lane melodramas, made a fortune from their successes. The continuing use and value of sensational tropes are explored by critics like Ben Singer and David Mayer, whose work on early film demonstrates its indebtedness to theatrical traditions.[67] Daly's sensation scene from *Under the Gaslight* is borrowed in the 1907 feature *The Bad Man*, in which the heroine escapes from her own difficulties to rescue a man tied to railway tracks. The 1917 film version of Joseph Arthur's play *Blue Jeans* (1890) moves the last-minute rescue scene to a sawmill, where the heroine saves the unconscious hero as

---

65. See Mayer (1996) for a discussion of *The Whip* and its filmic adaptations.
66. See Baugh (2005), p. 181.
67. Singer (2001); Mayer (2009). See also Brewster and Jacobs (1997).

the blade of a buzz-saw inches towards him.[68] It was not just theatrical content that film utilised; early filmmakers like David Belasco and D. W. Griffiths also borrowed directorial and managerial techniques from stage contexts in what Mayer explores as a 'long period of exchange between the stage and film' in the late nineteenth and early twentieth centuries.[69] Sensation dramatists were always adaptive and intertextual, continually renegotiating sensational tropes for their audiences. Sensation drama has not lost its cultural resonance and continues to be rewritten, reappropriated and restaged in the twenty-first century.[70]

The plays

The plays chosen for this anthology emphasise the fluidity of sensation drama between continents, social spaces and literary and theatrical cultures, and our general principle in selecting which variant of each play to transcribe has been to use the edition printed closest to the date of first performance, where possible. Notes accompanying each play record significant variations between the print version, any prompt or performance copies available and the deposit copy. Throughout the nineteenth century, theatres were obliged to deposit all plays intended for public performance at the Lord Chamberlain's Office, a system that, Sos Eltis argues, 'provided an inbuilt incentive for writers and managers to conform to orthodox standards'.[71] The scripts submitted to the Lord Chamberlain are usually hand-written and often lack information about staging and performance that might more frequently be found in a prompt copy. Neither the deposit scripts nor any textual version can capture the full sensory experience of the play, nor the necessarily shifting nature of performance that would have varied nightly.[72] However, these textual sources do allow us to trace important distinctions when comparing the deposit scripts with other sources and, as Radcliffe and Mattacks suggest, they 'construct an intricate web of connections between not just the specific textual variants, but also between themes, contemporary debates, visual cultures, theatres, families and business

---

68. The play was published by Samuel French in 1940 and the sawmill scene can be viewed on YouTube, available at <youtube.com/watch?v=XaKzQAOuSZA> (last accessed 1 May 2018).
69. Mayer (2009), p. 29.
70. Most recently, *The Woman in White* was adapted by Fiona Seres for a five-part BBC mini-series in 2018.
71. Eltis (2013), p. 4.
72. The Lord Chamberlain did not, for example, require accompanying musical scores to be deposited but music was significant to sensation drama.

networks to form an image of the theatre as multi-authored, collective cultural response'.[73]

The first play in the anthology is C. H. Hazlewood's *Never Too Late to Mend*. In both its style of representation and its production history, Hazlewood's drama squarely locates illegitimate melodrama at the root of sensation drama. Like earlier melodramas, *Never Too Late* aims 'to highlight some social ill or injustice' by mobilising a cast of closely connected, stock *dramatis personæ*.[74] Further, it is part of an established theatrical culture in which adaptation can be indistinguishable from piracy. As we have noted, the play is based on Charles Reade's 1856 novel, which was itself adapted from Reade's drama, *Gold*. Reade would himself readapt his novel for the stage in 1865, and its production at the Princess's Theatre in London quickly gained notoriety because of the verisimilitude of its prison scenes. Frederic Guest Tomlins, theatre critic for the *Morning Advertiser*, even interrupted the performance by jumping to his feet to shout: 'It's revolting!'[75] However, Reade's play was preceded by adaptations for London's Surrey, Britannia, Marylebone and Grecian theatres. The prolific Hazlewood wrote at least two of these dramas. The version chosen for this anthology (collected in *Lacy's Acting Edition of Plays, Vol. 2*) was originally staged at the Royal Marylebone Theatre in 1859.[76] This printed script is significantly different to the adaptation Hazlewood wrote for the Britannia in Hoxton, East London, in the same year. In the latter, Hazlewood changes the structure and *dramatis personæ* of Reade's tale; for instance, he adds a character called London Nan, who takes centre stage as the moral voice of the drama, while the heroic chaplain Mr Eden is elided. By contrast, the Lacy's edition is very similar to Reade's own dramatisation of the novel. Indeed, Reade sued the publisher for printing Hazlewood's unauthorised adaptation, and the printed play was found to be in infringement of Reade's copyright, even though Lacy's edition predates Reade's play.[77] For, although the year of publication is not stated on the script, Hazlewood's drama appears to have been performed internationally by 1861.[78] This performance history reveals that the shocked reaction to

---

73. Radcliffe and Mattacks (2009), n.p.
74. Pisani (2014), p. 169.
75. Maunder (2013), p. 61.
76. Lacy's editions were usually published soon after performance at an affordable price. They often contained lists of *dramatis personæ*, prop lists and guidance on staging, and advertisements for theatrical goods could be found within the covers of each volume. See Weig (2017) for recent work on Lacy's.
77. See Meer (2015), p. 31.
78. The Houghton Library holds a copy belonging to Edwin Adams of the Walnut Street Theatre, Philadelphia, which is hand-dated March 1861.

Reade's 1865 drama in fact built on the success of productions at less reputable theatres. Therefore, one reason for including Hazlewood's version in this anthology (rather than Reade's) was to reinforce how important this astonishingly productive dramatist is to histories of mid-nineteenth-century theatre, and to help to make his expansive œuvre more accessible.

The second drama, Boucicault's *The Colleen Bawn*, first premiered on 27 March 1860 at Laura Keene's Theatre in New York, before achieving a record-breaking long run at London's Adelphi Theatre from 10 September 1860 to November 1861. The drama is chosen for this collection because it was instrumental in popularising sensation internationally – to the extent that contemporaries recognised the genre as a new dramatic phenomenon. It is well known that Queen Victoria went to see *The Colleen Bawn* three times, and reviews of the Adelphi's production lauded the play as 'a great success', which 'will form an era in the history of the house'.[79] *The Colleen Bawn* was so popular that it inspired a variety of consumer products: sheet music transcribing the Irish melodies used in the play; songs celebrating the drama, such as 'The Colleen Bawn Gallop'; a fashion trend for red cloaks, of the kind worn by the heroine, Eily; and, of course, multiple theatrical imitations, burlesques and spin-offs.[80] The selection of variants discussed in the notes records examples of differences to Boucicault's printed script (such as in the hand-written licensing copy); adaptations/piracies by other dramatists (Hazlewood; Young); and satires (Byron; Brough and Halliday). The notes are necessarily limited, and readers may wish to consult further versions of the drama, such as Julius Benedict's opera, *The Lily of Killarney*, which has a libretto by John Oxenford. But the reasons for *The Colleen Bawn*'s international success and legacy also lie in its significance to changing how dramatists were valued and remunerated, and in Boucicault's challenging representation of stock theatrical types. Despite being criticised by playwrights of Dublin's Abbey Theatre in the early twentieth century, Boucicault's performance as Myles – and, later, as Conn in *The Shaughraun* – has since been analysed as presenting a reassessment of the stage Irishman, alongside more nuanced readings of Boucicault's wider engagement with political and colonial contexts.[81] Indeed, Deirdre McFeely argues that the version of

---

79. V&A, Colleen Bawn Production File, New Adelphi (1860), THM|LON|ADE|1861. Anon., 'New Adelphi' (hand-dated 15 Sep. 1860), newspaper cutting.
80. The Templeman Library holds a variety of such music in their Boucicault collection, much of which has illustrated cover pages. Readers may also wish to consult N. Daly (2009) for further information about the play's cultural and consumer legacies.
81. See Chiles (2004); Krause (1964); McFeely (2012).

rural Ireland presented in *The Colleen Bawn* was 'so successful as a commercial commodification of Ireland' that it marked 'the start of the internationalisation of Irish drama', and even sold 'a highly acceptable version of that aspect of Irish life' to Dubliners, despite the fact that the Great Famine was still relatively recent history when the production toured to Ireland in April 1861.[82]

Augustin Daly's *Under the Gaslight* is chosen as an example of American drama being exported and revised for international audiences. The version of the play presented in this anthology is the script originally copyrighted by Daly in 1867. The 1856 amendment to the 1831 Copyright Act gave dramatists 'the sole right to print and publish the said composition, the sole right also to act, perform, or represent the same, or cause it to be acted, performed, or represented, on any stage or public place' for the first time.[83] Managers who pirated the play after this date were liable for damages, but a discrepancy between the title given on Daly's copyright script and that of the published edition led to a copyright dispute in 1889. The subtitle given on the copyright script is *A Totally Original and Picturesque Drama of Life and Love in These Times*, but the later published book was altered to *Under the Gaslight, A Romantic Panorama of the Streets and Homes of New York*.[84] As Daly's later subtitle suggests, the play's New York setting was significant to the staging of the play in America, as the 'scenery [. . .] exhibited localities familiar to explorers of Old New York'.[85] Nevertheless, the textual variants discussed in the notes also record the drama's international success and indicate how performing the play in other countries could entail acts of cultural translation. Both Daly's script, and unauthorised revisions of it, thus emphasise the drama's immediacy for the audience through the evocation of known, adjacent locales.

Miss Chester is a sensation play without a sensation scene. Although we do see a duel on stage, it is a much less spectacular drama than the other plays in this collection. Its inclusion represents a conscious choice to take seriously the objections of Daly and others to the way in which the term 'sensation' threatened to reduce the significance of their work to a single gimmick. *Miss Chester* earns its place by providing many sensational tropes – illegitimacy, mistaken identity, violence and the *demi-monde* – but also for its most impressive *coup de théâtre* in the voicing of female discontent in the heroine's powerful speeches.[86] Critics were impressed by

---

82. McFeely (2012), p. 13, p. 24.
83. Qtd in Fawkes (2011 [1979]), p. 91.
84. See J. F. Daly (1917), pp. 474–5.
85. Ibid., p. 239.
86. See Kate Newey (2005), pp. 180–3, for one of the few recent critical discussions of the play.

the way in which Mrs Hermann (Eliza) Vezin, a mature actor who performed a wide repertoire of roles in London theatres during the 1850s and 1860s, took on the unusual and challenging role. Florence Marryat, herself an actor and novelist, as well as a playwright, had often given voice to difficult, wronged, law-breaking women in her writing, but this was newer terrain for Sir Charles Young, whose other work consists mainly of light comedic pieces.[87]

Collaboration was a frequent practice for dramatic writers of the nineteenth century, Charles Reade co-wrote *Masks and Faces* (1852) with Tom Taylor, Collins worked with Dickens on both the fiction and dramatic versions of *No Thoroughfare* (1867), and while Marryat mostly wrote her novels alone, she always collaborated on her dramatic writing.[88] Although we know little about the specific working practices of this particular pairing, the deposit copy does feature amendments and additions to both dialogue and staging, so it may have been used as a working copy by the authors. We follow French's Acting Edition of the play[89] but highlight significant variations between this and the deposit copy, most notably around which point in the play Rupert is revealed as Miss Chester's son and in the differing levels of explicitness about Montressor's connections to the *demi-monde*. The theatre collection of the Victoria and Albert Museum (V&A) holds a promptbook of the play, and the relatively small differences between this and the printed edition are also noted.

The Missing Witness offers a wonderful example of an extended sensation scene involving not one, but two hand-to-hand fight scenes on a treacherous mountain pass, the first ending with the hero seeming to plunge to his death and the second with an avalanche engulfing the heroine and the stage. Unfortunately, the play was hastily withdrawn when the actor playing Gustave, Mr J. F. Stephenson, misjudged his 'sensation leap' and broke his leg only three weeks after its opening at the Alexandra Theatre in Liverpool.[90] This inauspicious accident, alongside some 'little difficulty' in the terms of the engagement, meant that the play did not move down to the Adelphi in London after its run

---

87. Nicoll (2009) lists twenty-two plays by Young, most of them staged at small provincial theatres in the 1870s and 1880s: vol. V, p. 636.
88. *Her World Against a Lie* (1880) was co-written with George Neville and *The Gamekeeper* (1898) with Herbert McPherson.
89. Samuel French bought Lacy out in 1872 and became the primary publisher of playscripts for both professionals and amateurs for the rest of the nineteenth century; the firm remains an important theatrical publisher today.
90. 'On Saturday evening an actor, named Stephenson broke a leg in two places, in taking a sensation leap in Miss Braddon's play "Genevieve" at the Alexandra Theatre, Liverpool' (Anon. (1874b), p. 5).

in Liverpool, as had been planned.[91] The Alexandra was an important provincial theatre and we would not want to measure a play's success only by its presence in the capital, but Braddon, who had superintended the rehearsals, must have been disappointed.[92] Still, she was a woman used to the vicissitudes of theatrical life: from 1852 to 1860 she had pursued a career as an actor before turning to writing. She took the stage name Mary Seyton and met with some success travelling around the provinces and working at the Surrey Theatre in London. She acted in popular melodramas such as Tom Taylor's *Still Waters Run Deep* (on the Isle of Wight in 1855), as well as Shakespeare plays and pantomimes.[93] She transferred her energies to writing novels and plays in the early 1860s, achieving enormous success with *Lady Audley's Secret* (1862), which, as we know, was subsequently also a sensational hit on stage. Kerry Powell has argued that the odds were stacked against Victorian women playwrights and suggests that a woman's success in fiction writing was often used illogically as a reason for failure in writing for the stage.[94] Kate Newey, however, lists scores of female playwrights at work in the Victorian period who, until recently, have been largely neglected.[95] Many of these women, like Braddon, enjoyed multiple careers as writers, actors and journalists, and utilised networks of colleagues in order to maximise the chances of success. Indeed, it was Louise Swanborough (actor and lessee of the Strand) who gave Braddon her break as a playwright and staged her first play, *Loves of Arcadia*, in March 1860. Holder links Braddon's acting experience to the provocative content of *The Missing Witness*, arguing that she 'creat[ed] the characters she never got to play' and reworked Victorian drama 'from the actress's standpoint: the men learn their lessons and the women are vindicated'.[96] The play, like much of Braddon's fiction, challenges the idea of the morally righteous and passive heroine.

Here we follow the printed edition of the text as published by John and Robert Maxwell, Braddon's husband and stepson.[97] Aided by these familial arrangements, Braddon had become adept at managing and

---

91. Anon. (1891), p. 13. It was withdrawn from the Alexandra on 18 April, the same day as the accident.
92. Anon. (1874c), p. 3.
93. See Jennifer Carnell (2016), pp. 9–43, for further details on Braddon's acting career.
94. Powell (2004), p. 363.
95. Newey (2005).
96. Holder (2000), pp. 177–8.
97. Braddon married Maxwell in 1874 after his existing wife's death. They had, however, lived together as husband and wife for a decade at the time *The Missing Witness* was published.

maintaining control over her published work, so there was no need for her to engage with another theatrical publisher. Archival material on this production is relatively scant but the Mary Elizabeth Braddon Collection, held at the Harry Ransom Center, University of Texas, holds a copy of the printed John and Robert Maxwell edition of the play with hand-written revisions and annotations made around 1880. The annotated copy makes some significant changes, most notably the addition of a large Mount St Bernard dog, called Leo, and his handler. Animals, particularly dogs and horses, were often seen on the nineteenth-century stage and Ann Featherstone (2000) has explored the frequency with which theatrical animals are advertised in the stage's trade paper, the *Era*. Animals sometimes became celebrities, such as Carlo the Wonder Dog in Frederick Reynolds's *Caravan; or, The Driver and His Dog* (Drury Lane, 1803), who performed a similarly daring rescue to the later Leo. The notes highlight the ways in which the annotations speed up the action, condensing the latter sections of the play in particular.

Although each of the dramas collected in this anthology is selected on its own merits, this corpus, taken as a whole, also emphasises the interconnectedness of theatrical cultures in the period. There are many links between the plays and dramatists included in this volume, which go beyond this small selection. For example, Hazlewood and Daly both dramatised Reade's novels, and Hazlewood wrote versions of several of Boucicault's plays and adapted Braddon's fiction for the stage, most successfully with *Lady Audley's Secret* for the Victoria Theatre in 1863. Reade worked with Boucicault on both the novel and the stage versions of *Foul Play* (1868). As mentioned above, Boucicault and Daly worked together despite their hostile dealings in the law courts: in 1874 Boucicault co-wrote *Kentuck* with Bret Harte for Daly's theatre, in consultation with Daly.[98] Braddon played Nan in the Surrey Theatre's touring production of *Never Too Late to Mend*,[99] and Marryat's sister, Eva, played Anne Chute in *The Colleen Bawn* in Glasgow.[100] As we have suggested, sensation drama was highly mobile: tropes, ideas and personnel flowed between theatrical and literary cultures, and across national boundaries. The connections between these plays and dramatists underlie these assertions, and reinforce sensation's culture of exchange and appropriation in personal connections, as well as theatrical devices.

98. J. F. Daly (1917), pp. 170–1.
99. Theatre Royal, Doncaster, 23 May 1859; Carnell (2016), p. 439.
100. See Newey (2005), p. 181.

Throughout the anthology, characters' full names are used, rather than the abbreviated prefixes often found in Lacy's, French's or manuscript versions. Some obvious typographical errors in the originals have been silently corrected and some words that were hyphenated in the originals have been shifted to modern spellings. Some regularisation of the format of stage directions and title pages has been undertaken for consistency across the anthology. A key to the abbreviations used in the stage directions can be found at the end of the first play in the anthology. In the notes, the plays are sometimes referred to by self-explanatory abbreviations: for example, *NTL* for *Never Too Late to Mend*.

Sensation Drama

Figure 1 The Theatre Royal Marylebone c.1845, where *Never Too Late to Mend* was staged just over a decade later. Fenoulhet, engraved by J. Harwood, *View from the Stage, Theatre Royal Marylebone*. Westminster City Archives, London.

NEVER TOO LATE TO MEND[1]

A Drama of Real Life

IN

FOUR ACTS

FOUNDED ON MR. CHARLES READE'S POPULAR NOVEL

BY

COLIN HAZLEWOOD,

AUTHOR OF

The Return of the Wanderer – Jenny Foster – Trials of Poverty –
Going to Chobham, &c. &c.

———————

THOMAS HAILES LACY,
89 STRAND
(*Opposite Southampton Street, Covent Garden Market,*)
LONDON.

There is no charge for the performance of this Drama.

~*~

---

1. Other adaptations discussed in the notes are:
   CON: Add MS 52975 A. George Conquest (1858), 'Never too late to mend'.
   Licensing copy for production at 'the Royal Grecian on Monday 14 June 1858', where Conquest was 'Actual responsible Manager' (f. 1a). Reade successfully sued Conquest for copyright infringement, but won because this adaptation infringed the novel's theatrical antecedent, *Gold*, rather than his rights as a novelist (Hammet (1986), p. 13).
   HAZ2: Add MS 52980 K. C. H. Hazlewood (1859), 'Never to [*sic*] late to Mend. A Drama of Womans [*sic*] faith + Mans [*sic*] Treachery'.
   Licensing copy of Hazlewood's adaptation for the Britannia Theatre: performed in the same year as the Marylebone Theatre's production, but very different to the script published by Lacy. Particularly significant is the introduction of an additional character, London Nan, who takes centre stage.
   REA: Add MS 53044 D. Charles Reade, *It's Never Too Late to Mend.*
   Printed copy of Reade's adaptation submitted to the Lord Chamberlain on 20 July 1865, to be licensed for the Theatre Royal Manchester (f. 1). The copy includes some marginal annotations initialled 'C. R.', which usually suggest cuts to longer (often didactic) speeches, or scenes which explore the relationships between the *dramatis personæ*, rather than moving the plot forward.

DRAMATIS PERSONÆ
As performed at the ROYAL MARYLEBONE THEATRE, 1859

THE HONOURABLE MR. WINCHESTER . . .

Mr. Richards.

GEORGE FIELDING } . . . (*brothers and leaseholders of Grove Farm*) . . .

{ Mr. R. Thomas.

WILLIAM FIELDING } . . .

{ Mr. Andrews.

MR. JOHN MEADOWS . . . (*a land surveyor, a man with a cool head and iron hand and a body and mind alike indefatigable*) . . .

Mr. P. Hannan.

ISAAC LEVI . . . (*a Jew and money lender, but whose actions and sentiments are worthy of any Christian*) . . .

Mr. H. Forrester.

MR. MERTON . . . (*a farmer and father of Susan*) . . .

Mr. Baker.

PETER CRAWLEY . . . (*a crawling, sneaking, limb of the law, a tool of Mr. Meadows, and through circumstances compelled to do all his dirty work*) . . .

Mr. G. Belmore.

TOM ROBINSON . . . (*a London thief, and trying to pass himself off at the Grove as a London Gentleman*) . . .

Mr. J. F. Young.

MR. HAWES . . . (*Governor of the prison, an overbearing man*) . . .

Mr. Marshall.

JOSEPHS . . . (*victim of Hawes*) . . .

Miss J. Craven.[1]

MR. EDEN . . . (*the Chaplain of the prison*) . . .

Mr. Baildon.

EVANS and FRY . . . (*turnkeys*) . . .

Messrs. Skinner and Bond.

ABNER . . . (*a great scamp and not a faithful servant*) . . .

Mr. Jameson.

JACKY . . . (*a blacky, and staunch friend of George Fielding*) . . .

Mr. Bolton.[2]

JEM, BLACK WILL and BOB . . . (*bush rangers*) . . .

Messrs. Fredericks, Wilson, and James.

SUSAN MERTON . . . (*in love with George Fielding*) . . .

Miss Emma Barnett.

1. Josephs was often played as a cross-dress part: Louisa Moore took the role in the Princess's Theatre's 1865 production of **REA**.
2. In the 1865 production of **REA**, and probably in most other early productions, Jacky was played by a white actor in black-face. See Henderson (2004) for further discussion.

ACT FIRST.

SCENE FIRST.[3] – *Extensive View in Berkshire – corn fields, &c., in perspective – the Farm of George Fielding,* R.

Enter FRANK WINCHESTER *followed by* GEORGE *from farm.*

GEORGE. What, sir, is it possible you can be in earnest! Going all the way to Australia – a gentleman like you?

FRANK. Yes, George. The fact is, I'm deeply in love with a lady who returns my passion, but still she's hopelessly out of my reach because her friends think my money and expectations are not equal to hers. I'm going to Australia, where they tell me a little money turns to a great deal, instead of dissolving like a lozenge in the mouth, as it does in London.

GEORGE. (*aside*) Here's an earl's son, in this age of commonplace events, going to Australia with five thousand pounds, as sheep farmer and general speculator.

FRANK. I should like to persuade you to go with me as general adviser and manager. You know me, and I know you. I must have somebody to put me in the way. You once saved my life at the risk of your own, when I was seized with the cramp while bathing in the waters of Cleve Millpool, and my gratitude wishes to serve you in return.

GEORGE. Don't mention that trifling service, sir. That's an old story.

FRANK. Not quite. Come now, what do you say? I'll give you fifty sheep to begin with, and by industry, we shall both come home rich.

GEORGE. It's a handsome offer, sir, and a kind one. But to take me away from here would be like transplanting an oak that's been thirty years in the ground. Besides, there's Susan, sir – did you ever notice my cousin Susan?

---

3. **HAZ2** opens with dialogue between John Meadows and Peter Crawly, introducing Meadows's exploitation of Crawly's drunkenness. Crawly's humorously obsequious catch phrase is not used in this scene; instead, he goes so far as to refer to himself as Meadows's 'slave' (f. 2). Hazlewood's stark treatment of alcoholism in **HAZ2** likely responds to Teetotalism campaigns, which were linked with other working-class political movements like Chartism. However, the play is not politically radical. After Meadows exits, Nan – who is the moral voice of the drama – engages in witty repartee with Crawly, in which she laments social aspirations that cause people to be discontented with their lot in life. Nan's social conservatism in I.i is out of step with the grim injustice suffered by Josephs later on, particularly as she is the one who holds the prison staff to account.

FRANK. Notice her! do you think I've no eyes? She is, indeed, a lovely girl.

GEORGE. That's what everybody says, sir; so, you see, I should not like to leave her and go out to Australia to meet all kinds of dangers – to die, mayhap, for aught I know.

FRANK. Die! people don't go to Australia to die, but to make money – then come home and marry, and that's what you ought to do. This farm is unprofitable – it's a millstone round your neck.

GEORGE. Well, there may be some truth in that. Brother William and I have got four hundred acres between us, but most of it is poor, sour land. Mr. Meadows has often told me so, and he's as 'cute a judge as any about here, I take it.

FRANK. So I think, for everything he has done in life has prospered.

GEORGE. He was but a carter in his youth, and now at forty years of age he's a rich corn factor and land surveyor. He has a cool head, an iron will, and a sharp eye – always to be found by any man who wanted to do business, and when a man does find him, and has any dealings with him, he'll be pretty sure to get the sunny side of the bargain, and give you the windy.

FRANK. Here comes the man, and Farmer Merton with him. Have you any business with them?

GEORGE. Not I!

FRANK. Show me the blacksmith's shop, then. I want to learn how to shoe a horse.

GEORGE. (*aside*) Well, I never! the first nob in the country going to shoe a horse. The blacksmith's shop? oh, this is the way to it – this way, sir – this way.

[*Exeunt* L. U. E.

Enter JOHN MEADOWS *and* FARMER MERTON, R. 1 E.

JOHN. So you've been looking at the Fieldings' farm, eh, Mr. Merton? it wants some of your grass put to it, eh, Farmer?

MERTON. It lies cold. I never thought much of it. The land on the hill is as poor as death.

JOHN. And I fear George and his brother don't know how to make the best of it either. What do you think, farmer – they're threshing out new wheat for the rent.[4]

MERTON. You don't say so. Why, I didn't hear the flail going!

JOHN. They've just knocked off for dinner. You needn't say I told you; but – well, Fielding was at the bank this morning, trying to get money on their bill, and the bank said "No." (*aside*) Thanks to the hint I gave them.

MERTON. I wish my daughter Susan was not so fond of George; but you see, the young folks being first cousins –

JOHN. What of that? she's an obedient daughter, isn't she?

MERTON. Never gainsayed me in her life. My word is law with her.

JOHN. Well, then, a word from you would break off the acquaintance and save her from – but there, that's your affair, not mine. Think how bad George's circumstances look.

MERTON. That's true enough, Mr. Meadows, and I'm obliged to you for the hint, so I'll just step round to the barn and see what's doing. Servant, Mr. Meadows, and thank'ee too.

[*Exit behind farm,* R. U. E.

JOHN. I've raised his suspicions, and so far my first step is taken. Susan shall be mine. I have willed it so; and when once I am resolved, it is no easy matter to foil John Meadows.

Enter THATCHER, *a constable,* L.

THATCHER. I've news for you, sir. Your pocket was picked last Farnborough Fair, of three bank notes with your name on the back?

JOHN. It was.

THATCHER. (*shows notes*) Is this one of them?

JOHN. It is. Who passed it?

---

4. Threshing is the process which separates edible grain from the rest of the plant.

THATCHER. A chap that has got the rest – a stranger named Robinson, who lodges at the farm with George Fielding. They tell me he's a Londoner come down to take an airing.

JOHN. Who tells you so?

THATCHER. A gentleman from Bow Street,[5] who has come down to see if he knows him.

JOHN. (*aside*) Lucky chance! this will still further prejudice old Merton against George.

THATCHER. This Robinson is out fishing somewhere, or else we should have had him before this; but we'll hang about the farm and take him when he comes home.

JOHN. Do so. Any assistance that you require I will afford you.

THATCHER. Thank you, your honour.

[*Exit* L. U. E.

JOHN. (*rubbing his hands*) This is glorious! a network of adverse events is closing around George Fielding, and will make my rival powerless. But who comes here? (*looks* L.) It's that old rascal of a Jew. He's on the old story, I suppose.

ISAAC. Good day, Mr. Meadows. I was wishing to speak to you, sir.

JOHN. If you are come to talk to me about that house you are in, you may keep your breath to cool your porridge. I have bought the house, and given you warning to leave – let me hear no more of it, but when your time's up, turn out.

ISAAC. Mr. Meadows, I have lived there twenty years – I pay a fair rent, and I have come to treat with you, as the new landlord; but if you think it will fetch more, I will pay a little more, you shall lose nothing by me. You know your rent is sure?

JOHN. I do.

ISAAC. Thank you, sir. Well, then–

5. A colloquial reference to a London policeman.

JOHN. Well, then, next Lady-day[6] you turn out bag and baggage.

ISAAC. Nay, sir – nay, hear me. I have led a wandering life, and never found rest till I came here – here I was happy, for the god of my fathers gave me my wife, and here he took her to himself again.

JOHN. What the deuce is all this to me, man?

ISAAC. Much, if you are what people say – for men speak well of you. Two children were born to me in that house – they died there, and so did Leah, my dear loved wife, and there, at times, I seem to hear their voices speak comfort and blessings to me. In another house I shall never hear them. Oh, have pity on me, sir, an aged and lonely man! tear me not from the shadows of my dead! I beseech you let me prevail with you!

JOHN. (*sternly*) No, I tell you!

ISAAC. No! Then you are an enemy of Isaac Levi's.

JOHN. I am.

ISAAC. And why? What have I done to gain your enmity?

JOHN. You lend money.

ISAAC. A very little, sir – a very little.

JOHN. Well, what *you* are, *I* am – what *I* do on the sly, *you* do on the sly, eh, old Thirty-per-cent?

ISAAC. The world is wide enough for us both, good sir.

JOHN. It is, and it lies before you. Go where you like, for the little town of Farnborough is not wide enough for me and any man that works my business for his own pocket.

ISAAC. Let me stay, and I promise you you shall gain, and not lose. You'll trust me, won't you, sir?

JOHN. Yes, as far as I can fling a bull by the tail. You have told me your character, I will not tell you mine. I have always put my foot on whatever man or thing that has stood in my way – it is my course – my policy.

---

6. Lady Day was one of the traditional days for the quarterly payment of rents.

ISAAC. It is a frail policy, for be assured, sooner or later, some man will put his foot on you.

JOHN. Ha, do you threaten me?

ISAAC. No – but I tell you the strong man is sure to find one as strong as himself – the cunning man will meet one still as cunning and crafty. Be advised, then, and let me not have to curse, but to bless you. I have been driven to and fro these many years, like a withered leaf, and now I long for rest. Oh, let me die where those I have loved have died, and the despised Jew will kneel and bless you.

JOHN. Die on my premises if you like – nay, you may hang yourself there if you please, but it must be before next Lady-day, for after that time, no more Jewish dogs shall die in my house, nor be buried in my garden.

ISAAC. Irreverent cur! I spit upon ye, and I curse ye! Whatever is the secret wish of your life, may Heaven look on my grey hairs, and wither that wish. Ha, ha! have I touched you? you wince, do you? All men have secret wishes – and Heaven fights against yours. May you be near your wish – close to it, pant for it, stretch forth your hand for it, and – lose it – lose it – lose it!

JOHN. (*raising the riding whip he carries*) Dog of a Jew! I'll strike thee to the earth. (*raises butt end of whip to strike him*)

Music – GEORGE enters, R. and stays his arm.

GEORGE. Not if I know it – you are joking, Master Meadows. Why, the man is twice your age. (*to* ISAAC) Who are you, old man, and what do you want here?

JOHN. Who is he? Why, a villainous Jew, who insults me because I refuse to have him as a tenant.

ISAAC. Yes, young man, I am a Jew. (*to* JOHN) And what is *your* religion? The Christian creed is charity – that is not yours. The heathens were your superiors, for they respected both sorrow and grey hairs.[7]

JOHN. (*striving to reach him*) You shall smart for this. I'll show you what my religion is! (*raises whip*)

---

7. In **HAZ2** I:i, Isaac says: 'You are a Heathen, + have no respect for grey hairs' (f. 9b).

GEORGE. Not so fast, Mr. Meadows – and you, old man, don't be so aggravating. Mr. Meadows, you should know how to make light of an old man's tongue. Why, it's like a woman's – it's all he's got to hit with – you must not lift a hand to him on my premises, or you will have to settle with me first, and I don't think that would suit your book.

ISAAC. (*pointing to* JOHN) Look at him – he dare not look you in the face. Any man that has read men from east to west like I have, can see lion in your eye, young man, and cowardly wolf in his.

JOHN. Look to next Lady-day, old reptile.

ISAAC. Rascal – rascal! hard-hearted rascal! (*shaking his fist*)

GEORGE. (*to* ISAAC) There – there, don't be so spiteful, old man. Why, if he isn't all of a tremble! (*goes to farm house*) Sarah!

Enter SARAH, *a Female Farm Servant*, R.

Take the old man in, and give him a mug of ale, and whatever he likes to have – and mind you don't go lumping the china down under his nose – do you hear? (*to* SARAH)

ISAAC. I thank you, young man – I must not eat with you, but I will go in and rest, and compose myself, for passion is unseemly at my years.

GEORGE. (*taking him up to door*) Well, then, don't vex yourself any more about it – forget all your trouble awhile by my fireside, old man.

ISAAC. (*shaking his hand*) Bless you, young man – from this day forth Isaac Levi is your friend.

[*Exit to farm, following* SARAH.

JOHN. (*aside*) One more to your account, George Fielding – one more – one more!

GEORGE. The old man's words seemed somehow to knock against my bosom. Mr. Meadows and I – Eh – what, gone? Well, let him go, he's not a man whose company I care for. Who'd think he'd lift his hand against a man of three score and upwards? it makes me wild when I think of it. (*looks* L. U. E.) Oh, here's brother Will come back.

Enter WILLIAM FIELDING, L. U. E.

Well, Will, better late than never.

WILLIAM. Couldn't get away sooner, George. Here's the money for the sheep, thirteen pounds ten shillings. (*gives small bag*) No offer for the cow – Jem is driving her home again.

GEORGE. Well, but the money you went to borrow, the eighty pounds, Will?

WILLIAM. I haven't got it, George – there's your draft again – (*gives it*) the bank wouldn't take it.

GEORGE. Not take it! Oh, Will, then our credit is, indeed, down – and the whole town must know our rent is overdue. Well, the money must be got some way.

WILLIAM. Any way is better than threshing out new wheat at such a price. Ask a loan of a neighbour.

GEORGE. Oh, Will, to ask a loan of a neighbour, and then be denied, is a thought bitterer than death. *You* might do it, *I* can't.

WILLIAM. *I!* am I master here? The farm is not farmed my way, and never was! No – give me the plough handle, and I'd soon show you how to cut the furrow, George.

GEORGE. No doubt – no doubt. You'd like to draw the land dry with potato crops, and have fourscore hogs snoring in the farmyard – that's your idea of a farm. Oh, I know, you want to be elder brother. You'll have to kill me first though, Will Fielding.

WILLIAM. Oh, go on, go on – I don't mind your temper. But one thing is certain – we must raise the money somehow – you got us into the mud, elder brother, now get us out of the mire.

GEORGE. Well, well, it's no use being in a passion, I grant. Who shall I ask?

WILLIAM. Uncle Merton – or – or Mr. Meadows – he lends money to friends sometimes – ask either of 'em, it don't matter which.

GEORGE. What, show my empty pockets to Susan's father? Oh, Will, how can you be so cruel as to talk so?

WILLIAM. Ask Meadows, then.

GEORGE. I can't – I've just offended him. Besides, he's a man that never knew trouble or ill-luck in his life, and men of that kind are like flints.

WILLIAM. Well, look here – I think I stand pretty well in Meadows' books, so I'll ask him, if you'll try uncle.

GEORGE. Agreed.

WILLIAM. The first who meets his man shall be the first to ask.

GEORGE. That sounds fair – but I – (*looks off*) Well, yes, I agree. Set to work, then, brother Will, for here comes your man.

[*Exit into farm*, R.

WILLIAM. Confound it, I'm fairly caught!

Enter JOHN MEADOWS, L. U. E.

(*aside*) It goes sorely against the grain, but I must keep to my bargain! Good day, Mr. Meadows – I – I want to speak to you if you please.

JOHN. I am at your service, Mr. William.

WILLIAM. Well, sir, George and I are a little short of money at present, and George says he should take it very kind of you if you would lend us a hundred pounds for a week or two, just to help us over the stile like.

JOHN. I should have been delighted, William, to do it if I could. If you had only asked me yesterday I could have obliged you, but my business eats up a deal of money, and all my loose cash is laid out. I'm very sorry – perhaps, at some future time – I might, perhaps – but just now – I – I – Good morning, William.

[*Exit*, L. 1 E.

GEORGE *coming out of farm*, R.

Well, what luck?

WILLIAM. Oh, he says he is short of money and cannot.

GEORGE. He lies. He paid fifteen hundred into the bank yesterday, and you know that as well as I. Why didn't you tell him so?

WILLIAM. What would have been the use? a man that lies to avoid lending, won't be driven to it.

GEORGE. Why didn't you stick to him till you got it? – you could if you'd liked. But you want to drive your brother to beg of his sweetheart's father! You're a false lad, Will.

WILLIAM. You durstn't say so if you were not my brother.

GEORGE. If I wasn't your brother, I'd say a great deal more.

WILLIAM. Well, show your high spirit to Uncle Merton, for here he is. (*calls off*) Uncle! George wants to speak to you.

[*Exit into farm*, R.

FARMER MERTON *entering*, R. U. E.

MERTON. George wants to speak to me, does he? Well, that's luck, for I want to speak to him.

GEORGE. (L. *aside*) Who would have thought of his being about?

MERTON. You are threshing out new wheat, I see.

GEORGE. (*looking down*) Yes, yes.

MERTON. That's a bad look out! a farmer has no business to go to his barn door for his rent.

GEORGE. Where is he to go then? – to the church door, and ask for a miracle?

MERTON. No – to his sheep fold, to be sure.

GEORGE. Ah, *you* can if you like – you've got grass and water, and everything to hand.

MERTON. George, you are a fine lad, and I must speak to you seriously. I like you very well, George, and I respect you – but still I like my own daughter better than you, that's natural.

GEORGE. And *I* like your daughter better that *you* – that's natural again.

MERTON. I have seen for some time how matters are going on here, and if she marries you, she will have to keep you, instead of you her. You are too much of a man, I hope, to eat a woman's bread – and if you are not, *I* am man enough to keep the girl from it.

GEORGE. These are hard words to hear, old man, so near my own home.

MERTON. Plain speaking is best when the mind is made up.

GEORGE. Is this from Susan, as well as you?

MERTON. Susan is an obedient daughter – what I say she'll stand to. And I hope you know better than to tempt her to disobey me, for you won't succeed if you do. So, good day, young man.

GEORGE. Oh, enough said. I've no need to tempt any girl.

MERTON. I hope so, George – I hope so.

[*Exit,* L. 1 E.

GEORGE. Ungrateful old rascal!

Enter WILLIAM, R.

Our mother took him out of the dirt, Will, I've heard her say as much, or he'd not have had a sheep fold to brag of.

WILLIAM. Will he lend the money?

GEORGE. I never asked the old hunks.

WILLIAM. Never asked him!

GEORGE. Will, he began upon me in a moment. He sees we are going down hill, and he as good as told me to think no more of Susan.

WILLIAM. Well, you should have asked him for all that – it was your business to own the truth, and ask him to help us over the stile; he's our own blood.

GEORGE. You want to let me down lower than I'd let Carlo, that dog of yours. You're no brother of mine!

WILLIAM. A bargain is a bargain. *I* asked Meadows, and he said "No!" and when you met Uncle Merton you never asked him at all – that's playing false, George.

GEORGE. If you call me false, I'll knock your ugly head off.

WILLIAM. So you are, false, and a fool into the bargain.

GEORGE. What, you will have it, then?

WILLIAM. Yes, if you can give it me.

GEORGE. Look here – I'll give you something to put you on your mettle. The best man shall farm the grove, and the other shall be a servant on it, or go elsewhere, for I am sick of this. (*takes off his coat*)

WILLIAM. (*doing the same*) And so am I, and have been any time this two years – so here goes to settle it. (*Music – As they are rushing on each other*)

SUSAN *enters*, L. U. E. *down* C. *and interposes*,

SUSAN. Stay, William – hold your hand, George. What is all this?

GEORGE. What is it? Why – why – why, William was only going to show me a wrestling trick he learnt at the fair, that's all, Susan. (*they put on their coats*)

SUSAN. That is a falsehood, George – you were both going to fight, for I saw your eyes flash with rage and malice. Oh, shame, shame! brothers by one mother, fighting in a Christian land, within a stone's throw of a church, where brotherly love is preached as a debt we owe to strangers, let alone our own blood.

WILLIAM. I – I ask your pardon, Susan, I ought to have known better, I own, but I –

SUSAN. Oh, it wasn't your fault – it was you, George, I'll be bound. What, would you shed a brother's blood?

GEORGE. Why, how you're talking, Susan! I wasn't going to shed the fellow's blood, not I – I was only going to give him a hiding for his impudence.

WILLIAM. Or take one for your own, more likely.

GEORGE. What?

SUSAN. Silence, George, and take William's hand – take it, I say.

GEORGE. Well, don't go into a passion about nothing, Susan!

SUSAN. Then take William's hand while I say something to you.

GEORGE. (*takes his hand*) Well, there, we're friends now.

SUSAN. George Fielding, your character must change greatly before I can ever be your wife.

GEORGE. You don't know all I have to bear, Susan. Your father as good as told me not to speak to you any more, and that upset me, for it was more than I could stand.

SUSAN. George, I am very sorry my father was so unkind.

GEORGE. Thank ye kindly, Susan. That is the first drop of dew that has fallen on my heart today.

SUSAN. But obedience to parents is a great duty, and I hope I shall never disobey my father.

GEORGE. (*getting angry*) Oh, I don't want any girl to love me, if it's not agreeable. I'm so unlucky, you know! ha, ha, ha! it would not be worth any woman's while.

SUSAN. No, I don't think it *would* be worth any woman's while, George, till your temper undergoes a change.

GEORGE. Oh, I'll leave this place – I'm in everybody's way here.

TOM ROBINSON *entering,* L. U. E.

TOM. Everybody is in this country. California's the place. Come out of this country, and go into that, if you want to make your fortune.

SUSAN. You didn't make yours there?

TOM. I beg pardon, miss, I did make it, or how could I have spent it?

SUSAN. No doubt of it. What comes by the wind goes by the water, they say.

TOM. Alluding to the dust, miss?

SUSAN. Yes, the gold dust.

TOM. Ha, ha! the ladies are sharp, even in Berkshire. But let me tell you it's not so easy to get as people think! a crop of gold doesn't come by the wind, any more than a crop of corn.

GEORGE. No – it comes by digging, I suppose?

TOM. Ay, and harder digging than your potatoes ever saw, and harder work than you ever did – you make your oxen and horses perspire for you.

GEORGE. Did you ever see an ox or horse mow an acre of grass or barley?

TOM. Don't brag – they'll eat all you can mow, and never say a word about it.

WILLIAM. Bravo, Mr. Robinson – you had him there.

TOM. Gold is not to be got without hard toil even in California – the miners' shirts are wet through and through in their struggle for gold. Why, the little boys want a dollar a-piece for only half washing 'em – but the diggers won't submit to such extortion, so they send their linen to China in ships on Monday morning, and China sends them back on Saturday – only it's Saturday six months.

SUSAN. And you like that country so much, do you, sir?

TOM. I should think I did – one man's as good as another there, and a precious sight better. Why, I heard one of your clodhoppers say the other day, "The squire be very good to me – he do often give me a day's work." Now I should think it was the clodhopper gave the gentleman a day's work, and the gentleman gave him a shilling for it – and made five by it.[8]

WILLIAM. (*scratches his head*) Drat me if there isn't something in that, after all.

---

8. In line with Nan's arguments against social aspiration, Tom does not criticise class inequality in **HAZ2**.

TOM. Ay, rake that into your upper soil – and George, take your muscle, pluck, wind, and self, out of this miserable country, and come where the best man has a chance to win.

GEORGE. No, no – old England is the spot for me.

TOM. Old England's all very well if you happen to be married to a duke's daughter, and have got fifty thousand pounds a year – *and* a coach – *and* a brougham – *and* a curricle – *and* ten brace of pointers – *and* no end of pretty housemaids – *and* a butler, with a poultice round his neck, and whiskers like a mop-head – *and* a greenhouse full of peaches and green peas all the year round – *and* a carpet a foot thick – *and* a pianoforte in every blessed room in the house! But it's the dead sea to a poor man.

GEORGE. I'm afraid I begin to look at it in that light myself!

TOM. Anyone can see with half an eye what sort of land you're on! poor, hungry, arable ground! You know you can't work it to a profit.

GEORGE. (*sighing*) True – true!

TOM. I tell you what – steal, beg, or borrow five hundred pounds – carry out a cargo of pea jackets and fourpenny bits,[9] to swap for gold dust, a few tools, a stout heart, and a light pair of "Oh, no, we never mention 'em! their name is never heard." (*sings*)

GEORGE. But then, to live with all those thieves and ruffians that are settled down there, like crows on a dead horse! No, no! I thank you kindly all the same, but a crust of bread in old England before all the buffalo beef in California.

> SARAH, *the servant, enters, from farm,* R.

SARAH. Dinner's ready, master.

> [*Exit in farm.*

TOM. And I'm ready for your dinner, farmer. Come along, Will – come along, George.

> [*Exit in farm,* R. *followed by* WILLIAM.

---

9.   A short overcoat worn by sailors, and a small silver coin.

GEORGE. (*shakes hands with* SUSAN) Well, goodbye, Susan, and when I see you again, I hope you'll be in a better temper.

[*Going*

SUSAN. Stay, George – let me warn you against that man who has just left us. My father says he has no business nor trade, and is no gentleman, in spite of his fine clothes – be assured, George, he's a rogue of some sort.

GEORGE. Shall I tell you his greatest fault? he is *my* friend – the only creature that has spoken kind words to me today. Oh, I saw how disdainfully you looked at him!

SUSAN. You are a fool, George, and don't know how to read a woman, nor her words either. Farewell, and I trust some day you may judge me better.

[*Exit, L. U. E.*

GEORGE. Now *she's* turning against me. I feel as if everything was turning cold and slippery, and gliding from my hand. Old Merton's words have been like iron passing through my soul, and I almost wish the sun would set even now, at one o'clock, and bring this sorrowful day to an end.

[*Exit in farm.*

Enter JOHN MEADOWS, *followed by* PETER CRAWLEY, L. 1 E.

JOHN. (L.) Now, Mr. Crawley, oblige me by listening attentively to what I've got to say.

PETER. (C.) I will. You're a great man, Mr. Meadows – a very great man, sir.[10]

JOHN. I know you well, recollect – too well for your safety perhaps. You've done a deal of dirty work in your time.

PETER. I have – a very great deal. Isn't it astonishing – here's another year gone, and I'm not struck off the rolls?

JOHN. Those papers will give you every authority to do as I wish. I have bought this farm. (*points to farm*) George and William Fielding little guess that; they owe a twelvemonths' rent – it's a month overdue – demand it; they're not ready with it, I know.

---

10. Crawley's catch phrase is used in each of Hazlewood's adaptations, but not in **REA** or **CON**, indicating that Hazlewood developed the device.

PETER. (*lifting up his hands*) A wonderful man is Mr. Meadows – a wonderful man. Well, sir, what next?

JOHN. Put in an execution.

PETER. They'll be preciously put about!

JOHN. I hope so!

PETER. He's an astonishing man. Sir, may I ask what is the game with this young George Fielding?

JOHN. You ought to guess the game pretty well. Why, to get him in my power, and take his sweetheart from him to be sure.

PETER. He's a cunning man! a clever man is Mr. Meadows!

[*lifts up his hands.*

JOHN. Why, yes, I know how to play a close game, Crawley.

PETER. Nobody better, sir – nobody better. George Fielding won't be the only one in your power in these parts. Ha, ha! (*chuckling, and rubbing his hands*) Excuse my curiosity, sir, but when is the blow to fall?

JOHN. As soon as you like.

PETER. The sooner the better, sir. I shall be delighted, Mr. Meadows, for I too, have a grudge against the family.[11]

JOHN. Have you? then don't act upon it. I don't employ you to do your business, but mine.

PETER. Certainly, Mr. Meadows. You don't think I'd be so ungrateful as to spoil your admirable plans, by acting upon any little feeling of my own?

JOHN. If you did, we should part, Mr. Crawley.

PETER. Don't mention such an event.

JOHN. You've been drinking, Mr. Crawley.

---

11. Crawley does not bear George a grudge in **HAZ2**. He says: 'In my heart I dont [*sic*] dislike George [. . .] I shall do him no evil' (f. 5a).

PETER. Not a drop, sir, these two days. – Hic!

JOHN. You lie, sir – the smell of it comes through your skin. I won't have it – do you hear what I say? – I won't have it. No man that drinks can do business – especially mine.

PETER. He's a wonderful man – he's got an eye like a hawk.

JOHN. Hold your prate, and listen to me. The next time you look at a public-house, say to yourself "Peter Crawley, that is not a public-house to you, it is a hospital, a workhouse, or a dunghill" – for if you go in there, John Meadows that is your friend will be your enemy, so mark you that.

PETER. He's a surprising man, a long-headed man! Heaven forbid that I should offend you, Mr. Meadows.

JOHN. Then go and do my work, and don't do an atom more or an atom less than your task.

PETER. No, sir. Oh, Mr. Meadows, it's a pleasure to serve you, sir – you're as deep as the sea, sir, and as firm as the rock. You never drink, sir – you're a man of a thousand! No little weaknesses like the rest of us! You're a great man, sir – a model man, sir – a –

JOHN. There, that'll do, Mr. Crawley. Mind your business, and see that it is done properly.

[*Exit* L. 1 E.

PETER. Of course I will. (*knocks at Farmhouse door* R. 2 E.)

Enter WILLIAM – CRAWLEY *gives him paper.*

WILLIAM. (*looks at paper*) Has it come to this? (*goes to farm and calls*) George!

Enter GEORGE, R. 2 E.

George, I want to speak to you.

GEORGE. Some deadly ill-luck, I suppose. Out with it. I've felt it coming all day. But what can't I bear after the words I have borne this morning.

WILLIAM. George, there is a distress upon the farm for the rent.

GEORGE. (*staggered*) A distress upon the farm.

Enter SUSAN, L. U. E., *followed by* FARMER MERTON.

SUSAN. What do I hear?

PETER. Why, you hear what you might have expected to have heard a month ago. If folks don't pay they must turn out! (*goes to* L.)

MERTON. (C., *to* GEORGE) I told you how it would end.

GEORGE. Why do you come here to insult me? I must be a long way lower than I am, before I shall be as *you* were, when my mother took you up and made a man of you.

SUSAN. George, George, stay, for pity's sake, for you will say words that will separate us for ever. Father, how can you push poor George so hard, and he in such trouble. Oh, father, we have all been too unkind to him today.

Enter SERVANT, L. U. E., *with letter, which he gives to* GEORGE, R. C.

SERVANT. I was to wait for an answer, if you please. (*retires*)

GEORGE. (*looking at letter*) From Mr. Winchester! (*reads letter*) "George Fielding, – My fine fellow, think of it again – the ship sails from Southampton tomorrow. I will give you the five hundred sheep I said, to come with me, for I must have an honest man; and where can I find as honest a one as George Fielding?" Thank you, Mr. Winchester – George Fielding thanks you. "You are doing no good at the farm – everybody says so." He is right – everybody *does* say so. "Come with me, and let me be cheered by the face of a thoroughbred English yeoman, and – a – a – friend – and a – and –

SUSAN. (*finishing the letter, which* GEORGE *is unable to read from emotion*) "And an upright, honest man." And so you are, George! "If the answer is favourable, a word is enough. I will call upon you, and we can go up to town by the mail train."

GEORGE. (*to* SERVANT) The answer is "Yes!"

[*Exit* SERVANT, L. U. E.

SUSAN. No, no, George – you will not think of going.

PETER. (*aside, rubbing his hands*) We shall get rid of him – ha, ha! we shall get rid of him!

GEORGE. This nobleman's son, you see, respects me, if other folks don't. It's only the village curs that bark at misfortune's heels when all is done – so I'll go – I'll go!

SUSAN. Oh, father – father, what have you done?

MERTON. No more than my duty, girl; and I hope you will do no less than yours.

TOM ROBINSON *enters from house.*

TOM. Hollo! what's the row?

PETER. (*goes up and beckons on* THATCHER *and another* OFFICER *from* L. U. E.) Ha! there he is! that's the fellow they're after from London.

TOM. What's all this about?

WILLIAM. George is going to Australia!

TOM. What! To Australia? Au – stra – lia? Why, who ever goes there unless they're forced. I wouldn't go if my passage was paid, and a new suit of clothes given me, and the governor's gig to take me ashore to a mansion provided for my reception – fires lighted – beds aired, and pipes laid across the table.

Music. – The OFFICERS *advance, seize* TOM, *and put handcuffs on.*

PETER. To Australia you'll go, for all that, Tom Robinson, *alias* Scott, *alias* Lyon; and you shall have a new suit of clothes mostly one colour, and your voyage paid, and a large house waiting ashore for you, and the governor's barge will come alongside for you, providing they can't find the governor's gig – so, you see, you'll have most of the things you wish for, after all.

TOM. Gentlemen, what am I to understand by this violence from persons to whom I am an utter stranger? I am not acquainted with you, sir, and by the titles you give me, it seems you are not acquainted with me.

PETER. Ha, ha! show him you are not mistaken, Thatcher. (*they take pocket-book and notes from* TOM'S *pocket*) See! the stolen notes!

Enter JOHN MEADOWS, L. 1 E.

JOHN. Which I can identify.

TOM. Well, I suppose I'm nabbed at last.

GEORGE. What, and have I made the acquaintance of a thief?

TOM. Well, it's a business like any other.

GEORGE. If you have no shame, I have. The sooner I am gone now the better.

TOM. George, did I ever take anything of yours? You've got a silver caudle cup, a heavenly old coffee pot, no end of spoons, and they're all in a box under the bed in your room. Go and count them – you'll find them all right; and your bracelet, Miss Merton – (*to* SUSAN) the gold one with the cameo. I could have had it a hundred times. Do ask him to shake hands with me before I go.[12]

GEORGE. Shake hands with you! but there – you are not worth a thought at such a time. I forgive you, and hope I shall never see your face again. (*crosses* R.)

PETER. Honesty turns his back in theft's face!

TOM. Oh, carry me out of this as soon as you like. Any place is better than England. Let chaps that never saw the world and the beautiful countries

12. Tom engages the audience's sympathy from an early stage in **CON**, and is clearly represented as one of the heroes from the start. Tom presents himself as a Robin Hood-like figure: 'I openly rob the rich who dont [*sic*] feel it, you rob the poor and needy under the guise of the law, and ruin and bring them to distress' (f. 3b). More than mere posturing, Tom's protective interventions on behalf of Josephs in the opening scene indicate that his self-image is correct and his actions are justified – particularly after Meadows compels Crawley to arrest Josephs for stealing an apple from his orchard, even though Josephs pleads: 'Oh, forgive me, I was driven to it by want. I am starving and can get no work' (f. 5a). Still, despite the fact that **CON** introduces the prison narrative in I.i (unlike Hazlewood), this plotline receives no more attention in the rest of the script than in other adaptations. Although Josephs dies dramatically in Act II, unlike in the novel **CON** never returns to the prison after this scene.

that are in it, snivel at leaving this island of fogs, nobs, and taxes. England is the rich man's paradise, and the poor man's – Well, I won't swear – it's vulgar. (*sings*)[13]

> As I was going up the Strand,
>   Luddy fuddy! hi, poor luddy heigho!
> As I was going up the Strand,
> The beaks they took me out of hand,
>   Luddy fuddy! hi, poor luddy heigho!

[*Exit with* OFFICERS, L. U. E.

MERTON. Susan, mayhap the lad thinks me his enemy, but I'm not. My daughter shall not marry a bankrupt farmer, but bring home a thousand pounds, just to show me you are not a fool, and you shall have my daughter, and she shall have my blessing.

PETER. (*aside*) Do you hear that, Mr. Meadows?

JOHN. (L. C., *aside*) I do, and glory in the bargain.

SUSAN. Oh, father, your words are sending him away from me!

GEORGE. Susan, I am to go; but don't forget it is for your sake that I make the trial. Yes, for your sake, and to be a better man, I'll leave you.

Enter ISAAC LEVI *from farm,* R. 2 E.

ISAAC. No, you shall not!

JOHN. (*aside*) Ha! here to cross my wishes!

ISAAC. (R.) Young man you shall not wander forth from the home of your fathers. These old eyes see deeper than yours. You are honest – all men say so. I will lend you the money for your rent, and one who loves you will bless me.

---

13. The songs recorded in **HAZ2** differ from the printed script. The first is a non-diegetic love ballad, sung by Nan in I.i, which refers to her preceding dialogue about not wanting to be a lady. The second is an alternative comic song performed by Tom as he is led away by the police.

PETER. (*to* JOHN, *aside*) Oh, Mr. Meadows, here's all our web undone in a moment, through that old spider!

SUSAN. (C.) You will stay, George – you will stay?

GEORGE. (R. C.) No, Susan – no, old man! (*to* ISAAC) To borrow, without a chance of paying, is next door to stealing. Farewell, Susan! it was my hard luck there should be some bitter words between us this unlucky day. But you will think of me when the ocean rolls between us, if no villain undermines me, will you not, Susan?

SUSAN. Oh, George, you shall not go in doubt of me. We are betrothed these three years, and I never regretted my choice a single moment. I never saw – I never shall see – the man I could look on besides you, George – and while you are true to me, nothing shall part us twain. I love you – I honour you – I adore you.

PETER. (*aside to him*) Do you hear her, Mr. Meadows – do you hear her?

JOHN. (*aside*) I do – I do! but I'll triumph yet.

GEORGE. (*to* WILLIAM) Will, here is my life – my soul! (*pointing to* SUSAN) Let no man rob me of it, if one mother really bore us!

WILLIAM. Never, George, never! and may the red blight fall on my heart and arm, if *I* or any man takes her from you.[14]

GEORGE. (*grasping* WILLIAM'S *hand*) Give me your hand, Will – these fleshy compacts are stronger than bond, deed, or indenture, for they are written by moist eyes, stamped by the grip of eloquent hands – in those moments full of soul when men's hearts beat from their bosoms to their finger's ends. Goodbye, little village church, where I have worshipped, man and boy. Goodbye, churchyard, where my mother lies. There will be no church bells, Susan, where I am going – no happy peal, to remind me of soul and home! (*church bells heard till end of act*) What, are they mocking me?

WILLIAM. No, George – it is Tom Clarke and Esther Burgess, who were married this morning – only they couldn't have the ringers till afternoon.

---

14. In the novel, William is also in love with Susan.

GEORGE. And they have only kept company a year, and we have known each other twice as long, Susan! and while Tom and Esther are married today, what are George and Susan doing? Oh, Heaven help me! Heaven help me!

SUSAN. Oh, stay, George, stay! Don't go – don't go! Have pity on us both, and stay!

GEORGE. I cannot – I cannot! Farewell – farewell! I am with you, sir – I am with you.

[*Exit, rapidly*, L. U. E., *followed by* WILLIAM.

SUSAN. (*following*) George – George – Geo – (*fainting*)

JOHN. (*at back, exulting – raising his arms over her*) Mine – mine – mine!

ISAAC. (*catching her*) Not if I know it – not if I know it!

Tableau.

END OF ACT FIRST.[15]

––––––––––

15. There is a second scene in Act I of **HAZ2**, in which dialogue between Susan and Nan emphasises Susan's constancy to George during his absence, but also builds the audience's sense of dread, as Susan refuses to believe Nan's warnings about Meadows. Nan promises that she will 'be a Thorn in the way of that Meadows + trust me I'll match him yet' (f. 18a).

Close personal and family ties between the *dramatis personæ* are typical in melodrama. In I.ii, we also learn that Hawes is Meadows's cousin and Nan is Tom's sweetheart. Tom, Nan and Crawly form a love triangle which mirrors that between George, Susan and Meadows. But, unlike Meadows, Crawly openly tells Nan he is attracted to her.

The final exchange between Isaac and Nan in I.ii is a marked departure from the novel and Lacy's script. Nan is galvanised into action upon hearing that Tom is about to be transported to Australia, and swears that she will accompany Isaac 'to redeem Tom + make him again an honest man' (f. 21a).

By the end of I.ii, Nan has had more stage time than the primary romantic couple or Meadows, even though she does not feature in the novel, Lacy's script or other adaptations such as **CON**. However, Nan does appear in what is apparently the earliest dramatisation of the novel, licensed for the Surrey Theatre in April 1858, which toured provincial theatres in 1859. In this, as in **HAZ2**, Nan follows Tom to Australia with Isaac. This could indicate that Hazlewood's two versions respond to different but coexisting ideas about how the novel should be staged. Still, **HAZ2** is not a direct copy of the Surrey production, as the latter includes Mr Eden, Hawes and Jacky among the *dramatis personæ*, where Hazlewood does not.

ACT SECOND.

SCENE FIRST.[16] – *A Double Scene, representing the Interior of Two Prison Cells.*[17] *A door in flat in each cell – in cell,* L. *a small round table and stool, in each cell, on truckle bed, a mattress.*

TOM ROBINSON, *in prison dress, discovered, seated on stool in* L. *compartment, ruminating.*

TOM. And so I've got ten years of it! And I'm to begin with twelve months imprisonment, and then to go across the sea to finish the rest. How things are altered since I was last in quod[18] under the old system. *Then* the gaol was a finishing school of felony and petty larceny – now they make it a hospital for the cure of diseased morals.[19]

Enter EVANS, *the turnkey, (door* L. C.) *with* TOM'S *breakfast in a round tin with two compartments, containing gruel and bread.*

EVANS. There's your breakfast. (*gruffly, and putting down tin*)

TOM. How civil! like any one flinging tripe to a bear. I say, old fellow, how long am I to be kept here without being allowed to mix with the other prisoners in the yard?

EVANS. Talking is not allowed here.

TOM. (*whistling with astonishment*) My eye!

EVANS. (*aside*) He whistled! Shall I report him or not? I've a great mind.

[*Exit,* D. F. *leaving it open.*

16. Instead of opening Act II with a prison scene, II.i of **CON** is set in Farnborough and features Meadows's revelation to Crawley that he loves Susan. By contrast, **REA** stages Meadows's confession at the beginning of the play.
17. A split stage is also used in II.ii of **CON**. Stage directions describe the setting as: 'The Model Prison. Passage in C. and another Cell RH' (f. 23b). 'Joseph [*sic*] is thrown in LH Cell, he crouches down on Bed [. . .] Robinson is left in his Cell RH' (f. 24b).
18. Prison.
19. **CON** employs soliloquy to fill in narrative detail that Hazlewood's adaptation stages, and explicitly to condemn the prison system: 'When I first came here I had'nt [*sic*] a bad heart, I was a felon but I was a man, they turned me to a brute by cruelty and wrong. Mr. Eden came too late, it was'nt [*sic*] Tom Robinson he found in this cell. I had got to think all men were devils, they poisoned my soul. I hated Heaven and man, but he came his voice, his face, his eye were all pity and kindness. I hoped but I was afraid to hope. I had seen but two things in this place, Butchers & Hypocrisy' (f. 25a).

TOM. Here, you've left the door open. Don't you know manners?

EVANS. (*putting in his head*) Prisoners shut their own doors.

TOM. Well, I don't see what I shall gain by that!

EVANS. If you answer me again I'll tell you what you'll gain!

TOM. What's that?

EVANS. The black hole.[20]

[*Exit, door* L. C.

TOM. Oh, well I'm blessed! every man his own turnkey now! Oh, good luck to you, save the queen's pocket, whatever you do. Times are so precious hard! box at the opera costs no end of money. Well, it's no use being out of temper! I may as well get my breakfast. (*takes up tin, sits at table, and eats*) Bread and gruel! Ah, this is the sort of grub I had when I was in quod before. (*eats*) It's not very relishing, but I suppose I shall have something nicer at dinner time. They used to allow the prisoners three ounces of meat here, and no bone in it either – eight ounces of potatoes, and eight ounces of bread. Now that's what I call very tidy! It's twice as good as they give the poor devils in the workhouses – that pleases me! but it's the way. The beauty of Old England is, they always feed the thief better than they do the poor pauper in this country. Ah, I begin to find out that it's a great crime to be poor! If people respected a ragged honest man, instead of a rogue in a fine coat, the ragged man would often be saved from a place like this, into which he has been thrown by the wish to cut a swell in the eyes of those who worship the clothes and not the man.

EVANS, *re-entering,* D. F.

EVANS. Prisoners to open and shake bedding, wash face, hands, and neck, on pain of punishment – clean cells, and be ready to clean corridors.

[*Exit,* D. F.

TOM. All right – I shan't be sorry to clean the corridor, if it's only for a change. (*sings*) "Oh, bear him to some distant sphere, or solitary cell."

20. Reade based the abuse that Tom and Josephs suffer in prison on shocking details that emerged from an 1853 government enquiry reported in *The Times* (12 Sep.). Likewise, Josephs's suicide is inspired by a real case: Edward Andrews, who hanged himself in Birmingham Gaol. (See Henderson (2004), pp. 97–8.)

EVANS, *re-entering,* L. C.

EVANS. Prisoners who sing are put in the black hole.

[*Exit* L. C.

TOM. Oh, powder me blue! what a crib it is!

[*Exit, after* EVANS, L. C.

Music – JOSEPHS, *a convict lad, is dragged in by* TWO TURNKEYS, (*door* R. C.) HAWES, *the governor, follows, in the* R. *compartment which is the cell of Josephs.*[21]

HAWES. (*to* JOSEPHS) So you won't work at the crank, eh?

JOSEPHS. I can't, sir, I'm only just getting well of a fever. I'm as weak as water – I am, indeed, sir.

HAWES. And that's why you are not trying to do anything, eh?

JOSEPHS. I have tried, sir, and it's impossible. I'm not strong enough to turn that heavy crank.

HAWES. Well, I must try if I can't make you. (*calls off* R. C.) Bring the punishment jacket.

JOSEPHS. Oh, for Heaven's sake don't torture me, sir! there is nobody more willing to work than I am. Give me a day or two to get my strength after the fever, and then see how I'll work!

Enter EVANS, *with the jacket, door* R. C.

HAWES. There, hold your palaver! Strap him up!
(*Music – They seize him, and bind him in the jacket or straight waistcoat, and chain him to wall which divides the prisons*)

JOSEPHS. Oh, mercy, good gentlemen – mercy!

---

21. Hazlewood's printed script differs from each of the variants because Josephs is not introduced in I.i. As in **CON**, pity inspires Tom to attempt to prevent Josephs's capture in I.i of **REA** – this time by locking him in a barn. Likewise in **HAZ2**, the audience first encounters Josephs out of prison in I.i, but his relationship with Tom is staged differently: they are already allies, and Josephs hopes to warn Tom about the nearby policemen, so that they can escape together.

Enter MR. EDEN,[22] *the chaplain,* D. R. C.

EDEN. What is all this, Mr. Hawes?

HAWES. That's my business – mind your own, Mr. Parson.

EDEN. As chaplain of this jail, sir, I ask you this lad's offence?

HAWES. Refractory at the crank.

EDEN. Why, Josephs, you told me you would always do your best.

JOSEPHS. So I do, your reverence, but the crank is too heavy for a lad like me, and that is why I am put on it to get punished.

HAWES. Hold your tongue!

EDEN. Why is he to hold his tongue? How can he answer the questions I have a right to ask him if he holds his tongue? The crank is too heavy for him in my opinion, and I think he is strapped too tight.

HAWES. Will you take a bit of advice, sir? If you wish a prisoner well, don't come between him and me, for it will always be the worse for him – for I am master here, and master I will be.

EDEN. Mr. Hawes, I have never done or said anything in the prison to lessen your authority, but privately I must remonstrate against the uncommon severities practised upon the prisoners in the gaol – and if you will not listen to me, I must call the attention of the visiting justices to the question.

HAWES. Well, parson, the justices will be in the gaol today – you tell them your story, and I will tell them mine.

EDEN. This is a nice quiet boy. What is he in for?

HAWES. Stealing a piece of beef out of a butcher's shop.

EDEN. Poor boy! How old are you? (*to* JOSEPHS)

JOSEPHS. Sixteen, sir.

22. Mr Eden does not appear on stage in **HAZ2**, though he is spoken of several times as an eminently good man. In **CON**, however, Eden is introduced in II.i, prior to the prison scene in II.ii.

HAWES. He's a hardened ruffian – he's been in prison three times; once for throwing stones, once for orchard robbing, and this time for the beef.

JOSEPHS. I won't live such a life as this, and so I tell you. Why don't you hang me at once?

HAWES. You hear his impudence.

EVANS. (*to* HAWES) If you were to order him a flogging, sir, I think it would be all the better for him, sir, in the end.

HAWES. So do I, Evans. So let him have twenty lashes.

EVANS. I beg your pardon, sir, but will you allow me to make a remark?

HAWES. Certainly, Mr. Evans.

EVANS. I find twenty lashes, all at once, rather too much for a lad at his age. Now if you would allow me to divide the punishment into two, so that his health might not be endangered by it – then we could give him ten, or even twelve, and after a day or two as many more.

HAWES. That speaks a great deal for your humanity, Mr. Evans!

EDEN. Yes, a *very* great deal.

HAWES. Well, give him half the punishment, today, and half tomorrow.

JOSEPHS. No, no, sir! Oh, please flog me all at once, and have done with it, for I don't feel the cuts near so much when you're half way through it!

HAWES. Hold your tongue! You little beggars get no good by kicking up a row.

EDEN. Mr. Hawes, this punishment is too severe for this delicate lad!

HAWES. Oh, for the matter of that, you'll see lots of people punished like that here. You had better mind your own business in the gaol – you'll find work enough.

EDEN. No doubt – and to dissuade men like you from unnecessary cruelty, is part of my work!

HAWES. If you come between me and the prisoners, sir, you won't be here long!

EDEN. What does it matter whether I am here or elsewhere? I shall do my duty, sir, wherever I am.

JOSEPHS. (*faintly*) Mercy – mercy!

EDEN. Your victim is fainting, sir – release him!

HAWES. He's only shamming! he'd come to the moment a pail of water was thrown over him.

EDEN. On your peril be it, if any harm befalls this lad. I hold you responsible, sir, for this prisoner's life and wellbeing, and beware how you injure him!

HAWES. And what will you do?

EDEN. I have spoken to warn you, not to threaten. Will you release that boy?

HAWES. No, not for an hour yet.

EDEN. Then I know my course! And may Heaven forgive *you* and direct *me*.

[*Exit,* D. C. R.

HAWES. What's that sneak's object?

EVANS. Can't say, sir.

HAWES. I'll watch him, and see where he goes. Follow me, Evans.

Music – Exit HAWES, EVANS, *and* TURNKEYS, D. R. C.

JOSEPHS. Water – water! Oh, they are killing me! I shall die – I shall sir! Oh, death, be quick, and release me from this place! For here the living are tortured – the dying abandoned, and the dead kicked out of the way.

TOM. (*looks in* R. D. F.) Oh, what is this? What have they been doing to you?

Enter TOM ROBINSON, *and tries to loosen him.*

JOSEPHS. No, no! what are you about? Let me alone – let me alone! They'll give it me worse if you unloose me – and you will be punished too!

TOM. But you will die, boy – you will die!

JOSEPHS. No, no, I shan't die – no such luck! Who are you? tell me quickly, and go. I am Josephs, No. 15, corridor A.

TOM. And I am Robinson, No. 16, corridor A.

JOSEPHS. They are killing me inch by inch! Oh, I can't stand this much longer! I shall go to father!

TOM. And where is he?

JOSEPHS. He is dead – and I don't care how soon I am the same, for the head gaoler and governor are killing me. Oh, if I could only live and hope as his reverence, the clergyman, told me! But I fear I can't, for Mr. Hawes, the governor, is bent on killing me!

TOM. But he shan't. I know where there is a brick I think I can loosen, just outside the door. I'll try while there is no one about.

[*Goes out,* D. R. C.

JOSEPHS. No, no! Don't – don't, Robinson! They'll be sure to find you out, and then you'll suffer the worse for it. Come back – come back! I think I hear footsteps! Look out, Robinson – look out! Mind they don't see you! Quick – quick!

Re-enter TOM, *with brick.*

TOM. It's here – I have it!

JOSEPHS. And what will you with it?

TOM. Smash that beast's skull with it, and then he can torture you no more.

JOSEPHS. Oh, don't do that. Better that he should murder us than you him.

TOM. (*contemptuously*) Murder! don't the brute murder you day by day?

JOSEPHS. He does – he says he will make my life hell to me – and I'm sure it has been nothing else to me since I've been here. You don't know what a relief it is to me to speak to any one! But you and I shan't often speak together again – perhaps never! (*weeps*)

TOM. Don't speak so, lad – keep up your heart – never say die!

JOSEPHS. Why don't they kill me at once, and have done with it?

TOM. Poor lad! their devilish instrument of torture is killing you by inches. (*going to him*) Why, I can't get my finger between the straps and the poor fellow's flesh! I can feel that he has scarcely room to breathe. It's a black and burning shame, to use any Christian like this. I'll loosen you a bit, if they kill me for it!

JOSEPHS. You'll get in trouble, I tell you.

TOM. I don't care.

> *Music – As* TOM *is releasing him. – Enter* HAWES, *door* R. C.
> *followed by* EVANS *and* TURNKEYS.

HAWES. Hollo, what's this? seize that fellow!
(EVANS *and the* TURNKEYS *seize* TOM, *who, after a struggle, is overpowered*)

HAWES. What, you'll assist a prisoner to get loose, will you? You'll dearly pay for that, my lad![23] Away with him to his cell, and keep him in solitary confinement for a week. And as for that rascal, Josephs, take him into the yard, and give him a dozen lashes.

JOSEPHS. Mercy – mercy!

TOM. Devil!

> *Breaks from* TURNKEYS – *knocks down* HAWES, *and is rushing up to*
> *escape by door, when other* TURNKEYS *enter, and overpower him. –*
> *Picture, and closed in.*

---

23. Melodramas often explore broader social injustices through characters' betrayal or abuse of close relationships between the *dramatis personæ*. This is the case in **HAZ2**. Nan explains that 'Farnborough Prison [. . . is] where private malice usurps the place of Justice, Meadows owed Tom a grudge, + his Cousin Hawes will lend him a helping hand to pay it' (f. 17b).

SCENE SECOND. – *Country View* (*1ˢᵗ Grooves.*[24])

Enter SUSAN, *followed by* ISAAC LEVI, R.

ISAAC. Come, come, my dear, don't give way, you'll fret yourself to death.

SUSAN. Is it possible that Mr. Meadows wishes me to play George false and marry him! What, marry Mr. Meadows? No, no – I cannot think that. And yet his attentions to me, and the readiness with which he proffered to serve my father! Oh, Susan, Susan! guard well your heart against craft and treachery, and let it ever beat with true love and constancy for one who is far – far away, and depending on my promise.

Enter JOHN MEADOWS, R.

JOHN. Good day, my dear Susan. Any letter from George yet?

SUSAN. No, Mr. Meadows. (*sighing*)

JOHN. Um! very strange! you ought to have had one long before this!

SUSAN. Yes, sir, I ought – but who knows what may have been the reason? Perhaps sickness –

JOHN. Perhaps death.

SUSAN. Oh, Mr. Meadows, don't talk so, without you would wish to kill me.

JOHN. *I* wish to kill you, my dear Susan! Why, what an idea! I should like to see you happy – happy with the man of your heart, and trust he may return to make you so – in fact, it cut me to the heart to see him go!

SUSAN. You could have easily prevented his going if you had liked, sir.

JOHN. How, my dear Susan?

SUSAN. Why, by lending him the money he has gone to seek in other lands.

24. Grooves were a mechanism that allowed scenery to be changed quickly, simply by sliding new wings and shutters into place at the beginning of a scene and pulling the old scenery away. Grooves came as sets. Top grooves were attached to the underside of the lowest fly gallery on each side, and these corresponded to another pair of grooves on either side of the stage floor. Most theatres had four sets, arranged parallel to the proscenium. For further detail on backstage machinery, see Booth (1991), pp. 58–98.

JOHN. Um! well – I – you see – I hadn't got the money at hand. (*aside*) Not for that purpose. But never mind, Susan, if George is gone never to return, there may be others who love you quite as much as he, and who may perhaps have the means to make you happier. I know one who would yield up his very life to make you his.

SUSAN. And he is –

JOHN. Here, dear Susan – here (*taking her hand, and kissing it*)

SUSAN. (*recoiling*) You!

JOHN. Even I!

SUSAN. And still you say you wish George back again to marry me, and see me happy. I am but a simple country girl, sir, but I have sense enough to see your motive. Let George Fielding never return, and still I would reverence him dead a thousand times more than I would the rich John Meadows living.

[*Exit*, L.

JOHN. Ah, is it so? What the better am I for all my scheming? Susan seems farther from me than ever. So much for scheming. That old Jew's curse seems ever ringing in my ears – he said "May all your good luck turn to wormwood," those were his words – his very words. Why do I think of Susan? She loves that man, George, with every fibre of her body. How she clung to him when he went away – and how I stood there, and looked on it, and did not kill them both! I see their parting now – it is burnt into my eyes and my heart for ever. Perdition seize him! may he die, and rot before the year is out! may his ship sink to the bottom of the sea! may – But what right have I to curse the man, and drive him across the sea too? Curse yourself, John Meadows, for letting a girl master your heart. Oh, Heaven, pity me, for this love will make a villain of me, and sink my soul to hell. I have ruined her father to gain her. I have led him into speculations that I knew would fail, that his daughter might have no dependence but in marrying me – and now she scorns me – scorns me in the hope of George returning, and making her happy with his thousand pounds! but she shall never have a letter from him, I have settled that. By my interest, I have got old Merton, her father, appointed postmaster, and every letter that George writes to her must pass through my hands first. I have the father in my power, and he shall secure me the daughter.

Enter FARMER MERTON, R.

MERTON. Good day, Mr. Meadows.

JOHN. Good day, Mr. Merton. I've seen Susan, your daughter, farmer – she seems sadly out of spirits.

MERTON. At not hearing from George, I suppose?

JOHN. Merton, she must never hear from him – she must think him either dead or unfaithful.

MERTON. How can she think that, when she gets a letter from him to say that he is constant to her?

JOHN. She must never receive a letter from him.

MERTON. But suppose a letter reaches the post office?

JOHN. Well, suppose it does? it must never reach your daughter, Susan.

MERTON. Why not? Would you have me keep it back, Mr. Meadows?

JOHN. It would not be the first letter you've kept back, Mr. Merton. Do you know this five-pound note? (*shows it*)

MERTON. Can't say I do.

JOHN. Why, it has passed through your hands.

MERTON. Has it? Well, a good many pass through my hands, being post-master. I wish a few of 'em would stop on the road.

JOHN. This one did – it stuck to your fingers.

MERTON. I don't know what you mean, sir.

JOHN. You stole it.

MERTON. Take care what you say – I'll have my action of defamation against you, if you dare say such a thing of me.

JOHN. Hold your tongue, you fool, and don't make yourself a fool. One or two in this neighbourhood lost money coming through the post. I said to myself, "Merton is a man who often speaks of his conscience – he must be thief." So I baited six traps for you, and you took five. This note came over from Ireland – you remember it now?

MERTON. I am ruined – I am ruined!

JOHN. You changed it at the grocer's – you had four sovereigns and silver for it. The other baits were a note and two sovereigns – you spared one sovereign, the rest you stole – they were all marked by lawyer Crawley – they have been traced from your hand, and lie locked up till next assizes. Good morning, Mr. Merton, think over what I've said about your daughter, Susan.

[*Exit*, L.

MERTON. Lost, lost, lost! he has me in his power, and will make the most of it.

PETER *entering,* R.

PETER. Of course he will. A great man is Mr. Meadows, Mr. Merton – a wonderful man!

MERTON. Oh, Mr. Crawley, can nothing be done? No one knows my misfortune but you and Mr. Meadows. It's not for my sake, sir, but for my daughter's. If she knew I had been so tempted, and had fallen, she'd never hold up her head again. Oh, sir, if you and Mr. Meadows will let me off this once, I'll take an oath, on my bended knees, never to offend again.

PETER. What will you do for me if I succeed?

MERTON. I'd do anything in the world to serve you.

PETER. Well, Mr. Merton, I'm undertaking a difficult task when I try to turn such a man as Mr. Meadows – but I'll try, and I think I may succeed – but I must have terms.

MERTON. Anything, Mr. Crawley, anything.

PETER. Every letter that comes here from Australia you must bring to me with your own hands directly.

MERTON. I will, sir, I will. Here is one just arrived – give it Mr. Meadows.

PETER. (*takes letter*) And you must find me ten pounds. (*aside*) Meadows shan't have all the pull. I'll squeeze him a little on my own account.

MERTON. Ten pounds! I must pinch to get it.

PETER. Well, pinch, then – and let me have it directly.

MERTON. You shall – you shall, before the day is out.

PETER. And you must never let Meadows know I took this money of you.

MERTON. No, sir, I won't. Is that all?

PETER. That's all.

MERTON. Then I'm very grateful, sir, and won't fail, you may depend.

PETER. You'd better not.

[*Exit* MERTON, L.

This fellow's a shuttlecock, and Mr. Meadows and I are the battledores, who will knock him about to some tune. I've got this man's secret, and I'll squeeze him all I can, just like Mr. Meadows squeezes me. He works his business through me – makes me his human money bag, and goes behind a screen, and pulls the strings. I'm in Meadows's power – he knew I was in difficulties, so he bought up all my debts, sued me, got judgements out against me, and raising the axe of law over my head with his right hand, offered me the hand of fellowship with his left. So I was obliged to go down on my knees, and surrender my existence to this great man. Great man, did I say? Well, he is a great man in roguery. How I should like to be able to make him look little! He's got me like a fly in a spider's web – but, if I can break through it, good night to Mr. Meadows!

SONG, – PETER. – AIR – "Nice Young Maidens."

> He's got me tight within his clutch,
> Curse Mr. Meadows!
> No one can his conscience touch,
> Curse Mr. Meadows!
> All he touches turns to gold!
> The poor man up by him is sold!
> And he's worth thousands I am told!
> Skinflint Mr. Meadows!
> Skinflint Mr. Meadows!

He won't let me take my glass,
Curse Mr. Meadows!
He calls me drunken goof, and ass!
Curse Mr. Meadows!
I know he's got me just like bird lime!
But don't I mean to bide my time,
And serve out Mr. Meadows!
And serve out Mr. Meadows!

People when he calls for rent,
Curse Mr. Meadows!
Folks who borrow at cent. per cent.
Curse Mr. Meadows!
If Old Nick gave him his dues,
I wouldn't stand within his shoes!
More cunning than ten thousand Jews,
Is grinding Mr. Meadows!
Is grinding Mr. Meadows!

During symphony of third verse, JOHN *enters,* L. *unperceived by* PETER.

Every night I go to rest,
I – (*sees* JOHN, *who has advanced*)
I – I bless Mr. Meadows!
I'm sure of masters he's the best!
Bless Mr. Meadows!
He's a man of wealth and worth –
And though not given much to mirth,
There's not his equal on this earth!
Bless Mr. Meadows!

[*bowing.*

(*aside*) The devil seize old Meadows!

JOHN. What is that you were saying about me?

PETER. Why, you heard how I was admiring you, sir. I had been saying, that a clever man like you, knew everything, sir – even how far it is to the bottom of the sea. Oh! (*lifting up his hands*) A great man is Mr. Meadows!

JOHN. Crawley, the world calls me close-fisted, have you found me so?

PETER. Close-fisted, sir! why, you're as liberal as running water. I often say to myself, "How long will this last, before such a great man as Mr. Meadows flings away a poor talentless fellow like Peter Crawley, and looks out for a cleverer man?"

JOHN. I don't want any soft soap, Mr. Crawley – answer me plainly. How far dare you go along with me in my plans?

PETER. As far as your purse extends.

JOHN. Anything is nothing. Put it in figures.

PETER. I'll give twenty per cent off all you give me if you'll let me see the bottom – the motive – the what it is all to end in.

JOHN. Why not say at once you would like to read John Meadows's heart?

PETER. We all have our little vanities, sir, and like to be thought worthy of confidence. It puzzles me why you should stop every letter that comes here from Australia. Oh, bless me, here is a letter from there just come. To think me getting it from the post office, and then forgetting it.

JOHN. Give it me instantly. (*opens it and reads*)

PETER. Why, what is the matter, sir?

JOHN. Nothing – nothing! Is the writ ready to arrest William Fielding for the money he owes me?

PETER. Quite ready Mr. Meadows!

JOHN. Return, then, as quickly as you can with an officer and put it in execution.

PETER. Well, but I thought you were going to prove William's friend for Susan's sake.

JOHN. Go, and without daring to utter another word.

PETER. Certainly, Mr. Meadows. Your word is law with me. You know the very great respect I have for you, sir. (*aside, going* R.) D—d old thief!

[*Exit* R.

JOHN. (*looking at letter*) The thousand pounds that George despaired of now seems a certainty. He says that six months' work with average good fortune, will do it; and he will return and claim Susan. You'll come too late, George Fielding. I never longed for a thing yet but I always got it; and I'll have Susan Merton, though I trample a hundred George Fieldings dead on my way to her. How shall this be done? Let me think – let me think!

Enter SUSAN, R.

Susan! (*starts at seeing her, and conceals letter*)

SUSAN. Yes, Mr. Meadows, I am here again; my errand here is concerning Mr. Levi, the Jew. Mr. Meadows, do let me persuade you out of your bitter feeling towards the old man. Let him have his house again. You must excuse what he said to you some time past, for he has never been taught how wicked it is not to forgive.

JOHN. True, Susan – human nature is very revengeful! few of us are like you. It is my misfortune that I have not a lesson from you oftener. Perhaps you might charm away this unchristian spirit, which makes me unworthy to be your – your friend! (*takes her hand*)

SUSAN. And are you really our friend, Mr. Meadows?

JOHN. I am, dear Susan, therefore forget George, and –

Enter WILLIAM FIELDING, R.

WILLIAM. (C.) No, Mr. Meadows, that she will never do!

JOHN. Dog! what brings you this way?

WILLIAM. Sheep are no match for the wolves when the dog is away, so the dog is here. Susan, do you remember poor George's last words to me? Well, I mean to keep my promise to him. I mean to keep my eye upon such as I think capable of undermining my brother! This man is a schemer, Susan, and you are too simple to fathom him. But sooner than see that, I'd twist as good a man's neck as ever stood in your shoes Mr. Meadows! (*going up to him*)

Re-enter PETER *with* CONSTABLE, L.

PETER. Stop a moment, Mr. William – you are my prisoner, if you please!

WILLIAM. What for?

PETER. (*shows paper*) You are arrested on this judgement, at the suit of Mr. Meadows.

SUSAN. Oh, William, William, what is to be done? Mr. Meadows, I – I hope you won't be hard with him.

WILLIAM. Not a word to him, Susan – take me away – our family is doomed never to prosper. I am ready to go.

Enter ISAAC LEVI, R.

ISAAC. But you shall not go, Mr. William – not so fast if you please. Mr. Meadows, you're not going to have it all your own way. Which of you has the judgement?

PETER. (*shows it*) I have!

ISAAC. The amount!

PETER. A hundred and six pounds, thirteen and fourpence.

ISAAC. (*gives notes*) Here is the money – give me the document. (*gives* PETER *money, takes paper and tears it up*) There, there; and thus do I scatter your plans to the winds, Mr Meadows, and wish you a very good day. You see the old Jew is still a match for the hard-hearted Christian. Come, my children, come!

Exeunt ISAAC, SUSAN, *and* WILLIAM, R. – CONSTABLE, L. – MEADOWS *and* CRAWLEY *stand and look at each other.*

PETER. No go, Mr. Meadows!

JOHN. Crawley, you wanted to see the bottom of me just now.

PETER. Oh, Mr. Meadows, that is too far for me or any man to see with the naked eye.

JOHN. Not when it suits my book. I am going to show you my heart – to tell you my secret.

PETER. Are you really, Mr. Meadows?

JOHN. Know, then, Crawley, that – I – I love Susan Merton.

PETER. You, Mr. Meadows!

JOHN. I love her with all my heart, soul, and brain.

PETER. The devil you do, Mr. Meadows.

JOHN. And your fortune is made if you help me to win her.

PETER. The deuce it is, Mr. Meadows!

JOHN. Old Merton has promised Susan to George Fielding if he comes back with a thousand pounds – that he must never do – no, not if it costs me ten thousand to win the day.

PETER. He's a plucky man, is Mr. Meadows.

JOHN. Crawley, you must assist me; and the day that I walk out of church the husband of Susan, I'll put a thousand pounds into your hand, and set you up in business.

PETER. Oh, Mr. Meadows, I knew you were a great man, but I never knew you were such a good one. Your plan at once, sir, that I may co-operate, and not spoil your great scheme through ignorance.

JOHN. My plan has two hands. One must work here – another a long way off. *I* must be one hand – *you* the other. *I* work thus: – The post office here is under my thumb – I stop all letters from George to Susan. Presently there must be a letter from Australia saying that he gives up Susan and has married a girl out there with money.

PETER. But who is to write the letter?

JOHN. Can't you guess?

PETER. Haven't an idea! she won't believe it.

JOHN. Not at first, perhaps; but when she gets no more letters from him, she will. So when Susan thinks George married, I strike upon her disappointment and her father's distress – ask him for his daughter, and if I get her, pay my father-in-law's debts, and start him afresh.

PETER. Beautiful – beautiful! a wonderful man is Mr. Meadows!

JOHN. But suppose while I am working thus George should come back with the thousand pounds.

PETER. Ah! that would be awkward!

JOHN. I'm glad you see it – you must prevent him.

PETER. I, Mr. Meadows? how?

JOHN. Take that! (*gives paper*) that is a paper of instructions, and this is my bill-book! (*gives it*) You are going a journey, Mr. Crawley!

PETER. Am I, Mr. Meadows?

JOHN. And will draw on me for a hundred pounds a month.

PETER. No! shall I, though! you're a king, Mr. Meadows! but where am I to go to?

JOHN. What! don't you know?

PETER. No, is it a long journey?

JOHN. It is! you are not afraid of the sea and wind!

PETER. The sea be dashed and the wind be blowed. When I see your talent and energy, and hold your bill-book in my hand, and your instruction in my pocket, I feel as if I could play at football with the world. When shall I start, Mr. Meadows?

JOHN. Tonight, Mr. Crawley.

PETER. Where am I to go to?

JOHN. To Australia!

PETER. To – to Australia?

JOHN. Ay, don't turn pale. To Australia, I say, to crush George Fielding. Come, Mr. Crawley, come? (*takes him by the arm*)

PETER. But Mr. Meadows – Mr. Meadows!

JOHN. Not a word! think of your reward – think of the thousand pounds. No flinching – come, come!

[*Music. – drags him off,* R.

———————

SCENE THIRD. – *The Double Prison, as before.*

Music. – Enter at the door in Robinson's cell, EVANS, *followed by* TWO GAOLERS, *dragging in* TOM ROBINSON – *lights down – the cell,* R. *is empty – Exeunt* EVANS *and* GAOLERS.

TOM. (*beating at the door*) No, no! any punishment but that! Leave me my reason – you have robbed me of everything else. For pity's sake leave me my reason. Twenty-four hours in darkness and solitude! Well, I'll sleep! Oh, no – sleep is for those who are well and happy – it won't come to a wretch like me to save me from despair. I must tire myself. I'm too cold to sleep, so here goes for a warm. (*walks up and down*) They want to drive me mad, but I'll do my best to spite 'em – they shan't! Oh, what have I done to be used as I am here? They drive me to despair, and then drive me to hell for despairing. Oh, patience! or I shall go mad. My whole life seems passing before me in horrible reality. Every dark spot on my conscience rises within me; and Mary, the girl I wronged, who died through me, is there – there! (*pointing*) And that is why I am here. Do you see me, Mary? This is my grave – my grave! (*falls – pause*)

MR. EDEN *enters the* R. *cell and taps at the wall in which there is a door.*

EDEN. (*addressing* TOM) Brother!

TOM. Who – who – who – calls Tom Robinson brother?

EDEN. I, Francis Eden, the chaplain. Take courage – a friend is close by you.

TOM. (*rising and listening*) A friend! where are you?

EDEN. Here, within a hair's breadth of you!

TOM. Ah! don't go away – pray don't! Oh, sir, you don't know what a poor fellow suffers in this dark cell.

EDEN. Well, are you calmer now?

TOM. Oh, that I am, sir! This place seemed like a tomb till I heard your voice, which sounds like blessed music to me; but it isn't fair that a gentleman like you should be kept shivering at an unfortunate man's door like mine.

EDEN. It is never too late to mend, Robinson![25]

TOM. Sir, when I first came here I hadn't a bad heart. I was a felon, but I was a man. They've turned me to a brute by the cruelty I have experienced and seen here. They've poisoned my soul, and I seem abandoned by Heaven and man!

EDEN. Robinson, this is wrong!

TOM. Perhaps it is, sir, but you don't know what it is to lose hope. Treat a man like a god, and you make him one. Oh, my benefactor – my kind friend – my angel – my – Oh, give me words to speak that mean something, before my heart bursts within me! (*weeps*)

EDEN. Weep on, my poor sinning, suffering brother! Let those tears refresh you, and shed peace on your troubled heart. Drop, gentle dew from heaven, and prepare his spirit, and prepare the dry soul for the good seed.

TOM. Your reverence is weeping, too – I am sure of it – my heart tells me you are shedding a tear for me, and I am happy. Go home, sir, now – you have done your work – you have saved me. I feel at peace. I can sleep – you need not fear to leave me now.

EDEN. I will take your word. In half an hour I will return. Have hope for the future. Although you have led a wicked life, it is a long life that has no returning; and remember the words I mentioned before – "It is never too late to mend."

[*Exit* R. D. F.

TOM. "It is never too late to mend." Well, I will mend – yes, yes, I will – I will! Now, let me try and sleep. (*lies down on mattress on truckle bed,* L.) And may I go from here a better man. (*sleeps*)

---

25. Nan is the moral pillar of **HAZ2**, and first gives voice to the drama's title (and message) in a conversation with Crawley in I.i.

Music. – JOSEPHS *is thrust in by* EVANS *and* TURNKEYS,
and HAWES *follows,* R. D. F.

HAWES. So, you won't turn the crank, eh, you young ruffian.

JOSEPHS. I can't – I can't – it is too heavy for me. I am weak and ill. I am too hardly used – I am too hardly used. (*cries.*)

HAWES. You are hardly used, are you? All you have ever known isn't a stroke with a feather to what I'll make you know by-and-by. Wait till tomorrow, and you shall see what I can do when I'm put to it.

[*Exit whispering to* EVANS, R. D. F.

JOSEPHS. (*falling on his bed,* R.) Oh, what shall I do – what shall I do? My mother – my mother – oh, my mother!

EVANS. Come, get up out of that!

JOSEPHS. What is it you want with me?

EVANS. We don't want you – we want your bed.

JOSEPHS. (*kneels to him*) No, don't rob me of my bed.

EVANS. Rob you! you young dog, it's the governor's order – no bed for fourteen days.

JOSEPHS. Ha, ha, ha! for fourteen days – a poor worn out boy deprived of his bed for fourteen days!

EVANS. It makes you laugh, does it, you young scamp?

JOSEPHS. It does. Tell the governor I'll find a bed in spite of him before fourteen days are over my head – long before.

EVANS. Come, you mustn't chaff the officers – the governor will serve you out quite enough without giving us any of your sauce. Here's your supper – six ounces of bread and a can of water. (*puts it down*)

JOSEPHS. It's as much as I shall want, and perhaps more; but I forgive you all. Good night! I'll give you my hand – you'll perhaps be sorry if you don't take it.

EVANS. (*shakes hands*) There it is! what the better are you for that you young fool? I tell you what it is, you're turning soft. I don't know what to make of you. I shall come to your cell the first thing in the morning.

JOSEPHS. Do, and then you won't be sorry you shook hands with me tonight, perhaps, for I can't stand this much longer – 'tisn't in human nature to stand it, you know.

EVANS. That boy's getting cranky. I shall speak to the doctor about him.

[*Exeunt* EVANS *and* TURNKEY, R. D. F.

JOSEPHS. What are they going to do with me tomorrow? Something worse than all I have gone through yet, he said; but no, that's impossible! I feel I can bear no more – their cruelty has done for me – I feel it has. I shall be beyond their reach tomorrow – they won't let me live, and it's better I should die. It's hard – I'm only sixteen, but Hawes, the governor, won't let me live to be a man. Mr. Eden will be sorry. Bless him, for being so good to me. My mother will fret, but I hope someone will tell her what I went through, and then, perhaps, she'll say better that my boy should die so than live to be tortured every day of his life. Farewell, mother, farewell. (*kneels*) Forgive me, Heaven, for all my faults, for you know what I have suffered. Oh, I die, I die! Now, Mr. Hawes, I am beyond your reach for ever – for ever! (*dies*)[26]

Enter HAWES *and* EVANS, R. D. F.

HAWES. I've altered my mind – I'll send this boy to hard labour in the yard.

EVANS. Josephs, you're on the list for hard labour in the yard. (*looks round*) Why, where is he? (*recoils with a cry of horror, covering his face with his hands*)

HAWES. What the devil are you howling at?

EVANS. Look there, Mr. Hawes, look there! (*points*)

HAWES. (*looking*) Why, the young vagabond has killed himself. Here, Jones – Smith – Barker!

---

26. Henry Morley was unimpressed by Reade's play and called Josephs's death a 'repulsive excrescence, which does not advance the story by a syllable'. Morley's *Journal* is typically scathing of sensation dramas, but he nonetheless records their impressive scenic effects. In the case of **REA**, he states that: 'the most costly scene in the play [is] a perspective of radiating prison corridors seen from the centre of a model prison, with practicable tiers of galleries, and iron staircases, and cells, and gas-lights' (1866, p. 380).

TOM. (*waking up*) Hollo! what's the row, I wonder!

EVANS. The young viper has done this to spite us!

Enter MR. EDEN, R. C.

EDEN. What is this? (*sees* JOSEPHS) Great heavens! the boy dead!

TOM. What do I hear?

EDEN. (*kneels by* JOSEPHS) And who can wonder at it? Brutes! murderers!

TOM. (*kneeling*) Poor, suffering boy! May our Heavenly Father take thy soul into his blessing!

EDEN. (*to* HAWES) Unhappy man! your victim is at rest. Heaven is merciful it has not struck you dead by his side. It gives you, greatest sinner of all, a chance of escape – to your knees, and pray for mercy on your forfeited soul.

HAWES. It – it – it – was the boy's fault, not mine – he – he – was – was obstinate – he –

EDEN. Hope not to shift the weight of guilt upon poor Josephs, there. As men taken by pirates at sea, and stabbed with cold steel, till in despair and pain they throw themselves into the sea, so died Josephs, murdered by you. And so surely as the sun will rise tomorrow, so will the spirit of this poor boy rise up against you, and bear your guilty soul down to perdition for ever – for ever – for ever![27]

Slow Music – Tableau. – TOM *continuing on his knees in the other cell, picture.*

END OF ACT SECOND.

————

27. In the novel, Josephs's death is the final trigger before Mr Eden acts to remove Hawes from the prison. He drafts in a government inspector and proceeds to detail the many cruelties of which Hawes is guilty, before revealing Josephs's dead body. Hawes is disgraced but is not penitent, and Mr Eden delivers a fiery sermon advising him to repent. Nan adopts Eden's role in **HAZ2**: 'You will have to answer thus (officers enter) There's your Prisoner (to Hawes) read this authority, + you'll find in it the dismissal of Mr Hawes from the Gaol + a Warrant to detain him for cruelty to Prisoners under his charge' (f. 23a).

ACT THIRD.

SCENE FIRST. – *Australia.*[28] *Horizon at back, and set waters extending in the distance – set rocks from* R. U. E. *to* R. 1 E. *– a rude log hut,* L. *– a bank,* L. U. E. *– Half dark.*

Enter GEORGE *from hut,* L.

GEORGE. Oh, what a heavenly land after four months prison at sea. My heart beats high with hope – surely in such a place I may hope to make the thousand pounds. Heaven knows my heart was never much set on gain; but it is now that I may make the stipulated sum and hasten back to dear old England, and claim Susan. My friend, Mr. Winchester, has given me a hundred pounds to start with, and five hundred sheep – bless him for it – may he soon make a rapid fortune in the large tract of land he has purchased five miles from here. A thousand pounds! why it's nothing if a man has luck. Why there are men who gain that in a week by making clever bargains. And yet how many have toiled all their lives and never reached that sum, and yet I'm eighty pounds richer than I was a few weeks ago – come that's getting on.

JACKY. (*singing without* R. U. E.)

> Black man eat de white man up,
> Ting tong ting, ting tong tong.
> But Jacky like on 'coon to sup,
> Ting tong tong, ting tong tong.

GEORGE. Here comes my black servant, Jacky – servant did I say? it's little work Jacky does, except hunting racoons and kangaroos.

28. The action shifts to Australia in Act II of **HAZ2**. Tom and George are reunited early in II.i, when Tom saves George from being attacked by 'Indians'. Jacky does not feature in this version: Tom and George discover gold on their own. Another major difference is that Nan, having travelled to Australia with Isaac, is present when Black Jack [*sic*] and his associates set fire to George and Tom's tent. Moreover, the audience learns that Crawly masterminded this arson by report only in the next scene, which is the first time that Meadows explains his schemes explicitly. In Lacy's script, by contrast, Hazlewood foregrounds Meadows's machinations throughout.

    Some scenes in Act II of **HAZ2** are out of sequence and are labelled differently to those in the rest of the manuscript. This could imply that several versions of Hazlewood's adaptation are spliced together in the licensing script. In this case, **HAZ2** might represent a working copy of the drama. Alternatively, it is possible that scenes from Hazlewood's *NTL* were quickly put together with scenes from different plays to meet licensing deadlines. In II.v and II.vi, Meadows's and Susan's names replace those of characters who do not appear in the drama: Esther and Withers. These unfamiliar names have been crossed out, but the dialogue has not been changed beyond altering the name Beecher to Fielding when the characters discuss George.

Enter JACKY *down rocks,* R. U. E. *singing, with two coat sleeves*
attached to either end of a long stick, which he carries
yoke fashion across his shoulders – the coat sleeves
are supposed to be filled with game, &c.

JACKY. Good morning, massa George; hope you berry much better dan well, sar!

GEORGE. You've been hunting again then Jacky; you seem very fond of change.

JACKY. Yes, massa George – black fellow like another place, not every day the same.

GEORGE. But what have you done with your coat?

JACKY. Make bags of him, massa.

GEORGE. But where's the rest of the coat?

JACKY. Thrown it away, 'cause it good deal hot.

GEORGE. But then it won't be hot at night, and then you'll wish you hadn't been such a fool.

JACKY. Jacky too hot now, nebber mind being cold 'noder time.

GEORGE. Well, Jacky, it seems you're not inclined to make much of a shepherd to me, and yet you ought, for I suppose you've not quite forgotten Two Fold Bay?

JACKY. (*scratching his head*) Two Fold Bay, massa George?

GEORGE. You were not hunting then; you were hunted, and pretty close too – well! if he hasn't forgotten the whole thing, shark and all!

JACKY. Shark! shark! Oh, now Jacky remember; Jacky in water, shark come to Jacky, you throw rock on shark, kill him, and den he no bite Jacky, so den we get shark ashore, and cook him, and 'stead of shark eat Jacky, Jacky eat shark – yah, yah, yah! But (*touching his head*) dat a long way off – berry long way off to tink on – white man tink a long way off. Black fellow see berry little behind him back.

GEORGE. You are right lad, it was a long while ago, and I am vexed for mentioning it. Well, anyway, you *are* come back, and you are welcome. (*Music*)

ABNER *runs on from* R. U. E., *down rocks.*

ABNER. Oh, master, the sheep, the sheep!

GEORGE. What's the matter?

ABNER. The sheep, master – the sheep they're dying by the score – they've all got the rot.

GEORGE. I feared this – I dreaded this every night of my life; for days I suspected something of the kind, but dared not give utterance to my thoughts – sharpen your knife, Abner.

ABNER. What must they all –

GEORGE. Yes, they'll be worth nothing now, except for their wool, and the fat they'll boil down for. Jacky will help you – he likes to see the sight of blood. I can't abide it – I can't go and see their blood and my means spilt like water. Oh, Susan! this is a black day for us. But away with Jack, Abner, and see how many you can save.

ABNER. No, thank you, sir, you'd better look out for another shepherd.

GEORGE. Why, surely you wouldn't think to leave me in this plight?

ABNER. Well, ye see, I've got the offer of a place with Mr. Meredith, and he won't wait for me, if I don't go at once.[29]

GEORGE. Ah! he is a rich man, and I am a poor one.

ABNER. That's just the reason I'm going, sir!

JACKY. Den I tell you what, Abner, you tam rascal!

---

29. In **CON**, III.i opens with Crawley bribing Abner with £50 to leave the diseased sheep in with the rest of the flock, knowing the rot will spread to all of them.

ABNER. There's no agreement between us, you know – but I'll stay a week to oblige you.

GEORGE. How can I get another shepherd in a week? And you'll stay to *oblige* me, you say – then oblige me by taking yourself off – there are your wages. (*throws down money*) Out of my sight, and let me meet misfortune with only friends by my side.

ABNER. (*picks up money*) Well, I'm sure!

GEORGE. Away with you, and wherever you go, may sorrow and sickness – but, no, your own selfishness will be sufficient punishment for you some day.

[*Exit* ABNER, R. U. E.

The ungrateful rascal, to leave me in a fix like this.

JACKY. Massa George, suppose I get de make thunder, (*imitating gun*) and shoot him.

GEORGE. Shoot him? what for? No, Heaven forbid I should do the man any harm! I'm only angry that he should leave me in my trouble; I that was so kind to him; do you remember when he was ill, how you and I tended him, and now to leave us – and I in such trouble; but there, I'll think no more about it. Work is best for a sore heart, and mine is sore and heavy too this day.

JACKY. First you listen to me; this one time I speak a good many words. Dat fellow know nothing, and 'cause you not shoot him, you very stupid, he know nothing wid dese. (*touching his eyes*) Jacky know possum, Jacky know kangaroo, know turkey, know snake, know good many, some wid legs, like dis – (*shows two fingers*) some wid legs like dis – (*shows four fingers*) He stupid fellow, know nothing but de sheep, and dem he let die – you do him good things, he do you bad things, and dat make Jacky angry, so Jacky go hunting a little, not much, directly.

[*Going* R. U. E.

GEORGE. What today? no, no, Jacky, don't go today – don't set me against flesh and blood altogether.

JACKY. Jacky come back when sun dere. (*pointing to the east*) But must hunt a little, not much – Jacky a good deal uncomfortable.

GEORGE. Well, I'll say no more, I have no right – goodbye, take my hand, I shall never see you any more.

JACKY. Massa George, dis a good deal dam ridiculous. I shall come back when de sun dere. (*pointing eastward*)

GEORGE. Ah, well, I dare say you think you will. Goodbye, Jacky, don't stay to please me.

JACKY. (*going, singing*) "Black man eat de white man up," &c.

[*Exit* JACKY, R. U. E.

GEORGE. He thinks he'll come back to me; but when he finds himself in the forest, and gets on the track of the animals he likes to hunt, he'll follow them wherever they go, and his poor shallow head will neither remember this place nor me. I have left my Susan, and I have lost her – left the only friend I had, or ever shall have in this hard world. Oh, how my head swims! My limbs seem powerless! Heaven send I'm not going to have the fever and ague! Oh Susan, Susan! I shall never see you more! (*sinks on bank*)

Music. – Enter TOM ROBINSON, R. U. E.

TOM. Hollo, here's a hut! Anybody at home here? (*bawls*) No answer! Where's the proprietor, I wonder. (*sees* GEORGE) Is this he asleep? Hollo, mate! (*shaking him*)

GEORGE. (*rising*) What's your business?

TOM. What – George Fielding!

GEORGE. Ah, Robinson, is that you? (*coolly*)

TOM. Just the welcome I expected – but I'm a better man than I was. I'm getting to be quite respectable. I'm a ticket-of-leave[30] now; they sent me from England here 'cause I behaved myself so well. I heard you were here – I see you don't think much of me – but perhaps you don't know that I've walked sixty miles to bring you a letter, and from Mr. Eden, the chaplain of the stone jug I was in. (*shows letter*)

---

30. Tickets of leave were parole documents issued to convicts who were released before they had served their full sentence. These people were allowed to work for themselves, but still had to report to local authorities regularly and could not leave the country. Tom Taylor's sensation drama *The Ticket of Leave Man* was a runaway success in 1863.

GEORGE. (*takes letter and opens it*) Why does he write to me? I don't know the man!

TOM. But you'll find a letter inside from someone you *do* know.

GEORGE. (*taking out an enclosed letter*) 'Tis Susan's hand! (*kissing it*) You're a good fellow after all to bring me such a letter, and I'll never forget it as long as I live. There's something about you, Tom, in this letter.

TOM. About me?

GEORGE. Susan says you never had a father – not to say a father that –

TOM. She says true.

GEORGE. And Susan says, that is a great disadvantage to any man, and – poor fellow – she says, they came between your sweetheart and you, and you lost her. No wonder you went astray after that. What would become of me if I lost my Susan! She says that she and I have never been sore tempted like you.

TOM. Bless her little heart for making excuses for a poor fellow like me – but she was always a charitable, kind hearted young lady.

GEORGE. Wasn't she, Tom?

TOM. And what sweet eyes!

GEORGE. Ain't they, Tom? – brim-full of heaven, I call them.

TOM. And when she used to smile on you, George! Oh, the ivories!

GEORGE. Will you stay with me, Tom? I'm not a lucky man, but while I have a shilling, there's sixpence for the man that brought me this letter. Stop, Tom, there's something for you here. (*takes out another from enve-lope – reads direction on it*) "George Fielding is requested to give this to Thomas Robinson." Open it, Tom, and see what's inside. (*gives it*)

TOM. (*opening it*) A five pound note! (*takes it out and reads letter*) "If you have retained the name of an honest man, keep it." You see, George, I'm well paid for my journey. Who wouldn't be honest if they knew the sweets! This comes from Mr. Eden. Bless his kind heart – he *is* a man – a man? he's a brick! George, how far have you got towards your thousand pounds?

GEORGE. Oh! don't remind me of it, Tom. How can I ever make it? – no market within a thousand miles of any place in this confounded country. Forced to boil down sheep into tallow, and sell them for the price of a wild duck. I have left my Susan and have lost her. Oh! why do you remind me –

TOM. So much for the farming lay. Don't you be down hearted – there's better cards in the pack than the five of spades – and the more I see of this country the surer I am – for when I shut my eyes for a moment and then open them, I'm in California.

GEORGE. Dreaming?

TOM. No! wide awake – wider awake than you are now. Look at these hills – you couldn't tell them from the golden range of California. When you look into them they're made of the same stuff, too – granite, mica, and quartz.

GEORGE. Oh, nonsense, Tom! We'll drop gold – tell me what this is. (*gives him fossil*)

TOM. (*taking it and looking at it*) He bids me drop gold, and then shows me a proof of gold that never deceived me.

GEORGE. You are mad! how can this be a sign of gold? I tell you it's a shell.

TOM. And I tell you that where these things are found, gold is to be found, if men have the wit, the patience, and the skill to look for it!

GEORGE. Tom, if there is as much gold in this land as will make me a wedding ring, I'm a Dutchman!

TOM. (*excited*) George! (*stamping on ground*) If I don't stand on gold, I'm d–d!

GEORGE. No more of this – let us go down into the pasture.

TOM. Not I – prejudice is for babies, George – experience for men. I'll stay here and work for gold. Why, that very gully yonder – (*points,* R.) looks exactly like the mouth of a purse. Come with me, George.

GEORGE. Not I.

TOM. Why not?

GEORGE. You'll have a better chance if I'm not by to spoil it. Luck is all against me – if there's money to be made by a thing, I'm out of it. If there's money to be lost, I'm in it. If I loved a vixen, she'd drop into my arms like a medlar – I love an angel, and that is why I shall never have her – never! From a game of marbles to the game of life, I never had a grain of luck like other people. Leave me, Tom, and try if you can find gold – you'll have luck, perhaps, if unlucky George is not with you.

TOM. Leave you, George? Not if I know it!

GEORGE. You are to blame if you don't. Turn your back on me, as I did on you in England.

TOM. Never! I'd rather not find gold than part with honesty. You've got such a thing as a pickaxe and a spade, I suppose?

GEORGE. I have, in the hut.

TOM. Let's be quick, and get them. Lord, lord! What a twitter I'm in!
               [*Exeunt* TOM *and* GEORGE *in house,* L.

BLACK WILL *and* JEM *look on, from* R. U. E. *watching them.*

BLACK WILL. Curse their inquisitiveness! They've hit on the secret. A secret is no secret if all the world is to know it.

JEM. You remember our oath, captain?

BLACK WILL. Why should I forget it? Have you got your knife?

JEM. I have.

BLACK WILL. We'll soon settle them, then. Back! They return!

Enter TOM *and* GEORGE *with pickaxe and spade, from hut.*

GEORGE. Well, what are we to do? Go up that rock, and dig into its side?

TOM. Ay, and if we find a speck of gold in them, I'll believe that yonder river is the gold's home, and there we will wash for it!

GEORGE. Well, I own the sample mostly tells us what is in the barn.

TOM. Now, then, let us set to work and break every stone in the rock if we can.

> [*as they are going to rock* R., BLACK WILL *and* JEM *come down and confront them.*

BLACK WILL. Hold hard, mates – two words to that bargain. You've found out our secret, and it must die with you. Stick to me, Jem, and stop their tongues.

Music. – WILL *attacks* GEORGE, *and* JEM TOM *– they struggle –* JEM *and* WILL *are overcome.*

BALCK WILL. Bob Sutton – Bob, where are you?

> BOB SUTTON *enters,* R. U. E., *with a knife to stab* GEORGE.

BOB. Bob is here! (*raising knife to strike*)

> JACKY *enters and strikes him down with club.*

JACKY. And so'd Jacky, you tam thief!

BLACK WILL. ⎫
BOB.   ⎬   Quarter! Quarter! Quarter!
JEM.   ⎭

GEORGE. Give us your knives, then!

BLACK WILL. There! (*throws down his knife – the others do the same*)

TOM. Get up, while I show you the error of your ways. (*they rise*) I could forgive a rascal, but I hate a fool. You thought to keep this secret all to yourself, and you would spill blood sooner than your betters should know it. Now I tell you what it is, you're for keeping dark all you know, so be off, or else my pal and his nigger here shall make all dark with you in quick sticks!

BLACK WILL. Where are we to go to, mate?

GEORGE. (*points* R. U. E) Do you see that ridge about three miles west? Well, if we catch you on this side of it, we'll hang you like wild cats. Come, go!

BLACK WILL.
BOB.   } Well, but – (*grumbling*)
JEM.

GEORGE. Come, be off! No more words, or – (*presents pistol.*)

BLACK WILL. Well, if we must, we must. (*aside*) A time *will come*, lads!

TOM. Come, off you go.

> [*They exeunt,* R. U. E.

To work, George, to work! (*Music. – They dig in the side of rock,* R.) See, George, see! (*picks up a small nugget*) Here's a small sample to show you I was right.

JACKY. What you look for? you make all this row about yellow stone! Why, Jacky show you where to find large lump.

TOM. Large lump – of what?

JACKY. Yellow stone, massa!

GEORGE. Where, Jacky?

JACKY. Why, just here, massa! (*points to rock piece,* R. 2 E.)

TOM. I do believe he's right, George – set to work. (*Music. – They loosen the earth and the nugget of gold falls*) It must be full a hundredweight, George; but half the mass is quartz – but what of that – at least four-fifths of it must be gold. We're made men, George – we're made men.

GEORGE. (*kneels down to it*) Oh, you beauty! I see my Susan's eyes in you, that I do!

TOM. (*kneeling also on the other side*) You'll be the wonder of the world, that you will! (*patting nugget*) But stay – we must hide it somewhere. The most honest men in the world would turn villains at the sight of it. Oh, George! Let's shake hands over it. (*They do so and dance round it*)

GEORGE. (*suddenly*) Oh, lord!

TOM. What's the matter?

GEORGE. Why, it's Jacky's – he found it.

TOM. Eh? why so – no, I'm afraid one-third of it is though, for pals share, whether black or white.

JACKY. What for you dance? what for you make dis fuss? You turn white, you turn red, den you turn white again, and all because you pull up yellow stone. All dis a good deal dam ridiculous. Jacky give him to you.

GEORGE. Noble fellow – noble fellow! it's ours, Tom – ours.

TOM. Well, if it is, you needn't look so pale!

GEORGE. You'd be pale if you could see what a day this is for you and me – ay, and for all the world. Why, Tom, in a month there'll be five thousand men working round this little spot.

TOM. Let them come – there is plenty for all. Gold – gold – gold! I have found it, and I grudge it to no man. I, a thief that was, make it a present to its rightful owner, and that is all the world. Gold – gold – gold!

GEORGE. Blessings on it, for it will take me to Susan. We shall be rich men, Tom. We have it – we have it – the secret is ours. Gold – gold – gold!

*They shake hands over nugget as scene closes. The latter part of this
scene should be played excitedly, and as rapidly as possible,
to give an impression of their wild joy.*

———————

SCENE SECOND. – *Front View in Australia.* (*1ˢᵗ grooves*)

Enter PETER CRAWLEY, L.

PETER. Well, here I am in Australia! wonderful idea of Mr. Meadows to send me over here to ruin George Fielding. But the worst of it is, I can't find him anywhere – I've asked everybody. Hollo; here come two men – I wonder if they know! What rough-looking chaps! I'll consider a bit before I speak to them. (*retires,* R.)

Enter BLACK WILL *and* JEM, R. *followed by* BOB

BLACK WILL. Well, we've made a nice job of this, Jem.

JEM. Never say die – we'll have 'em yet. Who are the chaps?

BLACK WILL. One of 'em was a ticket-of-leave from London – the other is a farmer from the west of England, who has come out here, they say, to make a thousand pounds. His name is George Fielding.

PETER. (*aside*) Ah! that's my man, then!

BLACK WILL. What luck some men have, don't they?

JEM. Ah, there'll be a good lump of gold in their hut tonight!

BLACK WILL. He shall never take it home to his sweetheart, though!

JEM. I wish we had it instead of him.

PETER. (*advancing*, R.) So do I, gentlemen.

BLACK WILL. }
JEM.   } You! why?

PETER. That's a secret for the present, gentlemen; but I think that you and I might, perhaps, do business together. I have a friend in England who would give money to anyone that would take the gold away from this George Fielding and his friend.

BLACK WILL. And won't he ask for any share of the swag?

PETER. Not a farthing!

BLACK WILL. And what will he give if we do the trick?

PETER. A good price. Come here and I'll tell you
                                        [*goes up with them*, L.

Enter ISAAC LEVI, R.

ISAAC. (*sees them*) Ah! that man Crawley here! his visit bodes no good to George Fielding. Some villainy lies at the bottom of all this; but I will fathom it – ay, and thwart it – I swear it by the god of my fathers.

BLACK WILL. (*sees him*) Why, here's old Smouchy. What do you want here?

ISAAC. I came in this land to trade. It is as free for me as for you?

BLACK WILL. Trade in what?

ISAAC. In gold dust!

BLACK WILL. Ha! gold dust! what do *you* know –

ISAAC. Our people find out all things where money is concerned. You thought to keep your secret safe among three. It was never kept secret in any land, and never will be. The very birds in the air would carry it. If a thousand knew it today, would that lower the price of gold a penny an ounce? No! To all who find gold, Isaac Levi will find money to buy.

JEM. (*aside to* WILL) I'll be bound he carries a tidy swag with him. The quickest way to find gold will be to search for it in his pocket.

BLACK WILL. So I think!

ISAAC. If you should wish to trade with Isaac Levi in the article, he will give you a fair price, and so good day. (*going* L.)

BLACK WILL. Stay – we don't part so easily.

ISAAC. What do you want with me?

BLACK WILL. We don't want you, but we want your money.

PETER. That's right! rob the old heathen of all he's got, and I'll go shares with you!

ISAAC. Ha! are you there, base tool of a crafty villain? but craft shall meet craft, and honesty set its foot on villainy.

BLACK WILL. Silence, you old reptile, and fork out.

ISAAC. Never!

BLACK WILL. Then here goes to take it! (*seizes him, assisted by all but* CRAWLEY)

ISAAC. Help! help! murder!

> *Enter* GEORGE, R. *who fires pistol –* WILL *and the rest run off,*
> L. *having thrown* ISAAC *on the ground.*

GEORGE. What! Isaac Levi! and here in Australia!

ISAAC. Thanks, young man, thanks! you are the poor Jew's guardian angel! But beware – the villain Crawley is here!

GEORGE. Here!

ISAAC. Ay! sent by the villain Meadows to compass your destruction.

GEORGE. And why?

ISAAC. That he may rob you of your sweetheart, young man, and make her Mrs. Meadows.

GEORGE. The villain! but I shall foil him, Isaac, for I am rich now. I can return with the thousand pounds, and claim Susan in spite of him and all the world.

ISAAC. Ay, if you ever reach there; and he does not mean you should, or why has he sent his man, Crawley, here? Come with me, and let us think what is to be done? the old Jew is your friend, young man – the old Jew is your friend, who will not die happy till he has seen you and your Susan joined hand and heart together.

GEORGE. Bless you, old man – my friend – my more than father!

ISAAC. Time flies! Come come!

> *[Exeunt* R.

> PETER, JEM, *and* BOB *peep on,* L. *watching them off.*

PETER. There they go! Can't we follow 'em and drop a lump of rock on their heads, or something?

BLACK WILL. No, no, we'll get some pals, and track 'em as they pass the bush. It's thick, and just the place for such a job. I'll get two more pals and settle their hash out of hand!

PETER. No, no, no murder – it makes such a mess.

BLACK WILL. Do you think they'll give up their swag while they're alive?

PETER. Keep cool, and you shall have the swag, and not lose your revenge either.

BLACK WILL. How?

PETER. Do you know where their hut is?

BLACK WILL. I should think we ought to, eh, mates?

PETER. Suppose I show you how to make those two run out of their hut like two frightened women, and never once think of their swag!

BLACK WILL. How's that?

PETER. (*drawing them close together*) Look here – we must get a barrel of turpentine, and scatter the liquid all over their hut, and then set light to some tow steeped in the turpentine – their hut will be in a blaze, they'll run out, and in the confusion we get the gold.[31]

BLACK WILL. Well, you *are* a pal! What a head piece you have got! This is a dodge I never should have thought of.

PETER. You don't know what an ingenious man I am!

JEM. We must buy the turpentine directly then. There's only one store that sells it, and that shuts at nine.

BLACK WILL. (*to* PETER) Hand us out the blunt as sharp as you can then, if that's the case.

PETER. No, I'll not give the money towards such a thing as that – robbery's bad enough. Do you think I haven't got a conscience? I'll not *give* the money. (*winks, and touches his pocket*)

BLACK WILL. Why, what do you mean?

---

31. Stage fires were already a staple effect in melodramas, famously in *The Miller and His Men* (1813). The spectacular appeal of stage fires is recorded in an interview with the toy theatre publisher William West: '"The Miller and his Men" has sold better than any other play I ever published. [. . .] It's the last scene, with the grand explosion of the mill, as pleases the young uns, uncommon' (Mayhew (1850), n.p.).

JEM. Why, don't you see the move? He won't *give* the money, but if we like to *take* it, why then there's no questions asked.

BLACK WILL. The tarnation hypocrite! (*takes purse from Crawley's pocket*) My eyes, he's a greater villain than I am! This way – caution's the word.

[*Music – Exeunt*, L.

SCENE THIRD. – *Same as the First Scene – a vessel at anchor in perspective. On George's hut is a paper, on which is written* "First we fire – then inquire."

Enter PETER, BLACK WILL *with cask, and* JEM *and* BOB *following*, L. 1 E.

BLACK WILL. Here's the stuff to warm 'em!

PETER. Not a word – to business. Have you got a torch?

JEM. (*shows one not lighted*) All right – I can soon light it when you're ready.

BLACK WILL. Let's begin at the back of the hut, and soak the boards well.

JEM. Come along, then.

BLACK WILL. (*to* PETER) You keep a good look out!

PETER. Don't be long – for you see what they've written over their door. "First they fire, then inquire."

Exeunt BLACK WILL, BOB *and* JEM *behind hut*, L.

PETER. I hope they won't be long, for I'm getting nervous! It's a bold stroke, and a decisive one. I shall get my thousand pounds from Mr. Meadows – and so I ought, for the risk is worth double the money. What a time they are! That placard makes me nervous! Suppose they fire first, and then inquire afterwards? This is assuming a critical aspect!

Re-enter BLACK WILL *and the rest – they sprinkle the turpentine round hut, and leave barrel at door –* BLACK WILL *strikes match, and lights torch.*

BLACK WILL. Now, my lads, if we don't make your hole too hot to hold you, my name's not Black Will. (*sets light to turpentine – the hunt is enveloped in flames*)

PETER. Beautiful – beautiful! How fond I am of a good fire.

BLACK WILL. (*to* BOB *and* JEM) Place yourselves at each side of the door, and as they enter, strike them down. (*they place themselves at door*)

PETER. They don't seem to come out! can they be inside?

GEORGE *entering,* R. U. E. *with* TOM *and* JACKY.

GEORGE. No, villains, we are outside!

PETER. Kill 'em! knock 'em down! they will escape us!

BLACK WILL. Never mind, their gold's inside.

ISAAC *rows on from* R. U. E. *in boat*

ISAAC. No, it's outside, in my boat. (*to* TOM *and* GEORGE) In with you, lads!

Music – BLACK WILL, JEM, *and* BOB *rush upon* GEORGE, TOM, *and* JACKY, *and are worsted*

PETER. (*running about*) Stop 'em! stop 'em! stop 'em!

JACKY. Me stop you, tam thief!

Knocks PETER *down, pulls off his wig, and jumps into boat with* GEORGE *and* TOM, *who push off with a loud cheer, as the act descends*

END OF ACT THIRD.

———————

ACT FOURTH.

SCENE FIRST. – *Room in Merton's Cottage.* (*1ˢᵗ Grooves.*) *Door with window in flat – table and chairs.*

Music – Enter FARMER MERTON *and* SUSAN, R.

MERTON. Now don't thee take on so, Susan! Eight months and no letter from George! – he's false to thee, lass – false to thee. (*aside*) Heaven forgive me the falsehoods I am forced to tell to keep me from disgrace!

SUSAN. No, no, he is not false! He must be dead, father – he must be dead!

JOHN MEADOWS *entering, with letter,* L.

JOHN. No, he is not dead, Susan – I can answer for that.

SUSAN. Oh, thank you for saying those words, Mr. Meadows, you have made my heart bound with joy again. Poor George! You never will let him know I was so foolish as to doubt him, will you?

JOHN. And yet you were right to doubt him, Susan, for – No, no, I can never have the heart to tell you! He has been deceiving you, Susan – you placed your heart upon an unworthy object. (*shows letter*) Read that, and judge for yourself.

SUSAN. (*reads letter*) "What luck some have. There is George Fielding, of the Grove Farm, has made his fortune at the gold diggings, and married one of the prettiest girls in Sydney – I met them walking in the street today. She would not have looked at him, but for the gold." (*pauses – lets letter fall, and weeps bitterly*) He has forgotten me – he has abandoned me! But no, no, I will not weep for another woman's husband. From this moment I will never shed a tear for one who is unworthy of a thought!

JOHN. (*aside*) Success attends my stratagem! She'll be mine, mine, mine!

SUSAN. Have I wept and sighed all this time for a man who did not care for me – defied the sneers, and despised the advice of my friends – gloried openly in my love to be openly insulted and betrayed! grieved and prayed for one I thought was dead – but who is well, happy, and married to another! Father – (*to* MERTON) let us leave this place – I cannot stay here, to see the finger of scorn point towards Susan Merton as the cast off girl of any man!

MERTON. What, leave Grassmere – leave the cottage where your mother lived with me, and where you were born?

SUSAN. No, no, father – I am too selfish to ask it! You shall not leave it for me! Forgive me, I am a wretched, wayward girl!

JOHN. (*aside*) Now is the time to plead my suit. (*aloud*) Susan, for three years, you know not what I have suffered for your sake – how I have doted on you with all my soul. I never thought to be able to tell you this – I have struggled against my passion, and tried to subdue it, because I knew you were promised to another man – but now that he has deceived you, and you are free, I have no longer the power to hide my love – now that he has thrown away the jewel, let me be allowed, dear Susan, to take it up, and wear it in my heart.

SUSAN. Mr. Meadows! you surprise me – I – I did not expect this!

JOHN. Speak, Susan, can I at least have your regard – your affection?

SUSAN. Let no man ever hope for affection from me, for my heart is in the grave. Oh, would that I were there too! Oh, pardon me, sir, pardon me! I can stay no longer. Oh, this blow will kill me. I shall die – I shall die!

[*Exit*, R.

MERTON. Stay, Susan! stay, don't take on so, girl – don't take on so!

JOHN. It works – it works! The first blow is struck – it remains for me to clinch it!

PETER. (*opens window in flat, and looks in*) Mr. Meadows!

JOHN. Ha, who's that? Crawley?

PETER. Yes, Mr. Meadows.

Enter PETER, L.

JOHN. You returned! What made you come back without orders?

PETER. I've come to tell you they're on their road home.

JOHN. They? who?

PETER. George Fielding and his mate – they gave me the slip, and got away before me.

JOHN. Fool!

PETER. How could I help it, Mr. Meadows? I thought I should have died on the spot when I saw them put off for the ship with the gold they've found.

JOHN. Gold!

PETER. Yes, Mr. Meadows. George Fielding has found a lump of gold big enough to make a prince of him.

JOHN. Curses on him!

PETER. But then you've married his sweetheart, Susan, since I've been away, haven't you?

JOHN. No, fool – I've been obliged to work my way cautiously!

PETER. Oh lord – oh lord! Then we're ruined – we're undone! George will return, and spoil every plan we've formed!

JOHN. Hold your tongue, and let me think. They are not in England, Crawley, or we should have seen them – you sailed faster than they – I'll beat them yet – I'll be married tomorrow morning.

PETER. But is this girl really worthy of a great man like you, Mr. Meadows? If George Fielding does come home before you're prepared with your plans, give the girl up, and have no more to do with her. She's like all the women, Mr. Meadows – more trouble than she's worth.

JOHN. What, wade through all these crimes for nothing? Lie and intercept letters, lend myself to robbery and assassination, and fail! wade in crime up to my middle, and then go back without the prize? (*takes out pistol*) Do you see this pistol? it has two barrels! if she and I are ever parted, it shall be this way – I'll send her to heaven with one barrel, and myself to hell with the other.

PETER. (*trembling*) Lord, Mr. Meadows!

JOHN. You needn't look like a girl at me – most likely it won't come to that. It's not easy to beat me, and I'll first try every move that man's wit can devise. This – (*putting pistol on table*) shall be my last resource. I'll go and tell old Merton I want to speak to him. In the meantime, make yourself scarce, and meet me at my house in an hour.

PETER. Yes, Mr. Meadows.

[*Exit* JOHN MEADOWS, R.

Mr. Meadows is getting wildish. It frightens me to see such a man as he burst out like that. He is not to be trusted with a loaded pistol. Ha, and I am in his secrets – deep in his secrets! and sometimes great men sweep away little men, if they think they know too much! I never saw him with a pistol before, and in case he might feel inclined to have a pop at me, I'll take off the caps. (*takes caps of pistol*) And now I'll take myself off. I never give a chance away.

[*Exit*, L.

Re-enter JOHN, R. *who goes to table, and puts pistol in his pocket –*
SUSAN *and* MERTON *follow.*

MERTON. Well, but Susan, listen to Mr. Meadows – I'm sure he speaks fairly enough!

SUSAN. Others see they have a right to love me now, and they act upon it.

JOHN. Susan, I have been so long used to hide my feelings when they were unlawful, that you must excuse me if I press my suit now that no man stands in my way. I never would have spoken to you but for the unexpected treason of George, and now, seeing you insulted and despised I take this moment to show you how you are loved and honoured.

MERTON. (*aside to* SUSAN) John Meadows seems down a little! do give him a cheering word! (*aside*) John Meadows will set me on my legs again if he marries my Susan.[32]

SUSAN. (*aside to* MERTON) Father, you may think me an ungrateful girl, but I feel I can never love that man!

MERTON. (*aside*) Susan, will you break that man's heart? you know how good he has been to me.

---

32. Merton is more sympathetic to his daughter's feelings in **HAZ2**, though he is still under
    Meadows's control. 'Oh let my poor girl have this one [letter]. I cant [*sic*] carry this on
    much longer – I see my child's pale face every night in my dreams, and its [*sic*] killing
    me fast' (f. 31b).

SUSAN. (*aside*) Why should I hesitate? *I* can never be happy, but I can make two other persons so – my father and Mr. Meadows. And if I refuse to make my father and his friend happy, why do I live? what am I on the earth for at all?

MERTON. I'll leave you together – I'll soon return. (*aside*) This will come to be a match, I see it will. Meadows is a better catch than George – Susan may not think so, but these girls never know what's good for themselves.

[*Exit*, R.

JOHN. Come, dear Susan, your answer – all my happiness in this world depends on you.

SUSAN. Is it really true your happiness depends on me? Then take me – quick, before my courage fails, and leaves me stubborn and undecided!

JOHN. (*aside*) Mine, mine, mine! (*aloud*) But the day, Susan, the marriage day – pray name that?

SUSAN. No, no! I cannot – I cannot!

JOHN. Shall I name it then?

SUSAN. If you will – it is immaterial.

JOHN. (*aside*) I'll strike while the iron's hot. (*aloud*) What do you think of tomorrow?

SUSAN. When you please – when you please!

JOHN. I'll get the license then. And now, dear Susan –

[*going to take her hand.*

SUSAN. Pray let me go to my father. Don't speak any more to me now – I am not well – I – I – Oh, Susan, Susan! (*aside*) You have promised your hand to a man who is valueless, and hateful to you.

[*Exit*, R.

JOHN. I triumph – I triumph! What will not a strong will do? I see she does not love me, but I will make her – and then will tell her how I have risked my soul for her – how I have played the villain for her – all the crimes

I have committed to make her mine. So far, so good – and now to clinch the nail that shall hold fast George Fielding.

[*Exit*, L.

––––––––––

SCENE SECOND. – *Commercial Room at an Inn. Tables, chairs, &c. – candles on table – doors*, R. *and* L. *and* D. F. C. – *Time, night.*

Enter GEORGE, TOM, *and* JACKY, *in a long-tailed blue coat, and trousers of a showy pattern.*

GEORGE. Hurrah for old England once again, and the dear native village I was born in! Here, then, we stay tonight, and then the first thing in the morning I hasten to my dear Susan, and throwing the gold at her feet, I say, "Here I am, my dear Susan, with the one thousand pounds I went to gain, ready and willing to make you Mrs. George Fielding, and realise the dearest wish of my heart, the wish that has sustained me in sorrow and trouble, and which now lies within my grasp to gladden my pathway of life, and light me to happiness."

[*shows pocket book.*

JACKY. Dat's right, Massa George – and when you married, Jacky be de bridesmaid.

TOM. Hark at old Blackingbottle. Well, Jacky, what do you think of old England?

JACKY. Very too much houses, see no 'possums, no 'coons, no squirrel – nicee women, though; Jacky like to marry six or seven, and make 'em Mrs. Jackies.

GEORGE. We don't allow more than one wife here, Jacky.

JACKY. Dat very much stupid. How a man to pick out a good 'un?

MAID SERVANT *entering,* C. D.

MAID. Yonder are your rooms, gentlemen.

TOM. Alright, my dear – and bring us some brandy and water, hot, strong, and sweet.

JACKY. (*to* MAID) I say, missee, you be Mrs. Jacky number one?

MAID. Don't speak to me, you impudent nigger!

JACKY. What dat you say? Nigger! Leave the room, white trash!

MAID. Well, I'm sure, old Blackingbottle!

[*Exit.*

JACKY. Jacky's a gentleman, and he not be consulted.

GEORGE. Sit down, Jacky, and don't forget yourself in your new clothes.

JACKY. (*sits*) Iss, Massa George – new clothes berry much dam fine!

Re-enter MAID, *with three glasses of brandy and water.*

MAID. Here's the brandy and water, gentlemen.

TOM. Ah, that's the stuff for trousers.

[*Exit* MAID, D. F. C.

JACKY. (*drinking*) Dis berry much dam fine too.

GEORGE. Mind it don't get in your head, Jacky.

JACKY. How it get in my head, when I put it in my belly?

[PETER *and* JOHN *look in,* C. D.

GEORGE. But before we take our grog, let's see what sort of accommodation there is for us, and whether there are good locks to the bedroom doors – because a prize gained so hardly as this – (*places his hand on case*) should be well guarded.

JACKY. What make so much row about yellow stone for, Massa George – what use is him?

GEORGE. If you come to live here long, you'll find out. Money makes the man here, I'm sorry to say, Jacky, for poverty's about one of the greatest crimes a man can be found guilty of in this country, eh, Tom?[33]

---

33. George evokes the 1834 Poor Law Amendment Act, which introduced the notoriously cruel 'workhouse test'.

TOM. You're right, George – only let a goose have tin, and the people swear he's a goldfinch directly. But let's look at the hammock.

JACKY. That's right, Massa Tom. Jacky fond of hammock, it is so nicee, nicee, and softee, softee.

PETER *and* JOHN *advance.*

JOHN. How shall we manage this?

PETER. Let's try skill without force. Look here! (*shows phial*)

JOHN. What's that?

PETER. Put that in a man's glass, and he will never taste it, and in a few minutes he will sleep so sound you might take the very clothes off his back, and not wake him. You shall see the effect of it, Mr. Meadows. (*pours some in each of the glasses*)

JOHN. Quick – quick, Crawley – they are here! To ambush to ambush!

PETER. Yes, Mr. Meadows – yes, Mr. Meadows.

[*They go in room,* R.

Enter GEORGE, JACKY, *and* TOM.

TOM. Oh, those rooms will do slap up!

JACKY. Nice hammock – good, beautiful! Jacky sleep like squirrel – fast sound all de winter.

GEORGE. (*puts pocket book in his pocket*) Are the locks of the door in good condition, Tom? – for the prize I carry would be no trifle to lose! safe bind safe find you know.

JOHN *and* PETER *look out watching him.*

So the sooner we turn in the better, for I long to rise early in the morning, to claim the dear treasure that is in store for me.

[*drinks.*

JOHN. Indeed! we shall see!

[*Crosses behind, and goes in room,* L.

TOM. (*drinks*) And here's success, and long life to you, George.

JACKY. (*drinks*) And long life to Jacky, and a long wife, too!

PETER. (*aside*) They've drank – they've drank! (*rubbing his hands*) We shall do 'em – we shall do 'em![34]

GEORGE. Come, drink up, and let's go to bed. (*drinks*)

TOM. Ah, let's turn in, as you say, for I see you'll never be at rest till you reach Susan's side. (*drinks*)

GEORGE. Right, Tom, right! I long for tomorrow with all my heart and soul. When I show them the money I've made, I fancy they'll not call me unlucky George any more. Come along, Tom – come along, Jacky. Joy comes with the rising sun, dear Susan, and tomorrow we meet to part no more.

TOM. Success to you, George, and good luck to true hearts all over the world.

[*They exeunt,* L. D.

PETER. (*coming forward*) Joy comes with the rising sun, does it? Don't be too sure – perhaps your sun may rise in a fog. They've locked their door – but what of that? Mr. Meadows is on the right side of it. They must rise very early in the morning to do Mr. Meadows – I never saw the man yet who could do it! That stuff I put in the brandy and water will make them sleep as fast as a chancery suit. What a blessing it is that Providence sends us such things to work our ends with. Industry must prosper they say in everything. So success to us, I say, and to every man who tries to turn a penny, whether it is honest or not. Hark! Here he comes! Can he have done the trick already?

Music – Enter JOHN *from room,* L. *– he locks the door, taking
the key from inside.*

JOHN. (*with pocket book*) Victory – victory! the prize is mine!

PETER. He's a clever man, is Mr. Meadows – a wonderful man!

JOHN. (*pulling out notes on table*) Count them, Crawley – count them. See, they are all hundred pound notes, bright and crisp, fresh from the bank.

---

34. In both **REA** and **CON** this scene occurs off stage, and Meadows is wholly responsible for drugging and robbing Tom and George.

PETER. (*counting them*) Oh, what a great man you are, Mr. Meadows! Twenty, forty – a wonderful man! – sixty, seventy – an extraordinary man! – eighty, ninety – an astonishing man! Why, I declare, Mr. Meadows, there is altogether seven thousand pounds. Oh, Mr. Meadows, this is a glorious haul to you!

JOHN. Why, you fool, do you think I'll run the danger of keeping the money? no no! (*going to candle*) I mean to burn them, then they'll tell no tales!

PETER. Burn them? no, no, Mr. Meadows, don't think of it. What, burn the good money that the bountiful Heaven has given us for the good of man? no, no, don't, sir, don't!

JOHN. Why not? no more of this folly!

[*going to burn them*

PETER. No, no, don't! what does it matter what becomes of them, so that he never sees them again. Give them to me, and in twelve hours I'll be in France with them. You won't miss me, for I've done my work. Pray let me go, and take these with me – do, Mr. Meadows – do!

JOHN. (*aside*) Shall I? I shall get rid of him by doing so. It will stop his mouth by doing so, for the knave will drink himself to death in a twelve-month. (*aloud*) Well, Crawley, they are yours on these conditions – that you go at once to the railway – the mail train starts in half-an-hour – up to London tonight, and over to France tomorrow – do you agree?

PETER. I do, Mr. Meadows – I do, Mr. Meadows!

JOHN. (*gives notes*) There, then, away – away!

PETER. I will – I will! thank you, Mr. Meadows – bless you, Mr. Meadows – I worship you, Mr. Meadows – goodbye, Mr. Meadows!

[*Runs off* C. D.

JOHN. I triumph! I triumph! I triumph! Who can beat John Meadows? are there any more that hope to conquer him? then come on, a thousand strong, with the devil at your back, and then I'll beat you. You're done, George Fielding, and when you awake to consciousness, Susan Merton will be mine – mine – mine!

[*Music. – Exit* C. D.

———

SCENE THIRD. – *Roadside View. (1ˢᵗ grooves)*

Enter JOHN, *followed by* FARMER MERTON, L.

MERTON. Mr. Meadows, I can carry on this game no longer, and I won't, for any man living.

JOHN. What do you mean, fool?

MERTON. Susan, my poor daughter, has been crying all night, poor girl, over George's supposed falsehood to her, and I feel I can carry on the deception no longer. Better be poor and content, than rich and conscience-stricken.

JOHN. Perhaps you would like to blab, and confess your villainy.

MERTON. My villainy!

JOHN. Whose else? *you* have intercepted letters, not *I!* you have abused the public confidence, and if you are such a fool and sneak as to cut your throat, and peach on yourself, I'll give evidence against you, and show how you have opened letters, and stopped them, too.

MERTON. I know you are without mercy, Meadows, but villain as you are, I will beat you yet. I'll leave a note for Susan, confessing all, and blow out my brains this very morning.

JOHN. (*aside*) Those people never talk about it when they mean to do it. (*aloud*) Merton, you are not bold enough to take your own life.

MERTON. You'll know, perhaps, by night.

JOHN. No, I must know that before night!
                    [*seizes him, and places a pistol to his head.*

MERTON. No, no, Mr. Meadows – mercy, mercy!

JOHN. (*putting up pistol*) All right! you half imposed on me, and that is something for you to brag of. Give over shaking like an aspen, and look and listen. You're in debt – I've bought up two drafts of yours – they are here! (*shows them*) After the wedding I'll give them to you to light your pipe with.

MERTON. That, indeed, would be one load off my mind!

JOHN. You are short of cash, too, I suppose! come home with me, and I'll give you fifty pounds in cash.

MERTON. Thanks, Mr. Meadows, I –

JOHN. No time for words – time flies – and we must be at church. Keep your own counsel, and mine also; and when once I am your son-in-law, you may feel yourself secure. Rouse up, man – come, come!

PETER CRAWLEY *enters, L. followed by* ISAAC LEVI.

PETER. Seven thousand pounds! seven thousand, and mine – mine – mine! Luck's on my side! what a glorious thing is steam, when a man's in a hurry. I'm off – I'm off! (*going* R.)

ISAAC. (*coming down,* R.) Ah, Mr. Crawley, where are you going in such a hurry?

PETER. I've business – business!

ISAAC. So have I, with you, too, Mr. Crawley! It's my turn now. When I last saw you in Australia you set ruffians on to abuse and to rob me. It is my turn now – an eye for an eye – a tooth for a tooth.[35]

PETER. Don't bother me with your grievance now – call on me tomorrow.

ISAAC. No, no, I never postpone vengeance when it is ripe. I heard you say you had seven thousand pounds about you.

PETER. (R.) No, no, you made a mistake, Mr. Levi.

ISAAC. No, I didn't, Mr. Crawley. (*calling off,* L.) Here, officers!

Enter TWO OFFICERS, L.

I charge that man with being unlawfully possessed of seven thousand pounds. I'll be bound we shall soon find an owner for it.

35. Exodus 21: 24.

PETER. It's false, Mr. Levi, I have no money.

ISAAC. It's true, Mr. Crawley – it's in his right hand pocket. Search him! (OFFICERS *search him and pull out pocket book*) Aha, Mr. Crawley!

PETER. It's a mistake! send for Mr. Meadows – it belongs to him!

ISAAC. We'll take you to him and see. Bring him along!

PETER. But my dear, good Mr. Levi!

ISAAC. Ah, ha! soft words butter no parsnips, my dear. Bring him along!

PETER. Just as I was bolting, too! oh, lord! oh, lord!

ISAAC. Ah ha! what, I caught you, my dear, did I? away with him – away with him!

PETER. Oh, lord – oh, lord! Mr. Levi's a more wonderful man than Mr. Meadows!

[*They take him off,* R.

———————

SCENE FOURTH. – *Church Porch,* R. *with distant country at back.*

VILLAGERS *discovered,* L. *looking towards* R. U. E. –
church bells ringing.

VILLAGERS. Here they be – here they be! three cheers for the bride and bridegroom! Hooray – hooray – hooray!

Music. – Church bells and shouts. – Enter JOHN MEADOWS *with*
SUSAN, *dressed for the wedding, followed by* MERTON *and*
FRIENDS *with wedding favours,* R. U. E.

MERTON. Come, come, girl, cheer up! why, how pale you look, child.

SUSAN. And can you wonder at it? the life blood has been drained out of my heart by so many cruel blows – by the long waiting – the misgivings, and the deep woe, when I believed George dead, and the bitter grief, mortification, and sense of wrong I have experienced at the knowledge that he is married to another.

JOHN. Come, come, Susan, cheer up, my lass!

SUSAN. Pause, sir, and think what you are doing before you tie an icicle to your heart, and take an unworthy wife.

JOHN. Oh, fear not, Susan – love will come in time. Let us go in church. Why should you grieve for the man who has deceived you? Would he were here now to see you leaning on this faithful arm!

Enter GEORGE *and* TOM, R. U. E. *followed by* WILLIAM.

GEORGE. He *is* here, villain!

SUSAN. Ha! George! (*leans on her father's shoulder weeping.*)

GEORGE. (C.) Susan, Susan, what on earth is this? Oh, what have I done to you that I should see you about to marry another?

SUSAN. (L.) What have you done? You are false to me. You never wrote me a letter for twelve months, and you are married to another. Oh, George, George!

GEORGE. I married to another!

TOM. If he is, he must be slyer than I gave him credit for, for I have never left his side night or day, and I have never heard him say three civil words to a woman. Somebody has been making a fool of you, Miss Merton. Why, when we found the great nugget, he kisses it and says, "There! That is not because you are gold, but because you take me to Susan, you beauty." (R. C.)

GEORGE. Hold your tongue, Tom! who puts me on my defence? Is there any man here who has been telling her I have ever had a thought of any girl but her? If there is, let him stand out now and say it to my face if he dares! (*a pause*) So! there is a lie without a backer, it seems. And now, Susan, what are you doing by that man's side?

JOHN. (L. C.) Because we are to be married – that is why.

GEORGE. How is this, Susan? Speak! there's no man in the world can love you better than I do. Then speak your mind, my lass, now you know I'm true to you, and let your early promise be fulfilled.

MERTON. (L.) George, I have been an imprudent fool. I owe more than two thousand pounds. We heard you were married, and Mr. Meadows came forward like a man, and said –

GEORGE. But your promise, uncle – your promise. Remember I crossed the seas on the faith of it. "Bring back a thousand pounds," said you, "and my daughter is yours."

JOHN. That's right enough! I was present and heard the words. Well, and have you brought back the thousand pounds?

GEORGE. I have!

MERTON. (*to* JOHN) Then, Mr. Meadows, I must stand to my word.

JOHN. Yes, if he has the money. Produce it and let us see it!

GEORGE. (*takes out pocket-book and finds it empty*) Why, why, why, Tom!

TOM. What's up?

GEORGE. The money's gone!

TOM. Gone!

MERTON. George, cease this folly! go and leave me and my daughter in peace. If you had come home with the money to keep her, I was ready to give you Susan as I promised; but Susan is about to give her hand to a man who can make a lady of her, and set me on my legs again – you can only beggar us. Don't stand in the poor girl's light, but for pity's sake, George, leave us in peace.

GEORGE. You are right, old man – my head is confused – I hardly know what I'm about – but I'll – I'll go. Come, Tom; we'll go back again to Australia, only I shall have nothing to work for now. Goodbye, William. I'll go back – I'll go back!

SUSAN. And if you do, George, I'll go with you! (*going to him*)

JOHN. What, is the girl mad! will you marry a beggar?

ISAAC *enters, with notes,* R. U. E.

ISAAC. (C.) He is no beggar, the money is here! I have waited months and months and years and years, for vengeance, and it has come at last. The old Jew has been despised and insulted in many lands, but now it is *his* turn, and he can give blow for blow, and strike his enemy to the heart.

JOHN. Why does my very life blood turn to ice – am I to be beaten after all?

ISAAC. (*points to* JOHN) I accuse that man of theft. Crawley has confessed that he drugged the liquor while he stole the notes.

TOM. That's right! it must be right. You know what a light sleeper I am, George! I was hocussed, and no mistake.

JOHN. (*aside*) Crawley taken! (*aloud*) I am a man of property, why should I steal?

ISAAC. To beggar your rival, whose letters to the maiden he loved you intercepted. Ha, you see I know all. Bring in Mr. Crawley!

OFFICERS *bring on* PETER, R. U. E., *down* R.

JOHN. (L.) If I could only catch his eye! but he won't look at me, the traitor!

ISAAC. (*to* PETER) Tell these good folks if what you have confessed to me is true.

PETER. It is, and I'll swear it before any magistrate in the world. Oh, a wicked man is Mr. Meadows – a horrid man!

JOHN. So you'll split on me, will you? Die, you rascal! (*levels the pistol which* PETER *took the caps off in the preceding scene*) Foiled! (CONSTABLES *seize* JOHN.)[36]

---

36. In **CON**, Meadows says that he intended to give George back his £7,000 after he had married Susan: 'I am a sinner but not a villain!' (f. 40b).

PETER. Yes, Mr. Meadows, it was I who took the caps off. I thought I'd better clip your claws, and I was right, you see. So, this is the end of all your manœuvring. Oh, what a fool I was to side with a bungler like you against such a clever man as Mr. Levi. Here am I, an innocent man, ruined through knowing a thief; for you are a thief – yes, a thief – a thief – a thief – ah, a thief! (*pointing at him*)

JOHN. How am I fallen when this thing can trample on me! Take me where you will. I have lived respected all these years, and now I shall be called a felon. Take me where I can lay my head and die.

[*Rushes off, followed by* OFFICERS, R. 1 E.

PETER. (*following him in custody*) There goes a thief! (*calls after him*) Look at him – there goes a thief! he's ruined an honest man like me! there goes a thief! there goes a thief!

[*Exit in custody*, R. 1 E.

GEORGE. (*to* ISAAC) My friend – my more than father – we owe every-thing to you. Cheer up, Susan – grief has sadly altered you. But how can I wonder at it! Had I found you going to be married, with the roses on your cheeks, I should have turned on my heel and gone back to Australia; but you were miserable, and I saw at a glance that your heart was dead against it, and you still cherished in your heart a thought for George. (*bells heard*) Again the bells ring a merry peal; and happy may they ring on the morn when I call you my own – my dearest wife.

SUSAN. I was foolish, George. I was rash to believe, so easily, you were false; but we all have our errors. Father, I forgive you, for you were in the power of a bad man, who would have made you sacrifice your child. But who is without errors in this world? Let us, then, strive to purify our hearts, and ever bear in mind, though erring may have been our life, still it is "NEVER TOO LATE TO MEND."[37]

	VILLAGERS.			VILLAGERS.		
R.	ISAAC.	TOM.	GEORGE.	SUSAN.	MERTON.	L.

CURTAIN.

----

37. In both **REA** and **CON**, Tom evokes the title in the final line of the play. **HAZ2** gives Susan the final line and does not reprise the title. She says that her greatest ambition is: 'To prove to you George (advancing) and to all our friends that a true wife's love is like unto a well, sealed and kept secret – a deep hidden fount that flows when every other spring is dry –' (f. 45a).

STAGE DIRECTIONS.

R. means *Right of the Stage, facing the Audience*; L. *Left*; C. *Centre;*
R. C. *Right of Centre;* L. C. *Left of Centre*; D. F. *Door in the Flat; or*
Scene running across the Stage; C. D. F. *Centre Door in the Flat;*
D. R. C. *Right Door in the Flat*; D. L. C. *Left Door in the Flat*;
R. D. *Right Door*; L. D. *Left Door*; 2 E. *Second Entrance;*
U. E. *Upper Entrance.*[38]

38. For more on nineteenth-century stage directions, see Rowell (1988), p. xiii.

Figure 2 Cave scene from *The Colleen Bawn*, as painted by Egron Sellif Lundgren (1815–75). The original watercolour is held in the Royal Collection, but this black-and-white photograph belongs to the Pettingell Collection, Templeman Library, Kent.

Figure 3 Original playbill for Adelphi production of *The Colleen Bawn*. Theatre and Performance Archive, V&A, London.

THE COLLEEN BAWN;[1]

Or,

THE BRIDES OF GARRYOWEN.[2]

A Domestic Drama,

IN THREE ACTS.

BY

DION BOUCICAULT, ESQ.,

AUTHOR OF

The Pope of Rome – The Young Actress – The Poor of New York –
The Dublin Boy – Pauvrette – Life of an Actress – Jessie Brown –
The Octoroon – Azael – Blue Belle – Dot – &c.

PRINTED BUT NOT PUBLISHED

---

1. Variants discussed in the notes are:
   BOU: Add MS 52995 B. Dion Boucicault (1860), 'The Colleen Bawn'.
   Licensing copy of Boucicault's play, received by the Lord Chamberlain on 20 August and licensed on 31 August for the Adelphi Theatre (f. 1a).
   HAZ: Add MS 52995 T. C. H. Hazlewood (1860), 'Eily O Connor'.
   Licensing copy of Hazlewood's version for the Britannia Theatre in East London, submitted to the Lord Chamberlain just over one month after Boucicault's drama premiered at the Adelphi. Hazlewood significantly revised Boucicault's characterisation to appeal to the Britannia's audience, who were typically drawn from the working and lower-middle classes living in the neighbourhood (see Davis and Emeljanow (2001), i.e. p. 46).
   YOU: Add MS 53002 M. Henry Young (1861), 'The Bride of Garryowen'.
   Licensing script submitted by the Theatre Royal Wolverhampton, Staffordshire (Apr.). Boucicault later sued the manager, John Delafield, for copyright infringement. Cuttings and letters relating to the case are held in the Boucicault Collection at the Templeman Library, Kent.

Original Cast, at MISS LAURA KEENE'S THEATRE,[3] NEW YORK, MARCH 27TH, 1860.[4]

CAST OF CHARACTERS. – [THE COLLEEN BAWN.]

MYLES NA COPPALEEN . . .

Mr. Dion Boucicault.[5]

HARDRESS CREGAN . . .

Mr. H. F. Daly.

DANNY MANN . . .

Mr. Charles Wheatleigh.

BYR: Add MS 53009 I. [H. J. Byron] (1861), 'Miss Eily O'Connor'.
Anticipating an audience familiar with Boucicault's drama, this burlesque mocks its characters, actors and situations, particularly the sensation scene. Music heightens the comic effect throughout. In the cave scene, Danny and Eily sing a duet to the tune of 'Sally come up' (f. 37), as he repeatedly attempts to push her down and she rises back to the surface. Myles and Eily also sing a duet as they 'appear through the water bobbing up and down as if in the attempt to see each other' (f. 39).
B&H: Add MS 53014 Z. William Brough and Andrew Halliday (1862), 'The Colleen Bawn Settled at Last'.
The play combines *dramatis personæ* from two theatrical phenomena of the period: *TCB* and Tom Taylor's *Our American Cousin* (1858). Detailing the lives of the principle characters after marriage, the humour picks up on Boucicault's themes and characterisation, as well as mocking his sensation scene.
2. *TCB* is loosely based on Gerald Griffin's 1829 novel *The Collegians*, itself inspired by a real murder case that Griffin had covered as a journalist. Fifteen-year-old Ellen Hanley is the model for Eily. She had eloped with John Scanlan, a County Limerick gentleman, who later sought to get rid of her by employing his boatman to kill her. Scanlan was defended by the Irish parliamentarian Daniel O'Connell at his trial in 1819, but was found guilty and hanged in Limerick in 1820.
3. Laura Keene was the first woman in America to manage a theatre.
4. The original production was apparently written and produced in a matter of days to save a failing season at Laura Keene's Theatre: the actors rehearsed the script piecemeal as Boucicault penned the lines. Agnes and Dion Boucicault each described the idea for *TCB* as a fortuitous accident, born from a second-hand copy of *The Collegians* bought by chance on Broadway; however, the details of their individual recollections differ. Agnes indicates that she inspired the drama by asking: 'why not have an Irish play'? But Agnes is not even present in Boucicault's heavily romanticised account. In fact, it is likely that Boucicault had already been working on the idea for an adaptation of Griffin's book for a number of weeks, since the actor-manager Barney Williams approached him for an Irish play in the autumn of 1859. Williams's wife, Maria Pray, recounted that Boucicault breached his contract with Williams when the play was produced for Laura Keene. (The Boucicaults' and Pray's accounts are qtd in Fawkes (2011 [1979]), pp. 113–15.)
5. Boucicault was so popular as Myles that he continued to play the part well into his sixties.

KYRLE DALY ...

Mr. Charles Fisher.

FATHER TOM ...

Mr. D. W. Leeson.[6]

MR. CORRIGAN ...

Mr. J. G. Burnett.

BERTIE O'MOORE ...

Mr. Henry.

HYLAND CREAGH ...

Mr. Levick.

SERVANT ...

Mr. Goodrich.

CORPORAL ...

Mr. Clarke.

EILY O'CONNOR ...

Miss Agnes Robertson.[7]

ANNE CHUTE ...

Miss Laura Keene.

MRS. CREGAN ...

Madam Ponisi.

SHEELAH ...

Miss Mary Wells.

KATHLEEN CREAGH ...

Miss Josephine Henry.

DUCIE BLENNERHASSET ...

Miss Hamilton.[8]

6. Leeson, and other members of the New York cast, appeared in Boucicault's later touring productions in Britain alongside Adelphi actors.
7. Boucicault met his second wife Agnes (*née* Robertson) when he joined Charles Kean and Ellen Tree's company. The pair eloped for America in the summer of 1853. Boucicault acted as Agnes's manager in America and wrote parts to showcase her talents. Until the success of *The Poor of New York* (1857), Agnes's fame far outstripped his.
8. Cast lists for early UK productions – Adelphi Theatre, London (1860); Theatre Royal Birmingham (1869); Pavilion Theatre, London (1876); Surrey Theatre, London (1879) – are recorded in: Pettingell Collection, PETT B.186.

COSTUMES. – Period, 179– .[9]

HARDRESS. – Green broad-skirted body coat of the time; double-breasted light silk waistcoat, leather pantaloons, top boots, hair rather long, steeple-crowned gold-laced hat, and white muslin cravat. *2nd Dress:* Blue body coat, white waistcoat, white kerseymere breeches, silk stockings, and shoes.

DALY. – Brown coat, *etc.*, same fashion as above. *2nd Dress:* Full dress.

CREAGH O'MOORE, and GENTLEMEN. – Evening dress.

FATHER TOM. – Broad-brimmed, low-crowned hat, faded black suit, black riding boots, and white cravat.

DANNY. [*A hunchback.*] Blue frieze jacket, corduroy breeches, yellow waistcoat, gray stockings, shoes and buckles, and old seal-skin cap.

MYLES. – Drab great coat, with cape, red cloth waistcoat, old velveteen breeches, darned gray stockings, and shoes.

CORRIGAN. – Black suit, top boots, and brown wig.

MRS. CREGAN. – Puce silk dress of the time, white muslin neckerchief and powdered hair. *2nd Dress:* Handsome embroidered silk dress, jewels and fan.

ANNE. – Gold-laced riding habit, hat and veil. *2nd Dress:* White embroidered muslin dress, and colored sash.

EILY. – Blue merino petticoat, chintz tuck-up body and skirts, short sleeves, blue stockings, hair plain, with neat comb, red cloak, and hood.

---

9. The period costumes point to the play's picturesque aesthetic. Queen Victoria noted that the 'scenery was very pretty and the whole piece very characteristic and thrilling' (qtd in Fawkes (2011 [1979]), p. 123). Meanwhile, Irish ballads and a new overture composed by Thomas Baker reinforced the representation of an Irish rural idyll. For further discussion see N. Daly (2009), pp. 55–80.

THE COLLEEN BAWN.

ACT I.

SCENE I. – [*Night*] – *Torc Cregan, the Residence of Mrs. Cregan, on the Banks of Killarney. House, L. 2 E.; window facing Audience – light behind – light to work in drop at back. Stage open at back. Music – seven bars before curtain.*

Enter HARDRESS CREGAN, *from house,* L.

HARDRESS. (*Going up* C.) Hist! Danny, are you there?[10]

DANNY *appearing from below, at back.*

DANNY. Is it yourself, Masther Hardress?

HARDRESS. Is the boat ready?

DANNY. Snug under the blue rock, sir.

HARDRESS. Does Eily expect me tonight?

DANNY. Expict is it? Here is a lether she bade me give yez; sure the young thing is never aisy when you are away. Look, masther, dear, do ye see that light, no bigger than a star beyant on Muckross Head?

---

10. **YOU** begins with the soliloquy:

> <u>Hard</u>. So Kyrle Daley loves Anne Chute = well she is a creature to be loved = she is far above Eily = my Eily = why did I not think of this before = he will be courted and admired while I, Hardress Cregan am beggar'd and every hope blighted by this secret marriage = oh Eily, my devoted, loving Eily has the day so soon arrived that I should wish to be released from bonds that are so sweet – so soul entrancing. (f. 3)

Stated thus at the outset of the drama, Hardress's wish to leave Eily appears purely selfish, inspired by pride and ambition rather than any threat to his mother. Hardress, though, is not a stock cold-hearted villain, and is softened by Eily's arrival later in I.i. Still, the opening is an early indication of how Kyrle displaces Hardress as the romantic lead in **YOU**. Kyrle acts heroically throughout, and proactively investigates Hardress's secret because 'Love – duty and friendship – prompt me to exertion. I feel that the fate of Hardress – the lovely – unknown [&] dear Anne all depend on me' (f. 13). The extent and significance of this character revision is revealed by the fact that **BYR** mocks Kyrle's limpness in *TCB*: 'Indeed, my character's so weak my charmer / That I don't see I'm wanted in the Drama' (f. 9).

HARDRESS. Yes, it is the signal which my dear Eily leaves burning in our chamber.

DANNY. All night long she sits beside that light, wid her face fixed on that lamp in your windy above.

HARDRESS. Dear, dear Eily! After all here's asleep, I will leap from my window, and we'll cross the lake.

DANNY. (*Searching.*) Where did I put that lether?

Enter KYRLE DALY *from house,* L.

KYRLE. (L.) Hardress, who is that with you?

HARDRESS. (C.) Only Mann, my boatman.

KYRLE. That fellow is like your shadow.

DANNY. (R.) Is it a cripple like me, that would be the shadow of an illegant gintleman like Mr. Hardress Cregan?

KYRLE. (L.) Well, I mean that he never leaves your side.

HARDRESS. (C.) And he never *shall* leave me. Ten years ago he was a fine boy – we were foster-brothers, and playmates – in a moment of passion, while we were struggling, I flung him from the gap rock into the reeks below, and thus he was maimed for life.

DANNY. Arrah! Whist aroon! Wouldn't I die for yez? Didn't the same mother foster us? Why, wouldn't ye break my back if it plazed ye, and welkim! Oh, Masther Kyrle, if ye'd seen him nursin' me for months, and cryin' over me, and keenin'! Sin' that time, sir, my body's been crimpin' up smaller and smaller every year, but my heart is gettin' bigger for him every day.[11]

---

11. Another important difference in **YOU** is in Danny's feelings for Hardress. Far from loving Hardress in spite of his prior violence, Danny feels vengeful because Hardress has spoiled his chance ever to have a wife. Danny is a threatening figure – 'you have made my bones ache and wont [*sic*] I be the boy to make your heart ache' (f. 10) – but he is not two-dimensional; his dialogue rightly emphasises Hardress's culpability and abuse of his social position: 'for only one word he cast me to the ground – broke + disfigured me – and to heal the deadly wrong he makes me his drudge' (f. 10). By contrast, **HAZ** jokingly draws out the homoeroticism of Danny and Hardress's friendship. When Myles is asked whether 'Hardress Cregan is sincerely attached to any one', Myles replies 'Danny Mann the hunchback' (f. 4a).

HARDRESS. Go along, Danny.

DANNY. Long life t'ye, sir! I'm off.

[*Runs up and descends rocks C. to R.*

KYRLE. Hardress, a word with you. Be honest with me – do you love Anne Chute?

HARDRESS. Why do you ask?

KYRLE. Because we have been fellow-collegians and friends through life, and the five years that I have passed at sea have strengthened, but have not cooled, my feelings towards you.

[*Offers hand.*

Enter MRS. CREGAN, *from house*, L.

HARDRESS. (L.) Nor mine for you, Kyrle. You are the same noble fellow as ever. You ask me if I love my cousin Anne?

MRS. CREGAN. (C., *between them.*) And I will answer you, Mr. Daly.

HARDRESS. (R.) My mother!

MRS. CREGAN. (C.) My son and Miss Chute are engaged. Excuse me, Kyrle, for intruding on your secret, but I have observed your love for Anne with some regret. I hope your heart is not so far gone as to be beyond recovery.

KYRLE. (L.) Forgive me, Mrs. Cregan, but are you certain that Miss Chute really is in love with Hardress?

MRS. CREGAN. Look at him! I'm sure no girl could do that and doubt it.

KYRLE. But I'm not a girl, ma'am; and sure, if you are mistaken –

HARDRESS. My belief is that Anne does not care a token for me, and likes Kyrle better.

MRS. CREGAN. (C.) You are an old friend of my son, and I may confide to you a family secret. The extravagance of my husband left this estate deeply involved. By this marriage with Anne Chute we redeem every acre of our barony. My son and she have been brought up as children together, and don't know their true feelings yet.

HARDRESS. Stop, mother, I know this: I would not wed my cousin if she did not love me, not if she carried the whole county Kerry in her pocket, and the barony of Kenmare in the crown of her hat.[12]

MRS. CREGAN. Do you hear the proud blood of the Cregans?

HARDRESS. Woo her, Kyrle, if you like, and win her if you can. I'll back you.

Enter ANNE CHUTE, *from house,* L.

ANNE. (L. C.) So will I – what's the bet?

MRS. CREGAN. Hush!

ANNE. I'd like to have bet on Kyrle.

HARDRESS. Well, Anne, I'll tell you what it was.

MRS. CREGAN. (C.) Hardress!

ANNE. (L. C.) Pull in one side aunt, and let the boy go on.

HARDRESS. (R.) Kyrle wanted to know if the dark brown colt, Hardress Cregan, was going to walk over the course for the Anne Chute Stakes, or whether it was a scrub-race open to all.

ANNE. I'm free-trade – coppaleens, mules and biddys.

MRS. CREGAN. How can you trifle with a heart like Kyrle's?

12. Early in **HAZ**, it appears that Hardress intends to go through with the bigamous marriage. When pressed to marry Anne in Boucicault's version, Hardress's first concern is how to tell his mother that he is already married, and so extricate himself from the situation. In **HAZ**, however, Hardress asks what he can say to Eily: 'Hesitate – no, no – aside Poor Eily what can I say to her' (f. 3). This shift is evidence of how Hazlewood revised the drama's moral dynamics to emphasise Hardress's exploitation of his superior class status.

ANNE. Trifle! His heart can be no trifle, if he's all in proportion.

Enter SERVANT, *from house,* L.

SERVANT. Squire Corrigan, ma'am, begs to see you.

MRS. CREGAN. At this hour, what can the fellow want? Show Mr. Corrigan here. (*Exit* SERVANT *into house,* L.) I hate this man; he was my husband's agent, or what the people here call a middle-man – vulgarly polite, and impudently obsequious.

HARDRESS. (R.) Genus squireen – a half sir, and a whole scoundrel.

ANNE. I know – a potato on a silver plate: I'll leave you to peel him. Come, Mr. Daly, take me for a moonlight walk, and be funny.

KYRLE. Funny, ma'am, I'm afraid I am –

ANNE. You are heavy, you mean; you roll through the world like a hogshead of whisky; but you only want tapping for pure spirits to flow out spontaneously. Give me your arm. (*Crossing,* R.) Hold that glove now. You are from Ballinasloe, I think?

KYRLE. I'm Connaught to the core of my heart.

ANNE. To the roots of your hair, you mean. I bought a horse at Ballinasloe fair that deceived me; I hope you won't turn out to belong to the same family.

KYRLE. (R. C.) What did he do?

ANNE. Oh! like you, he looked well enough – deep in the chest as a pool – a dhiol, and broad in the back as the Gap of Dunloe – but after two days warm work he came all to pieces, and Larry, my groom, said he'd been stuck together with glue.

KYRLE. (R.) Really, Miss Chute!

[*Music. – Exeunt,* R. 1 E.

HARDRESS. (*Advancing, laughing.*) That girl is as wild as a coppaleen, – she won't leave him a hair on the head.

[*Goes up.*

Enter SERVANT, *showing in* CORRIGAN, *from house,* L.

[*Exit* SERVANT, L.

CORRIGAN. (L.) Your humble servant, Mrs. Cregan – my service t'ye, Squire – it's a fine night, entirely.

MRS. CREGAN. (C.) May I ask to what business, sir, we have the honor of your call?

CORRIGAN. (*Aside,* L. C.) Proud as a Lady Beelzebub, and as grand as a queen. (*Aloud.*) True for you, ma'am; I would not have come, but for a divil of a pinch I'm in entirely. I've got to pay £8,000 tomorrow or lose the Knockmakilty farms.

MRS. CREGAN. Well, sir?

CORRIGAN. And I wouldn't throuble ye –

MRS. CREGAN. Trouble me, sir?

CORRIGAN. Iss, ma'am – ye'd be forgettin' now that mortgage I have on this property. It ran out last May, and by rights –

MRS. CREGAN. It will be paid next month.

CORRIGAN. Are you reckonin' on the marriage of Mister Hardress and Miss Anne Chute?

HARDRESS. (*Advancing,* R.) Mr. Corrigan, you forget yourself.

MRS. CREGAN. Leave us, Hardress, a while. (HARDRESS *retires,* R.) Now, Mr. Corrigan, state, in as few words as possible, what you demand.

CORRIGAN. Mrs. Cregan, ma'am, you depend on Miss Anne Chute's fortune to pay me the money, but your son does not love the lady, or, if he does, he has a mighty quare way of showing it. He has another girl on hand, and betune the two he'll come to the ground, and so bedad will I.

MRS. CREGAN. That is false – it is a calumny, sir!

CORRIGAN. I wish it was, ma'am. D'ye see that light over the lake? Your son's eyes are fixed on it. What would Anne Chute say if she knew that her husband, that is to be, had a mistress beyant – that he slips out every night after you're all in bed, and like Leandher,[13] barrin' the wettin', he sails across to his sweetheart?

MRS. CREGAN. Is this the secret of his aversion to the marriage? Fool! Fool! What madness, and at such a moment.

CORRIGAN. That's what I say, and no lie in it.

MRS. CREGAN. He shall give up this girl – he must!

CORRIGAN. I would like to have some security for that. I want, by tomorrow, Anne Chute's written promise to marry him, or my £8,000.

MRS. CREGAN. It is impossible, sir; you hold ruin over our heads.

CORRIGAN. Madam, it's got to hang over your head or mine.

MRS. CREGAN. Stay; you know that what you ask is out of our power – you know it – therefore this demand only covers the true object of your visit.

CORRIGAN. 'Pon my honor! And you are as 'cute, ma'am, as you are beautiful!

MRS. CREGAN. Go on, sir.

CORRIGAN. Mrs. Cregan, I'm goin' to do a foolish thing – now, by gorra I am! I'm richer than ye think, maybe, and if you'll give me your *personal* security, I'll take it.

MRS. CREGAN. What do you mean?

CORRIGAN. I meant that I'll take a lien for life on *you*, instead of the mortgage I hold on the Cregan property. (*Aside.*) That's nate, I'm thinkin'.

MRS. CREGAN. Are you mad?

13. In Greek legend, Leander swam the Hellespont at night to visit his lover, Hero, guided by a light from her tower. One night, the light was extinguished in a storm and Leander drowned. Hero then drowned herself to be with him.

CORRIGAN. I am – mad in love with yourself, and that's what I've been these fifteen years.[14]

[*Music through dialogue, till* ANNE CHUTE *is off.*

MRS. CREGAN. Insolent wretch! My son shall answer and chastise you. (*Calls.*) Hardress!

HARDRESS. (*Advancing.*) Madam.

Enter ANNE CHUTE *and* KYRLE, R.

CORRIGAN. Miss Chute! ⎫

HARDRESS. Well, mother? ⎬   [*Together.*]

ANNE. Well, sir? ⎭

MRS. CREGAN. (*Aside.*) Scoundrel! He will tell her all and ruin us! (*Aloud.*) Nothing.

[*Turns aside.*

CORRIGAN. Your obedient.

ANNE. Oh!

[*Crosses with* KYRLE *and exit,* L. U. E. *– Music ceases.*

CORRIGAN. You are in my power, ma'am. See, now, not a sowl but myself knows of this secret love of Hardress Cregan, and I'll keep it as snug as a bug in a rug, if you'll only say the word.

MRS. CREGAN. Contemptible hound, I loathe and despise you!

CORRIGAN. I've known that fifteen years, but it hasn't cured my heart ache.

MRS. CREGAN. And you would buy my aversion and disgust!

CORRIGAN. Just as Anne Chute buys your son, if she knew but all. Can he love his girl beyant, widout haten this heiress he's obliged to swallow? –

14. In **HAZ**, Warner's [Corrigan's] desire to marry Mrs Cregan is presented as calculated social climbing, without any sexual motivation.

ain't you sthriven to sell him? But you didn't feel the hardship of being sold till you tried it on yourself.[15]

MRS. CREGAN. I beg you, sir, to leave me.

CORRIGAN. That's right, ma'am – think over it, sleep on it. Tomorrow I'll call for your answer. Good evenin' kindly.
                              [*Music. – Exit* CORRIGAN, *in house,* L.

MRS. CREGAN. Hardress.

HARDRESS. What did he want?

MRS. CREGAN. He came to tell me the meaning of yonder light upon Muckross Head.

HARDRESS. Ah! Has it been discovered? Well, mother, now you know the cause of my coldness, my indifference for Anne.

MRS. CREGAN. Are you in your senses, Hardress? Who is this girl?

HARDRESS. She is known at every fair and pattern in Munster as the Colleen Bawn – her name is Eily O'Connor.

MRS. CREGAN. A peasant girl – a vulgar, barefooted beggar!

HARDRESS. Whatever she is, love has made her my equal, and when you set your foot upon her you tread upon my heart.

MRS. CREGAN. 'Tis well, Hardress. I feel that perhaps I have no right to dispose of your life and your happiness – no, my dear son – I would not wound you – heaven knows how well I love my darling boy, and you shall feel it. Corrigan has made me an offer by which you may regain the estate, and without selling yourself to Anne Chute.

HARDRESS. What is it? Of course you accepted it?

MRS. CREGAN. No, but I will accept, yes, for your sake – I – I will. He offers to cancel this mortgage if – if – I will consent to – become his wife.

---

15. Corrigan evokes contemporary abolition debates, which Boucicault also addresses in *The Octoroon*. Both plays anticipate the 13th Amendment of the US Constitution (1865), banning slavery.

HARDRESS. You – you, mother? Has he dared –

MRS. CREGAN. Hush! He is right. A sacrifice must be made – either you or I must suffer. Life is before you – my days are well-nigh past – and for your sake, Hardress – for yours; my pride, my only one. – Oh! I would give you more than my life.

HARDRESS. Never – never! I will not – cannot accept it. I'll tear that dog's tongue from his throat that dared insult you with the offer.

MRS. CREGAN. Foolish boy, before tomorrow night we shall be beggars – outcasts from this estate. Humiliation and poverty stand like specters at yonder door – tomorrow they will be realities. Can you tear out the tongues that will wag over our fallen fortunes? You are a child, you cannot see beyond your happiness.

HARDRESS. Oh, mother, mother! What can be done? My marriage with Anne is impossible.

Enter DANNY MANN, *up rock, at back.*

DANNY. (R. C.) Whisht, if ye plaze – ye're talkin' so loud she'll hear ye say that – she's comin'.

MRS. CREGAN. Has this fellow overheard us?

HARDRESS. If he has, he is mine, body and soul. I'd rather trust him with a secret than keep it myself.

MRS. CREGAN. (L. C.) I cannot remain to see Anne; excuse me to my friends. The night perhaps will bring counsel, or at least resolution to hear the worst! Good night, my son.

[*Music. – Exit into house,* L.

DANNY. (R. C.) Oh, masther! She doesn't know the worst! She doesn't know that you are married to the Colleen Bawn.

HARDRESS. Hush! What fiend prompts you to thrust that act of folly in my face?

DANNY. Thrue for ye, masther! I'm a dirty mane scut to remind ye of it.

HARDRESS. What will my haughty, noble mother say, when she learns the truth! How can I ask her to receive Eily as a daughter? – Eily, with her awkward manners, her Kerry brogue, her ignorance of the usages of society. Oh, what have I done?

DANNY. Oh! vo – vo, has the ould family come to this! Is it the daughter of Mihil-na-Thradrucha, the old rope-maker of Garryowen, that 'ud take the flure as your wife?

HARDRESS. Be silent, scoundrel! How dare you speak thus of my love? – wretch that I am to blame her! – Poor, beautiful, angel-hearted Eily.

DANNY. Beautiful is it! Och – wurra – wurra, deelish! The looking-glass was never made that could do her justice; and if St. Patrick wanted a wife, where would he find an angel that 'ud compare with the Colleen Bawn? As I row her on the lake, the little fishes come up to look at her; and the wind from heaven lifts up her hair to see what the divil brings her down here at all – at all.

HARDRESS. The fault is mine – mine alone – I alone will suffer!

DANNY. Why isn't it mine? Why can't I suffer for yez, masther dear? Wouldn't I swally every tear in your body, and every bit of bad luck in your life, and then wid a stone round my neck, sink myself and your sorrows in the bottom of the lower lake.

HARDRESS. (*Placing hand on* DANNY.) Good Danny, away with you to the boat – be ready in a few moments; we will cross to Muckross Head.

[*Looks at light at back,*

[*Music. – Exit* HARDRESS *into house,* L.

DANNY. Never fear, sir. Oh! It isn't that spalpeen, Corrigan, that shall bring ruin on that ould place. Lave Danny alone. Danny, the fox, will lade yez round and about, and cross the scint. (*Takes off his hat – sees letter.*) Bedad, here's the letter from the Colleen Bawn that I couldn't find awhile ago – it's little use now. (*Goes to lower window, and reads by light from house.*) "Come to your own Eily, that has not seen you for two long days. Come, acushla agrah machree. I have forgotten how much you love me – Shule, shule agrah.[16] – Colleen Bawn." Divil an address is on it.

Enter KYRLE and ANNE, L. U. E.

ANNE. (C.) Have they gone?

KYRLE. (L. C.) It is nearly midnight.

ANNE. Before we go in, I insist on knowing who is this girl that possesses your heart. You confess that you are in love – deeply in love.

KYRLE. I do confess it – but not even your power can extract that secret from me – do not ask me, for I could not be false, yet dare not be true.

[Exit KYRLE into house, L.

ANNE. (L. C.) He loves me – oh! he loves me – the little bird is making a nest in my heart. Oh! I'm faint with joy.

DANNY. (As if calling after him.) Sir, sir!

ANNE. Who is that?

DANNY. I'm the boatman below, an' I'm waitin' for the gintleman.

ANNE. What gentleman?

DANNY. Him that's jist left me, ma'am – I'm waitin' on him.

ANNE. Does Mr. Kyrle Daly go out boating at this hour?

DANNY. It's not for me to say, ma'am, but every night at twelve o'clock I'm here wid my boat under the blue rock below, to put him across the lake to Muckross Head. I beg your pardon, ma'am, but here's a paper ye dropped on the walk beyant – if it's no vally I'd like to light my pipe wid it.

[Gives it

ANNE. A paper I dropped!

[Goes to window – reads.

16. Deriving from 'Siúl, siúl, a ghrá' ('Walk, walk [with me], my darling'); there is also a song of this name.

DANNY. (*Aside.*) Oh, Misther Corrigan, you'll ruin masther will ye? Aisy now, and see how I'll put the cross on ye.

ANNE. A love-letter from some peasant girl to Kyrle Daly! Can this be the love of which he spoke? Have I deceived myself?

DANNY. I must be off, ma'am; here comes the signal.

[*Music.*

ANNE. The signal?

DANNY. D'ye see yonder light upon Muckross Head? It is in a cottage windy; that light goes in and out three times winkin' that way, as much as to say, "Are ye comin'?" Then if the light in that room there (*points at house above,*) answers by a wink, it manes "No!" But if it goes out entirely, his honor jumps from the parlor windy into the garden behind, and we're off. Look! (*Light in cottage disappears.*) That's one. (*Light appears.*) Now again. (*Light disappears.*) That's two. (*Light appears.*) What did I tell you? (*Light disappears.*) That's three, and here it comes again. (*Light appears.*) Wait now, and ye'll see the answer. (*Light disappears from window, L.*) That's my gentleman. (*Music change.*) You see he's goin' – good night, ma'am.

ANNE. Stay, here's money; do not tell Mr. Daly that I know of this.

DANNY. Divil a word – long life t'ye.

[*Goes up.*

ANNE. I was not deceived; he meant me to understand that he loved me! Hark! I hear the sound of someone who leaped heavily on the garden walk.

[*Goes to house L. – looking at back.*

Enter HARDRESS, *wrapped in a boat cloak,* L. U. E.

DANNY. (*Going down,* R. C.) All right, yer honor.

[HARDRESS *crosses at back, and down rock,* R. C.

ANNE. (*Hiding,* L.) It is he, 'tis he.

[*Mistaking* HARDRESS *for* DALY – *closed in.*

SCENE II. – *The Gap of Dunloe. (1ˢᵗ grooves.) Hour before sunrise.*

Enter CORRIGAN, R. 1 E.

CORRIGAN. From the rock above I saw the boat leave Torc Cregan. It is now crossing the lake to the cottage. Who is this girl? What is this mysterious misthress of young Cregan? – that I'll find out.

[MYLES *sings outside,* L.

"Oh! Charley Mount is a pretty place,
In the month of July"

CORRIGAN. Who's that? – 'Tis that poaching scoundrel – that horse stealer, Myles na Coppaleen. Here he com's with a keg of illicit whisky, as bould as Nebuckadezzar.

Enter MYLES,[17] *singing, with keg on his shoulder,* L.

Is that you, Myles?

MYLES. No! It's my brother.

CORRIGAN. I know ye, my man.

MYLES. Then why the divil did ye ax?

CORRIGAN. You may as well answer me kindly – civility costs nothing.

17. **BYR** reprises this scene to mock conventional stage Irishmen:

> Behold in me that happy ragged rogue
> The stock stage Irishman without the Brogue
> To manufacture which this will you'll see
> Turn out a never failing recipe
> He must have lightish hair extremely curly
> His teeth must be particularly ~~curly~~ pearly
> Because he shows them all whene'er he grins
> Dilapidated hose must veil his shins
> Not having shaved he must be blackish muzzled
> And this must be his attitude when puzzled
> <u>Striking the stock attitude of the Stage Paddy, with his right hand in his hair</u> (f. 14).

MYLES. (L. C.) Ow now! Don't it? Civility to a lawyer manes six-and-eight-pence about.

CORRIGAN. (R. C.) What's that on your shoulder?

MYLES. What's that to you?

CORRIGAN. I am a magistrate, and can oblige you to answer.

MYLES. Well! It's a boulster, belongin' to my mother's feather bed.

CORRIGAN. Stuff'd with whisky!

MYLES. Bedad! How would I know what it's stuff'd wid? I'm not an upholsterer.

CORRIGAN. Come, Myles, I'm not so bad a fellow as ye may think.

MYLES. To think of that now!

CORRIGAN. I am not the mane creature you imagine!

MYLES. Ain't ye now, sir? You keep up appearances mighty well, indeed.

CORRIGAN. No, Myles! I am not that blackguard I've been represented.

MYLES. (*Sits on keg.*) See that now – how people take away a man's character. You are another sort of blackguard entirely.

CORRIGAN. You shall find me a gentleman – liberal, and ready to protect you.

MYLES. Long life t'ye sir.

CORRIGAN. Myles, you have come down in the world lately; a year ago you were a thriving horse-dealer, now you are a lazy, ragged fellow.

MYLES. Ah, it's the bad luck, sir, that's in it.

CORRIGAN. No, it's the love of Eily O'Connor that's in it – it's the pride of Garryowen that took your heart away, and made ye what ye are – a smuggler and a poacher.

MYLES. Thim's hard words.

CORRIGAN. But they are true. You live like a wild beast in some cave or hole in the rocks above; by night your gun is heard shootin' the otter as they lie out on the stones, or you snare the salmon in your nets; on a cloudy night your whisky-still is going – you see, I know your life.

MYLES. Better than the priest, and devil a lie in it.

CORRIGAN. Now, if I put ye in a snug farm – stock ye with pigs and cattle, and rowl you up comfortable – d'ye think the Colleen Bawn wouldn't jump at ye?

MYLES. Bedad, she'd make a lape, I b'lieve – and what would I do for all this luck?

CORRIGAN. Find out for me who it is that lives at the cottage on Muckross Head.

MYLES. That's aisy – it's Danny Mann – no less and his ould mother Sheelah.

CORRIGAN. Yes, Myles, but there's another – a girl who is hid there.

MYLES. Ah, now!

CORRIGAN. She only goes out at night.

MYLES. Like the owls.

CORRIGAN. She's the misthress of Hardress Cregan.

MYLES. (*Seizing* CORRIGAN.) Thurra moa dhiol, what's that?

CORRIGAN. Oh, lor! Myles – Myles – what's the matter – are you mad?

MYLES. No – that is – why – why did ye raise your hand at me in that way?

CORRIGAN. I didn't.

MYLES. I thought ye did – I'm mighty quick at takin thim hints, bein' on me keepin' agin the gangers – go on – I didn't hurt ye.

CORRIGAN. Not much.

MYLES. You want to find out who this girl is?

CORRIGAN. I'll give £20 for the information – there's ten on account.

[*Gives money.*

MYLES. Long life t'ye; that's the first money I iver got from a lawyer, and bad luck to me, but there's a cure for the evil eye in thim pieces.

CORRIGAN. You will watch tonight?

MYLES. In five minutes I'll be inside the cottage itself.

CORRIGAN. That's the lad.

MYLES. (*Aside.*) I was goin' there.

CORRIGAN. And tomorrow you will step down to my office with the par-ticulars?

MYLES. Tomorrow you shall breakfast on them.

CORRIGAN. Good night, entirely.

[*Exit* CORRIGAN, L.

MYLES. I'll give ye a cowstail to swally, and make ye think it's a chapter in St. Patrick, ye spalpeen! When he called Eily the misthress of Hardress Cregan, I nearly sthretched him – begorra, I was full of sudden death that minute! Oh, Eily! Acushla agrah asthore machree! As the stars watch over Innisfallen, and as the wathers go round it and keep it, so I watch and keep round you, avourneen!

Song. – MYLES.

Oh, Limerick is beautiful, as everybody knows,
The river Shannon's full of fish, beside that city flows;
But it is not the river, nor the fish that preys upon my mind,
Nor with the town of Limerick have I any fault te find.
The girl I love is beautiful, she's fairer than the dawn;
She lives in Garryowen, and she's called the Colleen Bawn.
As the river, proud and bold, goes by that famed city.
So proud and cold, without a word, that Colleen goes by me!
Oh, hone! Oh, hone!

Oh, if I was the Emperor of Russia to command.
Or, Julius Caesar, or the Lord Lieutenant of the land,
I'd give up all my wealth, my manes, I'd give up my army,
Both the horse, the fut, and the Royal Artillery;
I'd give the crown from off my head, the people on their knees,
I'd give my fleet of sailing ships upon the briny seas,
And a beggar I'd go to sleep, a happy man at dawn.
If by my side, fast for my bride, I'd the darlin' Colleen Bawn.
                                        Oh, hone! Oh, hone!

I must reach the cottage before the masther arrives; Father Tom is there waitin' for this keg o' starlight – it's my tithe; I call every tenth keg "his riverince." It's worth money to see the way it does the old man good, and brings the wather in his eyes, the only place I ever see any about him – heaven bless him!

                              [*Sings, Exit* MYLES, R. *– Music.*

————

SCENE III. *– Interior of Eily's Cottage on Muckross Head; fire burning,* R. 3 E.; *table* R. C.; *arm chair; two stools,* R. *of table; stool* L. *of table; basin, sugar spoon, two jugs, tobacco, plate, knife, and lemon on table.*

FATHER TOM *discovered smoking in arm chair,* R. C. – EILY *in balcony, watching over lake.*

FATHER TOM. (*Sings.*) "Tobacco is an Injun weed." And every weed want's wathering to make it come up; but tobacco bein' an' Injun weed that is accustomed to a hot climate, water is entirely too cold for its warrum nature – it's whisky and water it wants. I wonder if Myles has come; I'll ask Eily. (*Calls.*) Eily, alanna! Eily, a suilish machree!

EILY. (*Turning.*) Is it me, Father Tom?

FATHER TOM. Has he come?

EILY. No; his boat is half a mile off yet.

FATHER TOM. Half a mile! I'll choke before he's here.

EILY. Do you mean Hardress?

FATHER TOM. No, dear! Myles na Coppaleen – *cum spiritu Hiberneuse,* which manes in Irish, wid a keg of poteen.

Enter MYLES, R. U. E., *down* C.

MYLES. Here I am, your riverince, never fear. I tould Sheelah to hurry up with the materials, knowin' ye be dhry and hasty.

Enter SHEELAH, *with kettle of water,* R. U. E.

SHEELAH. Here's the hot water.

MYLES. Lave it there till I brew Father Tom a pint of mother's milk.

SHEELAH. Well thin, ye'll do your share of the work, an' not a ha'porth more.

MYLES. Didn't I bring the sperrits from two miles and more? And I deserve to have pref'rence to make the punch for his riverince.

SHEELAH. And didn't I watch the kettle all night, not to let it off the boil? – there now.

MYLES. (*Quarrelling with* SHEELAH.) No, you didn't, *etc.*

SHEELAH. (*Quarrelling.*) Yes, I did, *etc.*

EILY. No, no; I'll make it, and nobody else.

FATHER TOM. Aisy now, ye becauns, and whist; Myles shall put in the whisky, Sheelah shall put in the hot water, and Eily, my Colleen, shall put the sugar in the cruiskeen. A blessin' on ye all three that loves the ould man. (MYLES *takes off hat –* WOMEN *curtsey – they make punch.*) See now, my children. There's a moral in everthing, e'en in a jug of punch. There's the sperrit, which is the sowl and strength of the man. (MYLES *pours spirit from keg.*) That's the whisky. There's the sugar, which is the smile of woman; (EILY *puts sugar.*) without that life is without taste or sweet-ness. Then there's the lemon, (EILY *puts lemon.*) which is love; a squeeze now and again does a boy no harm; but not too much. And the hot water (SHEELAH *pours water*) which is adversity – as little as possible if ye plaze – that makes the good things better still.

MYLES. And it's complate, ye see, for it's a woman that gets into hot wather all the while.

[*Pours from jug to jug.*

SHEELAH. Myles, if I hadn't the kettle, I'd bate ye.

MYLES. Then, why didn't ye let me make the punch? There's a guinea fur your riverince that's come t'ye – one in ten I got a while ago – it's your tithe – put a hole in it, and hang it on your watch chain, for it's a mighty great charm entirely.

They sit, SHEELAH *near fire,* EILY *on stool beside her,* FATHER TOM *in chair,* MYLES *on stool,* L. *of table.*

FATHER TOM. Eily, look at that boy, and tell me, haven't ye a dale to answer for?

EILY. He isn't as bad about me as he used to be; he's getting over it.

MYLES. Yes, darlin', the storm has passed over, and I've got into settled bad weather.

FATHER TOM. Maybe, afther all, ye'd have done better to have married Myles there, than be the wife of a man that's ashamed to own ye.

EILY. He isn't – he's proud of me. It's only when I spake like the poor people, and say or do anything wrong, that he's hurt; but I'm gettin' clane of the brogue, and learnin' to do nothing – I'm to be changed entirely.

MYLES. Oh! If he'd lave me yer own self, and only take away wid him his improvements. Oh! murder – Eily, aroon, why wasn't ye twins, an' I could have one of ye, only nature couldn't make two like ye – it would be onreasonable to ax it.

EILY. Poor Myles, do you love me still so much?

MYLES. Didn't I lave the world to folley ye, and since then there's been neither night nor day in my life – I lay down on Glenna Point above, where I see this cottage, and I lived on the sight of it. Oh! Eily, if tears were pison to the grass there wouldn't be a green blade on Glenna Hill this day.[18]

18. Unlike Boucicault's drama, Myles's love for Eily is not stated explicitly in **HAZ.**

EILY. But you knew I was married, Myles.

MYLES. Not thin, aroon – Father Tom found me that way, and sat beside, and lifted up my sowl. Then I confessed to him, and, sez he, "Myles, go to Eily, she has something to say to you – say I sent you." I came, and ye tould me ye were Hardress Cregan's wife, and that was a great comfort entirely. Since I knew that (*Drinks – voice in cup.*) I haven't been the blackguard I was.

FATHER TOM. See the beauty of the priest, my darlin' – *videte et admirate* – see and admire it. It was at confession that Eily tould me she loved Cregan, and what did I do? – sez I, "Where did you meet your sweetheart?" "At Garryowen," sez she. "Well," says I; "that's not the place." "Thrue, your riverince, it's too public entirely," sez she. "Ye'll mate him only in one place," sez I; "and that's the stile that's behind my chapel," for, d'ye see, her mother's grave was forenint the spot, and there's a sperrit round the place, (MYLES *drinks,*) that kept her pure and strong. Myles, ye thafe, drink fair.

SHEELAH. Come now, Eily, couldn't ye cheer up his riverince wid the tail of a song?

EILY. Hardress bid me not sing any ould Irish songs, he says the words are vulgar.

SHEELAH. Father Tom will give ye absolution.

FATHER TOM. Put your lips to that jug; there's only the strippens left. Drink! And while that thrue Irish liquor warms your heart, take this wid it. May the brogue of ould Ireland niver forsake your tongue – may her music niver lave yer voice – and may a true Irishwoman's virtue niver die in your heart!

MYLES. Come, Eily, it's my liquor – haven't ye a word to say for it?

Song, EILY – *"Cruiskeen Lawn."*[19]

Let the farmer praise his grounds,
As the huntsman doth his hounds,
And the shepherd his fresh and dewy morn;
But I, more blest than they,
Spend each night and happy day.

---

19. The Templeman Library holds sheet music for a ballad entitled 'The Cruiskeen Lawn', 'As Sung by Mrs. Dion Boucicault in Colleen Bawn'. The ballad predates the drama.

With my smilin' little Cruiskeen Lawn, Lawn, Lawn.
Chorus [Repeat.] Gramachree, mavourneen, slanta gal avoumeen,
Graraachree ma Cruiskeen Lawn, Lawn, Lawn,
With my smiling little Cruiskeen Lawn.
    [*Chorused by* MYLES, FATHER TOM*, and* SHEELAH.

MYLES.

And when grim Death appears,
In long and happy years,
To tell me that my glass is run,
I'll say, begone you slave.
For great Bacchus[20] gave me lave
To have another Cruiskeen Lawn – Lawn – Lawn.

Chorus. – Repeat

Gramachree, &c., &c.

HARDRESS. (*Without,* L. U. E.) Ho! Sheelah – Sheelah!

SHEELAH. (*Rising.*) Whist! It's the master.

EILY. (*Frightened.*) Hardress! Oh, my! What will he say if he finds us
here – run, Myles – quick, Sheelah – clear away the things.

FATHER TOM. Hurry now, or we'll get Eily in throuble.
            [*Takes keg –* MYLES *takes jugs –* SHEELAH *kettle.*

HARDRESS. Sheelah, I say!
            [*Exeunt* FATHER TOM *and* MYLES, R. U. E., *quickly.*

SHEELAH. Comin', Sir, I'm puttin on my petticoat.
                    [*Exit* SHEELAH, R. U. E., *quickly.*

Enter HARDRESS *and* DANNY, L. U. E. *opening –* DANNY
        immediately goes off, R. U. E.

EILY. (C.) Oh, Hardress, asthore?

---

20. Bacchus, also called Dionysus, is a god of wine and ecstasy in Greco-Roman mythology.

HARDRESS. (L. C.) Don't call me by those confounded Irish words – what's the matter? You're trembling like a bird caught in a trap.

EILY. Am I, mavou – no I mean – is it tremblin' I am, dear?

HARDRESS. What a dreadful smell of tobacco there is here, and the fumes of whisky punch, too; the place smells like a shebeen.[21] Who has been here?

EILY. There was Father Tom, an' Myles dhropped in.

HARDRESS. Nice company for my wife – a vagabond.

EILY. Ah! Who made him so but me, dear? Before I saw you, Hardress, Myles coorted me, and I was kindly to the boy.

HARDRESS. Damn it, Eily, why will you remind me that my wife was ever in such a position?

EILY. I won't see him again – if yer angry, dear, I'll tell him to go away, and he will, because the poor boy loves me.

HARDRESS. Yes, better than I do you mean?

EILY. No, I don't – oh! Why do you spake so to your poor Eily!

HARDRESS. Spake so! Can't you say speak?

EILY. I'll thry, aroon – I'm sthrivin' – 'tis mighty hard, but what wouldn't I undert-tee-ta – undergo for your sa-se – for your seek.

HARDRESS. Sake – sake!

EILY. Sake – seek – oh, it is to bother people entirely they mixed 'em up! Why didn't they make them all one way?

HARDRESS. (*Aside.*) It is impossible! How can I present her as my wife? Oh! What an act of madness to tie myself to one so much beneath me – beautiful – good as she is –

---

21. In Boucicault's version Hardress's complaints relate to prior events on stage (drinking and smoking), but in **HAZ** the whiskey is never opened and Eily explains 'It's the chimney that's been smoking' (f. 5). This draws attention to Hardress's prejudice, his unfairness to Eily, and to her poor living conditions, in spite of her marriage to a wealthy man.

EILY. Hardress, you are pale – what has happened?

HARDRESS. Nothing – that is, nothing but what you will rejoice at.

EILY. What d'ye mane?

HARDRESS. What do I mane! Mean – mean!

EILY. I beg your pardon, dear.

HARDRESS. Well; I mean that after tomorrow there will be no necessity to hide our marriage, for I shall be a beggar, my mother will be an outcast, and amidst all the shame, who will care what wife a Cregan takes?

EILY. And d'ye think I'd like to see you dhragged down to my side – ye don't know me – see now – never call me wife again – don't let on to mortal that we're married – I'll go as a servant in your mother's house – I'll work for the smile ye'll give me in passing, and I'll be happy, if ye'll only let me stand outside and hear your voice.

HARDRESS. You're a fool. I told you that I was betrothed to the richest heiress in Kerry; her fortune alone can save us from ruin. Tonight my mother discovered my visits here, and I told her who you were.

EILY. Oh! What did she say?

HARDRESS. It broke her heart.

EILY. Hardress! Is there no hope?

HARDRESS. None. That is none – that – that I can name.

EILY. There is one – I see it.

HARDRESS. There is. We were children when we were married, and I could get no priest to join our hands but one, and he had been disgraced by his bishop. He is dead. There was no witness to the ceremony but Danny Mann – no proof but his word, and your certificate.

EILY. (*Takes paper from her breast.*) This!

HARDRESS. Eily! If you doubt my eternal love, keep that security; it gives you the right to the shelter of my roof; but oh! if you would be content with the shelter of my heart.

EILY. And will it save ye, Hardress? And will your mother forgive me?

HARDRESS. She will bless you – she will take you to her breast.

EILY. But you – another will take you to her breast.

HARDRESS. Oh, Eily, darling, d'ye think I could forget you, machree – forget the sacrifice more than blood you give me?

EILY. Oh! When you talk that way to me, ye might take my life, and heart, and all. Oh! Hardress, I love you – take the paper and tare it.

[HARDRESS *takes paper.*

ENTER MYLES C., *opening.*

MYLES. No. I'll be damned if he shall.

HARDRESS. Scoundrel! You have been listening?

MYLES. To every word. I saw Danny, wid his ear agin that dure, so as there was only one kay-hole, I adopted the windy. Eily, aroon, Mr. Cregan will giv' ye back that paper; you can't tare up an oath; will ye help him then to cheat this other girl, and to make her his mistress, for that's what she'll be if ye are his wife. An' after all, what is there agin' the crature? Only the money she's got. Will you stop lovin' him when his love belongs to another? No! I know it by myself; but if ye jine their hands together your love will be an adultry.

EILY. Oh, no!

HARDRESS. Vagabond! Outcast! Jail bird! Dare you prate of honor to me?

MYLES. (C.) I am an outlaw, Mr. Cregan – a felon, maybe – but if you do this thing to that poor girl that loves you so much – had I my neck in the rope – or my fut on the deck of a convict ship – I'd turn round and say to ye, "Hardress Cregan, I make ye a present of the contimpt of a rogue."

[*Snaps fingers.*

Music till end of Act. – Enter FATHER TOM, SHEELAH *and* DANNY,
R. U. E. – HARDRESS *throws down paper – goes to table – takes hat.*

HARDRESS. Be it so, Eily, farewell! Until my house is clear of these
vermin – (DANNY *appears at back*) – you will see me no more.

> [*Exit* HARDRESS, L. C., *followed by* DANNY.

EILY. Hardress – Hardress! (*Going up.*) Don't leave me, Hardress!

FATHER TOM. (*Intercepts her.*) Stop, Eily!

> [DANNY *returns and listens.*

EILY. He's gone – he's gone!

FATHER TOM. Give me that paper, Myles. (MYLES *picks it up – gives it.*)
Kneel down there, Eily, before me – put that paper in your breast.

EILY. (*Kneeling.*) Oh, what will I do – what will I do?

FATHER TOM. Put your hand upon it now.

EILY. Oh, my heart – my heart!

FATHER TOM. Be thee hush, and spake after me – by my mother that's
in heaven.

EILY. By my mother that's in heaven.

FATHER TOM. By the light and the word.

EILY. By the light and the word.

FATHER TOM. Sleepin' or wakin'.

EILY. Sleepin' or wakin'.

FATHER TOM. This proof of my truth.

EILY. This proof of my truth.

FATHER TOM. Shall never again quit my breast.

EILY. Shall never again quit my breast.

EILY *utters a cry and falls – Tableau.*

ACT II.

SCENE I. – (*1ˢᵗ Grooves.*) – *Gap of Dunloe; same as 2d Scene, Act I. – Music.*

Enter HARDRESS *and* DANNY, L. 1 E.

HARDRESS. (R.) Oh, what a giddy fool I've been! What would I give to recall this fatal act which bars my fortune?

DANNY. (L.) There's something throublin' yez, Masther Hardress. Can't Danny do something to aise ye? Spake the word, and I'll die for ye.

HARDRESS. Danny, I am troubled. I was a fool when I refused to listen to you at the chapel of Castle Island.

DANNY. When I warned ye to have no call to Eily O'Connor?

HARDRESS. I was mad to marry her.

DANNY. I knew she was no wife for you. A poor thing widout any manners, or money, or book larnin', or a ha'porth o' fortin'. Oh, worra! I told ye that, but ye bate me off, and here now is the way of it.

HARDRESS. Well, it's done, and can't be undone.

DANNY. Bedad, I dun know that. Wouldn't she untie the knot herself – couldn't ye coax her?

HARDRESS. No.

DANNY. Is that her love for you? You that give up the divil an' all for her. What's *her* ruin to yours? Ruin – goredoutha – ruin is it? Don't I pluck a shamrock and wear it a day for the glory of St. Patrick, and then throw it away when it's gone by my likin's. What is *she*, to be ruined by a gentleman? Whoo! Mighty good for the likes o' her.

HARDRESS. She would have yielded, but –

DANNY. Asy now, an' I'll tell ye. Pay her passage out to Quaybeck and put her aboord a three-master, widout sayin' a word. Lave it to me. Danny will clear the road foreninst ye.

HARDRESS. Fool, if she still possesses that certificate – the proof of my first marriage – how can I dare to wed another? Commit bigamy – disgrace my wife – bastardise my children?

DANNY. Den by the powers, I'd do by Eily as wid the glove there on yer hand; make it come off as it came on – an' if it fits too tight, take the knife to it.

HARDRESS. (*Turning to him.*) What do you mean?

DANNY. Only gi' me the word, an' I'll engage that the Colleen Bawn will never trouble ye any more; don't ax me any questions at all. Only – if you're agreeable, take off that glove from yer hand an' give it to me for a token – that's enough.

HARDRESS. (*Throws off cloak; seizes him; throws him down.*) Villain! Dare you utter a word or meditate a thought of violence towards that girl –

DANNY. Oh, murder! May I never die in sin, if –

HARDRESS. Begone! Away, at once, and quit my sight. I have chosen my doom! I must learn to endure it – but blood! – and hers! Shall I make cold and still that heart that beats alone for me? – quench those eyes that look so tenderly in mine? Monster! Am I so vile that you dare to whisper such a thought?

DANNY. Oh, masther! divil burn me if I meant any harm.

HARDRESS. Mark me well, now. Respect my wife as you would the queen of the land – whisper a word such as those you uttered to me, and it will be your last. I warn ye – remember and obey.

[*Exit* HARDRESS, R.

DANNY. (*Rises – picks up cloak.*) Oh, the darlin' crature! Would I harrum a hair of her blessed head? – no! Not unless you gave me that glove, and den I'd jump into the bottomless pit for ye.

[*Exit* DANNY, R. *Music – change.*

SCENE II. – *Room in Mrs. Cregan's house; window, R., in flat backed by landscape; door, L., in flat; backed by interior. Lights up.*

Enter ANNE CHUTE, L. *in flat.*

ANNE. That fellow runs in my head. (*Looking at window.*) There he is in the garden, smoking like a chimney-pot. (*Calls.*) Mr. Daly!

KYRLE. (*Outside window.*) Good morning!

ANNE. (*Aside.*) To think he'd smile that way, after going Leandering all night like a dissipated young owl. (*Aloud.*) Did you sleep well? (*Aside.*) Not a wink, you villain, and you know it.

KYRLE. I slept like a top.

ANNE. (*Aside.*) I'd like to have the whipping of ye. (*Aloud.*) When did you get back?

KYRLE. Get back! I've not been out.

ANNE. (*Aside.*) He's not been out! This is what men come to after a cruise at sea – they get sunburnt with love. Those foreign donnas teach them to make fire-places of their hearts, and chimney-pots of their mouths. (*Aloud.*) What are you doing down there? (*Aside.*) As if he was stretched out to dry.

[KYRLE *puts down pipe outside.*

Enter KYRLE *through window, R., in flat.*

KYRLE. (R. C.) I have been watching Hardress coming over from Divil's Island in his boat – the wind was dead against him.

ANNE. (L. C.) It was fair for going to Divil's Island last night, I believe.

KYRLE. Was it?

ANNE. You were up late, I think?

KYRLE. I was. I watched by my window for hours, thinking of her I loved – slumber overtook me, and I dreamed of a happiness I never can hope for.

ANNE. Look me straight in the face.

KYRLE. Oh! If some fairy could strike us into stone now – and leave us looking forever into each other's faces, like the blue lake below and the sky above it!

ANNE. Kyrle Daly! What would you say to a man who had two loves, one to whom he escaped at night, and the other to whom he devoted himself during the day – what would you say?

KYRLE. I'd say he had no chance.

ANNE. Oh, Captain Cautious! Well answered. Isn't he fit to take care of anybody! His cradle was cut out of a witness-box.

Enter HARDRESS *through window, R., in flat.*

KYRLE. (R.) Anne! I don't know what you mean, but that I know that I love you, and you are sporting with a wretchedness you cannot console. I was wrong to remain here so long, but I thought my friendship for Hardress would protect me against your invasion – now I will go.

[HARDRESS *advancing.*

HARDRESS. (C.) No, Kyrle, you will stay. Anne, he loves you, and I more than suspect you prefer him to me. From this moment you are free; I release you from all troth to me: in his presence I do this.

ANNE. (L.) Hardress!

HARDRESS. There is a bar between us which you should have known before, but I could not bring myself to confess. Forgive me, Anne – you deserve a better man than I am.

[*Exit,* L.

ANNE. A bar between us! What does he mean?

KYRLE. He means that he is on the verge of ruin: he did not know how bad things were till last night. His generous noble heart recoils from receiving anything from you but love.

ANNE. And does he think I'd let him be ruined anyway? Does he think I wouldn't sell the last rood of land – the gown off my back, and the hair off my head, before that boy that protected and loved me, the child, years ago, should come to a hap'orth of harrum?

[*Crosses to* R.

KYRLE. Miss Chute!

ANNE. Well, I can't help it. When I am angry the brogue comes out, and my Irish heart will burst through manners, and graces, and twenty stay-laces. (*Crosses to* L.) I'll give up my fortune – that I will!

KYRLE. You can't – you've got a guardian who cannot consent to such a sacrifice.

ANNE. Have I? Then I'll find a husband that will.

KYRLE. (*Aside.*) She means me – I see it her eyes.

ANNE. (*Aside.*) He's trying to look unconscious. (*Aloud.*) Kyrle Daly, on your honor and word as a gentleman, do you love me and nobody else?

KYRLE. Do you think me capable of contaminating your image by admitting a meaner passion into my breast?

ANNE. Yes, I do.

KYRLE. Then you wrong me.

ANNE. I'll prove that in one word. Take care, now; it's coming.

KYRLE. Go on.

ANNE. (*Aside.*) Now I'll astonish him. (*Aloud.*) Eily!

KYRLE. What's that?

ANNE. "Shule, shule, agrah!"

KYRLE. Where to?

ANNE. Three winks, as much as to say, "Are you coming?" and an extinguisher above here means "Yes." Now you see I know all about it.

KYRLE. You have the advantage of me.

ANNE. Confess now, and I'll forgive you.

KYRLE. I will; tell me what to confess, and I'll confess it – I don't care what it is.

ANNE. (*Aside.*) If I hadn't eye proof he'd brazen it out of me. Isn't he cunning? He's one of those that would get fat where a fox would starve.

KYRLE. That was a little excursion into my past life – a sudden descent on my antecedents, to see if you could not surprise an infidelity – but I defy you.

ANNE. You do? I accept that defiance; and, mind me, Kyrle, if I find you true as I once thought, there's my hand; but if you are false in this, Anne Chute will never change her name for yours. (*He kisses her hand.*) Leave me now.

KYRLE. Oh, the lightness you have given to my heart! The number of pipes I'll smoke this afternoon will make them think we've got a haystack on fire.

> [*Exit* KYRLE, *through window*, R.

ANNE. (*Rings bell on table,* R.) Here, Pat, Barney, someone.

Enter SERVANT, L. *door in flat.*

Tell Larry Dolan, my groom, to saddle the black mare, Fireball, but not bring her round the house – I'll mount in the stables.

> [*Exit* SERVANT, L. *door in flat.*

I'll ride over to Muckross Head, and draw that cottage; I'll know what's there. It mayn't be right, but I haven't a big brother to see after me – and self-protection is the first law of nature.

> [*Exit* ANNE, R. 1 E.

Music. Enter MRS. CREGAN *and* HARDRESS, L. *door in flat.*

MRS. CREGAN. (R. C.) What do you say, Hardress?

HARDRESS. (L. C.) I say, mother, that my heart and faith are both already pledged to another, and I cannot break my engagement.

MRS. CREGAN. And this is the end of all our pride!

HARDRESS. Repining is useless – thought and contrivance are of no avail – the die is cast.

MRS. CREGAN. Hardress, I speak not for myself, but for you – and I would rather see you in your coffin than married to this poor, lowborn, silly, vulgar creature. I know you, my son; you will be miserable when the infatuation of first love is past; when you turn from her and face the world, as one day you must do, you will blush to say, "This is my wife." Every word from her mouth will be a pang to your pride. You will follow her movements with terror – the contempt and derision she excites will rouse you first to remorse, and then to hatred – and from the bed to which you go with a blessing, you will rise with a curse.

HARDRESS. Mother! Mother!

[*Throws himself in chair.*

MRS. CREGAN. To Anne you have acted a heartless and dishonorable part – her name is already coupled with yours at every fireside in Kerry.

Enter SERVANT, L. *door in flat.*

SERVANT. Mr. Corrigan, ma'am.

MRS. CREGAN. He comes for his answer. Show him in.

[*Exit* SERVANT, L. *door in flat.*

The hour has come, Hardress – what answer shall I give him?

HARDRESS. Refuse him – let him do his worst.

MRS. CREGAN. And face beggary! On what shall we live? I tell you the prison for debt is open before us. Can you work? No! Will you enlist as a soldier, and send your wife into service? We are ruined – d'ye hear? – ruined! I must accept this man only to give you and yours a shelter, and under Corrigan's roof I may not be ashamed, perhaps, to receive your wife.

Enter SERVANT, *showing in* MR. CORRIGAN L. *door in flat.*

CORRIGAN. (L.) Good morning, ma'am; I am punctual, you perceive.

MRS. CREGAN. (C.) We have considered your offer, sir, and we see no alternative – but – but –

CORRIGAN. Mrs. Cregan, I'm proud, ma'am, to take your hand.

HARDRESS. (*Starting up.*) Begone – begone, I say; touch her, and I'll brain you!

CORRIGAN. Squire! Sir! Mr. Hardress!

HARDRESS. Must I hurl you from the house?

Enter two SERVANTS, *door in flat.*

MRS. CREGAN. Hardress, my darling boy, restrain yourself.

CORRIGAN. Good morning, ma'am. I have my answer, (*to* SERVANT) is Miss Chute within?

SERVANT. No, sir; she's just galloped out of the stable yard.

CORRIGAN. Say I called to see her. I will wait upon her at this hour tomorrow. (*Looking at the Cregans.*) Tomorrow! Tomorrow!
[*Exit, followed by* SERVANT, L. *door in flat.*

MRS. CREGAN. Tomorrow will see us in Limerick Jail, and this house in the hands of the sheriff.

HARDRESS. Mother, heaven guide and defend me! Let me rest for a while – you don't know all yet, and I have not the heart to tell you.
[*Crosses L.*

MRS. CREGAN. With you, Hardress, I can bear anything – anything – but your humiliation and your unhappiness –

HARDRESS. I know it, mother, I know it.
[*Exit, L. 1 E. Music.*

DANNY *appears at window, R., in flat.*

DANNY. Whisht – missiz – whisht.

MRS. CREGAN. (L. C.) Who's there?

DANNY. It's me, sure, Danny – that is – I know the throuble that's in it. I've been through it all wid him.

MRS. CREGAN. You know, then?

DANNY. Everything, ma'am; and, sure, I shtruv hard and long to impache him from doing it.

MRS. CREGAN. Is he, indeed, so involved with this girl that he will not give her up?

DANNY. No; he's got over the worst of it, but she holds him tight, and he feels kindly and soft-hearted for her, and daren't do what another would.

MRS. CREGAN. Dare not?

DANNY. Sure she might be packed off across the wather to Ameriky, or them parts beyant? Who'd ever ax a word afther her? – barrin' the masther, who'd murdher me if he knew I whispered such a thing.

MRS. CREGAN. But would she go?

DANNY. Ow, ma'am, wid a taste of persuasion, we'd mulvather her aboord. But there's another way again, and if ye'd only coax the masther to send me his glove, he'd know the manin' of that token, and so would I.

MRS. CREGAN. His glove?

DANNY. Sorra a ha'porth else. If he'll do that, I'll take my oath ye'll hear no more of the Colleen Bawn.

MRS. CREGAN. I'll see my son.

[*Exit* L. D. F.

DANNY. Tare an' 'ouns, that lively girl, Miss Chute, has gone the road to Muckross Head; I've watched her – I've got my eye on all of them. If she sees Eily – ow, ow, she'll get the ring itself in that helpin' maybe, of kale-canon. By the piper, I'll run across the lake, and get there first; she's got a long round to go, and the wind rising – a purty blast entirely.

[*Goes to window – Music.*

Re-enter MRS. CREGAN, L. D. F., *with glove.*

MRS. CREGAN. (*Aside.*) I found his gloves in the hall, where he had thrown them in his hat.

DANNY. Did ye ax him, ma'am?

MRS. CREGAN. I did – and here is the reply.[22]

[*Holds out glove.*

DANNY. He has changed his mind, then?

MRS. CREGAN. He has entirely.

DANNY. And – and – I am – to – do it?

MRS. CREGAN. That is the token.

DANNY. I know it – I'll keep my promise. I'm to make away with her?

MRS. CREGAN. Yes, yes – take her away – away with her!

[*Exit* MRS. CREGAN, L. *door in flat.*

DANNY. Never fear, ma'am. (*Going to window.*) He shall never see or hear again of the Colleen Bawn.

[*Exit* DANNY *through window – change.*

SCENE III. – *Exterior of Eily's Cottage; Cottage, R. 3. E.; set pieces, backed by Lake; table and two seats, R. C.*

SHEELAH *and* EILY *discovered, knitting.*

SHEELAH. (R.) Don't cry, darlin' – don't, alanna!

---

22. Hardress gives Danny the order in **YOU**, but then regrets it:

> Hard. Madly Ha! ha! I am bound to Anne and I am bound to Eily – I am wedded to one and am about to wed another = the deed is yet undone – the word that kill [*sic*] my Eily is yet unspoken = but the word shall be spoken – the token shall be given – the deed done /gives his glove to Danny Man do not harm her Danny = take her away from Ireland put the sea between us but do not harm her = never let me see her again – never – never
>
> Danny. I will do it good master and do it well
>
> Exit
>
> Mrs C. Hardress you forget me.
>
> Hardress. Away – who are you – I am mad. Danny – Danny – do not go – give me back my Eily – Eily my Eily
>
> Sinks Exhausted in chair (ff. 27–8)

Later, upon hearing of the discovery of Eily's cloak, Hardress threatens to kill himself. Hardress is wracked with grief, but Mrs Cregan reminds him that he must marry Anne.

EILY. (L.) He'll never come back to me – I'll never see him again, Sheelah!

SHEELAH. Is it lave his own wife?

EILY. I've sent him a letther by Myles, and Myles has never come back – I've got no answer – he won't spake to me – I am standin' betune him and fortune – I'm in the way of his happiness. I wish I was dead!

SHEELAH. Whisht! Be thee husht! What talk is that? When I'm tuk sad that way, I go down to the chapel and pray a turn – it lifts the cloud off my heart.

EILY. I can't pray; I've tried, but unless I pray for him, I can't bring my mind to it.

SHEELAH. I never saw a colleen that loved as you love; sorra come to me, but I b'lieve you've got enough to supply all Munster, and more left over than would choke ye if you wern't azed of it.

EILY. He'll come back – I'm sure he will; I was wicked to doubt. Oh! Sheelah! What becomes of the girls he doesn't love? Is there anything goin' on in the world where he isn't?

SHEELAH. There now – you're smilin' again.

EILY. I'm like the first mornin' when he met me – there was dew on the young day's eye – a smile on the lips o' the lake. Hardress will come back – oh! yes; he'll never leave his poor Eily all alone by herself in this place. Whisht, now, an' I'll tell you.

[*Music.*

Song. – Air, "Pretty Girl Milking her Cow."

'Twas on a bright morning in summer,
I first heard his voice speaking low,
As he said to a colleen beside me,
"Who's that pretty girl milking her cow?"
And many times after he met me,
And vowed that I always should be
His own little darling alanna,
Mavourneen a sweelish machree.

> I haven't the manners or graces
> Of the girls in the world where ye move,
> I haven't their beautiful faces,
> But I have a heart that can love.
> If it plase ye, I'll dress in satins.
> And jewels I'll put on my brow,
> But don't ye be after forgettin'
> Your pretty girl milking her cow.

SHEELAH. Ah, the birds sit still on the boughs to listen to her, an' the trees stop whisperin'; she leaves a mighty big silence behind her voice, that nothin' in nature wants to break. My blessin' on the path before her – there's an angel at the other end of it.

[*Exit* SHEELAH *in cottage,* R.

EILY. (*Repeats last line of song.*)

Enter ANNE CHUTE, L. U. E.

ANNE. There she is.

EILY. (*Sings till facing* ANNE – *stops* – *they examine each other.*)

ANNE. My name is Anne Chute.

EILY. I am Eily O'Connor.

ANNE. You are the Colleen Bawn – the pretty girl.

EILY. And you are the Colleen Ruaidh.

ANNE. (*Aside.*) She is beautiful.

EILY. (*Aside.*) How lovely she is.

ANNE. We are rivals.

EILY. I am sorry for it.

ANNE. So am I, for I feel that I could have loved you.

EILY. That's always the way of it; everybody wants to love me, but there's something spoils them off.

ANNE. (*Showing letter.*) Do you know that writing?

EILY. I do, ma'am, well, though I don't know how you came by it.

ANNE. I saw your signals last night – I saw his departure, and I have come here to convince myself of his falsehood to me. But now that I have seen you, you have no longer a rival in his love, for I despise him with all my heart, who could bring one so beautiful and simple as you are to ruin and shame!

EILY. He didn't – no – I am his wife! Oh, what have I said!

ANNE. What?

EILY. Oh, I didn't mane to confess it – no, I didn't! But you wrung it from me in defense of him.

ANNE. You his wife?

Enter DANNY, L. U. E.

DANNY. (*At back – aside.*) The divil! They're at it – an' I'm too late!

ANNE. I cannot believe this – show me your certificate.

EILY. Here it is.

DANNY. (*Advances between them.*) Didn't you swear to the priest that it should niver lave your breast?

ANNE. Oh! You're the boatman.

DANNY. Iss, ma'am!

ANNE. Eily, forgive me for doubting your goodness, and your purity. I believe you. Let me take your hand. (*Crosses to her.*) While the heart of Anne Chute beats, you have a friend that won't be spoiled off, but you have no longer a rival, mind that. All I ask of you is that you will never mention this visit to Mr. Daly – and for you (*To* DANNY) this will purchase your silence. (*Gives money.*) Goodbye.

[*Exit* ANNE, L. U. E.

DANNY. Long life t'ye. (*Aside.*) What does it mane? Hasn't she found me out?

EILY. Why did she ask me never to spake to Mr. Daly of her visit here? Sure I don't know any Mr. Daly.

DANNY. Didn't she spake of him before, dear?

EILY. Never!

DANNY. Nor didn't she name Master Hardress?

EILY. Well, I don't know; she spoke of him and of the letter I wrote to him, but I b'lieve she never named him intirely.

DANNY. (*Aside.*) The divil's in it for sport; she's got 'em mixed yet.

Enter SHEELAH *from cottage,* R.

SHEELAH. What brings you back, Danny?

DANNY. Nothing! But a word I have from the masther for the Colleen here.

EILY. Is it the answer to the letter I sent by Myles?

DANNY. That's it, jewel, he sent me wid a message.

SHEELAH. (C.) Somethin' bad has happened. Danny, you are as pale as milk, and your eye is full of blood – yez been drinkin'.

DANNY. Maybe I have.

SHEELAH. You thrimble, and can't spake straight to me. Oh! Danny, what is it, avick?

DANNY. Go on now, an' stop yer keenin'.

EILY. Faith, it isn't yourself that's in it, Danny; sure there's nothing happened to Hardress?

DANNY. Divil a word, good or bad, I'll say while the mother's there.

SHEELAH. I'm goin'. (*Aside.*) What's come to Danny this day, at all, at all; bedad, I don't know my own flesh and blood.

[*Runs into cottage.*

DANNY. Sorro' and ruin has come on the Cregans; they're broke intirely.

EILY. Oh, Danny.

DANNY. Whisht, now! You are to meet Masther Hardress this evenin', at a place on the Divil's Island, beyant. Yo'll niver breathe a word to a mortal where yer goin', d'ye mind, now; but slip down, unbeknown, to the landin' below, where I'll have the boat waitin' for yez.

EILY. At what hour?

DANNY. Just after dark; there's no moon tonight, an' no one will see us crossin' the water.

[*Music till end of scene.*

EILY. I will be there; I'll go down only to the little chapel by the shore, and pray there 'till ye come.

[*Exit EILY, into cottage, R.*

DANNY. I'm wake and cowld! What's this come over me? Mother, mother, acushla.[23]

Enter SHEELAH, R.

SHEELAH. What is it, Danny?

DANNY. (*Staggering to table.*) Give me a glass of spirits!

[*Falls in chair – Change quickly.*[24]

————

23. Danny's line is delivered after Sheelah's entrance in **BOU** (f. 59). This changes the dynamics of the scene. Instead of calling for his mother, Danny reacts to her entrance.
24. The direction in **BOU** reads 'Wipes his forehead as he still looks after Eily' (f. 59). This indicates that the scene ended with a 'picture', rather than the quick change suggested in the printed script.

SCENE IV. – *The old Weir Bridge, or a Wood on the verge of the Lake –* (*1ˢᵗ grooves.*)

Enter ANNE CHUTE, R.

ANNE. Married! The wretch is married! And with that crime already on his conscience he was ready for another and similar piece of villainy. It's the Navy that does it. It's my belief those sailors have a wife in every place they stop at.

MYLES. (*Sings outside*, R.)

> "Oh! Eily astoir, my love is all crost,
>   Like a bud in the frost."

ANNE. Here's a gentleman who has got my complaint – his love is all crost, like a bud in the frost.

Enter MYLES, R.

MYLES.

> "And there's no use at all in my goin' to bed,
>   For it's drames, and not sleep, that comes into my head,
>   And it's all about you," etc., etc.

ANNE. My good friend, since you can't catch your love, d'ye think you could catch my horse?

> [*Distant thunder.*

MYLES. Is it a black mare wid a white stockin' on the fore off leg?

ANNE. I dismounted to unhook a gate – a peal of thunder frightened her, and she broke away.

MYLES. She's at Torc Cregan stables by this time – it was an admiration to watch her stride across the Phil Dolan's bit of plough.

ANNE. And how am I to get home?

MYLES. If I had four legs, I wouldn't ax betther than to carry ye, and a proud baste I'd be.

> [*Thunder – rain.*

ANNE. The storm is coming down to the mountain – is there no shelter near?

MYLES. There may be a corner in this ould chapel. (*Rain.*) Here comes the rain – murdher! Ye'll be wet through. (*Music – pulls off coat.*) Put this round yez.

ANNE. What will you do? You'll catch your death of cold.

MYLES. (*Taking out bottle.*) Cowld is it? Here's a wardrobe of top coats. (*Thunder.*) Whoo! This is a fine time for the water – this way, ma'am.

> [*Exeunt* MYLES *and* ANNE, L.

Enter EILY, *cloak and hood,* R.

EILY. Here's the place where Danny was to meet me with the boat. Oh! Here he is.

Enter DANNY, L.

How pale you are!

DANNY. The thunder makes me sick.

EILY. Shall we not wait till the storm is over?

DANNY. If it comes on bad we can put into the Divil's Island Cave.

EILY. I feel so happy that I am going to see him, yet there is a weight about my heart that I can't account for.

DANNY. I can. (*Aside.*) Are you ready now?

EILY. Yes; come – come.

DANNY. (*Staggering.*) I'm wake yet. My throat is dry – if I'd a draught of whisky now.

EILY. Sheelah gave you a bottle.

DANNY. I forgot – it's in the boat.

> [*Rain.*

EILY. Here comes the rain – we shall get wet.

DANNY. There's the masther's boat cloak below.

EILY. Come, Danny, lean on me. I'm afraid you are not sober enough to sail the skiff.

DANNY. Sober! The dhrunker I am, the better I can do the work I've got to do.

EILY. Come, Danny, come – come.

[*Exeunt* EILY *and* DANNY, R. – *Music ceases.*

Re-enter ANNE CHUTE *and* MYLES, L.

MYLES. It was only a shower, I b'lieve – are ye wet, ma'am?

ANNE. Dry as a biscuit.

MYLES. Ah! Then it's yerself is the brave and beautiful lady – as bould an' proud as a ship before the blast.

[ANNE *looks off*, R.

ANNE. Why, there is my mare, and who comes with –

[*Crosses to* R.

MYLES. It's Mr. Hardress Cregan himself.

ANNE. Hardress here?

MYLES. Eily gave me a letter for him this morning.

Enter HARDRESS, R.

HARDRESS. Anne, what has happened? Your horse galloped wildly into the stable – we thought you had been thrown.

MYLES. Here is a lether Eily tould me to give him. (*To* HARDRESS.) I beg your pardon, sir, but here's the taste of a lether I was axed to give your honor.

[*Gives letter.*

HARDRESS. (*Aside.*) From Eily!

ANNE. Thanks, my good fellow, for your assistance.

MYLES. Not at all, ma'am. Sure, there isn't a boy in the County Kerry that would not give two thumbs off his hands to do a service to the Colleen Ruaidh, as you are called among us – iss indeed, ma'am. (*Going – aside.*) Ah! Then it's the purty gill she is, in them long clothes.

[*Exit* MYLES, R.

HARDRESS. (*Reads, aside.*) "I am the cause of your ruin; I can't live with that thought killin' me. If I do not see you before night you will never again be throubled with your poor Eily." Little simpleton! She is capable of doing herself an injury.

ANNE. Hardress! I have been very blind and very foolish, but today I have learned to know my own heart. There's my hand; I wish to seal my fate at once. I know the delicacy which prompted you to release me from my engagement to you. I don't accept that release; I am yours.

HARDRESS. Anne, you don't know all.

ANNE. I know more than I wanted, that's enough. I forbid you ever to speak on this subject.

HARDRESS. You don't know my past life.

ANNE. And I don't want to know. I've had enough of looking into past lives; don't tell me anything you wish to forget.

HARDRESS. Oh, Anne – my dear cousin; if I could forget – if silence could be oblivion.

[*Exeunt* HARDRESS *and* ANNE, L.

SCENE V.[25] – *Exterior of Myles' Hut.* (*1ˢᵗ grooves.*)

Enter MYLES, R., *singing "Brian O'Linn."*

"Brian O'Linn had no breeches to wear,
So he bought him a sheepskin to make him a pair;
The skinny side out, the woolly side in,
'They are cool and convanient,' said Brian O'Linn."

---

25. This scene is not in **BOU**.

(*Locks door of cabin.*) Now I'll go down to my whisky-still. It is under my feet this minute, bein' in a hole in the rocks they call O'Donoghue's stables, a sort of water cave; the people around here think that the cave is haunted with bad spirits, and they say that of a dark stormy night strange unearthly noises is heard comin' out of it – it is me singing, "The night before Larry was stretched." Now I'll go down to that cave, and wid a sod of live turf under a kettle of worty, I'll invoke them sperrits – and what's more, they'll come.

[*Exit* MYLES, *singing,* R. *Music till* MYLES
begins to speak next scene.

———————

SCENE VI. – *A Cave;*[26] *through large opening at back is seen the Lake and the Moon; rocks* R. *and* L. *– flat rock,* R. C.; *gauge waters all over stage; rope hanging from* C., *hitched on wing,* R. U. E.

Enter MYLES, *singing,*[27] *top of rock,* R. U. E.

MYLES. And this is a purty night for my work! The smoke of my whisky-still will not be seen; there's my distillery beyant in a snug hole up there, (*Unfastens rope,* L.) and here's my bridge to cross over to it. I think it would puzzle a ganger to folly me; this is a patent of my own – a tight-rope bridge. (*Swings across from* R. *to* L.) Now I tie up my drawbridge at this side till I want to go back – what's that – it was an otter I woke from a nap he was takin' on that bit of rock there – ow! Ye divil! If I had my gun I'd give ye a leaden supper. I'll go up and load it, maybe I'll get a shot; them stones is the place where they lie out of a night, and many a one I've shot of them.

[*Music.* – *Disappears up rock,* L. U. E.[28]

EILY. What place is this you have brought me to?

————————————————————————————————

26. Concerned that journalists' focus on *TCB*'s sensation scene seemed to devalue his work, Boucicault later claimed: 'These effects were after-thoughts' (1862, p. 203).
27. Song given in **BOU**: 'Oh Charleymount is a purty place' (f. 65). In both **B&H**'s and **BYR**'s comic revisions of this scene, Myles is introduced singing 'Charley Mount' and carrying a keg of whiskey, indicating a strong association between the song and the character.
28. Extra directions in **BOU** read: 'a pause. A pirogue or small boat containing Danny and Eily appears. R. H.' (f. 66). This suggests the illusion of Danny and Eily rowing onto the stage.

DANNY. Never fear – I know where I'm goin' – step out on that rock – mind yer footin'; 'tis wet there.

EILY. I don't like this place – it's like a tomb.

DANNY. Step out, I say; the boat is laking.

[EILY *steps on to rock,* R. C.

EILY. Why do you spake to me so rough and cruel?

DANNY. Eily, I have a word to say t'ye; listen now, and don't trimble that way.

EILY. I won't, Danny – I won't.

DANNY. Wonst, Eily, I was a fine brave boy, the pride of my ould mother, her white haired-darlin' – you wouldn't think it to look at me now. D'ye know how I got changed to this?

EILY. Yes, Hardress told me.

DANNY. He done it – but I loved him before it, an' I loved him after it – not a dhrop of blood I have, but I'd pour out like wather for the masther.

EILY. I know what you mean – as he has deformed your body ruined your life – made ye what ye are.

DANNY. Have you, a woman, less love for him than I, that you wouldn't give him what he wants of you, even if he broke your heart as he broke my back, both in a moment of passion? Did I ax him to ruin himself and his ould family, and all to mend my bones? No! I loved him, and I forgave him that.

EILY. Danny, what do you want me to do?

[DANNY *steps out on to rock.*

DANNY. Give me that paper in your breast?

[*Boat floats off slowly,* R.

EILY. I can't – I've sworn never to part with it! You know I have!

DANNY. Eily, that paper stands between Hardress Cregan and his fortune; that paper is the ruin of him. Give it, I tell yez.

EILY. Take me to the priest; let him lift the oath off me. Oh, Danny, I swore a blessed oath on my two knees, and would ye ax me to break that?

DANNY. (*Seizes her hands*) Give it up, and don't make me hurt ye.

EILY. I swore by my mother's grave, Danny. Oh! Danny dear, don't. Don't, acushla, and I'll do anything. See now, what good would it be? Sure, while I live I'm his wife.

[*Music changes.*

DANNY. Then you've lived too long. Take your marriage lines wid ye to the bottom of the lake.

[*He throws her from rock backwards into the water, L. C., with a cry; she reappears, clinging to rock.*

EILY. No! Save me! Don't kill me! Don't, Danny, I'll do anything – only let me live.

DANNY. He wants ye dead.

[*Pushes her off.*

EILY. Oh, heaven! Help me! Danny – Dan –

[*Sinks.*

DANNY. (*Looking down.*) I've done it – she's gone.[29]

[*Shot is fired, L. U. E.; he falls – rolls from the rock into the water, R. C.*

MYLES *appears with gun, on rock, L. U. E.*

MYLES. I hit one of them bastes that time. I could see well, though it was so dark. But there was somethin' moving on that stone. (*Swings across to R. U. E.*) Divil a sign of him. Stop! (*Looks down.*) What's this? It's a

---

29. In **HAZ**, Danny's attempt to murder Eily is not explicitly presented as a premeditated attack. Danny has not been drinking to get up his courage to murder her; rather, his violence escalates as they fight over her marriage lines.

woman – there's something white there. (*Figure rises near rock,* R. U. E.; *kneels down; tries to take the hand of figure.*) Ah! That dress! – it's Eily. My own darlin' Eily.

> *Pulls off waistcoat – jumps off rock.*[30] EILY *rises,* R.*; then* MYLES *and* EILY *rise up,* C.*; he turns and seizes rock,* R. C.*;* EILY *across left arm.*[31]

ACT III.

SCENE I. *– Interior of an Irish hut; door and small opening,* R. C. *Door* L. C. *in flat.*

Truckle bed and bedding, R. C., *on which* DANNY MANN *is discovered; table with jug of water; lighted candle stuck in bottle,* L.*; two stools –* SHEELAH *at table,* L. *Music.*

DANNY. (*In his sleep.*) Gi' me the paper, thin – Screeching won't save ye – down – down! (*Wakes.*) Oh, mother! Darlin' mother!

---

30. In his first account of *TCB*, Henry Morley calls the stunts in the sensation scene 'Adelphi effects', indicating that the term 'sensation' was still not in common usage (1866, p. 258).
31. The rescue is scripted differently in each of the variants.
    Fawkes suggests that the idea for Myles's 'running header' was first suggested by Laura Keene's stage carpenter (2011 [1979], p. 118); however, in **BOU**, Myles recognises Eily only after he has rescued her, and he does not dive into the lake: 'Stop there's something white there – <u>leans over and catches an end of Eily's dress</u> What's this. <u>he drags her on the rock insensible</u>' (f. 69).
    In **YOU**, Kyrle is Eily's rescuer. The scene that follows Danny's demand for her 'marriage lines' runs:

    <u>Eily</u>. Never. I will die sooner.

    <u>Danny</u>. Then you must die <u>/ Business of boat – Boat sinks with Eily = she rises he thrusts her into the water again = Danny rushes up the rocks . sinks exhausted as Kyrle Daly appears</u>

    <u>Kyrle</u>. Heavens, what do I see a woman in the water – I know that face. Tis Eily O'Connor = I'll save her <u>/ Jumps into the water and rescues Eily</u> (f. 36)

    HAZ is closer to Boucicault's original: even though the sensation scene takes place much earlier in the drama (I.v), it ends when Myles '<u>Eventually rescues [Eily] as the Act Drop falls</u>' (f. 9a).

SHEELAH. (*Waking.*) Eh! Did ye call me, Danny?

DANNY. Gi' me a dhrop of wather – it's the thirst that's a killin' me.

SHEELAH. (*Takes jug.*) The fever's on ye mighty bad.

DANNY. (*Drinks, falls back, groans.*) Oh, the fire in me won't go out! How long have I been here?

SHEELAH. Ten days this night.

DANNY. Ten days dis night! Have I been all that time out of my mind?

SHEELAH. Iss, Danny. Ten days ago, that stormy night, ye crawled in at that dure, wake an' like a ghost.

DANNY. I remind me now.

SHEELAH. Ye tould me that ye'd been poachin' salmon, and had been shot by the keepers.

DANNY. Who said I hadn't?

SHEELAH. Divil a one! Why did ye make me promise not to say a word about it? Didn't ye refuse even to see a doctor itself?

DANNY. Has anyone axed after me?

SHEELAH. No one but Mr. Hardress.

DANNY. Heaven bless him!

SHEELAH. I told him I hadn't seen ye, and here ye are this day groanin' when there's great doin's up at Castle Chute. Tomorrow the masther will be married to Miss Anne.

DANNY. Married! But – the – his –

SHEELAH. Poor Eily, ye mane?

DANNY. Hide the candle from my eyes – it's painin' me; shade it off. Go on, mother.

SHEELAH. The poor Colleen! Oh, no, Danny, I knew she'd die of the love that was chokin' her. He didn't know how tindher she was when he gave her the hard word. What was that message the masther sent to her, that he wouldn't let me hear? It was cruel, Danny, for it broke her heart entirely; she went away that night, and, two days after, a cloak was found floatin' in the reeds, under Brikeen Bridge; nobody knew it but me. I turned away, and never said – . The creature is drowned, Danny, and woe to them as dhruv her to it. She has no father, no mother to put a curse on him, but the Father above that niver spakes till the last day, and then – (*She turns and sees* DANNY *gasping, his eyes fixed on her, supporting himself on his arm.*) Danny! Danny! He's dyin' – he's dyin'!

[*Runs to him,* R. *of bed.*

DANNY. Who said that? Ye lie! I never killed her – sure he sent me the glove – where is it?

SHEELAH. He's ravin' again.

DANNY. The glove – he sent it to me full of blood. Oh, master, dear, there's your token. I told ye I would clear the path foreninst ye.

SHEELAH. Danny, what d'ye mane?

DANNY. I'll tell ye how I did it, masther; 'twas dis way – but don't smile like dat – don't, sir! She wouldn't give me de marriage lines, so I sunk her and her proofs wid her. She's gone! She came up wonst, but I put her down agin. Never fear – she'll never throuble yer again – never – never!

[*Lies down; mutters.* SHEELAH *on her knees, in horror and prayer.*

SHEELAH. 'Twas he! He! – my own son – he's murdered her, and he's dyin' now – dyin', wid blood on his hands! Danny! Danny! Spake to me!

DANNY. A docther! Will they let me die like a baste, and never a docther?

SHEELAH. I'll run for one that'll cure ye. Oh, weerasthrue, Danny! Is it for this I've loved ye? No, forgive, acushla, it isn't your own mother that 'ud add to yer heart-breakin' and pain. I'll fetch the docther avick. (*Music – puts on cloak, and pulls hood over her head.*) Oh, hone! Oh, hone!

[*Exit* SHEELAH, L. *door in flat – a pause – knock – pause – knock. Enter* CORRIGAN, *door in flat,* L. C.

CORRIGAN. Sheelah! Sheelah! Nobody here? I'm bothered entirely. The cottage on Muckross Head is empty – not a sowl in it but a cat. Myles has disappeared, and Danny gone – vanished, bedad, like a fog – Sheelah is the only one remaining. I called to see Miss Chute; I was kicked out. I sent her a letter; it was returned to me, unopened. Her lawyer has paid off the mortgage, and taxed my bill of costs – the spalpeen! (DANNY *groans*.) What's that? Someone is asleep there. 'Tis Danny!

DANNY. A docther! – gi' me a docther!

CORRIGAN. Danny here – concealed, too! Oh, there's something going on that's worth peepin' into. Whist! There's footsteps comin'. If I could hide a bit. I'm a magistrate, an' I ought to know what's goin' on – here's a turf-hole, wid a windy in it.

[*Exit* CORRIGAN, *opening in flat* R. C.

Enter SHEELAH *and* FATHER TOM, L. C. *door.*

SHEELAH. (*Goes to* DANNY.) Danny!

DANNY. Is that you, mother?

SHEELAH. I've brought the docther, asthore.

[DANNY *looks up.*

DANNY. The priest!

SHEELAH. (*On her knees,* R. *of bed.*) Oh, my darlin'! Don't be angry wid me, but dis is the docther you want; it isn't in your body where the hurt is; the wound is in your poor sowl – there's all the harrum.

FATHER TOM. Danny, my son – (*Sits* L. *of bed.*) – it's sore-hearted I am to see you down this way.

SHEELAH. And so good a son he was to his ould mother.

DANNY. Don't say that – don't!

[*Covering his face.*

SHEELAH. I will say it – my blessin' on ye – see that, now, he's cryin'.

FATHER TOM. Danny, the hand of death is on ye. Will ye lave your sins behind ye here below, or will ye take them with ye above, to show them on ye? Is there anything ye can do that'll mend a wrong? Leave that legacy to your friend, and he'll do it. Do ye want pardon of any one down here? Tell me, avick; I'll get it for ye and send it after you – maybe ye'll want it.

DANNY. (*Rising up on arm.*) I killed Eily O'Connor.

SHEELAH. (*Covers her face with her hands.*) Oh! Oh!

FATHER TOM. What harrum had ye agin the poor Colleen Bawn?

[CORRIGAN *takes notes.*

DANNY. She stud in *his* way, and he had my heart and sowl in his keeping.

FATHER TOM. Hardress?

DANNY. Hisself! I said I'd do it for him, if he'd give me the token.

FATHER TOM. Did Hardress employ you to kill the girl?

DANNY. He sent me the glove; that was to be the token that I was to put her away, and I did – I – in the Pool a Dhiol. She would not gi' me the marriage lines; I threw her in and then I was kilt.

FATHER TOM. Killed! By whose hand?

DANNY. I don't know, unless it was the hand of heaven.

FATHER TOM. (*Rising, goes down – aside.*) Myles na Coppaleen is at the bottom of this; his whisky-still is in that cave, and he has not been seen for ten days past.[32] (*Aloud – goes to* DANNY.) Danny, after ye fell, how did ye get home?

DANNY. I fell in the wather; the current carried me to a rock; how long I was there half drowned I don't know, but on wakin' I found my boat floatin' close by, an' it was still dark; I got in and crawled here.

FATHER TOM. (*Aside*) I'll go and see Myles – there's more in this than has come out.

---

32. In **BOU**, Myles has already sought absolution from Father Tom, for having 'killed a man – by accident he said' (f. 78).

SHEELAH. Won't yer riverince say a word of comfort to the poor boy? He's in great pain entirely.

FATHER TOM. Keep him quiet, Sheelah. (*Music*.) I'll be back again with the comfort for him. Danny, your time is short; make the most of it. (*Aside*.) I'm off to Myles na Coppaleen. Oh, Hardress Cregan – (*Going up*) – ye little think what a bridal day ye'll have!

[*Exit door in flat*. L. C.

CORRIGAN. (*Who has been writing in note-book, comes out at back*.) I've got down every word of the confession. Now, Hardress Cregan, there will be guests at your weddin' tonight ye little dhrame of.

[*Exit* L. *door in flat*, L. C.

DANNY. (*Rising up*.) Mother, mother! The pain is on me. Wather – quick – wather!

[SHEELAH *runs to* L. *table; takes jug; gives it to* DANNY;
he drinks; SHEELAH *takes jug;* DANNY *struggles –
falls back on bed; close on picture.*

———

SCENE II. – *Chamber in Castle Chute.* (*1ˢᵗ grooves*.)

Enter KYRLE DALY *and* SERVANT, R.

KYRLE. Inform Mrs. Cregan that I am waiting upon her.

Enter MRS. CREGAN, L.

MRS. CREGAN. I am glad to see you, Kyrle.

[*Exit* SERVANT, L.

KYRLE. (R. C.) You sent for me, Mrs. Cregan. My ship sails for Liverpool tomorrow. I never thought I could be so anxious to quit my native land.

MRS. CREGAN. I want you to see Hardress. For ten days past he shuns the society of his bride. By night he creeps out alone in his boat on the lake – by day he wanders round the neighbourhood, pale as death. He is heart-broken.

KYRLE. Has he asked to see me?

MRS. CREGAN. Yesterday he asked where you were.

KYRLE. Did he forget that I left your house when Miss Chute, without a word of explanation, behaved so unkindly to me?

MRS. CREGAN. She is not the same girl since she accepted Hardress. She quarrels – weeps – complains, and has lost her spirits.

KYRLE. She feels the neglect of Hardress.

ANNE. (*Without,* R.) Don't answer me! Obey, and hold your tongue!

MRS. CREGAN. Do you hear? She is ratin' one of the servants.

ANNE. (*Without.*) No words – I'll have no sulky looks, neither.

Enter ANNE, R., *dressed as a bride, with a veil and wreath in her hand.*

ANNE. Is that the veil and wreath I ordered? How dare you tell me that?
[Throws it off, R.

MRS. CREGAN. Anne!
[ANNE sees KYRLE – stands confused.

KYRLE. You are surprised to see me in your house. Miss Chute?

ANNE. You are welcome, sir.

KYRLE. (*Aside.*) She looks pale! She's not happy – that's gratifying.

ANNE. (*Aside.*) He doesn't look well – that's some comfort.

MRS. CREGAN. I'll try to find Hardress.
[Exit MRS. CREGAN, L.

KYRLE. I hope you don't think I intrude – that is – I came to see Mrs. Cregan.

ANNE. (*Sharply.*) I don't flatter myself you wished to see me; why should you?

KYRLE. Anne, I am sorry I offended you; I don't know what I did, but no matter.

ANNE. Not the slightest.

KYRLE. I released your neighborhood of my presence.

ANNE. Yes, and you released the neighborhood of the presence of some-body else – she and you disappeared together.

KYRLE. She!

ANNE. Never mind.

KYRLE. But I do mind. I love Hardress Cregan as a brother, and I hope the time may come, Anne, when I can love you as a sister.

ANNE. Do you! I don't.

KYRLE. I don't want the dislike of my friend's wife to part my friend and me.

ANNE. Why should it? I'm nobody.

KYRLE. If you were my wife, and asked me to hate any one, I'd do it – I couldn't help it.

ANNE. I believed words like that once when you spoke them, but I have been taught how basely you can deceive.

KYRLE. Who taught you?

ANNE. Who? – your wife.

KYRLE. My what?

ANNE. Your wife – the girl you concealed in the cottage on Muckross Head. Stop, now – don't speak – save a falsehood, however many ye may have to spare. I saw the girl – she confessed.

KYRLE. Confessed that she was my wife?

ANNE. Make a clean breast of it in a minute, which is more than you could do with a sixteen-foot wagon and a team of ten, in a week.

KYRLE. Anne, hear me; this is a frightful error – the girl will not repeat it.

ANNE. Bring her before me and let her speak.

KYRLE. How do I know where she is?

ANNE. Well, bring your boatman then, who told me the same.

KYRLE. I tell you it is false; I never saw – never knew the girl.

ANNE. You did not? (*Shows* EILY'S *letter.*) Do you know that? You dropped it, and I found it.

KYRLE. (*Takes letter*.) This!

[*Reads.*

Enter HARDRESS, L.

ANNE. Hardress!

[*Turns aside.*

KYRLE. Oh! (*Suddenly struck with the truth; glances towards* ANNE; *finding her looking away, places letter to* HARDRESS.) Do you know that? – you dropped it.

HARDRESS. (*Conceals letter.*) Eh? Oh!

KYRLE. 'Twas he. (*Looks from one to the other.*) She thinks me guilty; but if I stir to exculpate myself, he is in for it.

HARDRESS. You look distressed, Kyrle. Anne, what is the matter?

KYRLE. Nothing, Hardress. I was about to ask Miss Chute to forget a subject which was painful to her, and to beg of her never to mention it again – not even to you, Hardress.

HARDRESS. I am sure she will deny you nothing.

ANNE. I will forget, sir. (*Aside.*) But I will never forgive him – never.

KYRLE. (*Aside.*) She loves me still, and he loves another, and I am the most miserable dog that ever was kicked. (*Crosses to* L.) Hardress, a word with you.

[*Exeunt* KYRLE *and* HARDRESS, L.

ANNE. And this is my wedding day. There goes the only man I ever loved. When he's here nearby me, I could give him the worst treatment a man could desire, and when he goes away he takes the heart and all of me off with him, and I feel like an unfurnished house. This is pretty feelings for a girl to have, and she in her regimentals. Oh! If he wasn't married – but he is, and he'd have married me as well – the malignant! Oh! If he had, how I'd have made him swing for it – it would have afforded me the happiest moment of my life.

[*Exit* ANNE, L. *music.*

SCENE III. – *Exterior of Myles's Hut, door* R. *in flat.* (*2nd grooves.*)

Enter FATHER TOM, L.

FATHER TOM. Here's Myles's shanty. I'm nearly killed with climbin' the hill. I wonder is he at home? Yes, the door is locked inside. (*Knocks.*) Myles – Myles, are ye at home?

MYLES. (*Outside,* R. 2 E.) No – I'm out.

Enter MYLES, R. 2 E.

Arrah! Is it yourself. Father Tom, that's in it?

FATHER TOM. Let us go inside, Myles – I've a word to say t'ye.

MYLES. I – I've lost the key.

FATHER TOM. Sure it's stickin' inside.

MYLES. I always lock the dure inside and lave it there when I go out, for fear on losin' it.

FATHER TOM. Myles, come here to me. It's lyin' ye are. Look me in the face. What's come to ye these tin days past – three times I've been to your door and it was locked, but I heard ye stirrin' inside.

MYLES. It was the pig, yer riverince.

FATHER TOM. Myles, why did yer shoot Danny Mann?

MYLES. Oh, murther, who tould you that?

FATHER TOM. Himself.

MYLES. Oh, Father Tom! Have ye seen him?

FATHER TOM. I've just left him.

MYLES. Is it down there ye've been?

FATHER TOM. Down where?

MYLES. Below, where he's gone to – where would he be, afther murthering a poor crature?

FATHER TOM. How d'ye know that?

MYLES. How! How did I? – whist. Father Tom, it was his ghost.

FATHER TOM. He is not dead, but dyin' fast, from the wound ye gave him.

MYLES. I never knew 'twas himself 'till I was tould.

FATHER TOM. Who tould you?

MYLES. Is it who?

FATHER TOM. Who? Who? – not Danny, for he doesn't know who killed him.

MYLES. Wait, an' I'll tell you. It was nigh twelve that night, I was comin' home – I know the time, betoken Murty Dwyer made me step in his shebeen, bein' the wake of the ould Callaghan, his wife's uncle – and a dacent man he was. "Murty," sez I –

FATHER TOM. Myles, you're desavin' me.

MYLES. Is it afther desavin' yer riverence I'd be?

FATHER TOM. I see the lie in yer mouth. Who tould ye it was Danny Mann ye killed?

MYLES. You said so a while ago.

FATHER TOM. Who tould ye it was Danny Mann?

MYLES. I'm comin' to it. While I was at Murty's, yer riverince, as I was a-tellin' you – Dan Dayley was there – he had just kim'd in. "Good morrow, – good day" – ses he. "Good morrow, good Dan, ses I," – jest that ways entirely – "it's an opening to the heart to see you." Well, yer riverence, as I ware sayin' – "long life an' good wife to ye. Masther Dan," ses I. "Thank ye, ses he, and the likes to ye, anyway." The moment I speck them words, Dan got heart, an' up an' tould Murty about his love for Murty's darter – the Colleen Rue. The moment he heard that, he puts elbows in himself, an' stood lookin' at him out on the flure. "You flog Europe, for boldness," ses he – "get out of my sight," ses he, – "this moment," ses he, – "or I'll give yer a kick that will rise you from poverty to the highest pitch of affluence," ses he – "away out 'o that, you notorious delinquent; single your freedom, and double your distance," ses he. Well, Dan was forced to cut an' run. Poor boy! I was sorry for his trouble; there isn't a better son nor brother this moment goin' the road than what he is – said – said – there wasn't better, an', an'[33] – oh! Father Tom, don't ax me; I've got an oath on my lips. (*Music*.) Don't be hard on a poor boy.

FATHER TOM. I lift the oath from ye. Tell me, avick, oh! Tell me. Did ye search for the poor thing – the darlin' soft-eyed Colleen? Oh, Myles! Could ye lave her to lie in the cowld lake all alone?

Enter EILY *from door* R. *flat.*

MYLES. No, I couldn't.

FATHER TOM. (*Turns – sees* EILY.) Eily! Is it yourself, and alive – an' not – not – Oh! Eily, mavourneen. Come to my heart.

[*Embraces* EILY.

MYLES. (*Crosses to* L.) D'ye think ye'd see me alive if she wasn't? I thought ye knew me better – it's at the bottom of the Pool a Dhiol I'd be this minute if she wasn't to the fore.

FATHER TOM. (C.) Speak to me – let me hear your voice.

EILY. Oh, father, father! Won't ye take me far, far away from this place?

FATHER TOM. Why did ye hide yourself this way?

EILY. For fear *he'd* see me.

33. Myles's long explanation is cut in **BOU**.

FATHER TOM. Hardress? You knew then that he instigated Danny to get rid of ye?

EILY. Why didn't I die – why am I alive now for him to hate me?

FATHER TOM. D'ye know that in a few hours he is going to marry another?

EILY. I know it. Myles tould me – that's why I'm hiding myself.

FATHER TOM. What does she mean?

MYLES. (L.) She loves him still – that's what she manes.

FATHER TOM. Love the wretch who sought your life!

EILY. Isn't it his own? It isn't his fault if his love couldn't last as long as mine. I was a poor, mane creature – not up to him anyway; but if he'd only said, "Eily, put the grave between us and make me happy," sure I'd lain down, wid a big heart, in the loch.

FATHER TOM. And you are willing to pass a life of seclusion that he may live in his guilty joy?

EILY. If I was alive wouldn't I be a shame to him an' a ruin – ain't I in his way? Heaven help me – why would I trouble him? Oh! He was in great pain o' mind entirely when he let them put a hand on me – the poor darlin'.

FATHER TOM. And you mean to let him believe you dead?

EILY. Dead an' gone: then, perhaps, his love for me will come back, and the thought of his poor, foolish little Eily that worshiped the ground he stood on, will fill his heart a while.

FATHER TOM. And where will you go?

EILY. I don't know. Anywhere. What matters?

MYLES. (*Against wing*, L.) Love makes all places alike.

EILY. I am alone in the world now.

FATHER TOM. The villain – the monster! He sent her to heaven because he wanted her there to blot out with her tears the record of his iniquity. Eily, ye have but one home, and that's my poor house. You are not alone in the world – there's one beside ye, your father, and that's myself.

MYLES. Two – bad luck to me, two. I am her mother; sure I brought her into the world a second time.

FATHER TOM. (*Looking,* R.) Whisht! Look down there, Myles – what's that on the road?

MYLES. (*Crosses* R.) It's the sogers – a company of red-coats. What brings the army out? – who's that wid them? – it is ould Corrigan, and they are going towards Castle Chute. There's mischief in the wind.

FATHER TOM. In with you, an' keep close a while; I'll go down to the castle and see what's the matter.

[*Crosses* R.

EILY. Promise me that you'll not betray me – that none but yourself and Myles shall ever know I'm livin'; promise me that before you go.

FATHER TOM. I do, Eily; I'll never breathe a word of it – it is as sacred as an oath.

[*Exit* L. – *music.*

EILY. (*Going to cottage.*) Shut me in, Myles, and take the key wid ye, this time.

[*Exit in cottage,* R. C.

MYLES. (*Locks door.*) There ye are like a pearl in an oyster; now I'll go to my bed as usual on the mountain above – the bolster is stuffed wid rocks, and I'll have a cloud round me for a blanket.

[*Exit* MYLES, R. 2 E.

SCENE IV. – *Outside of Castle Chute.* (*1ˢᵗ grooves.*)

Enter CORRIGAN *and six* SOLDIERS, R. 1 E.

CORRIGAN. Quietly, boys; sthrew yourselves round the wood – some of ye at the gate beyant – two more this way – watch the windies; if he's there to escape at all, he'll jump from a windy. The house is surrounded.

Quadrille music under stage. – Air, "The Boulanger."

Oh, oh! They're dancin' – dancin' and merry-making, while the net is clo-sin' around 'em. Now Masther Hardress Cregan – I was kicked out, was I; but I'll come this time wid a call that ye'll answer wid your head instead of your foot. My letters were returned unopened; but here's a bit of writin' that ye'll not be able to hand back so easy.

Enter CORPORAL, R.

CORPORAL. All right, sir.

CORRIGAN. Did you find the woman, as I told ye?

CORPORAL. Here she is, sir.

Enter SHEELAH, *guarded by two* SOLDIERS, R.

SHEELAH. (*Crying.*) What's this? Why am I thrated this way – what have I done?

CORRIGAN. You are wanted a while – it's your testimony we require. Bring her this way. Follow me!

[*Exit,* L.

SHEELAH. (*Struggling.*) Let me go back to my boy. Ah! Good luck t'ye don't kape me from my poor boy! (*Struggling.*) Oh! You dirty blackguards, let me go – let me go!

[*Exit* SHEELAH *and* SOLDIERS, L.

———

SCENE V. – *Ball Room in Castle Chute. Steps,* C.; *platform – balustrade on top, backed by moonlight landscape – doors* R. *and* L., *table* L. C.; *writ-ing materials, books, papers, etc., on it; chairs; chair* L. 2 E., *chairs* R.; *chandeliers lighted.* LADIES *and* GENTLEMEN, WEDDING GUESTS *discovered.* HYLAND CREAGH, BERTIE O'MOORE, DUCIE, KATH-LEEN CREAGH, ADA CREAGH, PATSIE O'MOORE, BRIDESMAIDS *and* SERVANTS *discovered. – Music going on under stage.*

HYLAND. Ducie, they are dancing the Boulanger, and they can't see the figure unless you lend them the light of your eyes.

KATHLEEN. We have danced enough; it is nearly seven o'clock.

DUCIE. Mr. O'Moore; when is the ceremony to commence?

O'MOORE. The execution is fixed for seven – here's the scaffold, I presume.

[*Points to table.*

HYLAND. Hardress looks like a criminal. I've seen him fight three duels, and he never showed such a pale face as he exhibits tonight.

DUCIE. He looks as if he was frightened at being so happy.

HYLAND. And Kyrle Daly wears as gay an appearance.

Enter KYRLE DALY *down steps,* C.

DUCIE. Hush! Here he is.

KYRLE. That need not stop your speech, Hyland. I don't hide my love for Anne Chute, and it is my pride, and no fault of mine if she has found a better man.

HYLAND. He is not a better man.

KYRLE. He is – she thinks so – what she says becomes the truth.

Enter MRS. CREGAN, L. 2 E.

MRS. CREGAN. Who says the days of chivalry are over? Come, gentlemen, the bridesmaids must attend the bride. The guests will assemble in the hall.

Enter SERVANT, R. 2 E., *with letter and card on salver.*

SERVANT. Mr. Bertie O'Moore, if you plase. A gentlemen below asked me to hand you this card.

O'MOORE. A gentleman! What can he want? (*Reads card.*) Ah! Indeed; this is a serious matter, and excuses the intrusion.

HYLAND. What's the matter?

O'MOORE. A murder has been committed.

ALL. A murder?

O'MOORE. The perpetrator of the deed has been discovered, and the warrant for his arrest requires my signature.

HYLAND. Hang the rascal.

[*Goes up with* DUCIE.

O'MOORE. A magistrate, like a doctor, is called on at all hours.

MRS. CREGAN. We can excuse you for such a duty, Mr. O'Moore.

O'MOORE. (*Crossing,* R.) This is the result of some brawl at a fair, I suppose. Is Mr. Corrigan below?

MRS. CREGAN. (*Starting.*) Corrigan?

O'MOORE. Show me to him.

[*Exit* O'MOORE *and* SERVANT, R. 2 E. –
GUESTS *go up and off,* L. U. E.

MRS. CREGAN. Corrigan here! What brings that man to this house?

[*Exit* MRS. CREGAN, R. 3 E.

Enter HARDRESS, *down steps,* C. *from* R., *pale.*

HARDRESS. (*Sits,* L.) It is in vain – I cannot repress the terror with which I approach these nuptials – yet, what have I to fear? Oh! My heart is bursting with its load of misery.

Enter ANNE, *down steps,* C. *from* R.

ANNE. Hardress! What is the matter with you?

HARDRESS. (*Rising,* L. C.) I will tell you – yes, it may take this horrible oppression from my heart. At one time I thought you knew my secret: I was mistaken. The girl you saw at Muckross Head –

ANNE. (R. C.) Eily O'Connor?

HARDRESS. Was my wife!

ANNE. Your wife?

HARDRESS. Hush! Maddened with the miseries this act brought upon me, I treated her with cruelty – she committed suicide.

ANNE. Merciful powers!

HARDRESS. She wrote to me bidding me farewell forever, and the next day her cloak was found floating in the lake. (ANNE *sinks in chair*.) Since then I have neither slept nor waked – I have but one thought, one feeling; my love for her, wild and maddened, has come back upon my heart like a vengeance.

[*Music – tumult heard,* R.

ANNE. Heaven defend our hearts, what is that?

Enter MRS. CREGAN, *deadly pale,* R. 3 E. – *Locks door behind her.*

MRS. CREGAN. Hardress! My child!

HARDRESS. Mother!

ANNE. Mother, he is here. Look on him – speak to him – do not gasp and stare on your son in that horrid way. Oh, mother! Speak, or you will break my heart.

MRS. CREGAN. Fly – fly! (HARDRESS *going,* R.) Not that way. No – the doors are defended! There is a soldier placed at every entrance! You – are trapped and caught – what shall we do? – the window in my chamber – come – come – quick – quick!

ANNE. Of what is he accused?

HARDRESS. Of murder. I see it in her face.

[*Noise,* R.

MRS. CREGAN. Hush! They come – begone! Your boat is below that window. Don't speak! When oceans are between you and danger – write! Till then not a word.

[*Forcing him off,* R. 3 E. – *noise,* R.

ANNE. Accused of murder! He is innocent!

MRS. CREGAN. Go to your room! Go quickly to your room, you will betray him – you can't command your features.

ANNE. Dear mother, I will.

MRS. CREGAN. Away, I say – you will drive me frantic, girl. My brain is stretched to cracking. Ha!

[*Noise,* R.

ANNE. There is a tumult in the drawing room.

MRS. CREGAN. They come! You tremble! Go – take away your puny love; hide it where it will not injure him – leave me to face this danger!

ANNE. He is not guilty.

MRS. CREGAN. What's that to me, woman? I am his mother – the hunters are after my blood! Sit there – look away from this door. They come!

[*Knocking loudly – crash – door* R. 3 E. *opened – enter* CORPORAL *and* SOLDIERS, *who cross stage, facing up to charge –* GENTLEMEN *with drawn swords on steps,* C.; LADIES *on at back –* O'MOORE, R. 3 E. *– enter* CORRIGAN, R. 3 E. – KYRLE *on steps,* C.[34]

CORRIGAN. Gentlemen, put up your swords; the house is surrounded by a military force, and we are here in the king's name.

ANNE. (R.) Gentlemen, come on, there was a time in Ireland when neither king nor faction could call on Castle Chute without a bloody welcome.[35]

GUESTS. Clear them out!

KYRLE. (*Interposing.*) Anne, are you mad? Put up your swords; stand back there – speak – O'Moore, what does this strange outrage mean?

[SOLDIERS *fall back*; – GENTLEMEN *on steps*; KYRLE *comes forward.*

O'MOORE. Mrs. Cregan, a fearful charge is made against your son; I know – I believe he is innocent; I suggest, then, that the matter be

---

34. Directions in **BOU** read: 'Knocking again. / The tumult increases. / The crowd of ladies and gentlemen promiscuously with servants +c rush on by the stairs. The Gentlemen with swords drawn – The door is beaten in. A file of soldiers and Corrigan – enter – Ducie – Ada + Patrice. – Hyland and Kyrle – Tableau' (ff. 97–8).
35. Mrs Cregan echoes Anne's sentiments in **BOU** (f. 98).

investigated here at once, amongst his friends, so that this scandal may be crushed in its birth.

KYRLE. Where is Hardress?

CORRIGAN. Where? – why, he's escaping while we are jabbering here. Search the house.

[*Exit two* SOLDIERS, R. 3 E.

MRS. CREGAN. (L.) Must we submit to this, sir? Will you, a magistrate, permit –

O'MOORE. I regret Mrs. Cregan, but as a form –

MRS. CREGAN. Go on, sir!

CORRIGAN. (*At door,* L. 3 E.) What room is this? 'Tis locked –

MRS. CREGAN. That is my sleeping chamber.

CORRIGAN. My duty compels me –

MRS. CREGAN. (*Throws key down on ground.*) Be it so, sir.

CORRIGAN. (*Picks up key – unlocks door.*) She had the key – he's there.

[*Exit* CORPORAL *and two* SOLDIERS.

MRS. CREGAN. He has escaped by this time.

O'MOORE. (*At* L. *table.*) I hope Miss Chute will pardon me for my share in this transaction – believe me, I regret –

ANNE. Don't talk to me of your regret, while you are doing your worst. It is hate, not justice, that brings this accusation against Hardress, and this disgrace upon me.

KYRLE. Anne!

ANNE. Hold your tongue – his life's in danger, and if I can't love him, I'll fight for him, and that's more than any of you men can do. (*To* O'MOORE.) Go on with your dirty work. You have done the worst now – you have dismayed our guests, scattered terror amid our festival, and made the remembrance of this night, which should have been a happy one, a thought of gloom and shame.

MRS. CREGAN. Hark! I hear – I hear his voice. It cannot be.

Re-enter CORRIGAN, L. 3 E.

CORRIGAN. The prisoner is here!

MRS. CREGAN. (C.) Ah, (*Utters a cry.*) is he? Dark bloodhound, have you found him? May the tongue that tells me so be withered from the roots, and the eye that first detected him be darkened in its socket!

KYRLE. Oh, madam! For heaven's sake!

ANNE. Mother! Mother!

MRS. CREGAN. What! Shall it be for nothing he has stung the mother's heart, and set her brain on fire?

Enter HARDRESS, *handcuffed, and two* SOLDIERS, L. 3 E.

I tell you that my tongue may hold its peace, but there is not a vein in all my frame but curses him. (*Turns – sees* HARDRESS; *falls on his breast.*) My boy! My boy!

HARDRESS. (L.) Mother, I entreat you to be calm. (*Crosses to* C.) Kyrle, there are my hands, do you think there is blood upon them?

KYRLE *seizes his hand –* GENTLEMEN *press round him,
take his hand, and retire up.*

HARDRESS. I thank you, gentlemen; your hands acquit me. Mother, be calm – sit there.

[*Points to chair,* L.

ANNE. Come here, Hardress; your place is here by me.

HARDRESS. (R. C.) Now, sir, I am ready.

CORRIGAN. (L. *of table.*) I will lay before you, sir, the deposition upon which the warrant issues against the prisoner. Here is the confession of

Daniel or Danny Mann, a person in the service of the accused, taken on his death-bed – in *articulo mortis*, you'll observe.

O'MOORE. But not witnessed.

CORRIGAN. (*Calling.*) Bring in that woman.

Enter SHEELAH *and two* SOLDIERS, R. 3 E.

I have witnesses. Your worship will find the form of the law in perfect shape.

O'MOORE. Read the confession, sir.

CORRIGAN. (*Reads.*) "The deponent being on his death-bed, in the presence of Sheelah Mann and Thomas O'Brien, parish priest of Kenmare, deposed and said" –

Enter FATHER TOM, R. 3

Oh, you are come in time, sir.

FATHER TOM. I hope I am.

CORRIGAN. We may have to call your evidence.

FATHER TOM. (C.) I have brought it with me.

CORRIGAN. "Deposed and said, that he, deponent, killed Eily O'Connor; that said Eily was the wife of Hardress Cregan, and stood in the way of his marriage with Miss Anne Chute; deponent offered to put away the girl, and his master employed him to do so.

O'MOORE. Sheelah, did Danny confess this crime?

SHEELAH. (L. C.) Divil a word – it's a lie from end to end; that ould thief was niver in my cabin – he invented the whole of it – sure you're the divil's own parverter of the truth.

CORRIGAN. Am I? Oh, oh! Father Tom will scarcely say as much? (*To him.*) Did Danny Mann confess this in your presence?

FATHER TOM. I decline to answer that question!

CORRIGAN. Aha! You must – the law will compel you!

FATHER TOM. I'd like to see the law that can unseal the lips of the priest, and make him reveal the secrets of heaven.

ANNE. So much for your two witnesses. Ladies, stand close. Gentlemen, give us room here.

[BRIDESMAIDS *down,* R. *Exit* FATHER TOM, R. 3 E.

CORRIGAN. We have abundant proof, your worship – enough to hang a whole country. Danny isn't dead yet. Deponent agreed with Cregan that if the deed was to be done, that he, Cregan, should give his glove as a token.

MRS. CREGAN. Ah!

HARDRESS. Hold! I confess that what he has read is true. Danny did make the offer, and I repelled his horrible proposition.

CORRIGAN. Aha! But you gave him the glove.

HARDRESS. Never, by my immortal soul – never!

MRS. CREGAN. (*Advancing.*) But *I – I* did! (*Movement of surprise.*) I your wretched mother – I gave it to him – I am guilty! Thank heaven for that! Remove those bonds from his hands and put them here on mine.

HARDRESS. 'Tis false, mother, you did not know his purpose – you could not know it.

[CORPORAL *takes off handcuffs.*

MRS. CREGAN. I will not say anything that takes the welcome guilt from off me.

Enter MYLES *from steps,* C. *from* R.

MYLES. Won't ye, ma'am? Well, if ye won't, I will.

ALL. Myles!

MYLES. Save all here. If you plaze, I'd like to say a word; there's been a murder done, and I done it.

ALL. You!

MYLES. Myself. Danny was killed by my hand. (*To* CORRIGAN.) Were yez any way nigh that time?

CORRIGAN. (*Quickly.*) No.

MYLES. (*Quickly.*) That's lucky; then take down what I'm sayin'. I shot the poor boy – but widout manin' to hurt him. It's lucky I killed him that time, for it's lifted a mighty sin off the sowl of the crature.

O'MOORE. What does he mean?

MYLES. I mane, that if you found one witness to Eily O'Connor's death, I found another that knows a little more about it, and here she is.

> *Enter* EILY *and* FATHER TOM *down steps*, C. *from* R.

ALL. Eily!

MYLES. The Colleen Bawn herself!

EILY. Hardress!   ⎫
HARDRESS. My wife – my own Eily. ⎬
                                    ⎭

EILY. Here, darlin', take the paper, and tear it if you like.

> [*Offers him the certificate.*

HARDRESS. Eily, I could not live without you.

MRS. CREGAN. If ever he blamed you, it was my foolish pride spoke in his hard words – he loves you with all his heart. Forgive me, Eily.

EILY. Forgive!

MRS. CREGAN. Forgive your mother, Eily.

EILY. (*Embracing her.*) Mother!

[MRS. CREGAN, HARDRESS, EILY, FATHER TOM, *group together – ANNE, KYRLE, and* GENTLEMEN – LADIES *together – their backs to* CORRIGAN – CORRIGAN *takes bag, puts in papers, looks about, puts on hat, buttons coat, slinks up stage, runs upstairs, and off* R. – MYLES *points off after him – several* GENTLEMEN *run after* CORRIGAN.

ANNE. But what's to become of me? Is all my emotion to be summoned for nothing? Is my wedding dress to go to waste, and here's all my blushes ready? I must have a husband.

HYLAND and GENTLEMEN. Take me.

O'MOORE. Take me.

ANNE. Don't all speak at once! Where's Mr. Daly?

KYRLE. (R.) Here I am, Anne!

ANNE. (R. C.) Kyrle, come here! You said you loved me, and I think you do.

KYRLE. Oh!

ANNE. Behave yourself now. If you'll ask me, I'll have you.[36]

KYRLE. (*Embracing* ANNE.) Anne!

[*Shouts outside,* L. U. E.

ALL. What's that?

MYLES. (*Looking off out at back.*) Don't be uneasy! It's only the boys outside that's caught ould Corrigan thryin' to get off, and they've got him in the horse-pond.[37]

KYRLE. They'll drown him.

---

36. Anne is not dominant in **YOU**. After Mrs Cregan has welcomed Eily as a daughter, it is Kyrle who suggests his and Anne's union. Anne replies that she is 'happy and content' (f. 48).
37. Warner [Corrigan] escapes unpunished at the end of **HAZ.**

MYLES. Niver fear, he wasn't born to be drowned – he won't sink – he'll rise out of the world, and divil a fut nearer heaven he'll get than the top o' the gallows.

EILY. (*To* HARDRESS.) And ye won't be ashamed of me?

ANNE. I'll be ashamed of him if he does.

EILY. And when I spake – no – speak –

ANNE. Spake is the right sound. Kyrle Daly, pronounce that word.

KYRLE. That's right; if you ever spake it any other way I'll divorce ye – mind that.[38]

FATHER TOM. Eily, darlin', in the middle of your joy, sure you would not forget one who never forsook you in your sorrow.

EILY. Oh, Father Tom!

FATHER TOM. Oh, it's not myself I mane.

ANNE. No, it's that marauder there, that lent me his top coat in the thunder storm.

[*Pointing to* MYLES.

MYLES. Bedad, ma'am, your beauty left a linin' in it that has kept me warm ever since.

EILY. Myles, you saved my life – it belongs to you. There's my hand – what will you do with it?

MYLES. (*Takes her hand and* HARDRESS'S.) Take her, wid all my heart. I may say that, for ye can't take her without. I am like the boy who had a penny to put in the poor-box – I'd rather keep it for myself. It's a shamrock itself ye have got, sir; and like that flower she'll come up every year fresh and green foreninst ye. When ye cease to love her may dyin' become ye, and when ye do die, lave yer money to the poor, your widdy to me, and we'll both forgive ye.[39]

[*Joins hands.*

38. **BOU** reinforces Anne's power over Daly by giving her this line. Kyrle only says 'Spake' on her command (f. 106).
39. **BOU** ends here.

EILY. I'm only a poor simple girl, and it's frightened I am to be surrounded by so many –

ANNE. Friends, Eily, friends.

EILY. Oh, if I could think so – if I could hope that I had established myself in a little corner of their hearts, there wouldn't be a happier girl alive than THE COLLEEN BAWN.[40]

SOLDIERS.   SOLDIERS.
GUESTS.   GUESTS.
HYLAND.
O'MOORE. SHEELAH.

KYRLE. ANNE. MYLES. HARDRESS. EILY. FATHER TOM. MRS. CREGAN.
R.   L.

THE END.

40. **HAZ** also gives the final line to Eily, who – though the title character – gets little time on stage: 'In faith and truth I ask your smiles for Eily the happy bride of dear Killarney' (f. 16a).

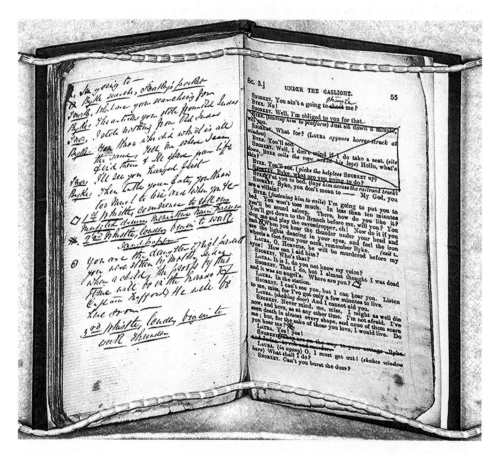

Figure 4 Annotated pages of *Under the Gaslight* prompt copy. Pettingell Collection, Templeman Library, Kent.

UNDER THE GASLIGHT;[1]

A Totally Original and Picturesque

Drama of Life and Love in These Times,

IN FIVE ACTS.

BY

AUGUSTIN DALY,

AUTHOR OF

Leah the Forsaken – Griffith Gaunt – Taming a Butterfly – &c., &c.

As originally played at the NEW YORK THEATER[2] IN THE MONTHS
OF AUGUST, SEPTEMBER AND OCTOBER, 1867.[3]

NEW YORK;

PRINTED FOR THE AUTHOR,
1867.

Entered according to Act of Congress in the year 1867, by

AUGUSTIN DALY,

In the Clerk's Office of the District Court of the United States for the
Southern District of New York.

———

1. Other scripts discussed in the notes are:
   RRR: Add MS 53070 T. Anon. (1868), 'Rail, River and Road'.
   Licensing copy for a version of Daly's play, adapted and localised for a London audience:
   specifically, the audience of the New East London Theatre on Whitechapel Road. Several
   of the scenes are set in close proximity to this playhouse.
   PRT: PETT D.9. Augustin Daly (n.d.), *Under the Gaslight*.
   Unlike the licensing copy of 'Rail, River and Road', which is mostly hand-written, this
   prompt copy is printed. Still, regular annotations and ex libris (*el*) inserts record significant alterations which relocate the drama to Britain. The setting is less specific than **RRR**,

DRAMATIS PERSONÆ

————————

RAY TRAFFORD. – One of the New York "bloods."

DEMILT. – Of the rising Wall Street generation.

WINDEL. – His friend – Sound on the street.

BYKE. – One of the men whom the law is always reaching for, and never touches.

SNORKEY. – A returned veteran, established as a soldier messenger, but open to anything else.

JUSTICE BOWLING. – Of the Tombs Police Court.

COUNSELLOR SPLINTER. – An attorney of the same court.

BERMUDAS. – One of the under crust, and one of the sidewalk merchant princes.

PEANUTS. – A rival operator in papers and matches.

SAM. – A coloured citizen, ready for suffrage when it is ready for him.

THE SIGNAL MAN AT SHREWSBURY BEND.

RAFFERDI (*né Rafferty*). – An Italian organist from Cork.

SERGEANT OF THE RIVER PATROL.

POLICEMAN 9-9-9.

---

      however. **PRT** documents a touring production, so the generic text can be suitable for many places, or allow actors to improvise specific local references on the night.

2. '[A] grotesque structure [. . .] converted from a church' (J. F. Daly (1917), p. 71).

3. The drama was reproduced at this theatre in December 1867 with a slightly different cast. Actors' names for both productions are printed in: Houghton Library, 2016T-469, p. 2. **PRT** details casts for some English performances: Tyne Theatre Newcastle (Apr. 1868); Leeds Amphitheatre (Jul. 1868); Grecian, London (1874); Pavilion, London (1876) (*el*).

MARTIN. – Servant to the Courtlands.

PETER RICH. – The boy who was committed.

LAURA COURTLAND. – The belle of Society.

PEARL COURTLAND. – Pretty, but no heart.

PEACHBLOSSOM. – A girl who was never brought up.

OLD JUDAS. – The right hand of Byke.

MRS. VAN DAM. – One of the voices of society.

SUE EARLIE. – One of the echoes of the voice.

LIZZIE LISTON. – Another echo.

DOCK BOYS, POLICEMEN, COURT OFFICERS, PRISONERS AND GENTLEMEN AND LADIES OF THE TUESDAY SOCIABLE.

The scene of the first three Acts is New York.
The scene of the last two Acts is Long Branch.

Time: – The Present.

A lapse of four months between first and second Acts, and of one month between third and fourth Acts.

TIME OF REPRESENTATION:

1st Act, . . . 35 minutes.
2nd Act, . . . 30 minutes.
3rd Act, . . . 34 minutes.
4th Act, . . . 30 minutes.
5th Act, . . . 15 minutes.

ACT I.

SCENE I. – *Parlour at the Courtlands;*[4] *deep window at back showing snowy exterior; street lamp lighted; time, night; the place elegantly furnished; chandelier.*

RAY TRAFFORD *is discovered lounging on tête-à-tête* (C.) PEARL *is at* (L.) *door taking leave of* DEMILT, WINDEL, MRS. VAN DAM, *and* SUE EARLIE, *who are all dressed and muffled to go out.*

MRS. VAN DAM. Good night! Of course we'll see you on Tuesday.

PEARL. To be sure you will.

DEMILT. Never spent a jollier hour. Good night, Ray.

RAY. (*On sofa.*) Goodnight.

MRS. VAN DAM. You won't forget the Sociable[5] on Tuesday, Ray?

RAY. O, I won't forget.

ALL. (*At door.*) Goodnight – Goodnight!

[*Exit* L.

PEARL. Goodnight. (*Coming forward.*) O, dear! Now they're gone, and the holiday's gone with them. (*Goes to window.*) There they go. (*Laughter without.*) Ray, do come and look at the Van Dam's new sleigh. How they have come out.

RAY. Yes, it's the gayest thing in the Park!

PEARL. (*Still at window* C.) I wonder where they got the money! I thought you said Van Dam had failed!

RAY. Well, yes. He failed to pay, but he continues to spend.

4. **RRR** locates the Hawleys' [Courtlands'] home in Hyde Park.
5. **PRT** changes 'sociable' to 'ball' to indicate an English rather than American setting (p. 3). Other minor alterations are made throughout for consistency: for example, 'brougham' replaces 'sleigh' (p. 3). Britishisms also substitute Americanisms in **RRR**.

PEARL. (*As if to those outside.*) Goodnight! (*Response from without as sleigh bells jingle – "Goodnight."*) I wish I was in there with you. It's delightful for a sleigh ride, if it wasn't New Year's. O! There's Demilt over! (*Laughter outside – cracking of whips – RAY saunters up to window. Sleigh bells jingle, sleigh music heard to die away. RAY and PEARL wave their handkerchiefs. RAY comes down and sits C.*)

PEARL. (*Closing lace curtains.*) Isn't it a frightful thing to be shut up here on such a beautiful night, and New Year's of all others. Pshaw! We've had nothing but mopes all day. O, dear! I hate mourning, though it does become me, and I hate everything but fun, larks and dancing. (*Comes down.*)

RAY. Where in the world is Laura?

PEARL. O! Do forget her for a second, can't you? She'll be here presently. You're not in the house a minute but it's, "Where's Laura?" "Why don't Laura come?"

RAY. (*Taking her hand.*) Well, if anybody in the world could make me forget her, it would be you. But if you had a lover, wouldn't you like him to be as constant as that?

PEARL. That's quite another thing.

RAY. But this doesn't answer my question – where is she?

PEARL. I sent for her as soon as I saw you coming. She has hardly been down here a moment all this evening. O, dear! Now don't you think I'm a victim, to be cooped up in this way instead of receiving calls as we used to?

RAY. You forget that your mother died only last summer. (*Rising.*)

PEARL. No, I don't forget. Pshaw! You're just like Laura. She's only my cousin, and yet she keeps always saying – "Poor Aunt Mary! Let us not forget how she would have sorrowed for us."

RAY. (*Going towards back.*) Well, don't you know she would, too?

PEARL. I don't know anything about it. I was always at boarding school, and she only saw me once a year. Laura was always at home, and it's very different. But don't let's talk about it. To die – ugh! I don't want to die till

I don't want to live – and that'll not be for a million of years. Come, tell me, – where have you been today? How many calls did you make? (*Sitting in tête-à-tête.*)

RAY. About sixty.

PEARL. That all? You're lazy. Demilt and Windel made a hundred and thirty, and they say that's nothing. Won't you have a cup of coffee?

RAY. No.

PEARL. Ain't you hungry?

RAY. No, – you torment.

PEARL. O, dear! I suppose it's because you're going to be married shortly to Laura. If there's one time that a man's stupid to his friends, it's when he's going to be married shortly. Tell me whom you saw. (RAY *has sauntered off L., and is looking over cards on table.*) Where are you? Oh, you needn't be so impatient to see her. Do be agreeable; sit here and tell me something funny, or I shall drop down and fall asleep.

RAY. (*Over her shoulder.*) You witch! Why didn't I fall in love with you?

PEARL. (*Laughing.*) I don't know; why didn't you?[6]

RAY. You never keep me waiting. (*Listening off* R.) Ah, that's her step! No.

PEARL. Do sit down.

RAY. (*Sitting.*) This calling's a great bore; but as you and Laura insisted I should go through it, I did. First I – (*Jumping up.*) I knew it was she. (*Goes to door,* R. H.; *meets* LAURA, *who enters.*) How you did keep me waiting. (*Kisses both her hands.*)

LAURA. And you, sir, we have been looking for you since eight o'clock.

---

6. The emotional dynamics of this love triangle are played differently in each variant. In **PRT**, Pearl is less frivolous and a genuine attraction between her and Ray is implied. In this early scene, significant cuts to the dialogue play down Ray's anxiety to see Laura, and some of Pearl's more dismissive comments are elided (such as those about her mother's death).

RAY. O, I was fulfilling your orders. I've been engaged in the business of calling, from ten o'clock in the morning, till now – (*looks at watch –*) ten at night.

LAURA. Well, you can make this your last one, for you have leave to spend a nice long hour chatting here before you go. Won't you have some supper? (*Goes to bell* L. 2 E. *on table.*)

RAY. I don't care if I do. I'm rather famished.

PEARL. Well, I declare! Did Laura bring your appetite with her?

[LAURA *rings.*

RAY. I don't know how it is, but she brings me a relish for everything in life, I believe. Laura, I think if I were to lose you I'd mope to death and starve to death.

LAURA. Well, that's as much as to say I'm a sort of Life Pill. (MARTIN *enters door* L. H.) Supper. (MARTIN *exits.*)

RAY. You may joke about it – but it's so. You take the lounge. (LAURA *and* PEARL *sit on tête-à-tête.*)

PEARL. You don't want me to go away, do you? (*Putting her head on* LAURA's *shoulder.*)

LAURA. Certainly not. What an idea!

PEARL. I'm sure you'll have time enough to be alone when you are married. And I do so want to talk and be talked to.

LAURA. Well, Ray shall talk to you.

PEARL. He was just going to tell me about his calls today.

LAURA. That's exactly what we want to hear about. Did you call on everyone we told you to?

RAY. Everyone. There was Miss –

PEARL. Did you go to Henrietta Liston's first?

RAY. Yes, and wasn't she dressed. Speaking of dress, are you going to have your new pink for the Sociable, Tuesday?

LAURA. Yes, Pearl and I will do credit to the occasion, as it is our first for a year.

RAY. (*Taking* LAURA'S *hand.*) And *our* last.

PEARL. Our last!

RAY. Laura's and mine. For when we are married, you know, we shall be tabooed – where maids and bachelors only are permitted.

PEARL. O bless me! (*rising*) How do you do Mrs. Trafford.

LAURA. (*rising*) (*sadly*) I wish you hadn't said that Pearl. You know the old Proverb: "Call a maid by a married name."

RAY. Nonsense! (*Putting his arm about* LAURA's *waist.*) It's only a few days to wait, and we'll live long enough, you know. For nothing but death shall separate us.

[MARTIN *appears at door* L.

PEARL. O here's supper.

MARTIN. Beg pardon Miss.

LAURA. What's the matter?

MARTIN. There's a person below, Miss, who says he's been sent with a bouquet for you, Miss, and must deliver it in person.

LAURA. For me? Whose servant is it?

MARTIN. I don't know, Miss, he looks like one of those Soldier Messengers – red cap and all that.

LAURA. Show him up here.

[*Exit* MARTIN, D. 2 E. L.

PEARL. How romantic. So late at night. It's a rival in disguise, Ray.

MARTIN *re-enters showing in* SNORKEY, *with an air of disdain.*
SNORKEY *has a large bouquet in his hand, and his hat is under*
the stump of his right arm, which is cut off.

LAURA. You wished to see me?

SNORKEY. (L. H.) Are you Miss Laura Courtland?

LAURA. Yes.

SNORKEY. Then I was told to give you this.

LAURA. (*Taking it from* RAY, *who has crossed* L. C. *and received it from* SNORKEY.) By whom?

SNORKEY. Now that's what I don't know myself! You see I was down by the steps of the Fifth Avenue Hotel, taking a light supper off a small tooth-pick, when a big chap dressed in black came by, and says he: "Hallo, come with me if you want to earn a quarter." That (*confidentially to all*) being my very frame of mind, I went up one street and down another, till we came here. "Just you take this up there" says he, "and ask for Miss Laura Court-land, and give it to her and no one else."

LAURA. It is some folly of our late visitors.

SNORKEY. I'm one of the Soldier Messengers, Miss. We take to it very well, considering we had so little running in Uncle Sam's service.

RAY. (*As* SNORKEY *is going* L.) Stop a moment, my man. Were you not one of the Twenty-second's recruits?

SNORKEY. Yes, Captain; I remember you joined us in New York, and left us at Washington. Real fighting wasn't funny you thought, and I began to think so too at Fredericksburg.

RAY. Poor devil.

SNORKEY. There was a South Carolina gentleman took such a fancy to me at Fredericksburg![7] Wouldn't have no denial, – cut off my arm to remember me by; he was very fond of me. I wasn't any use to Uncle Sam then, so I came home, put a red band round my blue cap, and with my empty sleeve, as a character from my last place, set up for light porter and general messenger. All orders executed with neatness and dispatch.

PEARL. And Uncle Sam has forgotten you.

SNORKEY. Ah! Miss, don't blame Uncle Sam for that, he's got such a big family to look after, I can't find fault if he don't happen to remember all us poor stumps of fellows.

RAY. (L. H.) So it seems.

LAURA. (C.) (PEARL *takes bouquet.*) Poor fellow! (*To servant.*) Martin, be sure and give him a glass of wine before he goes.

SNORKEY. (L. C.) I'm much obliged, Miss – but I don't think it would be good for me on an empty stomach – after fasting all day.

LAURA. Well, Martin shall find you some supper, too.

SNORKEY. Is this Martin? What a nice young man. Mayn't he have a drop of something, too? He must have caught cold letting me in, he has got such a dreadful stiffness in the back of his neck.

[MARTIN *exit.*

RAY. (*Giving pencilled address.*) Call on me at this place tomorrow, and you shan't regret it.

SNORKEY. All right, Cap'n! I haven't forgot the Army Regulations about punctuality and promotion. Ladies, if ever either of you should want a Light Porter, think of Joe Snorkey – wages no objection.

[*Exit* L. H. *door.*

---

7. **RRR** and **PRT** each alter Snorkey's back story to engage the sympathies of an English audience. In the former, Wadlow [Snorkey] relates that he lost his arm in 'the Crimea' (f. 5a), and the latter sets his story 'at Lucknow' (*el*). In each, references to 'Uncle Sam' are replaced by 'John Bull'.

PEARL. (C.) (*Who has been examining the bouquet.*) O! Laura, only look – here's a *billet-doux*!

RAY. Nonsense! Crazy head! Who would dare (*takes bouquet*) – a letter! (*Takes a paper from bouquet.*)

LAURA. A letter?

PEARL. I am crazy – am I?

RAY. (*Reads superscription.*) "For Miss Laura Courtland. Confidential."

LAURA. (*Laughs.*) Ha! Ha! From some goose who has made one call too many today. Read it, Ray – (*Offering letter.*)

RAY. "Dear Laura – (*Refusing the letter, and going to* PEARL.)

LAURA. (*Looks at it a moment, when the whole expression of face changes. Then reads slowly and deliberately.* RAY *down* R. C. *with* PEARL.) "I respectfully beg you to grant me the favour of an interview tonight. I have waited until your company retired. I am waiting across the street, now."

PEARL. (*Runs to window.*) A tall man in black is just walking away.

LAURA. "If you will have the door opened as soon as you get this, I will step over; if you don't, I will ring; under all circumstances I will get in. There is no need to sign my name; you will remember me as the strange man whom you once saw talking with your mother in the parlour, and who frightened you so much." What can be the meaning of this? – Pearl – no – (*goes to bell on table* L. H.*, and rings.*)

RAY. Laura, you –

LAURA. Ask me nothing. I will tell you by-and-by.

[*Enter* MARTIN, L. *door*

MARTIN. Missit –

LAURA. Admit no one till you bring me the name.

MARTIN. I was about to tell you, Miss, that a strange man has forced himself in at the door and asks to see you, but will give no name.

RAY. Kick the rascal out!

[*Cross to* L.

PEARL. Oh! Don't let him come here.

MARTIN. He's a very strange-looking person, Miss.

RAY. I'll find out what this means! (*Is going to door* L., *when* BYKE *appears at it smiling and bowing.*)

BYKE. (L. H.) I'll spare you the trouble, if you'll hear me a minute.

RAY. (L. C.) (*Violently*) Who are you, fellow?

BYKE. Don't, I beg of you. Don't speak so crossly; I might answer back – then you'd kick me out – and you'd never forgive yourself for it as long as I lived.

RAY. Your business? Come! Speak quickly and begone.

BYKE. (*Coming down*, L.) Business! On this happy day! I came for pleasure – to see Miss Courtland, my little pupil grown so – only think, sir! I knew her when she was only a little child. I taught her music – she was so musical – and so beautiful – I adored her, and her mother[8] told me I needn't come again. But I did – and her mother was glad to see me. Wasn't she, little pupil? – (*to* LAURA, *who is pale with terror, leaning on* PEARL. RAY, C. BYKE, L.) – and begged me to stay – but I said no – I'd call occasionally – to see my dear little pupil, and to receive any trifling contribution her mother might give me. Won't you shake hands, little pupil? (*Advances suddenly, when* RAY *grasps him by the collar –* BYKE *glares at him a moment. Then quickly, as before.*) Don't! Please, don't! The stuff is old, and I've no other.

RAY. The fellow's drunk! Leave the house!

BYKE. What! After sending that touching bouquet?

---

8. **PRT** alters 'mother' to 'aunt' (p. 9).

LAURA. It was you, then? I knew it.

BYKE. You see she knows me. Ah! Memory how it blooms again where the plough of time has passed.

LAURA. Leave this house at once.

BYKE. Not until I have spoken with you.

RAY. (*Seizing him.*) You miserable rascal.

BYKE. Don't, pray don't! I weigh a hundred and ninety eight pounds, and if you attempt to throw me about you'll strain yourself.

LAURA. (*Crossing.*) Go. Tomorrow in the morning I will see you.

BYKE. Thanks! I thank you, Miss, for your forbearance. (*To* RAY.) I am also obliged to you sir, for not throwing me out at the window. I am indeed. I wish you goodnight, and many happy returns of the day. (*Bows, and turns to go. Then familiarly to servant.*) Many calls today, John?

[*Exit* L.

RAY. (*Runs to* LAURA, *who is pale.*)

LAURA. (*Pointing after* BYKE.) See that he goes.

[*Exit* RAY, L. *door.*

LAURA. (*Taking both of* PEARL's *hands in her own.*) Pearl, he must know everything.

PEARL. O, dear! This is dreadful! I do hate scenes.

LAURA. He must know everything, I tell you; and you must relate all. He will question – he will ponder – leave him nothing to ask.

PEARL. If you wish it, but –

LAURA. I desire it; speak of me as you will – but tell him the truth. (RAY *enters hastily,* L.) Stay with her. Don't follow me.

[*Exit* R.

RAY. (*Down,* R. H.) Pearl, what does this mean?

PEARL. O, it's only a little cloud that I want to clear up for you.

RAY. Cloud – how? Where?

PEARL. Don't I tell you I'm going to tell you? Sit down here by me. (*She sinks into tête-à-tête, C.*)

RAY. (*Promenading.*) He said he knew her. And she gave him an interview for tomorrow. That drunken wretch –

PEARL. Do sit down. I can never speak while you are walking about so. (*Gets up, brings him to chair, R. H. and makes him sit.*) Sit by me, won't you? For I've got something strange to tell you.

RAY. *You* serious! I'd as soon expect to see the lightning tamed. Well, I listen.

PEARL. I have something to say to you, Ray, which you must settle with your own heart. You love Laura, do you not?

RAY. Pearl I do more, I adore her. I adore the very air that she breathes. I will never be happy without her. I can swear *that*.

PEARL. Laura is twenty now. How do you think she looked when I first saw her?

RAY. Were you at home when she first came into this earthly sphere?

PEARL. Yes.

RAY. Well then I suppose she looked very small and very pink.

PEARL. She was covered with rags, barefooted, unkempt, crying and six years old.

RAY. (*Shocked.*) Explain.

PEARL. One night father and mother were going to the Opera. When they were crossing Broadway,[9] the usual crowd of children accosted them for

9. Broadway is changed to 'the Haymarket' in **PRT** (p. 11/*el*), and 'Kensington Gardens' in **RRR** (f. 7b).

alms. As mother felt in her pocket for some change, her fingers touched a cold and trembling hand which had clutched her purse.

RAY. A pickpocket! Well.

PEARL. This hand my mother grasped in her own, and so tightly that a small, feeble voice uttered an exclamation of pain. Mother looked down, and there beside her was a little ragged girl.

RAY. The thief.

PEARL. Yes, but a thief hardly six years old, with a face like an angel's. "Stop!" said my mother. "What are you doing?" "Trying to steal," said the child. "Don't you know that it's wicked to do so?" asked my father. "No" said the girl, "but it's dreadful to be hungry." "Who told you to steal?" asked my mother. "She, – there?" said the child, pointing to a squalid woman in a doorway opposite, who fled suddenly down the street. "That is Old Judas," said the girl.

RAY. Old Judas! – what a name! But how does this story interest us?

PEARL. This child was Laura. My father was about to let her go – unharmed – but my mother said "No, it is not enough. We have a duty to perform, even to her," and acting on a sudden impulse took her to our home. On being questioned there, the child seemed to have no recollection, save of misery and blows. My mother persuaded father, and the girl was sent to a country clergyman's for instruction, and there she remained for several years.

RAY. Pearl, you are joking with me.

PEARL. In beauty, and accomplishments and dignity, Laura (as mother named her), exceeded every girl of her age. In gratitude she was all that father could have wished. She was introduced, as you know, into society as my cousin, and no one dreams of her origin.

RAY. (*Starting up.*) Laura, an outcast – a thief!

PEARL. (*Rising.*) No, that is what she might have been.

RAY. And this man – tonight.

PEARL. All I know about him is that four years ago this man came with a cruel-looking woman, to see mother. There was a fearful scene between them, for Laura and I sat trembling on the stairs, and overheard some awful words. At last they went away, the man putting money into his pocket as he left.

RAY. But who were they?

PEARL. Laura never told me, and mother would not. But of course they must have been Laura's father and mother. (RAY *sinks on chair, as if overcome.*)

PEARL. Mother made me promise never to tell anybody this, and you would have known nothing had not Laura made me speak. You see, she would not conceal anything from you. (*Going to him.*) Ray, why don't you speak – shall I go after Laura? Shall I tell her to come to you? Why don't you answer? (*Going.*) I'll go and tell her you want to see her. (*Pausing as she goes* R.) I'm going to send her to you, Ray.

[*Goes off* R. *still looking back at him.*

RAY. (*Starting up.*) What a frightful story. Laura Courtland a thief! A drunken wretch who knows her history, and a squalid beggar woman who can claim her at any moment as their child. And I was about to marry her. Yes, and I love her. But what would my mother think? My friends? Society? No – no – no – I cannot think of it. I will write her – I will tell her – pshaw! She knows of course that I cannot wed her now! (*Goes to the table* L. U. E.) Here is paper. (*Sits.*) What am I about to do? What will be said of me? But I owe a duty to myself – to society – I must perform it. (*Writes.*) "Laura, I have heard of all from your sister." What have I said – (*crosses out last word*) – "from Pearl. You know that I love you, but my mother will demand of me a wife who will not blush to own her kindred, and who is not the daughter of obscurity and crime." It is just; it is I who have been deceived. (*Folds letter and addresses it*) I will leave it for her. (*Puts on light overcoat, which hangs on chair at back.*) I must go before she returns. Her step – – too late! (*Crams the letter into pocket of overcoat.* LAURA *enters,* R. H.)

LAURA. (*Gently.*) Ray.

RAY. Miss – Miss Courtland. (LAURA *looks at him a moment, smiles, and then crosses* C. *without further noticing him, and sits down on tête-à-tête.*) What have I said? What ought I to have said? (*He takes a step towards her – she rises, without looking at him goes to window – looks out, then looks over books on table* R. H.)

RAY. Laura – I –

LAURA. Pshaw, where is my book?

RAY. What book do you want, Laura?

LAURA. Sir.

RAY. (*repulsed*) Oh! – (*pause*) – I've been a fool. How lovely she looks. (*He follows her mechanically to table* L.) Can I find it for you?

[LAURA *picks up a book and reseats herself* C.

LAURA. Don't trouble yourself, I beg.

RAY. (*Coming forward and leaning over her seat.*) Laura.

LAURA. (*Without lifting her head.*) Well.

RAY. (*Toying with her hair.*) Look at me.

LAURA. (*Turns round and looks full at him.*)

RAY. No, no, not that way; as you used to. You act as if I were a stranger.

LAURA. They are only strangers who call me Miss Courtland. (*Resumes reading.*)

RAY. Forgive me, I beg you to forgive me. (*Coming round and sitting beside her.*) I was mad – it was so sudden – this miserable story – but I don't care what they say. O! Do listen to me. I thought you hated reading.

LAURA. I often wish that I were ugly, wretched, and repulsive like the heroine in this story. (*Seats herself.*)

RAY. (*Behind her.*) Why?

LAURA. Because then I could tell who really loved me.

RAY. And don't you know?

LAURA. No; I do not.

RAY. Well, I know.

LAURA. Do tell me then, please.

RAY. He has told you so himself, a hundred times.

LAURA. You.

RAY. I.

LAURA. (*Laughing heartily at him, then seriously.*) How happy must those women be, who are poor and friendless and plain, when some true heart comes and says: I wish to marry you?

RAY. Laura you act very strangely tonight.

LAURA. Will you put this book away?

RAY. (*Throws it on table.*) There Laura. (*Seats himself beside her.*)

LAURA. (*Rising.*) There's Pearl calling me.

RAY. (*Rising and taking her hand.*) Laura, why don't you let me speak to you?

LAURA. About what?

RAY. About my love.

LAURA. For whom? Not me. This is only marriage and giving in marriage. I hate the very word.

RAY. You did not think so once.

LAURA. I wish I had. I am frightened now, I begin to understand myself better.

RAY. And I am frightened because I understand you less.

LAURA. Do not try to; goodnight. (*Up R. C. stops by door as she is going out.*) Goodnight Mr. Trafford.

[*Exit laughing,* R. 2 E.

RAY. I've been an ass. No, I wrong that noble animal. The ass recognised the angel, and I, like Balaam,[10] was blind. But I see now. After all what have I to fear? (*Takes letter from pocket.*) No one knows of this. (*Puts it in his pocket again.*) Let things go on; we'll be married, go straight to Europe,[11] and live there ten years. That's the way we'll fix it.[12]

[*Exit L. 2 E. Scene closes in.*

SCENE II. (*1ˢᵗ Grooves.*) – *The Gentlemen's coat-room at* DELMONICO'S *opening* (C.) *for hat and coat. Chairs* (L. H.) *Pier-glass on flat.*

Enter WINDEL *and* DEMILT *muffled, and with umbrellas* L. 2 E. *they proceed to disrobe.*

DEMILT. Phew! Wet as the deuce, and cold, too. There'll be nobody here.

WINDEL. It's an awful night. The rooms are almost empty.

DEMILT. Sam! Where the dickens is that darkey? (*Enter* SAM, R. *fetching in a chair, and boot black, box and brush.*)

SAM. Here, sah.[13]

DEMILT. (*Sitting in chair.*) Hurry up with my boots. Who's here?

SAM. Berry few gemman, sah; only lebben overcoats and ten over-shoes. Bless de Lord – dem obershoes is spilin the polishin business.

DEMILT. Look out and don't give me any knocks.

WINDEL. (*Handing in his coat at window and getting check for it.*) I wonder if the Courtland girls have come yet.

---

10. An Old Testament prophet described in the book of Numbers. Balaam disobeys God's counsel and then fails to recognise an angel three times, although his donkey perceives the angel straight away and attempts to divert Balaam from his current path.
11. **PRT** changes 'Europe' to 'France' (p. 14).
12. Although **RRR** makes regular modifications to evoke a London setting, the dialogue is at first very similar to Daly's original. However, revisions to the end of I.i reveal how significantly the emotional dynamics of the central love triangle are revised: May [Laura] almost immediately forgives Frank [Ray], and the scene ends with their embrace. This is an early indication that the parts were rewritten to fit stock types, particularly as the additional dialogue employs high-flown melodramatic diction.
13. Black racial stereotyping is removed from **RRR** and **PRT**; for example, 'sah' is changed to 'Sir', and 'darkey' to 'servant' (**PRT**, p. 14).

DEMILT. What did Laura Courtland ever see in Trafford to fall in love with? The Van Dam party is my fancy.

WINDEL. (*Brushing his hair at glass.*) She's ten years older than you, and has a husband.

DEMILT. Yes, a fine old banker, on whom she can draw for everything but attention and affection. She has to get that by her own business tact.

Other parties enter, exchange goodnights, and deposit their coats; some go out at once, some arrange themselves at glass.

DEMILT. That'll do, Sam, take my coat. (*Enter* RAY, L. 1. E.)

WINDEL. Hallo! Trafford, this is a night, ain't it? Have the Courtlands come?

RAY. Not with me. Here, Sam, take my coat. (*His coat is pulled off by* SAM, *and four letters drop out.*) Stupid.

DEMILT. Save the pieces. Mind the love letters.

RAY. (*Picking them up.*) Look out well next time. There's that cursed letter I was going to send to Laura. Confound it, I must destroy it when I go home. (*Puts letters back in overcoat pocket.* RAY *gets his boots touched up.*)

DEMILT. I say, Trafford, what'll you take, and let a fellow read those? Windel, I guess if the girls could get into the cloak-room, it would be better than the Dead-letter Office. What a time they'd have! Are you ready?

WINDEL. What's the use of hurrying? There's no life in the party till Laura Courtland comes. By Jove, Trafford! You're in luck. She's the prettiest girl in New York.

RAY. And the best. (*March music heard.*)

DEMILT. There's the march music; let's go. (*Gets a final brush as they all go off,* A. 1. E.)

RAY. Come along – .

[*Exeunt.*

SAM. (*Picking up a letter dropped from* RAY'S *pocket.*) Dare's anoder of dem billy dooses; wonder if it am Mist' Trafford's. Eh, golly! Musn't mix dem gentlemen's letters, – musn't mix 'em nohow, – or an oberruling providence wouldn't be able to stop fighting in dis city for de nex month.

[*Exit, carrying a chair,* R. 1. E.

Scene draws off to dance music.
Wait till change of music before change of Scene.

———

SCENE III. – *The Blue Room at* DELMONICO'S. *Waltz-music as the Scene opens. Waltzers in motion.* PEARL *is dancing with* MRS. VAN DAM.

Enter RAY, DEMILT, *and* WINDEL, R. 1. R.

PEARL. There's Ray. I've had enough; I want to speak with him.

Bursts away from MRS. VAN DAM, *runs up to* RAY. DEMILT *goes up to* MRS. VAN DAM.

PEARL. (*To* RAY.) You lazy fellow, where have you been?

DEMILT. You're not tired, are you?

MRS. VAN DAM. I feel as fresh as a daisy.

DEMILT. Have a waltz with me. (*Waltz music, piano, as they dance,* WINDEL *goes to* SUE EARLIE.)

RAY. (*Coming down with* PEARL.) Where's Laura?

PEARL. She wasn't ready, and I was dying to come. Been fixed since eight o'clock; so I came with Sue Earlie. So you made it up with Laura.

RAY. Yes. Don't say anything more about the horrid subject. We've made it all up. But what on earth keeps her tonight? It's eleven already. (*Looking at watch.*) Confound it, I tremble every moment she's out of my sight. I fear that terrible man and his secret.

MRS. VAN DAM. (*Coming up with* DEMILT.) Trafford, you look very uneasy. What's the matter?

RAY. O, nothing. I think I ought to go for Laura. I will, too. (SERVANT *passes at back.*) Here! Go upstairs for my overcoat. (*Gives the man a card, and he goes out.*)

MRS. VAN DAM. Nonsense! She'll be here in good time. You shan't leave us. Hold him, Pearl. We want a nine-pin quadrille; we haven't half enough gentlemen. Come, be jolly about it. You lovers are always afraid someone will carry your girls away.

RAY. (*Uneasy.*) I? I'm not afraid.

PEARL. Come, come! I never saw such a restless fellow.

SERVANT *enters with coat*, C.

SERVANT. Here's your coat, sir.

MRS. VAN DAM. Give it to me. I'm determined you shan't go. (*Takes coat carelessly.*) I'll make you a promise – if Laura isn't here in fifteen minutes you shall have your coat, and may go for her.

RAY. Well, I suppose I'll have to wait.

MRS. VAN DAM. There; take him off, Pearl. (RAY *goes up with* PEARL.) (*To* SERVANT) Here, take this back. (*Flings coat to* SERVANT. *As she does so, letters drop from it.*) Well, there's a mess! (SUE EARLIE *and another lady run forward and pick up letters.*) Love letters, of course! – (*smelling them.*) Perfumed to suffocation.

SUE EARLIE. Here's one for Laura. It's unsealed and not delivered.

MRS. VAN DAM. (*Tremolo waltz music.*) A fair prize! Let's see it, (*Music. Takes and opens it. Puts on eye-glass and reads.*) "Laura" – well, come! That's cool for a lover. "I have heard all from" – – – something scratched out – ah! – "your sister, Pearl – your obscure origin – terrible family connexions – the secret of the tie which binds you to a drunken wretch – My mother, Society – will demand of me a wife who will not blush to own her kindred, – or start at the name of outcast and thief!" Signed,

Ray Trafford.

All stand speechless and look at each other. All this time
the rest have been dancing.

SUE EARLIE. What can it mean?

MRS. VAN DAM. It means that the rumours of ten years ago are proven. It was then suspected that the girl whom Mrs. Courtland brought every year from some unnamed place in the country, and introduced to everybody as her niece, was an imposter, which that foolish woman, in a freak of generosity, was thrusting upon society. The rumours died out for want of proof – and before Laura's beauty and dignity – but now they are confirmed. She is some beggar's child.

SUE EARLIE. What do you think we ought to do? (RAY *surrenders* PEARL *to* DEMILT, *and comes down.*)

MRS. VAN DAM. Tell it – tell it everywhere, of course. The best blood of New York is insulted by that girl's presence. (RAY *coming down.*)

RAY. (R. H.) What have you three girls got your heads together for? – some conspiracy, I know.

MRS. VAN DAM. (*To ladies.*) Go, girls – tell it everywhere.

RAY. (*As the ladies distribute themselves about the groups.*) What is it all about? Your face is like a portrait of mystery.

MRS. VAN DAM. (*Showing letter.*) Look at this, and tell me what it means.

RAY. (*Quickly.*) Where did you get this?

MRS. VAN DAM. It is you who must answer – and Society that will question. So Laura is not a Courtland.

RAY. (*Overcome.*) You know, then –

MRS. VAN DAM. Everything; and will you marry this creature? You cannot. Society will not permit your sacrifice.[14]

RAY. This is not your business. Give me that letter.

MRS. VAN DAM. Certainly; take it. But let me say one word, – its contents are known. In an hour every tongue will question you about this secret, – every eye will inquire.

14. Frank addresses Lady Tynedale [Mrs. Van Dam] as 'Aunt' in **RRR** (f. 11b), reframing how her interference is staged and playing down Daly's satire.

RAY. I implore you! Do not breathe a word for her sake. (*She turns scornfully away.*)

MRS. VAN DAM. The secret's not mine.

RAY. Who knows it?

MRS. VAN DAM. Look! (*Points to others who are grouped about whispering and motioning towards* RAY. PEARL *enters here* E., *and speaks to ladies and gents* L. C.)

RAY. (*Wildly.*) What will they do?

MRS. VAN DAM. Expose her! Expel her from Society in which she is an intruder!

RAY. You dare not!

[PEARL *comes forward,* L.

PEARL. O, Ray! What is the meaning of this?

RAY. (*Bitterly.*) It means that Society is a terrible avenger of insult. Have you ever heard of the Siberian wolves? When one of the pack falls through weakness, the others devour him. It is not an elegant comparison – but there is something wolfish in society. Laura has mocked it with a pretence, and Society, which is made up of pretences, will bitterly resent the mockery.

MRS. VAN DAM. Very good! This handsome thief has stolen your breeding as well as your brains, I see.

RAY. If you speak a word against her, I will say that what you utter is a lie!

MRS. VAN DAM. As you please, we will be silent. But you will find that the world speaks most forcibly when it utters no sound.

PEARL. O, go and prevent her coming here.

RAY. That I can do. (*Going up hastily, sees* LAURA *entering at* C. D.) Too late. (*He retreats* R. C.)

MRS. VAN DAM. Come girls! Let us look after our things. They are no longer safe when such an accomplished thief enters.

Music low as LAURA *enters, continues while all except* PEARL *and*
RAY *pass out, eyeing her superciliously.* LAURA C., PEARL R.

PEARL. Ray, Ray, why do you not come to her?

MRS. VAN DAM. (*Up* C. *of stage, surrounded by others.*) Are you not
coming with us Ray?

PEARL. (*To* LAURA.) Let us go home.

LAURA. No; stay with him. (*Pointing to* RAY, *who has held off.*) He
shall not suffer the disgrace long! (*About to faint,* RAY *runs forward, she
proudly waves him away.*) It is Heaven's own blow.[15]

---

15. **RRR** follows Daly's script for I.iii fairly closely until the end of the scene:

> Lady T. Come, Ladies, let us look after our jewellery – it is no longer safe when an
> accomplished thief enters.
>
> Frank. Silence woman – obscure as might have been May's origin – o'ershadowed
> as her infant years were by the dark cloud of mystery – she has rested on your proud
> bosom – been the accepted playmate of your daughter, and is the affianced Bride
> of your Brother's son. The tie of love has bound my heart to hers – it shall not be
> unduly torn asunder by the harmful mandate of society or pride to May May before
> all here – my relations and friends I proudly take you to my heart – the sharer of my
> fortunes – my title and my life.
>
> May shrinking from him And I, Frank, with love as deep as yours, and pride as great –
> decline the house you propose.
>
> Frank. Decline
>
> May. Rather would I own a miserable existence dependent upon my own exertions –
> than borrow a life of opulence to be obtained only at the sacrifice of my pride. Pride
> is not an attribute of the rich alone – honest pride is a quality inherent in the lowly
> born. I possess it and it tells me I must not accept the position of wife in a family –
> where, notwithstanding the fond love of a husband – scorn and contempt would be
> but the welcome of his friends.
>
> Frank. May – think of my love – this blow.
>
> May. Is from above – and boldly must be borne breaks down / Frank, Frank, my
> heart will break – swoons – Frank is going when is restrained by Friends
>
> Frank. Ah – avert your faces – turn your backs – proud recipients of titles and of
> fortunes – but not of hearts – that beat as Heaven ordained with clarity and love – see
> what you've done – broken a spirit – laid prostrate at your feet a frame superior to
> you all. – Inferior alone perhaps in birth – your peer in all beside – waltz – go join
> the whirling waltz forget you have a mission here on earth – forget that it's 'neath
> fashions eye you reign its idols – still 'neath the gaze of one more powerful you
> seem but the patterns of a cold and selfish clique – Society.
>
> Frank supporting May. Company prepare for waltz – Picture – End of Act 1st.
> (ff. 12b-13b)

Picture – Quick Curtain.
E. RAY, LAURA AND PEARL, C. *Party at back.*

ACT II.

(Green Cloth down.)

SCENE I. – *Interior of a Basement. Street and railings seen through window at back. Entrance* to F. *from* D. F. L. H. *Stove with long pipe in fire-place,* R. U. E. *Table between two windows at back, with flowers, &c. Humble furniture. Table* C. *Three chairs. Closet* U. E. L. H.

PEACHBLOSSOM *is discovered polishing stove* R. H. – *a slip-shod girl à la Fanchon.*

SONG – PEACHBLOSSOM:[16]

A lordly knight and a lovely dame, were walking in the meadow,
  But a jealous rival creeping came a-watching in the shadow;
They heeded not, but he whet his knife and dogg'd them in the shadow.
The knight was brave, and the dame was true, the rival fared but badly;
For the knight he drew and ran him through, and left him groaning sadly;
  The knight and dame soon wedded were, with bells a-chiming gladly.

PEACHBLOSSOM. (*Talking while working.*) The stove won't shine. It's the fault of the polish I know. That boy that comes here, just fills the bottles with mud, and calls it stove polish. Only let me catch him, ah! Ah! (*Threatening gesture with brush.*) I declare I'd give it up if I didn't want to make everything look smart before Miss Nina comes in. Miss Nina is the only friend I ever had since I ran away from Mother Judas, I wonder where Old Judas is now? I know she's drunk; she always was; perhaps that's why she never tried to find out what became of me. If she died she could not take me away. Miss Nina begged me off a policeman. I belong to her. I wonder why she ain't got any other friends? She's awful mysterious. Tells me never to let any strangers see her. She's afraid of somebody, I know. It looks just as if she was hiding. I thought only bad girls, such as I, had to hide. If I was good and pretty like her, I wouldn't hide from the President. (*Still polishing.* JUDAS *appears at window with basket of ornaments, &c.*)

---

16. Printed pages from Daly's script are inserted into the hand-written MS at the beginning of **RRR** II.i. Peachblossom's opening song is crossed through, as are her references to Rafferdi having sold her bad polish.

JUDAS. Hum! Is your ma in my dear?

PEACHBLOSSOM. (*Starting.*) Oh! (*aside.*) Old Judas! She's found me out at last. No she h'aint, or she'd have got me by the hair before she spoke. That's *her* way.

JUDAS. (*Coming in at door.* PEACHBLOSSOM *keeps her back towards her.*) Any old clothes to change for chany, my dear? Where's your ma's old skirts and shawls, my pet? Get 'em quick before mother comes in, and I'll give you a beautiful chany mug or a tea-pot for them. Come here my ducky – see the pretty – (*recognises* PEACHBLOSSOM.) Eh! Why you jail-bird, what are you doing here? Are you sneakin' it? Answer me, or I'll knock your head agin the wall (*Catches her by the hair.*)

PEACHBLOSSOM. You just leave me be! I'm honest, I am! I'm good.

JUDAS. You're good? Where's my shoe? I'll take the goodness out of you.

PEACHBLOSSOM. Oh, oh! Please don't beat me. I ain't good, I'm only trying to be.

JUDAS. You're only trying to be, eh? Trying to be good, and here's me as was a-weeping every night, thinking as you was sent up for six months. Who're you living with – you ain't a-keeping house, are you?

PEACHBLOSSOM. I'm living with Miss Nina.

JUDAS. Nina, what's she, concert-saloon girl?

PEACHBLOSSOM. No, she's a lady.

JUDAS. A lady – and have such baggage as you about. Where's my shoe? I'll make you speak the truth.

PEACHBLOSSOM. I don't know what she is. She met me when the police was taking me up for loafin' down Hudson Street,[17] and she begged me off.

17. **PRT** alters 'loafin' down Hudson street' to 'hanging about the Strand' (p. 20/*el*). In **RRR**, the location is changed to 'Mile End', a road very close to the New East London Theatre, for which house the play was licensed in September 1868 (f. 14b). References to nearby landmarks indicate that the play was staged as a 'Local' drama (see Introduction).

JUDAS. Has she any money?

PEACHBLOSSOM. No, she's poor.

JUDAS. Any nice clothes?

PEACHBLOSSOM. O, she's got good clothes.

JUDAS. Where are they?

PEACHBLOSSOM. Locked up, and she's got the key.

JUDAS. You're lying, I see it in your eye. You're always shame-faced when you are telling the truth, and now you're as bold as brass. Where's my shoe? (*Making a dash at her.*)

PEACHBLOSSOM. (*Shouting.*) There's Miss Nina. (*As if curtseying to someone behind* JUDAS.) Good morning, miss.

JUDAS. (*Changing her tone.*) Ah! My pretty dear! What a good lady to take you in and give you a home. (*Turns and discovers the deception – in a rage.*) You hussy, (PEACHBLOSSOM *retreats*) wait till I get you in my clutches again, my lady; and it won't be long. Miss Nina takes care of you, does she? Who will take care of her? Let her look to it. (LAURA *enters* D. F. *plainly dressed, at back.*) Beg pardon, Miss, I just called to see if you had any old clothes you'd like to exchange.

LAURA. No, I don't want anything, my good woman.

JUDAS. (*Eyeing her sharply and going to door.*) That's her – I'd know her anywheres!

[*Malicious glance, and exit* D. F.

LAURA. You've been very good this morning, Blossom. The room is as nice as I could wish.

PEACHBLOSSOM. Please 'm, I tried because you are so good to me. (LAURA *taking off her shawl and things.*) Shall I sweep out the airy? (LAURA *does not answer.*) I guess I'd better – then she'll be alone, as she loves to be.

[*Takes broom and exit,* D. F.

LAURA. (*Solus. Opening a package and taking out photographs.*) No pay yet for colouring, 'till I have practiced a week longer. Then I shall have all the work I can do. They say at the Photographers I colour well, and the best pictures will be given me. The best! Already I have had beneath my brush so many faces that I know, friends of the old days. The silent eyes seem to wonder at me for bringing them to this strange and lowly home. (*Picking up letters from table.*) Letters; ah! Answers to my advertisement for employment. No, only a circular "To the lady of this house." What's that! (*Starting.*) Only Blossom sweeping. Every time there is a noise I dread the entrance of someone that knows me. But they could never find me in New York, I left them all too secretly and suddenly. None of them can suspect I would have descended to this. But it is natural, everything will find its level. I sprang from poverty, and I return to it. Poor Pearl. How she must have wondered the next morning – Laura gone? But three months have passed, and they have forgotten me. Ray will cheer her.

[*Wrangling outside,* PEACHBLOSSOM *bursts in dragging* BERMU-DAS, *with his professional tape, pins, blacking and baskets,* D. F.

PEACHBLOSSOM. Here he is m'm.

BERMUDAS. Leave go, I tell yer, or I'll make yer.

LAURA. What is the matter?

PEACHBLOSSOM. He's the boy that sold me that stove polish what isn't stove polish.

BERMUDAS. What is it then – s-a-a-y?[18]

PEACHBLOSSOM. It's mud! It's mud at ten pence a bottle.

BERMUDAS. Ah! Where could I get mud? Ain't the streets clean? Mud's dearer than stove-polish now.[19]

PEACHBLOSSOM. And your matches is wet, and your pins won't stick, and your shoe-strings is rotten, there now!

18. Bermudas's catch phrase, 's-a-a-y', is deleted throughout **PRT**.
19. Racism is not elided when Sam is cut from **PRT**. Bermudas's line continues: 'It's the very polish I used to sell to the King of Abyssinia when he wanted to brighten his face up' (p. 22/*el*).

BERMUDAS. Well, how am I to live; it ain't my fault, it's the taxes. Ain't I got to pay my income tax, and how am I to pay it if I gives you your money's worth? Do you think I'm Stewart[20] – Sa-a-y?

LAURA. Do let the boy alone, Blossom. Send him away. (*Enter* PEANUTS *at door flat.*)

PEANUTS. Extra! Hollo, Bermudas! How's your sister? Papers Miss. Extra! Revolution in Mexico!

LAURA. Dear, dear, this is the way I'm worried from morning till night.

BERMUDAS. Here, just you get out! This is my beat.

PEANUTS. Vell, I ain't blacking or hairpins now, I'm papers – How'm I hurting you?

BERMUDAS. Vell, I'm papers at four o'clock, and this is my beat. Take care of me, I'm in training for a fight. I'm a bruiser, I am.

PEANUTS. Hold yer jaw. (*They fight.*)

PEACHBLOSSOM. (*Beats them with broom.*) Get out with you. Both of you.
[*Grand escapade and exit of boys,* D. F.

LAURA. Don't let me be troubled in this way again. Have you got the things for dinner?

PEACHBLOSSOM. Lor, no, miss! It's twelve o'clock, and I forgot!

PEACHBLOSSOM *gets shawl, big bonnet from hooks on the wall, basket from closet, while* LAURA *opens her pocket-book for money.*

LAURA. What did we have for dinner yesterday, Blossom?

PEACHBLOSSOM. Beefsteak, 'm. Let's have some leg o'mutton today. We've never had that.

---

20. Probably a reference to the multimillionaire entrepreneur A. T. Stewart. **PRT** alters the reference to 'the Bank of England or Baron Rothschild or Mr Peabody or any of them swells' (p. 22/*el*).

LAURA. But I don't know how to cook it. Do you?

PEACHBLOSSOM. No, but I'd just slap it on, and it's sure to come out right.

LAURA. Slap it on what?

PEACHBLOSSOM. The gridiron.

LAURA. (*Giving money.*) No, we'd better not try a leg of mutton today. Get some lamb chops, we know how to manage them.

PEACHBLOSSOM. (*As she is going.*) Taters as usual, 'mum?

LAURA. Yes; and, stop Blossom – while you're buying the chops, just ask the butcher – off hand – you know – how he would cook a leg of mutton, if he were going to eat it himself – as if you wanted to know for yourself.

PEACHBLOSSOM. Yes'm – but I'm sure it's just as good broiled as fried.

[*Exit* D. F.

LAURA. Now to be cook. (*Laughing.*) "The Tuesday Sociable" ought to see me now. Artist in the morning, cook at noon, artist in the afternoon. (SNORKEY *raps at door* F. *and enters.*)

SNORKEY. (*With letter.*) Beg pardon, is there anybody here as answers to the name of A. B. C.?

LAURA. (*Aside.*) My advertisement for work. – Yes, give it to me.

SNORKEY. (*Seeing her face.*) If I'd been taking something this morning, I'd say that I'd seen that face in a different sort of place from this.

LAURA. Is there anything to pay? Why do you wait?

SNORKEY. Nothing, Miss. It's all right. (*Going – and aside.*) But it ain't all right, Snorkey, old boy! (*Goes out after looking at her, stops at window, and gazes in.*)

LAURA. (*Without noticing him, opening letter.*) Yes, an answer to my advertisement. (*Reads.*) To A. B. C.: "Your advertisement promises that you are a good linguist, and can teach children of any age. I have two daughters for whom I desire to engage your services while on a tour of Europe. Call at seven o'clock, this evening at No. 207 W 34th Street. ANNERSLEY." – Hope at last – a home, and in another land soon. I was sure the clouds would not always be black above me. (*Kisses letter.* SNOR-KEY *re-entering.*)

SNORKEY. Miss, I say Miss. (LAURA *starts.*) – Sh –

LAURA. What do you want?

SNORKEY. Only one word – and perhaps it may be of service to you. I'd do anything to serve you.

LAURA. And why me?

SNORKEY. I'm a blunt fellow, Miss, but I hope my way don't offend. Ain't you the lady that I brought a bouquet to on New Year's night – not here, but in a big house, all bright and rich – and who was so kind to a poor soldier?

LAURA. (*Faint and leaning against chair.*) Whoever you may be promise to tell no one you saw me here.

SNORKEY. No fear Miss! I promise.

LAURA. Sacredly!

SNORKEY. No need to do more than promise. Miss – I keeps my word. I promised Uncle Sam I'd stick to the flag – though they tore my arm off, and by darnation I stuck. I don't want to tell on you Miss. I want to tell on someone else.

LAURA. What do you mean?

SNORKEY. They're looking for you.

LAURA. Who?

SNORKEY. Byke! (LAURA *utters a loud cry and sinks on chair.*) He's on it day and night. I've got his money in my pocket now and you've got his letter in your hand this minute.

[LAURA *drops the letter in dismay.*

LAURA. This?

SNORKEY. Yes, it's his writin' – looks like a woman's, don't it? Lord! The snuff that man's up to, would make Barnum[21] sneeze his head off. He's kept me in hand, 'cause he thinks I know you, having seen you that once. Every day he reads the advertisements, and picks out a dozen or so and says to me: "Snorkey, that's like my little pet," and then he sits down and answers them, and gets the advertisers to make appointments with him, which he keeps regularly, and regularly comes back cussing at his ill luck. See here Miss, I've a bundle of answers to deliver, as usual, to advertisers. I calls 'em Byke's Target Practice, and this time, you see, he's accidentally hit the mark.

LAURA. For Heaven's sake do not betray me to him! I've got very little money, I earn it hardly; but take it, take it – and save me. (*Offers money.*)

SNORKEY. No, Miss; not a cent of it. Though Byke is a devil, and would kick me hard if he thought I would betray him.

LAURA. I don't want you to suffer for my sake, take the money.

SNORKEY. No, I stood up to be shot at for thirteen dollars a month, and I can take my chances of a kickin' for nothing. But Byke ain't the only one Miss, there's another's looking for you.

LAURA. (*Her look of joy changing to fear.*) Another! Who?

SNORKEY. (*Approaching smiling and confidential.*) Mr. Trafford. (LAURA *turns aside despairingly.*) He's been at me every day for more than six weeks, "Snorkey" says he, "do you remember that beautiful young lady, you brought the bouquet to on New Year's night?" "Well," says I "Capt'n, the young lady I slightly disremember, but the cakes and wine I got there that night I shall never forget." "Search for that young lady" says he, "and when you find her – "

LAURA. No, no, no; not even he must know. Do you hear – not he – not anyone. You have served them well; serve me and be silent.

SNORKEY. Just as you please, Miss, but I hate to serve you by putting your friends off the track – it don't seem natural – Byke I don't mind; but

21. P. T. Barnum: a famous American showman.

the Capt'n he wouldn't do you any harm. Just let me give him a bit of a hint. (LAURA *makes an entreating gesture.*) Well I'm mum, but as I've only got one hand, its hard work to hold my tongue. (*Going.*) Not the least bit of a hint. (LAURA *appealingly and then turns away.*) They say when a woman says no, she means yes! I wonder if I dare tell her that he's not far off. Perhaps I'd better not. But I can tell him.

[*Exit* D. F.

LAURA. How shall I ever escape that dreadful man? And Ray searching for me too! Our friends then remember us as well as our enemies. (PEACHBLOSSOM *enters quickly* D. F. *shutting the door behind her, with basket which she places on table* C.)

PEACHBLOSSOM. O, Miss Nina, whatever is into the people? There's a strange man coming down the entry. I heard him asking that red cap fellow about you.

LAURA. Byke! Fasten the door quick. (PEACHBLOSSOM *runs to door, it is slightly opened, she pushes it against someone on the other side.*)

PEACHBLOSSOM. O dear! He's powerful strong, I can't keep it shut. Go away you willin! Oh! (*The door is forced and* RAY *enters.*)

RAY. (*Advancing,* C.) Laura – It is I.

LAURA. (R.H.) Ray! (*Shrinks from him.*)

RAY. Dear Laura! (*He stops as he becomes conscious that* PEACHBLOS-SOM *with her basket on her arm and her bonnet hanging on her back is staring at him.*) I say, my girl, haven't you some particular business somewhere else to attend to?

PEACHBLOSSOM. (*Seriously,* L. H.) No, sir; I've swept the sidewalk and gone a marketing, and now I'm indoors and I mean to stay.

RAY. And wouldn't you oblige me by going for a sheet of paper and an envelope? Here's a dollar – try and see how slow you can be.

PEACHBLOSSOM. (*Firmly.*) You can't sheet of paper me, mister; I'm protecting Miss Nina, and I'm not to be enveloped.

LAURA. Go as the gentleman asks you, Blossom.

PEACHBLOSSOM. Oh! (*Takes money, fixes her bonnet.*) First it's "Keep the man out," now it's "Let him stay in alone with me." But I suppose she's like all of us – it makes a great difference which man it is.

[*Exit* D. F.

RAY. (*After watching* PEACHBLOSSOM *out.*) Laura, when I approached you, you shrank from me. Why did you so?

LAURA. Look around you and find your answer.

RAY. (*Shuddering.*) Pardon me, I did not come here to insult your misery. When I saw you I forgot everything else.

LAURA. (R. C.) And now it's time for us to remember everything. I told you to look around that you might understand that in such a place I am no longer Laura Courtland, nor anything I used to be. But I did not ask your pity. There is no misery here.

RAY. Alone, without means, exposed to every rudeness, unprotected, is this not misery for you?

LAURA. (*Laughing.*) Oh, it's not so bad as that.

RAY. Laura, don't trifle with me. You cannot have exchanged everything that made you happy, for this squalid poverty, and not feel it deeply.

LAURA. I have not time to feel anything deeply. (*Takes basket up goes to table, busies herself about preparing dinner.*) I work from sunrise till night, and I sleep so soundly that I have not even dreams to recall the past. Just as you came in I was about to cook our dinner. Only think – lamb chops!

RAY. Lamb chops! It makes me shudder to hear you speak.

LAURA. Does it? Then wait till I get the gridiron on the fire, and you'll shiver. And if you want to be transfixed with horror, stop and take dinner.

RAY. I will not hear you mock yourself thus, Laura. I tell you in this self-banishment you have acted thoughtlessly – you have done wrong.

LAURA. Why?

RAY. Because, let the miserable creatures who slandered you say what they might, you had still a home and friends.

LAURA. A home! Where the very servants would whisper and point. Friends who would be ashamed to acknowledge me. You are mistaken. That is neither home nor friendship.

RAY. And you are resolved to surrender the past forever.

LAURA. The past has forgotten me in spite of myself.

RAY. Look at me.

LAURA. (*Coming down* C.) Well then, there's one who has not forgotten me, but I desire that he may. You speak to me of bitterness. Your presence, your words, cause me the first pang I have felt since the night I fled unnoticed from my chamber, and began my life anew. Therefore I entreat you to leave me, to forget me.

RAY. Laura, by the tie that once bound us! –

LAURA (*Going up*.) Yes, once. It is a long time ago.

RAY. What have I said? – the tie which still –

LAURA. (*Sharply, turning*.) Mr. Trafford, must I remind you of that night when all arrayed themselves so pitilessly against me? When a gesture from you might have saved me! And you saw me sink without stretching a finger to the woman who had felt the beating of your heart. No, you made your choice then – the world without me. I make my choice now – the wide, wide, world without you.

RAY. I have been bitterly punished, for we are never so humiliated as when we despise ourselves. But, by the Heaven above us both, I love you Laura, I have never ceased to love you.

LAURA. I thank you. I know how to construe the love which you deny in the face of society, to offer me behind its back.

RAY. Will you drive me mad! I tell you Laura, your misery, your solitude, is as nothing to the anguish I have suffered. The maniac who in his mental darkness stabs to the heart the friend he loved, never felt in returning reason the remorse my error has earned me. Every day it says to me. "You have been false to the heart that loved you, and you shall account for it to your conscience all your life. You shall find that the bitterest drops in the cup of sorrow, are the tears of the woman you have forsaken." And it is true, O, forgive me – have pity on me.

LAURA. (*Moved.*) I forgive you. Yes, and I pity you – and so goodbye, forever.

RAY. Of course I am nothing to you now. That is some comfort to me. I have only to be sorry on my own account. But I come to you on behalf of others.

LAURA. Whom?

RAY. My mother and Pearl. They ask for you. For them I have sought you, to urge you to return to them.

LAURA. Dear little Pearl.

RAY. Yes, she has been quite ill.

LAURA. She has been ill?

RAY. Think of those two hearts which you have caused to suffer and do not drive me from you. It is not only wealth, luxury and refinement which you have surrendered – you have also cast away those greater riches: loving and devoted friends. But they shall persuade you themselves. Yes, I'll go and bring them to you, you cannot resist their entreaties.

LAURA. No, no, they must not come here. They must never know where I hide my shame, and you must never reveal it.

RAY. I promise it, if you will go to them with me. Think, they will insist on coming unless you do.

LAURA. Poor Pearl! If I go with you, you promise not to detain me – to permit me to come back, and to trouble me and my poor life no more?

RAY. I promise; but I know you will release me from it when you see them. I will get a carriage. So that no one will meet you. Wait for me, I shall not be long. Is it agreed?

LAURA. (*Smiling.*) Yes, it is agreed.

>   *Enter* PEACHBLOSSOM, D. F. *with a sheet of paper* (*foolscap,*)
>   *and some enormous envelopes.*

PEACHBLOSSOM. (L. H.) Here they are.

RAY. (C.) That's a good girl, keep them till I come back. In half an hour, Laura be ready.

>   [*Exit* D. F.

PEACHBLOSSOM. (*With an air.*) What's he going to do in half an hour?

LAURA. He's going to take me away with him for a little while, Blossom, and while I'm gone, I wish you to be a good girl, and watch the house, and take care of it till I return.

PEACHBLOSSOM. I don't believe it. You won't return. (*Crying.*) That's what our Sal said when she went off with her young man, and she never came back at all. You shan't go; I hate him. He shan't take you away.

LAURA. Blossom! (*Who is getting ready, putting her hat on, &c.*)

PEACHBLOSSOM. I don't care. If you go away, I'll go away; I'll bite and scratch him if he comes back. (*Fiercely tearing up the paper and envelopes.*) Let him come back. Let him dare come back.

LAURA. Blossom, you're very wicked. Go into the corner this minute, and put your apron over your head.

PEACHBLOSSOM. (*Crying, at* LAURA's *feet.*) O, please, Miss Nina, let me go with you, and I'll be so good and not say a word to anyone. Do let me go with you; let me ask him to let me go with you. (*Figure passes the window.*) Here he is; I see him coming.

LAURA. Run! Run! Open the door. (PEACHBLOSSOM *runs to door; throws it open, disclosing* BYKE. *Exclamation of horror from* LAURA.)

BYKE. (*Advancing.*) Ah, my dear little runaway! Found you at last, – and just going out. How lucky! I wanted you to take a walk with me.

LAURA. Instantly leave this place.

BYKE. How singular! You are always ordering me out, and I am always coming in. We want a change. I will go out, and I request you to come with me.

LAURA. Blossom, go find an officer. Tell him this wretch is insulting me.

BYKE. Blossom? Ah, – exactly! Here you, Judas! (JUDAS *appears at door, down* L. H.) (PEACHBLOSSOM *crosses to* LAURA, R.)

PEACHBLOSSOM. O, Miss, save me!

BYKE. (*Throws* PEACHBLOSSOM *over to* JUDAS, L.) Take care of that brat. And as for you, daughter, – come with me.

LAURA. Daughter!

BYKE. Yes; it is time to declare myself. Paternal feeling has been too long smothered in my breast. Come to my arms, my child, my long-estranged child! (*Takes out dirty handkerchief and presses his eyes with pretended feeling.*)

LAURA. God! Is there no help coming? (*She attempts to escape.* BYKE *seizes her.*)

BYKE. What, unfilial girl! You take advantage of a father's weakness, and try to bolt! (*Clutching her by the arm.*) Come, go with me; and cheer my old age. Ain't I good, to take you back after all these years?[22]

PICTURE. – *Quick Curtain.*

---

22. Lacy's script ends this scene with the direction '*drags her out* L. C., *she calling "help! help!"*' (p. 29), but this is crossed through in **PRT**, and the scene is extended *el*. Snorkey enters and places Laura under 'military protection' until Byke can prove his paternity before a magistrate (p. 29/*el*).

II.i is also lengthened in **RRR**. Covey [Byke] does not drag May away. Instead, Wadlow enters and releases May and Peachblossom, just as Covey reveals he is May's father. Wadlow accuses Covey of abduction but there is no trial scene. Instead, Covey calls a policeman with whom he is already acquainted to question May, as in the trial. Covey is ultimately given permission to take May away, even though Frank tries to prevent him.

ACT III.

SCENE I. – *The Tombs Police Court. Long high desk, with three seats, across back from* R. *to* L. *on Platform. Railing in front. Railing around* L. H., *with opening* C. *In front of railing, a bench* R. *and* L. H. *Gate in* C. *of railing.*

JUDGE BOWLING *and another Justice seated behind high desk,* C. *with Clerk on his* L. H. *Justice is reading paper, with his feet upon desk,* R. H. *Policemen at* R. *and* L., 1, 2, E.

POLICEMAN 9-9-9 *at gate,* C. *Hard-looking set of men and women on benches,* R. *and* L. *Lawyer* SPLINTER *is talking to* RAFFERDI, *who is in crowd down* R.

As the Curtain rises, noisy buzz is heard.

BOWLING. Smithers, keep those people quiet. (9-9-9 *handling people roughly.*) Here, – easy, officer; treat those poor people decently. Well, whom have you got there?

9-9-9. (*Going to* 1. E. L. H., *and dragging urchin within railing.*) Pick-pocket, your Honour. Caught in the act.

BOWLING. What's he got to say for himself? Nothing, eh? What's his name?

9-9-9. (*Stooping down to boy, as if asking him.*) Says his name is Peter Rich.

BOWLING. You stand a poor chance, Rich! Take him away (BOWLING *consults with other Justice as the boy is taken off* E. R. H.)

SPLINTER. (*To* RAFFERDI, *who has his monkey and organ.*) So you want to get out, eh? How much money have you got?[23]

RAFFERDI. Be jabers! Half a dollar in cents is all the money I'm worth in the world.

SPLINTER. Give it to me. I thought you organ fellows were Italians.

---

23. *El* additions and annotations in **PRT** extend Rafferdi's comic dialogue and cross through Sam's section.

RAFFERDI. Divil doubt it! Ain't I got a monkey?

9-9-9. Here, you; come up here. (*Takes* RAFFERDI *inside the railing,* L. H.)

BOWLING. Now, then; what's this, officer?

9-9-9. (RAFFERDI *takes stand,* R.) Complaint of disturbing the neighbourhood.

BOWLING. What have you got to say for yourself?

SPLINTER. (R. H.) If your Honour please, I appear for this man.

BOWLING. Well, what have you got to say for him?

SPLINTER. Here is an unfortunate man, your Honour – a native of Sunny Italy. He came to our free and happy country, and being a votary of music, he bought an organ and a monkey, and tried to earn his bread. But the myrmidons of the law were upon him, and the Eagle of Liberty drooped his pinions as Rafferdi was hurried to his dungeon.

BOWLING. Rafferdi? – You're an Irishman, ain't you? What do you mean by deceiving us?

RAFFERDI. Sure I didn't. It's the lawyer chap there. I paid him fifty cints and he's lying out the worth of it.

BOWLING. You fellows are regular nuisances! I've a great mind to commit you.

SPLINTER. Commit him! If the Court please – reflect – commit him – to prison – what will become of his monkey?

BOWLING. Well, I'll commit him too.

SPLINTER. You cannot. I defy the Court to find anything in the Statutes authorizing the committal of the monkey.

BOWLING. Well, we'll leave out the monkey.

SPLINTER. And if the Court please, what is the monkey to do in the wide world, with his natural protector in prison? I appeal to those kindlier feelings in your honour's breast – which must ever temper justice with mercy. This monkey is perhaps an orphan!

BOWLING. (*Laughing.*) Take them both away, and don't let me catch you here again Mr. Rafferdi or you'll go to jail.

Exit RAFFERDI 1 E. L. H. SPLINTER *goes down,* RAFFERDI *Exits.*

9-9-9. (*Pulling* SAM *who is drunk out of a crowd.*) Get up here.

SAM. (*Noisily.*) Look Yah – don't pull me around.

BOWLING. Silence there! What's all this noise about?

SAM. Whar's de Court? I want to see de Judge.

SPLINTER. (*Approaching him.*) My coloured friend, can I assist you?

SAM. Am you a Counsellor-at-Law?

SPLINTER. Yes, retain me! How much money have you got?

SAM. I ain't got no money – but I've got a policy ticket. It's bound to draw a prize.

SPLINTER. Got any pawn tickets?

SAM. Ob course. (*Giving him a handful.*)

BOWLING. Well, what's the charge?

9-9-9. (R. H. C.) Drunk and disorderly.

BOWLING. Well, my man, what have you to say?

SAM. Dis here gemman represents me.

SPLINTER. We admit, if the Court please, that we were slightly intoxicated, but we claim the privilege, as the equal of the white man.

BOWLING. (*To Clerk.*) Very good! Commit him for ten days.

SPLINTER. But this is an outrage your honour

BOWLING. (*To officer.*) Take him off! (*Motioning to* SAM.) (SPLINTER *sits down discomfited,* SAM *very wroth.*)

SAM. What?

BOWLING. Take him away.

SAM. Look here judge, hab you read the Civil Rights Bill? You can't send dis nigger to prison while dat bill am de law of de land.

BOWLING. That'll do – remove him.

SAM. I ain't no gypsy, I'm one of de Bureau niggers, I am! Where am de law! Don't touch me white man! Dis am corruption – dis am 'ficial delinquency!

9-9-9. (*Collars him and carries him off.*)

SAM. Mr. Stephens! Thaddeus! (*Exit* R. H. 1 E.)

BOWLING. Any more prisoners? (*Noise* L. 1 E.) What noise is that?

> *Officer goes out.* BYKE *enters followed by the officer*
> *who escorts* LAURA.[24]

BYKE. Where is the judge? O, where is the good kind judge?

BOWLING. Well, my dear sir, what is the matter?

BYKE. O, sir, forgive my tears. I'm a broken-hearted man.

BOWLING. Be calm, my dear sir. Officer, bring this gentleman a chair.

> [*Officer hands chair* R. C.

BYKE. Ah, sir, you are very good to a poor distressed father, whose existence has been made a desert on account of his child.

---

24. **PRT** changes Byke's dialogue to emphasise his obsequiousness and make his pretended parenthood even more farcical: for example, he calls Laura's feet her 'pretty little tootsies' (p. 35/*el*).

BOWLING. Repress your emotion, and tell me what you want.

BYKE. I want my child.

BOWLING. Where is she?

BYKE. She is here, sir – here – my darling, my beautiful child, and so unfilial – so unnatural.

BOWLING. How is this, young lady?

LAURA. (*Standing inside railing* L. H.) It is all a lie. He is not my father.

BYKE. Not your father! Oh, dear, oh, dear, you will break my heart.

BOWLING. This needs some explanation. If not his child, who are you?

LAURA. I am – I dare not say it. I know not who I am, but I feel that he cannot be my father.

BYKE. O, dear – O –

BOWLING. (*Sharply.*) Silence! (*To* LAURA, *sternly.*) You say you don't know who you are. Do you know this man?

LAURA. Yes.

BOWLING. Where and with whom do you live?

LAURA. I have lived alone for four months.

BOWLING. And with whom did you live before that?

LAURA. O, forgive me if I seem disobedient – but I cannot tell.

BOWLING. Then I must look to this gentleman for information.

BYKE. And I will gladly give it. Yes, sir, I will gladly tell. She was taken from me years ago, when she was but a little child, by rich people who wanted to adopt her. I refused – they paid me – I was poor – I was starving – I forbore to claim her – she was happy, but they turned her forth four months ago into the street. I could not see her suffer – my child – the prop of my declining days. I begged her to come – she refused. My enemies had poisoned my daughter's mind against me, her father. I am still poor. I taught school, but I have saved a little money, only for her.

BOWLING. How old is she?

BYKE. Nineteen.

BOWLING. (*To* LAURA.) Your father is your legal guardian during your minority, and is entitled to your custody. Why are you so undutiful? Try to correct this.

BYKE. Oh, bless you, dear good judge for those words.

LAURA. O, have I no friends, must I go with him?

BOWLING. Certainly.

LAURA. Anything then. Exposure! Disgrace rather than that.

> [*Judges consult. Enter* SNORKEY L. *goes opposite to* LAURA *and signals her.*

BYKE. (*Aside.*) Snorkey! The devil!

SNORKEY. (*Crossing to* LAURA, L. C.) Can I help you, miss? Only tell me what to do, and if it takes my other arm off I'll save you.

LAURA. Yes, yes, you can help me! (*To Judge.*) Will you let me send a message?

BOWLING. You may do that.

LAURA. Run to that house – not my house – but the one in which you saw me first. Do you remember it?

SNORKEY. Don't I, and the wine and cakes.

LAURA. Ask for Miss Pearl. Tell her where I am. Tell her to come instantly. (SNORKEY *going.*) Stay – tell her to bring the ebony box in mother's cabinet. Can you recollect?

SNORKEY. Can I what? Gaze at this giant intellect and don't ask me! The ebony box! All right – I'm off.

[*Exit* L.

BOWLING. It would have been as well, young lady, to have answered frankly at first.

BYKE. O, sir! Don't be harsh with her! Don't be harsh with my poor child.

BOWLING. Your father has a most Christian disposition.

LAURA. Sir, I have told you, and I now solemnly repeat it, that this man is no relation of mine. I desired to remain unknown, for I am most unfortunate; but the injustice you are about to commit forces me to reveal myself, though in doing so I shall increase a sorrow already hard to bear. (SPLINTER *talks with* LAURA *aside.*)

BOWLING. We sit here to do right, according to facts before us. And let me tell you, young lady, that your obstinate silence has more than convinced us that your father's statement is correct. Further, unless the witnesses you have sent for can directly contradict him, we shall not alter our decision.

LAURA. Let it be so. He says he gave me into the care of certain wealthy people when I was a little child.

BYKE. I am willing to swear it.

LAURA. (SPLINTER *watching effect of question.*) Then he will be able to describe the clothes in which I was dressed at the time. They were safely kept. I have sent for them.

BYKE. Let them be produced – and I will recognise every little precious garment. (*Aside.*) This is getting ferociously hot for me! Ha! (*Re-enter* SNORKEY *with* RAY *hastily* L. 1 E.)

SNORKEY. (*Excitedly.*) Here's a witness! Here's evidence!

[9-9-9 *admonishes him.*

LAURA. (RAY *takes her hand through rail.*) Ray?

BOWLING. Who is this?

RAY. I am a friend, sir, of this lady.

BYKE. He is a dreadful character – a villain who wants to lead my child astray! Don't – please don't let him contaminate her!

BOWLING. Silence! (*To* RAY.) Can you disprove that this young lady is his daughter?

RAY. His daughter? (*Looks at* LAURA.)

LAURA. He knows nothing.

BOWLING. Let him answer. Come – have you any knowledge of this matter?

RAY. I had been told, sir, that – (LAURA *looks at him.*) No – I know nothing.

LAURA. Have you brought the ebony box? It contained the clothes which I wore when –

RAY. I understand; but in my haste, and not knowing your peril I brought nothing. But can you not remember them yourself?

LAURA. Perfectly.

RAY. Write, then! (*Handing her a memorandum book. To* BOWLING.) Sir, this lady will hand you a description of those articles which she wore when she was found, thirteen years ago. Then let this scoundrel be questioned – and if he fail to answer, I will accuse him of an attempted abduction.

BOWLING. That's the way!

BYKE. (*Aside.*) It will not be a great effort for me to remember.

BOWLING. (*Taking the book from* RAY.) Now, sir, I will listen to you.

> RAY *and* LAURA *are eager and expectant.*

BYKE (*Deliberately.*) A soiled gingham frock, patched and torn. (LAURA *gives a shudder and turns aside.*)

BOWLING. What kind of shoes and stockings?

BYKE. Her feet were bare.

BOWLING. And the colour of her hood?

BYKE. Her dear little head was uncovered.

BOWLING. (*Handing book back.*) He has answered correctly.

LAURA. It is useless to struggle more! Heaven alone can help me!

RAY. You can see, sir, that this lady cannot be his daughter. Look at her and at him!

BOWLING. I only see that he has pretty well proven his case. She must go with him, and let her learn to love him as a daughter should.

RAY. She shall not! I will follow him wherever he goes.

BYKE. (*Taking* LAURA's *hand.*) I appeal to the Court.

BOWLING. Officer, take charge of that person, until this gentleman is gone.

BYKE. (*Coming forward with* LAURA *who is dumb and despairing.*) My child, try and remember the words of the good Judge. "You must learn to love me as a daughter should." (*Leading her towards* R. H.)

SNORKEY. (*To* RAY.) Stay here sir, I'll track him. No one suspects me!

[*Music, Tableau, – Scene closes in.*

LAURA, R. H.   BYKE, R. C.   SNORKEY, C.   RAY, L. H.

SCENE II. – *Exterior of the Tombs, with ballads on strings upon the railings. Enter* JUDAS *followed by* PEACHBLOSSOM, L. H. 1 E.

PEACHBLOSSOM. Only tell me where he has taken her, and I'll go with you – indeed I will.

JUDAS. We don't want you, we wouldn't be bothered with you; she's our game.

PEACHBLOSSOM. What are you going to do with her?

JUDAS. Do? Why we'll coin her. Turn her into dollars. We've had it on foot for a long time.

PEACHBLOSSOM. What! Is she the rich young lady I heard you and Byke speak of so often before I got away from you?

JUDAS. (*Savagely.*) Heard me speak of! What did you hear?

PEACHBLOSSOM. (*Dancing off.*) O, I know! I know more than you suppose. When you used to lock me up in the back cellar for running away, you forgot that doors had keyholes.

JUDAS. (*Aside.*) This girl must be silenced.

PEACHBLOSSOM. What are you muttering about – don't you know how Byke used to throw you down and trample on you for muttering.

JUDAS. I'll have you yet, my beauty.

PEACHBLOSSOM. I think you are a great fool, Judas.

JUDAS. Likely. Likely.

PEACHBLOSSOM. Why don't you give up Miss Nina to that handsome young gentleman? He'd pay you well for the secret. He'd give his whole fortune for her I know, I saw it in his face. And he'd treat you better than Byke does.

JUDAS. Not yet my chicken; besides, what does he care for her now? Isn't he going to marry the other girl – she's the one will pay when the time comes[25] – but we intend to hold the goods 'till the price is high.

PEACHBLOSSOM. Then if you won't, I'll tell all as I knows. I'll tell him all I used to overhear about babies and cradles, and he'll understand it perhaps, if I don't.

JUDAS. (*Aside.*) Hang her – she'll make mischief. (*Aloud.*) Well, come along with me, my beauty, and I'll talk it over with you.

---

25. The final twist in Daly's script – that Laura and Pearl were swapped in their cradles – is removed in **PRT**. Consequently, such hints of further secrets are omitted.

PEACHBLOSSOM. Don't touch me, I won't trust you with your hands on me. (JUDAS *makes a dart at her.*) I knew that was your game. But I'll be even with you yet. (*Dancing off tantalizingly before* JUDAS. *Both Exit* R. H.)

Enter SNORKEY, R. 1 E.

SNORKEY. (*Despondent.*) I'm no more use than a gun without a trigger. I tried to follow Byke, but he smoked me in a minute. Then I tried to make up with him, but he swore that I went against him in Court, and so he wouldn't have me at no price. Then I ran after the carriage that he got into with the lady, till a damn'd old woman caught me for upsetting her apple stand and bursting up her business. What am I to do now? I'm afraid to go back to the Cap'n, he won't have me at any price either, I suppose. (*Gazing at ballads, hand in his pockets – going from one to the other. Enter* BER-MUDAS L. 1 E. *with ballads in his hands and preparing to take others off the line as if to shut up shop.*)

BERMUDAS. (*After gazing at* SNORKEY.) What are you a doing of – sa-a-y? (SNORKEY *takes no notice.*) This here's one of the fellows as steals the bread of the poor man. Reading all the songs for nothin', and got bags of gold at home.[26] Sa-a-y!

SNORKEY. Well, youngster, what are you groaning about? Have you got the cholera?

BERMUDAS. Ah! What are you doing? Taking the bloom off my songs? You've read them 'ere ballads till they're in rags.

SNORKEY. I was looking for the "Prairie Bird."

BERMUDAS. Perary Bird! eh? There ain't no perary bird. There's a "Perary Flower."[27]

---

26. **PRT** employs repeated musical gags to heighten the comic effect of this scene. Bermudas sings 'You're no pal of mine' to Snorkey twice as they spar over the ballads (p. 37/*el*).
27. Bermudas appears to be right. The Bodleian Libraries' *Broadside Ballads Online* database holds numerous copies of 'The Prairie Flower' (or, 'Rosalie, The Prairie Flower'), but no copies of a ballad titled 'The Prairie Bird'.
  In **RRR**, Wadlow says he is 'looking for the Sabre of my Sire' rather than 'Prairie Bird' (f. 28a). It is likely that this is altered either to localise the drama further for a British audience, or to satirise music hall clichés, as Sweeds [comic character] also asks: 'Have you seen my Polly with Oxford Joe Tommy Dodd, as he play'd on the Indian Down' (f. 27a). (Our thanks to Dr Oskar Cox Jensen for this insight.)

SNORKEY. Now don't go into convulsions. I'll find it. (*Turns to songs.*)

BERMUDAS. Sa-a-ay – you needn't look no further for that bird! I've found him, and no mistake. He's a big Shanghae with a red comb and no feathers.

SNORKEY. He's dropped on me.

BERMUDAS. Ain't you a mean cuss, sa-ay? Why don't you come down with your two cents, and support trade?

SNORKEY. But I ain't got two cents. What's a fellow to do if he hasn't got a red?

BERMUDAS. (*Toning down.*) Haint you? Where's your messages?

SNORKEY. Haven't had one go today.

BERMUDAS. Where do you hang out?

SNORKEY. Nowheres.

BERMUDAS. My eye – no roost?

SNORKEY. No.

BERMUDAS. I tell you what, come along with us – we've got a bully place – no rent – no taxes – no nothin'.

SNORKEY. Where is it?

BERMUDAS. Down under the pier! – I discovered it. I was in swimmin' and seed a hole and I went in. Lo'-s of room, just the place for a quiet roost. We has jolly times every night I tell you on the dock; and when it's time to turn in we goes below, and has it as snug as a hotel; come down with us.

SNORKEY. I will! These young rascals will help me track that scoundrel yet.

BERMUDAS. Now, help me to take in my show windows; it's time to shut up shop.

Enter RAY, L.

RAY. If what that crazy girl has told me can be true, Laura may yet be restored to her friends if not to me, for I have dispelled that dream for ever. But that villain must be traced immediately, or he will convey his victim far beyond our reach or rescue.

> [SNORKEY *helping to take down songs, sees* RAY,
> *who has crossed to* R. H.

SNORKEY. Hollo! Cap'n!

RAY. The man of all I wanted. You tracked him?

SNORKEY. They was too much for me sir – two horses was – but I saw them turn into Greenwich Street, near Jay.[28]

RAY. This may give us a clue. I have learned from a girl who knows this fellow, that he has some hiding-place over the river, and owns a boat which is always fastened near the pier where the Boston Steamers are.

SNORKEY. Well Cap'n, if anything's to be done, you'll find me at Pier – what's the number of our pier, Shorty?

BERMUDAS. Pier 30! – Down stairs!

SNORKEY. Pier 30. That's my new home, and if you want me, say the word.

RAY. You will help me?

SNORKEY. You bet Cap'n. I was on Columbia's side for four years, and I'll fight for her daughters for the rest of my life, if you say so. If there's any fightin' count me in, Cap'n.

---

28. **PRT** swaps the locale for generic directions: 'towards the bridge' (p. 38/*el*), but **RRR** specifically evokes a dockside setting near to the New East London Theatre:

> Wadlow. [. . .] the last I saw of it was turning down by the Railway Arch in the Commercial Road.

> Sir Frank. This may give us a clue – this girl tells me he has a hiding place across the river, and owns a boat which is fastened near Blackwall Pier. (f. 30a)

RAY. Thank you, brave fellow. Here take this – no nonsense – take it. Pier thirty is it?

SNORKEY. Pier thirty.

[*Exit* RAY, R. 1 E.

BERMUDAS. (*Eyeing money.*) How much Perary?

SNORKEY. One – two – three – four – four dollars.

BERMUDAS. Four dollars! Sa-ay – Don't you want to buy a share in a paying business? I'm looking out for a partner with a cash capital, for the ballad business. Or I tell you what to do. Lay your money on me in a mill. I'm going to be a prize fighter, and get reported in the respectable dailies. "Rattling Mill, 99th round, Bermudas the victor, having knocked his antagonist into nowheres."

SNORKEY. Come along you young imp. I could floor you with my one arm, and then the report would be: "25th round – Snorkey came up first, while his antagonist showed great signs of distress."

BERMUDAS. Say, Perary, what are you going to do with all that money?

SNORKEY. I won't bet it on you, sure.

BERMUDAS. I'll tell you what to do, let's go and board at the Metropolitan Hotel for an hour.

SNORKEY. What will we do for toothpicks?

BERMUDAS. Oh, go along. You can't get anything to eat for four dollars.[29]

[*Exit* SNORKEY, BERMUDAS *squaring off,* L. 1. E.

---

29. III.i of **RRR** ends with all the characters setting off to find May at Blackwall Pier, where Covey is known to keep a boat (including Peachblossom, who enters already in company with Frank). A romantic sub-plot is also introduced: Paper Boy and Sweeds (comic characters who replace Bermudas, Rafferdi and Peanuts) compete for Peachblossom's attention.

SCENE III. – *Foot of Pier 30, North River. Sea cloth down and working – A pier projecting into the river. A large cavity in front. Bow of a vessel at back, and other steamers, vessels and piers in perspective on either side. The flat gives view of Jersey City and the river shipping by starlight. Music of distant serenade heard.*

BYKE *enters sculling a boat,* R. 2d. E. *and fastens his boat to the pier* L. H. JUDAS *is on the pier, smoking pipe, looking down.*

JUDAS. Have you fixed everything across the river?

BYKE. Yes, I have a horse and wagon waiting near the shore to carry her to the farm. Has anyone been around here?

JUDAS. Not a soul. I've been waiting here for an hour. What made you so long?

BYKE. I pulled down the river for a spell to throw any spies off the track. It was necessary after what you told me of that girl's threat to blab about the Boston pier.

JUDAS. Pshaw! She'd never dare.

BYKE. Never mind, it's best to be certain. Is the prize safe?

JUDAS. Yes, she was worn out, and slept when I came away. How her blood tells – she wouldn't shed a tear.

BYKE. Bah! If she'd been more of a woman and set up a screaming, we shouldn't have been able to get her at all. Success to all girls of spirit, say I.

JUDAS. Don't you think it might be worthwhile to treat with this young spark, Trafford, and hear what he has to offer?

BYKE. Satan take him! No. That'll spoil your game about the other girl, Pearl. He was making up to her all right, and if he gets this one back he'll upset the whole game by marrying her. I tell you he's got the old feeling for her, spite of her running away. Now you can judge for yourself, and do as you please.

JUDAS. Then I do as you do – get her out of the city. When Pearl is married to him we can treat for Laura's ransom, by threatening them with the real secret.

BYKE. Then that's settled. (*Taking out flask.*) Here's the precious infant's health. Do you think she'll go easy, or shall we drug her?

JUDAS. Just tell her it's to meet her beau and get her ransom, or give her a reason and she'll be as mild as a lamb.

BYKE. Ha! Let me get hold of her, and I'll answer she goes across, reason or no reason. (BERMUDAS *calls outside* L. H.) There's a noise.

JUDAS. It's only the market boys coming down for a swim.

BYKE. Softly then, come along.

[*Music. Exeunt* L.

Enter BERMUDAS, PEANUTS, *and a couple other boys,* L.

BERMUDAS. Say Peanuts, go down and see if any of the fellows is come yet. (PEANUTS *scrambles down to hole in front on side of dock; comes out again.*)

PEANUTS. There's nobody there.

SNORKEY. (*Without.*) Hollo!

BERMUDAS. Hollo! That's our new chum. Hollo! Follow your front teeth, and you'll get here afore you knows it.

Enter SNORKEY *with more boys,* L.

SNORKEY. What a very airy location.

BERMUDAS. It's a very convenient hotel. Hot and cold saltwater baths at the very door of your bedrooms, and sometime when the tide rises we has the bath brought to us in bed – doesn't we Peanuts?

PEANUTS. That's so.

SNORKEY. Come, what do you do before you go to bed?

BERMUDAS. We has a swarry.[30] Say, one of you fellows, go down and bring up the piany forty. (PEANUTS *goes into hole and gets banjo.*) What'll I give you?

---

30. *Swarry*: a mispronunciation of *soirée*. The word recalls Sam Weller in Charles Dickens's *Pickwick Papers*.

SNORKEY. Something lively. (*Music, and dance by boys, ensue, – given according to capacity and talent. At the end of it, a general shout of jubilee; when –* [31]

SERGEANT OF PATROL. (*Outside.*) Here, boys! Less noise.

BERMUDAS. It's Acton and the police. Let's go to bed. (BERMUDAS *and boys get down into hole.*)

SERGEANT. (*Entering* L. *in patrol boat.*) If you boys don't make less noise, I'll have to clear you out.

BERMUDAS. (*On the pier.*) It's an extra occasion, Mr. Acton; – we're having a distinguished military guest, and we're entertaining him. (*Boat passes out,* R.) Come along, Perary, let's go to bed. (SNORKEY *is about to descend.*)[32]

Enter RAY, L. *on pier.*

RAY. Is that you, Snorkey?

SNORKEY. (*Quickly whispering.*) Here, sir. Anything turned up?

RAY. Byke was overheard to say he intended crossing the river tonight; he will doubtless use that boat which he keeps by the Boston Pier. The river patrol are on the watch for him. But I will meet him before he can embark.

SNORKEY. Which Boston pier is it, Cap'n? There are three on this river.

RAY. Three!

SNORKEY. Yes; one of them is two slips below. I tell you what, Cap'n: You get the officers, go by the shore way, search all the slips; I'll find a boat about here, and will drop down the river, and keep an eye around generally.

31. Samuel French's edition indicates that these entertainments may include '*trained dogs, street acrobats, &c., ending with dance by boys*' (Pettingell Collection, PETT BND.125(5), p. 40). In **PRT**, Peachblossom takes the lead in a song, while 'all chorus [and] dance round' (p. 40/*el*).
32. **PRT** again employs ballads for comic effect. Bermudas begins a celebratory naval song, 'Mother be proud of your boy in blue', as an amusing misdirection, before switching to 'And she married a nasty policeman' (p. 41/*el*).

VOICE. (*Without,* L. H.) This way, sir.

RAY. That's the Patrol calling me. Your idea is a good one. Keep a sharp eye down the stream.

[*Exit,* L.

SNORKEY. (*Alone.*) Now for my lay.

BERMUDAS. (*Popping his head up.*) Say, can't I do nothin'? I'm the Fifth-Ward Chicken, and if there's any muss, let me have a shy.[33]

SNORKEY. No; get in, and keep quiet. (BERMUDAS *disappears.*) I wonder where I can find a boat. There ought to be plenty tied up about here. My eye! (*Discovering* BYKE's) Here's one for the wishin'; sculls too. I'm in luck. Say, Bermude, whose boat is this?

BERMUDAS. Yours, if you like. Tie it loose.

[*Jumps down, enters boat, pushes off towards* R.

BERMUDAS. (*Inside.*) Keep your toe out of my ear!

(*Pause.*)

[BYKE, LAURA, *and* JUDAS, *enter on pier from* L.

LAURA. Is this the place? There is no one here; you have deceived me.

BYKE. Well, we have but we won't do so any longer.

LAURA. What do you mean?

BYKE. (*Drawing pistol.*) Do you see this? It is my dog Trusty. It has a very loud voice and a sharp bite; and if you scream out, I'll try if it can't out scream you. Judas, unfasten the boat.

LAURA. What are you about to do? You will not murder me?

BYKE. No; we only mean to take you to the other shore, where your friends won't think of finding you. Quick, Judas.

JUDAS. The boat's gone.

---

33. *Shy*: 'Generic for a piece of action' (Farmer and Henley (1905), p. 410).

BYKE. Damn you, what do you mean? Where is it? Here; hold her. (JUDAS *clutches* LAURA.) Where the devil is that boat?

SNORKEY. (*Re-appearing in boat from* R.) Here!

BYKE. Snorkey! We're betrayed. Come. (*Drags* LAURA *towards* L.)

SNORKEY. The police are there! Turn, you coward! Don't run from a one-armed man!

BYKE. Judas, take her! (SNORKEY *strikes at him with oar. BYKE takes oar from him and strikes him; he falls in boat. The boys hear the noise, and scramble up at back. The patrol boat appears at* R., *with lights.*)

SNORKEY. Help! Bermudas!

BERMUDAS. Hi! Ninety-ninth round! First blood for Bermudas! (*Jumps at* BYKE.)

BYKE. (*Flinging* BERMUDAS *off.*) Judas, toss her over!

JUDAS *throws* LAURA *over back of pier.* RAY *enters* L. *Boys all get on pier and surround* BYKE, *fighting him.* Officers *enter at* L. RAY *leaps into water after* LAURA.

CURTAIN.
MOONLIGHT ON DURING SCENE.

ACT IV.

No carpet.

SCENE I.[34] *Long Branch. Ground floor of an elegant residence – open windows from floor to ceiling at back – opening upon a balcony or promenade. Perspective of the shore and sea in distance. Doors* R. *and* L. *Sunset.*

As the curtain rises to lively music, from R. *enter* PEARL, MRS. VAN DAM, SUE EARLIE, *and other ladies in summer costume,* DEMILT *and* WINDEL *with them.*

---

34. Annotations in **PRT** indicate that this scene was edited differently for separate performances. One set makes detailed textual alterations and *el* additions, but other marks cross through the scene entirely.

PEARL. And so the distinguished foreigner is in love with me? I thought he looked excessively solemn at the hop last night. Do you know I can't imagine a more serious spectacle than a Frenchman or an Italian in love. One always imagines them to be sick. (*To* MRS. VAN DAM) Do fasten my glove – there's a dear.

MRS. VAN DAM. Where's Ray?

PEARL. O, he's somewhere! I never saw such another. Isn't he cheerful? He never smiles, and seldom talks.

MRS. VAN DAM. But the foreigner does. What an ecstasy he was in over your singing; sing us a verse won't you, while we're waiting for Ray.

ALL. It will be delightful – do.

PEARL. Well!

[*Song introduced.*

(Air; *When the war is over, Mary.*)

I.

Now the summer days are fading,
Autumn sends its dreary blast
Moaning through the silent forest
Where the leaves are falling fast.
Soon dread winter will enfold us –
Chilling in its arras of snow,
Flowers that the summer cherished,
Birds that sing, and streams that flow.

II.

Say, shall all things droop and wither,
That are born this summer day?
Shall the happy love it brought us –
Like the flowers fade away?
No; be still thou flutt'ring bosom –
Seasons change and years glide by,
They may not harm what is immortal –
Darling, – love shall never die!

PEARL. Now, I've sung that to Ray a dozen times, and he never even said it was nice. He hasn't any soul for music; O, dear! What a creature.

MRS. VAN DAM. Yes, and what a victim you will be with a husband who has $60,000 per annum income.

PEARL. That's some comfort, isn't it?

RAY. (*Enters* L. H. *bowing to others.*) Going out, Pearl?

PEARL. Yes, we're off to Shrewsbury. Quite a party's going – four carriages – and we mean to stay and ride home by moonlight.

RAY. Couldn't you return a little earlier?

MRS. VAN DAM. Earlier! Pshaw! What's in you Ray? (*The ladies and gent. go up.*)

RAY. (PEARL, C.) You know that Laura will be quite alone, and she is still suffering.

PEARL. Well, she'll read and read, as she always did, and never miss me.

RAY. But, at least, she ought to have some little attention.

PEARL. Dear, dear, what an unreasonable fellow you are. Isn't she happy now – didn't you save her from drowning, and haven't I been as good to her as I can be – what more do you want?

RAY. I don't like to hear you talk so Pearl, and remember what she and you were once. And you know that she was something else once – something that you are now to me. And yet how cheerful, how gentle she is. She has lost everything and does not complain.

PEARL. Well, what a sermon! There, I know you're hurt and I'm a fool. But I can't help it. People say she's good-looking, but she's got no heart! I'd give anything for one, but they ain't to be bought.

RAY. Well don't moan about it, I didn't mean to reprove you.

PEARL. But you do reprove me. I'm sure I haven't been the cause of Laura's troubles. I didn't tell the big, ugly man to come and take her away, although I was once glad he did.

RAY. Pearl!

PEARL. Because I thought I had gained you by it. (RAY *turns away.*) But now I've got you, I don't seem to make you happy. But I might as well complain that you don't make me happy – but I don't complain, I am satisfied, and I want you to be satisfied. There, are you satisfied?

MRS. VAN DAM. (*Who with others has been promenading up and down balcony.*) Here are the carriages.

PEARL. I'm coming. Can't you get me my shawl Ray? (RAY *gets it from chair.*)

MRS. VAN DAM. And here's your foreign admirer on horseback.

[SUE EARLIE, DEMILT *and* WINDEL, *exit.*

PEARL. (*Up stage* C.) Bye, bye, Ray. (*Exit.*)

MRS. VAN DAM. Are you not coming Ray?

RAY. I? No!

MRS. VAN DAM. Do come on horseback, here's a horse ready for you.

PEARL. (*Without.*) Ray, Ray.

MRS. VAN DAM. Pearl's calling you. Be quick or Count Carom will be before you, and hand her in the carriage.

RAY. (*Taking his hat slowly.*) O, by all means, let the Count have some amusement.

MRS. VAN DAM. (*Taking* RAY's *arm.*) You're a perfect icicle.

[*They Exit.*

Noise of whips and laughter. Plaintive music as LAURA *enters.*
L., goes to C. *and gazes out at them.*

LAURA. Poor Pearl. It is a sad thing to want for happiness, but it is a terrible thing to see another groping about blindly for it when it is almost within the grasp. And yet she can be very happy with him. Her sunny temper, and her joyous face will brighten any home. (*Sits at table* C., *on which are books.*) How happy I feel to be alone with these friends, who are ever ready to talk to me – with no longings for what I may not have, – my existence hidden from all, save two in the wide world, and making my joy out of the joy of that innocent child who will soon be his wife.

>PEACHBLOSSOM *appears at back looking in cautiously,*
>*grotesquely attired.*

PEACHBLOSSOM. If you please.

LAURA. (*Aloud.*) Who is there?

PEACHBLOSSOM. (*Running in window* F.) O, it's Miss Nina! O, I'm so glad. I've had such a hunt for you. Don't ask me nothing yet. I'm so happy. I've been looking for you so long, and I've had such hard luck. Lord what a tramp – miles on miles.

LAURA. Did anyone see you come here? How did you find me?

PEACHBLOSSOM. I asked 'em at the Hotel where Mr. Trafford was, and they said at Courtland's and I asked 'em where Courtland's was, and they said down the shore, and I walked down lookin' at every place till I came here.

LAURA. Speak low Blossom. My existence is a secret, and no one must hear you.

PEACHBLOSSOM. Well, Miss, I says to Snorkey – says I –

LAURA. Is he with you?

PEACHBLOSSOM. No Miss, but we are great friends. He wants me to keep house for him some day. I said to him – "I want to find out where Miss Nina's gone," and so he went to Mr. Trafford's and found he was come to Long Branch, but never a word could we hear of you.

LAURA. And the others – those dreadful people.

PEACHBLOSSOM. Byke and Old Judas? Clean gone! They hasn't been seen since they was took up for throwing you in the water, and let off because no one came to Court agin 'em. Bermudas says he's seen 'em in Barnum's wax-work show, but Bermudas is such a liar. He brought me up here.

LAURA. Brought you up here.

PEACHBLOSSOM. Yes, he sells papers at Stetson's; he's got the exclusive trade here, and he has a little wagon and a horse, and goes down to the junction every night to catch the extras from the Express train what don't come here. He says he'll give me lots of nice rides if I'll stay here.

LAURA. But you must not stay here. You must go back to New York this very evening.

PEACHBLOSSOM. Back! No I won't.

LAURA. Blossom.

PEACHBLOSSOM. I won't, I won't, I won't! I'll never let you away again. I did it once and you was took away and dragged about and chucked overboard and almost drowned. I won't be any trouble, indeed I won't. I'll hire out at the hotel, and run over when my work is done at night, when nobody can see me, to look up at your window. Don't send me away. You're the only one as ever was good to me.

LAURA. (*Aside.*) It's too dangerous. She certainly would reveal me sooner or later. I must send her back.

PEACHBLOSSOM. Besides I've got something to tell you. Dreadful! Dreadful! About Old Judas and Byke – a secret.

LAURA. A secret? What in the world are you saying?

PEACHBLOSSOM. Is it wicked to listen at doors when people talk?

LAURA. It is very wicked.

PEACHBLOSSOM. Well, I suppose that's why I did it. I used to listen to Byke and Judas when they used to talk about a rich lady whom they called Mrs. Courtland.

LAURA. Ah!

PEACHBLOSSOM. Judas used to be a nurse at Mrs. Courtland's, and was turned off for stealing. And wasn't she and Byke going to make money off her! And Byke was to pretend to be some beautiful lady's father. Then, when they took you, Judas says to me: "Did you ever hear of children being changed in their cradles?" – and that you wasn't her child, but she was going to make money off the real one at the proper time."

LAURA. What do you tell me?

PEACHBLOSSOM. Oh! I'm not crazy. I know a heap, don't I? And I want you to think I'm somebody, and not send me away –

LAURA. (*To herself.*) She must speak the truth. And yet if I were to repeat her strange words here, I should be suspected of forging some tale to abuse the ear of Society. No! Better let it rest as it is. She must go – and I must go too.

PEACHBLOSSOM. You ain't mad with me?

LAURA. No, no; but you must go away from here. Go back to the hotel to your friend – anywhere, and wait for me; I will come to you.

PEACHBLOSSOM. Is it a promise?

LAURA. (*Nervously.*) Yes, go.

PEACHBLOSSOM. Then I'll go; for I know you always keep your word – you ain't angry, cause I came after you? I did it because I loved you – because I wanted to see you put in the right place. Honour bright, you ain't sending me away now? Well, I'll go; goodbye!

[*Exit* C.

LAURA. (*Animated.*) I must return to the city, no matter what dangers may lurk there. It is dangerous enough to be concealed here, with a hundred Argus-eyed women about me every day, but with this girl, detection would be certain. I must go – secretly if I can – openly if I must.

RAY. (*Outside.*) No, I shall not ride again. Put him up. (*Entering.*) Laura, I knew I should find you here.

LAURA. (*Sitting and pretending composure.*) I thought you had gone with Pearl.

RAY. I did go part of the way, but I left the party a mile down the road.

LAURA. You and Pearl had no disagreement?

RAY. No – yes; that is, we always have. Our social barometer always stands at "cloudy" and "overcast."

LAURA. (*Rising.*) And whose fault is that?

RAY. (*Pettishly.*) Not mine. I know I do all I can – I say all I can – but she – (*Crossing.*)

LAURA. But she is to be your wife. Ray – my friend – courtship is the text from which the whole solemn sermon of married life takes its theme. Do not let yours be discontented and unhappy.

RAY. To be my wife; yes. In a moment of foolishness, dazzled by her airs, and teased by her coquettishness, I asked her to be my wife.

LAURA. And you repent already?

RAY. (*Taking her hand.*) I lost you, and I was at the mercy of any flirt that chose to give me an inviting look. It was your fault – you know it was! Why did you leave me?

LAURA. (*After conflict with her feelings.*) Ray, the greatest happiness I have ever felt has been the thought that all your affections were forever bestowed upon a virtuous lady, your equal in family, fortune and accomplishments. What a revelation do you make to me, now! What is it makes you continually war with your happiness?

RAY. I don't know what it is, I was wrong to accuse you. Forgive me! I have only my own cowardice to blame for my misery.[35] But Pearl –

---

35. 'Pearl enters at back unobserved' at this point in **PRT** (p. 48/*el*). Here, she remains unperceived, but her entrance triggers the action in a new scene added after IV.ii: Pearl chooses to release Ray from their engagement and makes him promise to marry Laura instead. The new scene reinforces Pearl's softer characterisation in this version. Although she delivers a couple of humorous quips, the majority of her dialogue is moralistic: 'I will not permit that dear girl's generous sacrifice' (*el*). The new scene also permits Ray to appear in a more positive light, as he eagerly agrees to marry Laura before he is told that she is a lady by birth.

LAURA. You must not accuse her.

RAY. When you were gone, she seemed to have no thought – no wish – but for my happiness. She constantly invited me to her house, and when I tried to avoid her, met me at every turn. Was she altogether blameless?

LAURA. Yes, it was her happiness she sought, and she had a right to seek it.

RAY. Oh! Men are the veriest fools on earth; a little attention, a little sympathy, and they are caught, – caught by a thing without soul or brains, while some noble woman is forsaken and forgotten.

LAURA. (RAY *throws himself into a seat.*) Ray will you hear me?

RAY. (*Looking to her hopefully.*) Yes, speak to me as you used to speak. Be to me as you used to be.

LAURA. (*Smiling sadly.*) I cannot be that to you, but I can speak as the spirit of the Laura who is dead to you forever.

RAY. Be it as you will.

LAURA. (*Standing beside him.*) Let the woman you look upon be wise or vain, beautiful or homely, rich or poor, she has but one thing she can really give or refuse – her heart! Her beauty, her wit, her accomplishments, she may sell to you – but her love is the treasure without money and without price.

RAY. How well I have learned that.

LAURA. She only asks in return, that when you look upon her, your eyes shall speak a mute devotion; that when you address her, your voice shall be gentle, loving and kind. That you shall not despise her, because she cannot understand, all at once, your vigorous thoughts and ambitious designs; for when misfortune and evil have defeated your greatest purposes – her love remains to console you. You look to the trees for strength and grandeur – do not despise the flowers, because their fragrance is all they have to give. Remember, – love is all a woman has to give; but it is the only earthly thing which God permits us to carry beyond the grave.

RAY. (*Rising.*) You are right. You are always right. I asked Pearl to be my wife, knowing what she was, and I will be just to her. I will do my duty though it break my heart.

LAURA. Spoken like a hero.

RAY. But it is to you I owe the new light that guides me; and I will tell her –

LAURA. Tell her nothing – never speak of me. And when you see her, say to her it is she, and she alone, whom you consult and to whom you listen.

RAY. And you –

LAURA. You will see me no more.

RAY. You will leave me?

LAURA. Something of me will always be with you – my parting words – my prayers for your happiness. (*Distant music heard.*)

RAY. (*Falling on his knees.*) O, Laura, you leave me to despair.

LAURA (C.) No; to the happiness which follows duty well performed. Such happiness as I feel in doing mine.

PICTURE.

Scene closes in. During last of this scene the sun has set,
and night come on. Stage dark.

SCENE II. – *Woods near Shrewsbury Station – Night.*

Enter BYKE *shabbily dressed,* L. 1 E.

BYKE. It's getting darker and darker, and I'm like to lose my way. Where the devil is Judas? It must be nine o'clock, and she was to be at the bend with the wagon half an hour ago. (*Rumble of wheels heard.*) Humph – at last.

JUDAS. (*Entering L.*) Is that you Byke?

BYKE. Who did you suppose it was? I've been tramping about the wet grass for an hour.

JUDAS. It was a hard job to get the horse and wagon.

BYKE. Give me a match. (*Lights pipe and leans against a tree.*) Did you get the bearings of the crib?

JUDAS. Yes, it is on the shore, well away from the other cottages and hotels.

BYKE. That's good. Nothing like peace and quietness. Who's in the house?

JUDAS. Only the two girls and the servants.

BYKE. How many of them?

JUDAS. Four.

BYKE. It'll be mere child's play to go through that house. Have you spied about the swag?

JUDAS. They have all their diamonds and jewels there; Pearl wears them constantly; they're the talk of the whole place.[36]

BYKE. We'll live in luxury off that girl all our lives. She'll settle a handsome thing on us, won't she? When she knows what we know, and pays us to keep dark; – if t'other one don't spoil the game.

JUDAS. Curse her! I could cut her throat.

BYKE. O, I'll take care of that!

JUDAS. You always do things for the best, dear old Byke!

BYKE. Of course I do. What time is it?

---

36. The scene is rewritten in **PRT** from this point on. Characters secure proof (trinkets and a letter) that Laura's real parents are aristocratic (given that the cradle-swapping storyline is removed in this version).

JUDAS. Not ten yet.

BYKE. An hour to wait.

JUDAS. But, Byke, you won't peach on me before my little pet is married, will you?

BYKE. What's the fool about now?

JUDAS. I can't help trembling; nothing is safe while Laura is there.

BYKE. I've provided for that. I've had the same idea as you; – while she's in the way, and Ray unmarried, our plans are all smoke, and we might as well be sitting on the hob with a keg of powder in the coals.

JUDAS. That we might. But what have you thought to do?

BYKE. Why, I've thought what an unfortunate creature Laura is, – robbed of her mother, her home, and her lover; nothing to live for; it would be a mercy to put her out of the way.

JUDAS. That's it; but how – how – how –

BYKE. It's plain she wasn't born to be drowned, or the materials are very handy down here. What made you talk about cutting her throat? It was very wrong; when a thing gets into my head, it sticks there.

JUDAS. You oughtn't to mind me.

BYKE. Make your mind easy on that score.

JUDAS. (*Alarmed.*) Byke, I heard someone in the bushes just there. (*Points off* R.)

BYKE. (*Nervously and quickly.*) Who? Where? (*Going* R.)

JUDAS. Where the hedge is broken. I could swear I saw the shadow of a man.

BYKE. Stop here. I'll see.

[*Off* R.

JUDAS. (*Solus.*) I begin to shiver. But it must be done or we starve. Why should I tremble? It's the safest job we ever planned. If they discover us, our secret will save us; – we know too much to be sent to jail.

Re-enter BYKE, *slowly.*

BYKE. There are traces, but I can see no one. (*Looking off* R.)

JUDAS. Suppose we should have been overheard!

BYKE. (*Glaring at her.*) Overheard? Bah! No one could understand.

JUDAS. Come, let us go to the wagon and be off.

BYKE. (*Always looking off* R.) Go you, I will follow. Bring it round by the station, and wait for me in the shadows of the trees. I will follow. (JUDAS *goes off* L. BYKE, *after a moment, – still looking* R., – *buttons up his coat, and hides behind wood,* R. H.) Heigho! I must be off.

Enter SNORKEY, *slowly,* R.

SNORKEY. Tracked 'em again! We're the latest fashionable arrivals at Long-Branch. "Mr. Byke and Lady, and Brigadier-General Snorkey, of New-York"; – there's an item for the papers! With a horse and wagon, they'll be at the seaside in two hours; but in the train I think I'll beat 'em. Then to find Cap'n Trafford, and give him the wink, and be ready to receive the distinguished visitors with all the honours. Robbery; Burglary; Murder; – that's Byke's catechism: – "What's to be done when you're hard up? Steal! What's to be done if you're caught at it? Kill!" It's short and easy, and he lives up to it like a good many Christians don't live up to their laws. (*Looking off* L.) They're out of sight. Phew! It's midsummer, but I'm chilled to the bone; something like a piece of ice has been stuck between my shoulders all day, and something like a black mist is always before me. (BYKE *is behind tree.*) Just like old Nettly told me he felt, the night before Fredericksburg; – and next day he was past all feeling, – hit with a shell, and knocked into so many pieces, I didn't know which to call my old friend. Well, (*slapping his chest,*) we've all got to go; and if I can save them, I'll have some little capital to start the next world on. The next world! Perhaps I shan't be the maimed beggar there that I am in this. (*Takes out pistol, examines cap; goes off* L., BYKE *gliding after him.*)

———————

SCENE III. – *Railroad Station at Shrewsbury Bend. Up* R. *the Station shed* R. H. *Platform around it, and door at side, window in front. At* L. L. E. *clump of shrubs and tree. The Railroad track runs from* L. 4 E. *to* R. 4 E. *View of Shrewsbury River in perspective. Night, Moonlight. The switch, with a red lantern and Signalman's coat hanging on it* L. C. *The Signal lamp and post beside it.*

As the scene opens, several packages are lying about the Stage, among them a bundle of axes. The Signalman is wheeling in a small barrel from L. *whistling at his work.*

Enter LAURA *in walking dress, coming feebly from* L. U. E.

LAURA. It is impossible for me to go further. A second time I've fled from home and friends, but now they will never find me. The trains must all have passed, and there are no conveyances till tomorrow. (*She sits at clump* L. U. E.)

SIGNALMAN. Beg pardon, ma'am, looking for anybody?

LAURA. Thank you, no. Are you the man in charge of this station?

SIGNALMAN. Yes, ma'am.

LAURA. When is there another train for New York?

SIGNALMAN. New York? Not till morning. We've only one more train tonight; that's the down one; it'll be here in about twenty minutes – "Express Train."

LAURA. What place is that?

SIGNALMAN. That? That's the signal station shed. It serves for store-room, depot, baggage-room, and everything.

LAURA. Can I stay there tonight?

SIGNALMAN. There? Well it's an odd place, and I should think you would hardly like it. Why don't you go to the hotel?

LAURA. I have my reasons – urgent ones. It is not because I want money. You shall have this (*producing portemonnaie*) if you let me remain here.

SIGNALMAN. Well, I've locked up a good many things in there over night, but I never had a young lady for freight before. Besides ma'am, I don't know anything about you. You know it's odd that you won't go to a decent hotel, and plenty of money in your pocket.

LAURA. You refuse me – well – I shall only have to sit here all night.

SIGNALMAN. Here in the open air? Why it would kill you.

LAURA. So much the better.

SIGNALMAN. Excuse me for questions, Miss, but you're a running away from someone, ain't you?

LAURA. Yes.

SIGNALMAN. Well, I'd like to help you. I'm a plain man you know, and I'd like to help you, but there's one thing it would go agin' me to assist in. (LAURA *interested*.) I'm on to fifty years of age, and I've many children, some on 'em daughters grown. There's a-many temptations for young gals, and sometimes the old man has to put on the brakes a bit, for some young men are wicked enough to persuade the gals to steal out of their father's house in the dead of night, and go to shame and misery. So tell me this – it ain't the old man, and the old man's home you've left, young lady?

LAURA. No; you good, honest, fellow – no – I have no father.

SIGNALMAN. Then by Jerusalem! I'll do for you what I can. Anything but run away from them, that have not their interest but yours at heart. Come, you may stay there, but I'll have to lock you in.

LAURA. I desire that you should.

SIGNALMAN. It's for your safety as much as mine. I've got a patent lock on that door that would give a skeleton key the rheumatism to fool with it. You don't mind the baggage. I'll have to put it in with you, hoes, shovels, mowing machines and what's this – axes. Yes a bundle of axes. If the Superintendent finds me out, I'll ask him if he was afraid you'd run off with these. (*Laughs.*) So if you please I'll first tumble 'em in. (*Puts goods in house,* LAURA *sitting on platform R. H. looking at him. When all in, he comes towards her, taking up cheese-box to put it in Station.*) I say Miss, I ain't curious – but of course it's a *young man* you're a going to?

LAURA. So far from that, it's a young man I'm running away from.

SIGNALMAN. (*Dropping box.*) Running away from a young man! Let me shake hands with you. (*Shakes her hand.*) Lord, it does my heart good! At your age too! (*Seriously.*) I wish you'd come and live down in my neighbourhood a while, among my gals. (*Shaking his head.*) You'd do a power of good. (*Putting box in station.*)

LAURA. I've met an excellent friend. And here at least I can be concealed until tomorrow; – then for New York. My heart feels lighter already – it's a good omen.

SIGNALMAN. Now Miss, bless your heart, here's your hotel ready.

> [*Goes to switch and takes coat off, putting it on.*

LAURA. Thanks my good friend; but not a word to anyone – till tomorrow; not even – not even to your girls.

SIGNALMAN. Not a word, I promise you. If I told my girls it would be over the whole village before morning. (*She goes in. He locks door. LAURA appears at window facing audience.*)

LAURA. Lock me in safely.

SIGNALMAN. Ah! Be sure I will. There! (*Tries door.*) Safe as a jail. (*Pulls out watch, and then looking at track with lantern.*) Ten minutes and down she comes. It's all safe this way my noisy beauty, and you may come as soon as you like. Goodnight, Miss!

LAURA. (*At window.*) Goodnight.

SIGNALMAN. Running away from a young man, Ha! ha! ha!

He goes to track, then looks down R. – lights his pipe and is trudging off R., then enter SNORKEY from L. U. E.

SNORKEY. Ten minutes before the train comes. I'll wait here for it. (*To SIGNALMAN who re-enters.*) Hollo I say, the train won't stop here too long will it?

SIGNALMAN. Too long? It won't stop here at all.

SNORKEY. I must reach the shore tonight. There'll be murder done, unless I can prevent it!

SIGNALMAN. Murder, or no murder, the train can't be stopped.

SNORKEY. It's a lie. By waving the red signal for danger, the engineer must stop, I tell you!

SIGNALMAN. Do you think I'm a fool? What? Disobey orders and lose my place; then what's to become of my family?

[*Exit* R. U. E.

SNORKEY. I won't be foiled. I will confiscate some farmer's horse about here, and get there before them somehow. (BYKE *enters at back with loose coil of rope in his hand.*) Then when Byke arrives in his donkey cart he'll be ready to sit for a picture of surprise. (BYKE *enters* L. U. E. *suddenly throwing the coil over* SNORKEY.)

BYKE. Will he?

SNORKEY. Byke!

BYKE. Yes, Byke. Where's that pistol of yours? (*Tightening rope round his arm.*)

SNORKEY. In my breast pocket.

BYKE. (*Taking it.*) Just what I wanted.

SNORKEY. You ain't a going to shoot me?

BYKE. No!

SNORKEY. Well, I'm obliged to you for that.

BYKE. (*Leading him to platform.*) Just sit down a minute will you.

SNORKEY. What for? (LAURA *appears horror struck at window.*)

BYKE. You'll see.

SNORKEY. Well, I don't mind if I do take a seat. (*Sits down.* BYKE *coils the rope round his legs.*) Hollo! What's this?

BYKE. You'll see. (*Picks the helpless* SNORKEY *up.*)

SNORKEY. Byke what are you going to do?

BYKE. Put you to bed. (*Lays him across the R. R. track.*)

SNORKEY. Byke, you don't mean to – . My God, you are a villain!

BYKE. (*Fastening him to rails.*[37]) I'm going to put you to bed. You won't toss much. In less than ten minutes you'll be sound asleep. There, how do you like it? You'll get down to the Branch before me, will you? You dog me and play the eavesdropper, eh! Now do it if you can. When you hear the thunder under your head and see the lights dancing in your eyes, and feel the iron wheels a foot from your neck, remember Byke!

[*Exit* L. H. E.

LAURA. O, Heavens! he will be murdered before my eyes! How can I aid him?

SNORKEY. Who's that?

LAURA. It is I. Do you not know my voice?

SNORKEY. That I do; but I almost thought I was dead, and it was an angel's. Where are you?[38]

37. *The Life of Augustin Daly* describes the first performance: 'On the first night the audience was breathless. In spite of many drawbacks, – the insufficiency of the stage, the nervousness of the stage hands, and all the accidents of a first performance, – the play gained its decisive victory. The intensely wrought feelings of the spectators found vent in almost hysterical laughter when the 'railroad train' parted in the middle and disclosed the flying legs of the human motor who was propelling the first half of the express. Had the effect of the scene depended not upon the suspense and emotion created by the whole situation, but upon the machinery, the piece had been irretrievably lost; but the real sensation was beyond chance of accident' (J. F. Daly (1917), p. 75).
38. **PRT** introduces sounds of the approaching train earlier than Daly, heightening tension through repetition. Here: '1st Whistle, com[?]mence to roll on muffled drum, M[idwestern] train passes –' (p. 55/*el*).

LAURA. In the station.

SNORKEY. I can't see you, but I can hear you. Listen to me, Miss, for I've got only a few minutes to live.

LAURA. (*Shaking door*) God help me! and I cannot aid you.

SNORKEY. Never mind me, Miss. I might as well die now, and here, as at any other time. I'm not afraid. I've seen death in almost every shape, and none of them scare me; but, for the sake of those you love, I would live. Do you hear me?[39]

LAURA. Yes! Yes!

SNORKEY. They are on the way to your cottage – Byke and Judas – to rob and murder![40]

LAURA. (*In agony*) O, I must get out! (*Shakes window-bars.*) What shall I do?

SNORKEY. Can't you burst the door?

LAURA. It is locked fast.

SNORKEY. Is there nothing in there? – no hammer? – no crowbar?

LAURA. Nothing! (*Faint steam whistle heard in the distance*) O, Heavens! The train! (*Paralyzed for an instant.*) The axe!!!

SNORKEY. Cut the woodwork! Don't mind the lock – cut round it! How my neck tingles! (*A blow at door is heard*) Courage! (*Another*) Courage! (*The steam whistle heard again – nearer and rumble of train on track. Another blow*) That's a true woman! Courage! (*Noise of locomotive heard – with*

39. **PRT** increases the audience's sense of dread as '2<u>nd</u> Whistle, louder begin to work sand-paper' (p. 55/*el*).
40. Laura is informed of her true parentage as sounds of the approaching train continue to escalate tension in **PRT**: '3<u>rd</u> Whistle, louder, begin to work thunder' (p. 55/*el*).

*whistle. A last blow; the door swings open, mutilated – the lock hanging –
and* LAURA *appears, axe in hand.*)

SNORKEY. Here – quick! (*She runs and unfastens him. The locomotive
lights glare on scene.*) Victory! Saved! Hooray! (LAURA *leans exhausted
against switch.*) And these are the women who ain't to have a vote![41]

> [*As* LAURA *takes his head from the track, the train of cars rushes
> past with roar and whistle from* L. *to* R. H.[42]

ACT V.

SCENE I. – *An elegant boudoir at* COURTLAND'*s cottage, Long Branch;
open window and balcony at back; moonlight exterior; tree overhanging
balcony.*

Bed is at U. E. L.; *toilette table* R.; *arm-chair* C.; *door* L. 2 E.; *lighted
lamp on toilette table; dresses on chair by bed* L. H., *and by window on* R.
(*Music.*)

> PEARL *is discovered* (*en negligée*) *brushing her hair out
> at table* R. H. *before mirror.*

PEARL. I don't feel a bit sleepy. What a splendid drive we had! I like that
foreigner. What an elegant fellow he is! Ray is nothing to him. I wonder if
I'm in love with him? Pshaw! What an idea! I don't believe I could love
anybody much. How sweetly he writes! – (*picks up letter and sits on chair*
C.) "You were more lovely than ever tonight; with one more thing, you'd
be an angel" – Now that's perfectly splendid – "with one more thing,
you'd be an angel" – that one thing is Love. "They tell me Mr. Trafford is
your professed admirer. I'm sure he could never be called your lover – for
he seems incapable of any passion but Melancholy." It's quite true. Ray

---

41. Women's voting rights were not secured in the USA until 1920. This reference to wom-
en's suffrage is deleted in **PRT** (p. 56).
42. The final act is elided in **PRT**. A sentimental ending is inserted at this point, in which
Ray and Laura are united, Byke is taken into custody, and it is reported that Judas has
been killed in a road accident (p. 56/*el*).

does not comprehend me. (*Takes up another letter*) – "Pearl, forgive me if I have been cross and cold. For the future, I will do my duty, as your affianced husband, better." Now, did ever anyone hear such talk as that from a lover? Lover? – O, dear! I begin to feel that he can love, but not me. Well, I'd just as soon break – if he'd be the first to speak. How nice and fresh the air is! – (*she turns down lamp.*) It's much nicer here than going to bed. – (*settles herself in tête-à-tête for a nap. Pause.*)

> [*Moonbeams fall on* BYKE, *who appears above the balcony.*
> *He gets over the rail and enters.*

BYKE. Safely down! I've made no mistake – no, this is her room. What a figure I am for a lady's chamber. (*Goes to table, picks up delicate lace handkerchief, and wipes his face.*) Phew! Hot! (*Puts handkerchief in his pocket.*) Now for my bearings. (*Taking huge clasp-knife from his pocket.*) There's the bed where she's sleeping like a precious infant, and here – (*Sees* PEARL *in chair, and steals round at back, looking down at her.*) It's so dark – I can't recognise the face. It's a wonder she don't feel me in the air and dream of me. If she does she'll wake sure – but it's easy to settle that. (*Takes phial of chloroform from his pocket – saturates the handkerchief he picked up, and applies it.*) So! – now my charmer – we'll have the earrings. (*Takes them out.*) What's here? (*Going to table.*) Bracelets – diamonds! (*Going to dresses, and feeling in the pockets.*) Money! That's handy. (*He puts all in a bag, and hands them over balcony.*) Now for the drawers, there's where the treasure must be. Locked? (*Tries them with bunch of keys.*) Patent lock, of course! It amuses me to see people buying patent locks, when there's one key will fit 'em all. (*Produces small crowbar, and just as he is about to force the drawer, a shout is heard, and noise of wagon.*) What's that? (*Jumps, catching at bureau, which falls over.*) Damnation!

PEARL. (*Starting up*) Who's there? What's that?

BYKE. Silence or I'll kill you!

PEARL. Help! Help!

BYKE. (*Running to bureau for knife.*) You will have it my pretty one. (PEARL *runs to door* L.)

PEARL. Save me! Save me! (BYKE *pursues her, the door bursts open and* RAY *and* LAURA *enter.* BYKE *turns and runs to balcony, and confronts* SNORKEY *and* BERMUDAS, *who have clambered over.*)

LAURA. Just in time.

RAY. (*Seizing* BYKE.) Scoundrel.

SNORKEY. Hold him, Governor! Hold him. (*Assists* RAY *to bind* BYKE *in chair* R. H.)

BERMUDAS. Sixty-sixth and last round. The big 'un floored, and Bermudas as fresh as a daisy.

PEARL. Dear, dear Laura, you have saved me.

RAY. Yes, Pearl; from more than you can tell.

LAURA. No, no, her saviours are there. (*Pointing to* BERMUDAS *and* SNORKEY.) Had it not been for the one, I should never have learned your danger, and but for the other, we could never have reached you in time.

SNORKEY. Bermudas and his fourth editions did it. Business enterprise and Bermudas' pony express worked the oracle this time.

BERMUDAS. The way we galloped! Sa-ay, my pony must have thought the extras was full of lively intelligence.

PEARL. Darling Laura, you shall never leave us again.

RAY. No! Never.

SNORKEY. Beg pardon, Cap'n, what are we to do with this here game we've brought down?

RAY. The Magistrates shall settle with him.

SNORKEY. Come old fellow.

BYKE. One word, I beg. My conduct I know, has been highly reprehensible. I have acted injudiciously, and have been the occasion of more or less inconvenience to everyone here. But I wish to make amends, and therefore I tender you all in this public manner my sincere apologies. I trust this will be entirely satisfactory.

RAY. Villain!

BYKE. I have a word to say to you sir.

SNORKEY. Come, that's enough.

BYKE. My good fellow, don't interrupt gentlemen who are conversing together. (*To* RAY.) I address you, sir – you design to commit me to the care of the officers of the law?

RAY. Most certainly.

BYKE. And you will do your best towards having me incarcerated in the correctional establishments of this country? (RAY *bows.*)

SNORKEY. How very genteel!

BYKE. Then I have to say if you will, I shall make a public exposure of certain matters connected to a certain young lady.

LAURA. Do not think that will deter us from your punishment. I can bear even more than I have – for the sake of justice.

BYKE. Excuse me, but I did not even remotely refer to you.

LAURA. To whom, then?

BYKE. (*Pointing to* PEARL.) To her.

RAY. Miss Courtland?

BYKE. O, dear! No, sir. The daughter of old Judas – the spurious child placed in your cradle. Miss Laura Courtland, when you were abducted from it by your nurse.

PEARL. What does he say?

BYKE. That you're a beggar's child – we have the proofs! Deliver me to prison, and I produce them.

RAY. Wretch!

PEARL. Then it's you, dear Laura, have been wronged – while –

LAURA. You are my sister still – whatever befalls!

PEARL. I'm so glad it's so! Ray won't want to marry me, now – at least, I hope so; for I know he loves you – he always loved you – and you will be happy together.

RAY. Pearl, what are you saying?

PEARL. Don't interrupt me! I mean every word of it. Laura I've been very foolish, I know. I ought to have tried to reunite you – but there is time.

RAY. Dear Laura! Is there, indeed, still time? (*She gives her hand.*)

BYKE. Allow me to suggest that a certain proposition I had the honour to submit has not yet been answered.

RAY. Release him. (SNORKEY *undoes his cords.*)

BYKE. Thank you – not so rough! Thank you.

RAY. Now, go – but remember, if you ever return to these parts, you shall be tried, not only for this burglary, but for the attempt to kill that poor fellow.

BYKE. Thank you. Goodbye. (*To* SNORKEY.) Goodbye, my dear friend; overlook our little dispute, and write to me. (*Aside.*) They haven't caught Judas, and she shall make them pay handsomely for her silence, yet.[43]

---

43. **RRR** inserts heroic business at this point. Covey attacks Wadlow, and is subsequently tackled by Frank, Sweeds and Post Boy (ff. 50b–51a).

Enter PEACHBLOSSOM, L. 1 E.

PEACHBLOSSOM. Miss! O, such an accident – Old Judas!

LAURA and BYKE. Well?

PEACHBLOSSOM. She was driving along the road away from here – just now, when her horse dashed close to the cliff and tumbled her down all of a heap. They've picked her up, and they tell me she is stone dead.

BYKE. (*Aside*) Dead! And carried her secret with her! All's up. I'll have to emigrate. (*Aloud.*) My friends, pardon my emotion – this melancholy event has made me a widower. I solicit your sympathies in my bereavement.

[*Exit* L.

BERMUDAS. Go to Hoboken[44] and climb a tree! I guess I'll follow him and see he don't pick up anything on his way out.[45]

[*Exit* BERMUDAS, L. E.

SNORKEY. Well there goes a pretty monument of grief. Ain't he a cool 'un? If I ever sets up an ice cream saloon, I'll have him for head freezer.

PEACHBLOSSOM. O, Miss Laura, mayn't I live with you now, and never leave no more?

LAURA. Yes, you shall live with me as long as you please.

SNORKEY. That won't be long if I can help it. (PEACHBLOSSOM *blushes*.) Beg pardon! I suppose we'd better be going! The ladies must be tired Cap'n at this time of night.

RAY. Yes, it is night! It is night always for me. (*Moving towards door* L.)

LAURA. (*Placing one hand on his shoulder, taking his hand.*) But there is a tomorrow. You see it cannot be dark forever.

44. A city in Hudson County, New Jersey.
45. **RRR** refuses to offer a clear resolution, and perhaps hints at the possibility of a sequel. Covey says: 'a few years I hope to ~~return~~ resume my acquaintance with you when the work I now leave undone will probably be accomplished – so not farewell but au revoir my friends' (ff. 51a–b).

PEARL. Hope for tomorrow Ray.

LAURA. We shall have cause to bless it, for it will bring the long sought sunlight of our lives.[46]

CURTAIN.

R. SNORKEY. LAURA. RAY. PEARL. PEACHBLOSSOM. L. H.

---

46. Unlike in **PRT** and Daly's script, **RRR** ends with Frank placed centre stage as the hero, while May and Kate [Pearl] are silent.

THE ILLUSTRATED

SPORTING & DRAMATIC

· NEWS ·

REGISTERED AT THE GENERAL POST-OFFICE FOR TRANSMISSION ABROAD.

No. 4.—VOL. I. SATURDAY, MARCH 21, 1874. PRICE SIXPENCE.
By Post, 6½d.

Holborn oct 6 1872

MRS. HERMANN VEZIN IN "MISS CHESTER."

(Drawn by W. R. Buckman, from a Photograph by Messrs. Downey & Co.)

Figure 5 'Mrs Hermann Vezin in "Miss Chester"', *The Illustrated Sporting & Dramatic News*, Saturday, 21 March 1874. Theatre and Performance Archive, V&A, London.

MISS CHESTER[1,2]

A Drama in Three Acts

BY FLORENCE MARRYAT
and
SIR CHARLES YOUNG, BART.[3]

LONDON: SAMUEL FRENCH,
Publisher,
89, Strand

NEW YORK: SAMUEL FRENCH & SON,
Publishers,
122, Nassau Street.[4]

First performed at the Holborn Theatre (under the management of
Joseph Fell, Esq) on Saturday, October 6th 1872.[5]

1. Variants discussed in the notes are:
   LCC: British Library, Lord Chamberlain's Collection. Add MS 53112 C.
   The deposit copy states 'The property of Sir Charles L Young, Bart, 84 Inverness Terrace,
   Kensington Gardens.' It was read on 2 October 1872.
   V&A: Victoria & Albert Theatre and Performance Archive, PLAYS/MAR/PROMPT.
   This is a promptbook owned by William Cuthbert, not a member of the original cast.
2. In **LCC**, a subtitle has been given but crossed out and rendered indecipherable (f. 2).
3. Young's reputation as a playwright seems to have suffered from class bias against his
   inherited title (baronet). He rebuked such critics in print: 'From the tone that has been
   adopted recently by some of my critics, it really would seem as if I had personally
   offended them by presuming to attempt to write a drama at all [. . .]. I am not repentant,
   and I see no sufficient reason at present why I should not pursue my career' (qtd in Young
   (1873), p. 320).
4. *French's Acting Edition of Plays, Dramas, Extravaganzas, Farces, etc. etc. as performed
   at various theatres*, vol. 104, contains fifteen other dramas too, including *Charms*, also
   by Charles Young.
5. Frequent changes in management and ownership mark the history of the Holborn Theatre. See Howard (1970), p. 114. During the 1860s it had frequently featured equestrian
   and acrobatic acts, but the early 1870s saw a turn towards drama and the Holborn followed standard practice in presenting several pieces each evening. *Miss Chester* was
   'Preceded by a new farce, called A FALSE ALARM; and followed by the popular farce
   of SLASHER AND CRASHER' (Anon. (1872a), *Bell's Life in London and Sporting
   Chronical*, 19 Oct., p. 2).

CAST OF CHARACTERS.

EARL OF MONTRESSOR ...

Mr. Sydney Dyneley.

RUPERT ...

Mr. Lin Rayne.

ARMISHAW ...

Mr. Alfred Young.

MICHAEL FORTESCUE ...

Mr. John Nelson.

PIETI ...

Mr. Reeves.

VICENZI ...

Mr. Bennett.

VITOZZI ...

Mr. E. Hastings, Jun.

HENRY ...

Mr. R. Barrier.

MISS CHESTER ...

Mrs. Hermann Vezin.[6]

ISABEL, *an orphan. The Countess's niece and Ward* ...

Miss Edith Bertram.

COUNTESS OF MONTRESSOR ...

Mrs. St. Henry.[7]

———————

6. Jane (Eliza) Vezin premiered on the stage in 1857 under her first husband's name (Mrs Charles Young). On her divorce and remarriage, she was usually billed as Mrs Hermann Vezin and often played alongside her actor husband. The presence of such a well-known and experienced actor flavoured critical reactions in the press. For example, while the *Athenaeum* reviewer found the other characters insipid, 'Miss Chester has, however, abundant vitality and her rich and soured nature is cleverly described. This character found an admirable exponent in Mrs. Vezin, and to the force of her acting was due in a large measure the success of the piece, for successful it must be pronounced' (Anon. (1872b), 'Holborn Theatre', *Athenaeum*, 12 Oct., p. 476. See also Fig. 5 on p. 252).
7. In **LCC**, the Italian gentlemen are not listed individually (f. 2).

S C E N E R Y:–

ACT I.
Exterior of Castle Montressor.

ACT II.
Cascine Gardens at Bryano, Florence.

ACT III.
Drawing room at Castle Montressor.[8]

Costumes – Modern.

—————

8. *Bell's Life in London and Sporting Chronical* advertises 'The new and beautiful scenery by Julian Hicks' as one of the attractions of the piece (Anon., (1872a), 19 Oct., p. 2). *Punch* actually makes fun of the tasteless wallpaper displayed in the interior of Montressor Castle in 'Our Representative Man' (Anon., (1872c), 2 Nov., p. 185).

ACT I.[9]

SCENE. – *Gardens at Castle Montressor. Castle door on* R. *of stage; steps down from garden terrace* C., *distant view from terrace* L.; *thick shrubbery.*[10]

Enter by steps from castle, LORD MONTRESSOR, *followed by a servant.*

MONTRESSOR. And you have seen Miss Vivian nowhere?[11]

SERVANT. Not in the house, my Lord.

MONTRESSOR. If she should come in by the front door, let me know.

SERVANT. Yes, my Lord. (*Exit* SERVANT R.)

MONTRESSOR. I cannot stand this state of suspense. I must know my fate, I am quite sure she is very fond of me, but is she fond enough to become my wife? She treats me as if I were her brother. I can bear it no longer. My mother shall join her entreaties to mine, come what may.

> MONTRESSOR *goes out by terrace* C. *to* L., *when he is off stage*
> MICHAEL FORTESCUE *pushes his way through the shrubs* L.
> *but does not come out upon the stage, he contemplates*
> *the scene with a half-smile.*

FORTESCUE. Humph! Foliage in the shrubbery rather thicker than it used to be, and a trifle more of ivy and creepers about the walls. Otherwise, not much change here in three-and-twenty years. Can it really be so long as that? Now, if I carried about me anything so inconvenient as a heart, I suppose I should become rather sentimental. Shed a tear or two, perhaps, to wet the green that grows upon the mound that hides the past. I wonder if

---

9. **V&A** is marked by a stamp here reading 'William Cuthbert. Low comedian & character actor'. Cuthbert may have played the comic character Armishaw in the play but no records to confirm this have been found.
10. **LCC** gives slightly different staging: 'Scene: Gardens at Castle Montressor – Castle door on L of stage – steps down from open garden door. C distant views from terrace. L-R thick shrubbery' (f. 3). The amendments to these and further stage directions in the first scene may be the result of adjustments when rehearsing on stage, indicating that the **LCC** copy was not written purely for deposit.
11. Isabel is given the more formal name 'Miss Vivian' here and again late in the play. Michael Fortescue is also referred to by the name given in the *dramatis personæ* early on, but this changes to Sir Arthur when his identity is revealed. This double naming is symptomatic of the play's interest in identity as unstable and socially constructed.

I am a fool to come. Well, I have yielded to an impulse which I can't resist. I have long felt that I should like to get something out of this noble family of Montressor after all; and brute instincts are generally right. Someone coming? I must not anticipate a formal introduction. (*Disappears through foliage* R.)

Enter LADY MONTRESSOR *and the* EARL *by terrace* C. *from* L.

LADY MONTRESSOR. My dear Montressor, what is the good of your beating about the bush in this sort of way?[12] You have had something on your mind for days past.

MONTRESSOR. You have remarked it?

LADY MONTRESSOR. Could I fail to do so? I have lavished upon you my best affections, my whole heart, with the exception, of course, of that portion which was naturally due to your lamented father.

MONTRESSOR. And my brother, Rupert.

LADY MONTRESSOR. Rupert? Oh, yes, he is well enough, poor fellow. But you have the first place, Montressor.

MONTRESSOR. And – and – my cousin Isabel, she too enjoys a share of your affection, mother?

LADY MONTRESSOR. My own brother's child! What more natural than that she should do so, especially since she has lived so much with us? Oh, Montressor, you are blushing now; what, is the little bird beginning to flutter in the bush you have been beating about so long? I see you have taken too much Isabel, and you have got an attack of cousin on the heart.

MONTRESSOR. Ah, don't laugh about it, mother. I am desperately in love with her, and want to marry her, there.

LADY MONTRESSOR. Well?

12. **LCC** inserts in square brackets 'I never do such a thing. If I think Black is White I say so, no power on earth could induce me to say that it was grey' (f. 4). This and other remarks in the opening scene give Lady Montressor a slightly more ridiculous and belligerent edge in the **LCC** version.

MONTRESSOR. Well! You are not surprised?

LADY MONTRESSOR. Not in the least, my dear boy, it is what I have been silently longing for. Isabel is a sweet, docile girl, who will be to *me* an excellent and obedient daughter.

MONTRESSOR. And to me a charming wife.

LADY MONTRESSOR. Oh! that of course.

MONTRESSOR. If –

LADY MONTRESSOR. If! What ifs can there be in the way?

MONTRESSOR. There are two sides to this question, mother. I may offer her my heart, but will she listen to my suit?

LADY MONTRESSOR. If you offer her a coronet, do you suppose she will not take it and put it on her head at once? Only speak out your mind, and Isabel will no longer hesitate to let her happiness be seen.[13] (MONTRESSOR *shakes his head sadly*) Why, Montressor, what in the name of wonder do you suspect? (*rises*)

MONTRESSOR. That her affections are engaged elsewhere.

LADY MONTRESSOR. Impossible! Living all her life down here in the strict seclusion which you and I both love to keep, whom could Isabel have

---

13. **LCC** gives additional dialogue:

> MONTRESSOR: I think she loves me, Mother, but not in the same way that I love her! I am her brother – nothing more. But I ceased to think of her as a sister twelve long months ago.

> LADY MONTRESSOR: Your cousin loves you as a brother! What, in days like these when you may marry your deceased wife's something or other's deceased somebody else as soon as you like, provided you don't commit bigamy! Oh no my dear child, it is absurd. (f. 5)

This comment provides a comic topical reference to the ongoing debate surrounding the legality of men marrying their deceased wife's sister and a nod to Marryat's own sensation fiction, in which bigamy was a frequent plot point: for example, in *Veronique* (1869). See Eltis (2013), pp. 47–80.

seen to compare with yourself? There is only the old clergyman, and he has had two wives and seven children by each. Oh! the notion is utterly absurd, dismiss it from your mind at once.

MONTRESSOR. (*moodily*) I have a brother.

LADY MONTRESSOR. (*starting*) Rupert! Do you suppose for an instant that Isabel can dare to think of Rupert in any other light than as a brother?

MONTRESSOR. Brother! Mother you said just now –

LADY MONTRESSOR. Oh, but that is quite another thing. Isabel love Rupert! Rupert presume to think of Isabel! Why, the idea is positively ridiculous. She, an orphan, almost entirely dependent on me, and he, by his father's will, condemned to subsist upon three hundred a year or so. Their marriage is impossible. I would never give my consent to it.

MONTRESSOR. But Isabel has not forgotten him. (*crossing to* R.)

LADY MONTRESSOR. My dear Montressor, whatever foolish fancies Isabel and Rupert may have entertained in days gone by must all be over by this time. Your brother has now been absent, travelling, for more than a year; he never cared about his home, as you well know; has always been a wild and boisterous spirit, causing me the greatest anxiety, and at his age –

MONTRESSOR. (*interrupting*) Twenty-one today, mother, is he not?

LADY MONTRESSOR. Ah, by-the-bye, so he is!

MONTRESSOR. (*looking off* C.) Ah, here she comes. Oh, how beautiful she is! The very thought that another man should possess her drives me mad. If ever that should come to pass –

LADY MONTRESSOR. Trust me, it never shall. Leave us, I will speak to her at once. All will be right before we meet again. (*Kisses him hastily.*) MONTRESSOR *goes into the Castle*, R. ISABEL *enters* (*making up a bouquet by terrace* C. *from* R.) My Isabel, (ISABEL *comes from terrace.*) I have scarcely seen you this morning. (*They embrace.*) Montressor and I have been enjoying this sweet sunshine together, and talking about you. (*sitting* L. H.)

ISABEL. About me? (*seated* L.)

LADY MONTRESSOR. Yes; do we not both love you dearly? Whom, indeed, else have we to care for – to love – if not yourself, my Isabel?

ISABEL. Dear aunt, you have indeed supplied the place of a mother to me. How can I thank you sufficiently for all your kindness?[14]

LADY MONTRESSOR. This has always been your home. I should like to think that it might ever be so. (ISABEL *starts slightly*. LADY MON- TRESSOR *appears to take no notice*.) You have no wish to leave it, Isabel?

ISABEL. Oh, no.

LADY MONTRESSOR. You have no desire for more society than such as you have been accustomed to in the friendship of Miss Chester, and the affection of Montressor and myself?

ISABEL. Dear aunt, I am quite happy.

LADY MONTRESSOR. I am rejoiced to hear you say so, Isabel; *he* is not.

ISABEL. Montressor not happy?

LADY MONTRESSOR. You are now a woman, Isabel, and can you ask the question? Are not your eyes yet opened? Can they still be blind to the great affection that he bears for you?

ISABEL. Oh, do not say that.

LADY MONTRESSOR. Why not? You could not dare to trifle with his happiness – with mine! After all these years of tender solicitude and love, you would not break from us. Think how we have cherished you since you came to us, a hapless orphan. Think of the love and care we have lavished upon you. You would not repay it with what might seem ingratitude?

ISABEL. (*much agitated*) Oh no, aunt; not for worlds. But yet –

LADY MONTRESSOR. Think how happy it would make my remaining years to know my son had won the woman whom, out of all the world, his

14. **LCC** (ff. 9–10) gives further dialogue between Lady Montressor and Isabel which has the effect of enhancing the degree to which Isabel is browbeaten and emotionally black- mailed by her aunt.

mother would have chosen for his bride. Think of all this, sweet Isabel, and tell me you will let him hope.

ISABEL. I cannot tell him *not* to hope.

LADY MONTRESSOR. (*joyfully*) I ask no more. There, dry your eyes, my child. You may yet look back upon this as the happiest day of your life. (LADY MONTRESSOR *goes to door, turns, and extends her arms.* ISABEL *runs to her embraces. Kisses her fondly, and exit into Castle L.*)

ISABEL. The happiest day of my life. Ah, is there any happiness left in the world for me! Oh, Rupert! (*dashing away her tears*) Shame on my weakness. Have I no pride – no self-respect? What does it matter? If he ever loved me – he said he did. Oh, yes, he said he did! He has forgotten it long since; everything goes to prove it. Absent for more than a year, he has scarcely sent me one line to say that I am still held in his remembrance. Our love was but a childish folly, the natural affection of a boy and girl brought up together. I have been a fool to think it otherwise. It is best forgot, blotted from my memory forever. And yet – (*goes up stage, her face covered in her hand. Enter* MISS CHESTER *from Castle L.; she pauses on the steps, watching* ISABEL, *then comes down*)

MISS CHESTER. What, Isabel in tears? Has anything occurred to vex you?

ISABEL. Oh, it is nothing – nothing. I shall be myself again in a moment.[15]

MISS CHESTER. I know those tears spring from a wounded heart.

ISABEL. I do not know what right you have to say so.

MISS CHESTER. The right of knowledge and of long observation. Do you think your life has been so short among us that a friend like myself has not gained an insight into your character?

---

15. **LCC** gives further dialogue here which showcases Miss Chester's readiness to debunk gendered stereotypes.

> MISS CHESTER. When a woman, for you are a woman, ordinarily so quiet + calm as you are, declares that her emotion proceeds from nothing, the inference I draw is that she has reached a crisis in her life.
>
> ISABEL. Do you think so badly of your sex's candour?
>
> MISS CHESTER. I have learned to think as my experience of the world has taught me. And I know that we will shrink from nothing that will save our pride. (ff. 12–13)

ISABEL. (*aside*) She reads my thoughts, as she has ever done, like opened pages. (*crosses to* L. C.)

MISS CHESTER. Isabel, the time may seem short to you, but it is long to me; for ten years we have lived under the same roof.

ISABEL. I know it, and I have heard that my late uncle, for the sake of some dead memories, reckoned you as a second charge.

MISS CHESTER. He did, Heaven bless him! and I have always loved you.

ISABEL. Yes, and when I remember that, and the affection you always felt for my younger cousin, I am not surprised.

MISS CHESTER. (*breaking in*) Your younger cousin? Surely I have shown no preference between the three?

ISABEL. (*confusedly*) I have always fancied that you liked Rupert best. (*going a little to* R.)

MISS CHESTER. Your fancy is the reflection of your own mind. Though I confess I have always taken a strong interest in Rupert's character, it may be because no one else seemed to do so, which is wild and fitful enough to make an anxious study. Too wild and fitful it may be for a husband. Isabel, Montressor will bring more peace into your domestic life.

ISABEL. (*starting*) Montressor, Miss Chester, do you then guess?

MISS CHESTER. That you have been made the offer of his hand, and you hesitate about accepting, because you still cherish some foolish fancies of the past. No, I do not *guess*, I *know*.

ISABEL. And would advise me?

MISS CHESTER. Never to look further than today. Never to remember that yesterday has been, or that tomorrow inevitably must come. That is a foolish trick into which your heart would tempt you; but if you wish to fight successfully the battle of the world, you must ignore the very existence of a heart. It can never lead you on to any happiness. It may plunge you into irremediable error – might even persuade you to place your faith in such a lie as love!

ISABEL. (*amazed*) Miss Chester!

MISS CHESTER. (*continuing vehemently*) To believe that it exists! That the fables we hear of its delights, its purity, its trust, are not huge frauds, invented to tempt fools to their destruction! To believe that man is not the natural enemy of woman, and the thing he calls love the commonest weapon with which he strikes her to the ground![16]

ISABEL. (*alarmed*) You frighten me. I have never seen you look like this before.

MISS CHESTER. (*calming down*) Forgive me. I am afraid I have forgotten my part of monitor. Isabel, my counsel to you is to do as your aunt wishes. Marry Montressor, please the world, take all the satisfaction that wealth and distinction offer you, and be happy.

ISABEL. Not on such terms as those.

MISS CHESTER. Think, too, of the gratitude you owe to both your aunt and cousin – think how happy your consent would make them – and think of me, dear Isabel. I, too, take a great interest in your welfare, and for your own sake I would not that you should be cast out upon the world and meet temptations which might prove too strong for you. Once married to Montressor, I shall feel that you are safe. (*folds her in her arms*)

Enter LADY MONTRESSOR, *from Castle, with letters in her hand.*

LADY MONTRESSOR. One kiss for me, Isabel – Miss Chester must not monopolise them all. (*Isabel runs to her*) What tears – and yet a smile – like rain in sunshine? Ah, I see it all – you have thought over what we were talking about, and will follow your aunt's advice.

ISABEL. (*hiding her face*) I will try.

LADY MONTRESSOR. That's right. You've made me so happy. Now for my letters – the business of the day commences. I never feel as if the sun had really risen until the post comes in. (*opening letters*) Hum – from

16. Miss Chester's views gesture towards New Woman writing of the 1890s and 1900s, which sought to reveal the misogyny and inequality behind heterosexual romance plots. See, for example, novelists including Sarah Grand and Mona Caird, and playwrights such as Elizabeth Robins and Cicely Hamilton. Newey (2005) elaborates that, although Marryat's writings 'lack the explicit political dimension' of New Woman writing, it is 'all the more interesting for its location in the popular theatre, rather than the emerging "fringe"' (p. 182).

Mr. Armishaw – going to call here today on business. I have not the slightest idea what business he can have.

MISS CHESTER. Perhaps his business is connected with the coming of age of your second son.

LADY MONTRESSOR. (*laughing ironically*) Oh, doubtless. Rupert's vast estate and heavy income will require a great deal of legal attention before they are finally made over into the rightful owner's hands. What is this? The Brussels postmark. I declare it is from Rupert himself (ISABEL *starts* – MISS CHESTER *lifts her eyebrows*) to say that he is on his way home, and will be here almost as soon as his letter. Now, how excessively provoking – if there is one thing I dislike more than another, it is being taken by surprise. Why couldn't the boy have given us longer notice; but it is just like Rupert, so utterly thoughtless.

ISABEL. (*agitated to* MISS CHESTER) What shall I do?

MISS CHESTER. Behave yourself as the future Countess of Montressor should behave.

Enter LORD MONTRESSOR.

LADY MONTRESSOR. There is news, Montressor. Your brother Rupert returns home today.

MONTRESSOR. Rupert! returns today! (*aside*) Oh mother! this is what I have feared.

LADY MONTRESSOR. Hush! leave all to me.

Enter SERVANT *from Castle*, R. H.

SERVANT. Mr. Armishaw desires to speak with your ladyship.

LADY MONTRESSOR. Show him this way. (*exit* SERVANT) Dear me, I don't feel inclined for business. I am afraid the old man will bore me very much.

Enter ARMISHAW, R. H.

Oh, good morning, Mr. Armishaw. I am delighted to see you. Your letter has but just preceeded you.

ARMISHAW. Just so; I calculated on the post being punctual. Your ladyship is quite well?

LADY MONTRESSOR. Oh, yes, same as usual.

ARMISHAW. And my Lord? Miss Vivian – Miss Chester, your servant. I hope I haven't disturbed you too early?

LADY MONTRESSOR. Oh, dear no. It's always better to get business over early. You are not the only visitor arriving somewhat unexpectedly, I have just heard that Rupert will arrive today.

ARMISHAW. Oh, indeed! On the 15th of May too. Very odd! Just so.

LADY MONTRESSOR. And you have really come upon business! The very word always gives me palpitation of the heart.

ARMISHAW. You don't say so. Of the heart. Just so. Delicate and sensitive organ, I am told. Don't think I have got one myself.

LORD MONTRESSOR. The world says that lawyers never have.

MISS CHESTER. And the world is sure to be right.

ARMISHAW. Just so! A heart is a luxury which we can't afford.

MONTRESSOR. And wouldn't know how to use if you had it?

ARMISHAW. Then, we are better without it. Personal property which you can't invest is always unremunerative, and, so far, useless.[17]

LADY MONTRESSOR. You have come from London this morning?

---

17. **LCC** gives further dialogue between Lady Montressor and Armishaw, subsequently crossed through:

> LADY MONTRESSOR. But this business, what is it?

> ARMISHAW. Thought your ladyship would ask the question. But there is no hurry. Nice day, for the country. Not half as nice as London, though. Talk of air, this is thin – fog is substantial. Talk of fields, there are no fields, like Lincolns Inn Fields. (f. 18)

Here, and elsewhere, Armishaw's speeches are cut in the published version, presumably to move the plot more quickly. The pedantic lawyer was a typical character in sensation texts: for example, Matthew Bruff in Collins's *The Moonstone* (1868).

ARMISHAW. No, came into these parts last night, on business with your neighbour, Sir Hugh Ashton. (*slight movement on the part of* MISS CHESTER) Flesh is weak. His is failing. No doubt of that. Failing fast.

LADY MONTRESSOR. I suppose I ought to say I am sorry to hear it; but we know nothing of Sir Hugh. He has secluded himself from the world so long.

ARMISHAW. Just so. Odd that, isn't it? At least some folks might think so. Has his reasons, no doubt. Fine property, but bad sons. Elder drinking himself rapidly to death, younger nobody knows where. (MISS CHESTER *listening attentively*) Ah, fine fellow that younger son. Used to be so, at least many years ago. Sad story his.

LADY MONTRESSOR. I have heard my late husband speak of him once only, I think, and that was before our marriage.

ARMISHAW. Just so – bad job, very! When very young – mere boy, he was entrapped into a marriage with – well (*looking towards* ISABEL *and* MISS CHESTER) with a young person who, on the whole, was scarcely –

LADY MONTRESSOR. (*interrupting*) Well, well, Mr. Armishaw, I understand.

ARMISHAW. Just so. But odd, very. Then he got into a further scrape, and then – he disappeared. Fine property, and Sir Hugh failing. Disappeared – just so.

SERVANT *appears* R., *and announces.*

SERVANT. Mr. Rupert has arrived, my lady.

[*Exit* SERVANT.

Enter RUPERT *from Castle* L.

RUPERT. (*coming down quickly and embracing* LADY MONTRESSOR) My dear mother, how rejoiced I am to see you again. Montressor, old fellow, how are you? Pale and book-wormy as usual. You have been overdoing it, old boy, you have. Ah, Miss Chester, you have not forgotten your troublesome charge, I hope. And my cousin Isabel. (*goes to her and takes her hand*) This won't do, you are almost as pale as my brother.

ARMISHAW. How do you do? Glad you are come back. Ah, don't remember me, I suppose? Just so.

RUPERT *crosses to him.*

RUPERT. Really, I am compelled to say that I have not the honour. Stay – I *do* remember. Mr. Armishaw, my father's solicitor, I think?

ARMISHAW. Your father's? Oh yes, just so, just so.

RUPERT. And you are all flourishing – going along easily in the same grooves I left you in twelve months ago, when I ungratefully could bear the monotony no longer. After all, I have no doubt you have enjoyed yourselves as much as I have. By the way, my dear mother, I have a friend with me; he is now waiting at the Montressor Arms, and will follow me shortly – whom I am anxious to present to you. We have been travelling together for the last three months, and he is most desirous of making your acquaintance.

LADY MONTRESSOR. (*carelessly*) Any friend of yours, Rupert, will, of course, be welcome.

RUPERT. I knew you would say so. Montressor, you jolly old snail, he will help me to wake you up. His name is Fortescue – Michael Fortescue. He knows everything and has travelled everywhere.

MISS CHESTER. What a paragon!

RUPERT. He will be up very shortly. He wanted me to get over the "scene" of domestic felicitations first. Come, Montressor, show me the new billiard-room, conservatory, and all the rest, at once. I am longing to see all the improvements I have heard of.

MONTRESSOR. I hope you will approve. (*pause*) (RUPERT *looks entreatingly at* ISABEL, *and he follows*)

MONTRESSOR *out C. to L.* ISABEL, *with emotion, follows them.*

LADY MONTRESSOR. Wild and boisterous as ever. His travels do not appear to have tamed his unmanageable spirit.

MISS CHESTER. You should make some allowance for his youth. Experience and the world will be sure to tame him by-and-by.

LADY MONTRESSOR. Meanwhile, we are to be inconvenienced by his want of thought. What on earth could have possessed him to bring down his cosmopolitan friend to Castle Montressor, I wonder. He knows that we hate strangers. This is his one-and-twentieth birthday, Mr. Armishaw. (*sitting* C.)

ARMISHAW. Just so. Odd, as you will see. I have no time to spare. Your referring to his birthday recalls my business. Shall I proceed at once?

LADY MONTRESSOR. Oh, by all means, and get it over. It can't be long or very important if it has to do with him.

ARMISHAW. Just so. Very natural that you should think so. Will your ladyship step in doors?

LADY MONTRESSOR. Oh, no. (*seating herself*) It would be a sin to go in this lovely morning. We are quite private. Pray, go on.

ARMISHAW. Just so; but perhaps – (*glancing at* MISS CHESTER)

LADY MONTRESSOR. Oh, don't mind Miss Chester.[18] Go on, Mr. Armishaw, and don't be prosy, I beg.

ARMISHAW. Just so. (*sits*) The instructions upon which I am now acting I have had by me for some time. Indeed, ever since the late Earl's death, five years ago. Among his papers I found a sealed packet directed to me, and marked private, and not to be opened until the fifteenth of May of the present year. That is today.

LADY MONTRESSOR. You don't say so.

ARMISHAW. Yes I do. Just so. Well, yesterday, the fourteenth, I was summoned to Ashton Hall, to see my client, Sir Hugh, as I have already told you. I took the packet with me, guessing that it related to this estate, and that I might have to come on here at once. I wrote, announcing my visit. When I awoke this morning, the fifteenth of May, I opened the packet.

18. **LCC** complicates this dismissive implication with further bracketed dialogue in which Lady Montressor insists 'there are no secrets' from Miss Chester and asks her to help her comprehend Mr Armishaw (f. 22).

LADY MONTRESSOR. You are getting prosy. Be quick. What did it contain?

ARMISHAW. Certain information with reference to a young gentleman known as the Hon. Rupert Challinor.

LADY MONTRESSOR. (MISS CHESTER *much interested*)[19] Nothing to the detriment of my dear Montressor, I hope?

ARMISHAW. Just so, very natural. To the detriment of the Earl? Oh, no!

LADY MONTRESSOR. What then? For Heaven's sake, go on!

ARMISHAW. Just so, a little patience. Lady Montressor and Miss Chester, you are both women of the world. You have probably heard and seen strange things in your time, and I am of opinion that you are both what is usually termed strong-minded. I am not flattering, it is only the truth, I can assure you. Well, I learned from the papers I perused this morning, and I am instructed to impart my information to you, my lady, that Rupert is *not your son.*

LADY MONTRESSOR. Rupert *not my son*! You are dreaming. (MISS CHESTER *much amazed*)

ARMISHAW. I never dream. I haven't time. I thought you would make precisely that remark. You must bear in mind that I was not my Lord's legal adviser at the time of his marriage with yourself, and was therefore unacquainted with a certain family event that occurred just before that epoch. (MISS CHESTER *turns faint, and grasps a garden chair for support.*) Not well, Miss Chester?

MISS CHESTER. (*recovering herself with an effort*) Pray, go on.

ARMISHAW. Just so. It appears, then, that Lord Montressor had an only sister, the Lady Gertrude Challinor.

LADY MONTRESSOR. Yes. I have heard of her. But she and Montressor were not on good terms, I believe. At least, I never saw her.

---

19. This stage direction also reads 'to RUPERT' but this must be an error as Rupert is off stage.

ARMISHAW. She fell in love with an individual, whose name I have no means of ascertaining. He was a wild, harum-scarum dog, apparently, and Lord Montressor would not hear of the connection. Lady Gertrude, however, was a self-willed young lady – eloped with this nameless person – married him.

LADY MONTRESSOR. Shameless creature! But what has this to do with Rupert?

ARMISHAW. I am coming to that. Lady Gertrude believed that the man she married was at least an honourable man. She was mistaken; her union with him was but an empty ceremony – for shortly afterwards she discovered that her lover had already been entrapped into a marriage with an intriguing adventuress.[20] Learning this, Lady Gertrude left him at once.

LADY MONTRESSOR. But I do not comprehend. On the fifteenth of May, twenty-one years ago, I had a son born – my second son.

ARMISHAW. Just so. I am coming to that, too. You were very ill on that occasion – you were delirious with fever for weeks. Your life was despaired of. Your child died.

LADY MONTRESSOR. *My child died!* Why, Rupert is that child. You must be raving.

ARMISHAW. Just so. I mean quite the contrary. When you began to recover the doctors feared lest your convalescence should be retarded by the announcement of your infant's death, so another child of the same age was substituted for your own.

LADY MONTRESSOR. And that child was –

ARMISHAW. The infant Rupert.

LADY MONTRESSOR. Yes – but Rupert *what*? Whose child is he?

ARMISHAW. Just so – whose child? There's the puzzle. My instructions on this point are not so accurate as I could wish them to be.[21] But I believe

20. **LCC** gives 'courtesan', a term more evocative of prostitution than that used in the published version (f. 24).
21. **LCC** gives a marginal note, 'Miss C should be out and not know it is her son yet', and further dialogue between Armishaw and Lady Montressor at this point (f. 25). This may have been an effort to increase the suspense as the audience must wait for their suspicions to be confirmed regarding Rupert's parentage.

I am not far wrong in surmising that his mother was no other than the unhappy Lady Gertrude Challinor, who had given birth to a child after returning to the protection of her brother, and which the Earl, in order to save the reputation of his family, had caused to be hidden from her.

LADY MONTRESSOR. Good Heavens! How very shocking for the family.

ARMISHAW. Perhaps it would be as well that I should show your ladyship the papers. My bag is in the library.

LADY MONTRESSOR. As you please; but I do not think they will change my opinion.

Exeunt LADY MONTRESSOR *and* ARMISHAW *into Castle* L. MISS CHESTER *watches them out; when they are gone the cold expression of her countenance gives way.*

MISS CHESTER. (*passionately*)[22] My child! my child! how did they dare to tell me you were dead! my living, breathing child, my Rupert! Ah, who can wonder that I have been drawn to him as no other living creature has had the power to draw me! It was the strength of motherhood, mighty even in its agony. Rupert – mine! Oh, dead brother, now do I understood why you left me, a false-named legacy, to the family of Montressor, and so placed me, unknowing and unknown, beside my son. Oh, priceless joy, to know he lives! and yet, never to acknowledge him by the name of mother.[23] Oh, Heaven help me, the weary years that I have passed in silent, hopeless agony have dwindled down to nothing! My punishment has but descended on my head. Hush! voices. (*looks off* C.) He comes. I dare not meet him now.

L. *exit into Castle. Enter* RUPERT *and* ISABEL, C. *from* R. *terrace.*

RUPERT. Oh, Isabel, my sweetest cousin, why do you appear so changed to me? So far less warm and cordial than you used to be. Have you forgotten all our childhood's love – the deeper affection of our later years? Speak, Isabel; your silence tortures me.

---

22. **LCC** marginal note: 'This speech should be altered that the audience might not know Rupert is <u>her</u> son until 2nd [half] of second act' (f. 27). Specific mention of Rupert is replaced with: 'Better had my brother abandoned me to the obloquy my error had deservedly brought down upon my head, than left his cruel legacy to stir up all the passions I had hoped were lulled to rest forever!' (f. 27).
23. This may be an oblique reference to the incredibly popular stage version of *East Lynne*, which featured the famous line: 'dead, dead, dead! And he never knew me, never called me mother' (Palmer (1874), p. 38).

ISABEL. Oh, Rupert, I scarcely understand what you would have me say.

RUPERT. Not understand? You are trifling with me, Isabel. Would you shatter the hope that cheered me in my absence, and has smiled upon my homeward path – the hope that you comprehended and returned my love?

ISABEL. What was I to think of your long voluntary absence and your silence? (*sits* L. *on garden seat*)

RUPERT. (*follows her and sits beside her*) Think that I was learning lessons in life, that I might lay the results at your feet; and it was impossible for me to write, much, travelling incessantly, as I have been doing. Oh, Isabel, tell me that you love me still!

ISABEL. Oh, hush, Rupert! You must not speak these words to me. I cannot listen to them any longer. Your mother forbids it.

RUPERT. My mother! What right has she to interfere? This day sees me independent; and, as a man, I offer my heart to the woman whom I love.

ISABEL. I cannot, dare not take it. Pray, Rupert, say no more.

RUPERT. (*rises*) Say no more. Keep my lips closed when my heart is bursting! But I see through your precaution, Isabel. You would silence me because you fear to tell the reason that makes you disinclined to hear me press my suit. You do not hesitate to prove inconsistent, fickle, heartless, but you turn coward at the thought of crushing at one blow, all the hopes of the man whom, if not by word, at least, by deed, you once professed to love.

ISABEL. Oh, cruel! cruel!

RUPERT. But you mistake me. (*leans on garden seat*) I may have been weak in imagining that you would deign to remember so insignificant a being as myself during the tedious space of twelve months. It was next to impossible, being woman, that you should do so. But I am strong enough to bear with perfect equanimity the reason of the change, even to the extent of hearing that you have already decided on accepting a wealthier and more important suitor.

ISABEL. (*weeping*) Oh, Rupert! how unkind you are.

RUPERT. It is not impossible that you have set your heart on becoming Countess of Montressor, and to think, as a younger son, I have but little chance of being able to place the coronet upon your brow.

ISABEL. I will not listen to you further.

RUPERT. For you cannot deny the truth of the insinuation.

ISABEL. Let me pass. (*cross to* R.) You have insulted me too much already.

Exit ISABEL *into Castle* R., *sobbing bitterly.*

RUPERT. I have guessed aright, her open face could never hide her feelings, and it has spoken to some purpose now. Well, well, that hope is over. (*sits* R.) Better that I should learn the truth at once, (*sits at table*) however rudely. (*paces the stage in agitation*) Montressor, too, he of all others, who knew my affection for my cousin. My brother! No, not brother, Coward! Traitor! Thief! (*rises*) How dared he lay his hand on what he knew was mine. But he shall answer that question to myself. I never cared about my home, there are few sweet memories of childhood in my breast, and those it must now be my greatest effort to forget. I will leave the Castle; I will return to those scenes which have no power to torture me by recollections of the past.[24]

Enter MICHAEL FORTESCUE C. *from* L.

FORTESCUE. (*gaily*) Why, Rupert, what are you stamping about in this way for? Are you rehearsing to the shrubs and garden benches? What's up? Have they seized upon you the moment you returned home, and insist upon your standing for the county?

RUPERT. (*moodily*) My rehearsal is for the acting of a more serious drama than you anticipate.

FORTESCUE. Not a tragedy, I hope. (*up* C.)

RUPERT. More unlikely things have happened. Any way it must prove a tragedy for me.

---

24. **LCC** adds in square brackets: '[But not until I and he who was my brother, have had our reckoning together!]' (f. 31).

FORTESCUE. (*coming forward*) Then, of course, there is a woman at the bottom of it.

RUPERT. Why, of course?

FORTESCUE. Because, my dear fellow, women have formed the mainspring of all the plots of all the tragedies this world has ever seen, since the first female nuisance was created. At eighteen, we think them angels; at five-and-twenty, they have dwindled into ordinary comforts; at thirty we pronounce them to be extraordinary curses; and I should be sorry to say what name we give them by the time we are forty. (*crosses* R.)

RUPERT. Were you always such a cynic, Fortescue?

FORTESCUE. Oh, dear no. (*crosses to* R. *sitting on table*) I did not find them out for a long time. And how do you feel about them? Are you disposed to bless the sex entirely at this moment?

RUPERT. No. Heaven knows that I am not. (*sighs*)

FORTESCUE. That's a real sigh, and I don't like to hear it. Come, since it seems that I have guessed right as to your melancholy, let me hear the whole story.

RUPERT. (*places his hand on* FORTESCUE's *shoulder*) (*to him*) You have a strange influence over me, Fortescue. I know no man that I can talk to as I can to you. You have hinted before at your suspicion that I loved my cousin Isabel – and you were right. I did love her, and I have returned home to find my love is vain – for her faith is gone from me – wooed to my elder brother.

FORTESCUE. *Elder* brother! (*rises and goes forward* R. H.) How like a woman! And what do you propose to do?

RUPERT. Do? I will never give her up. I will pursue her wherever she may go. I will force her from his arms at the very altar. I will –

FORTESCUE. Gently – gently.

> LADY MONTRESSOR, MONTRESSOR, and ARMISHAW
> *enter from Castle* L.

LADY MONTRESSOR. (*regarding* FORTESCUE, *who takes his hat off*) Rupert, will you introduce your friend?

RUPERT. Mr. Fortescue, Lady Montressor, Lord Montressor (*they bow,* FORTESCUE *with great courtesy, the others coldly*)

FORTESCUE. (*crosses to* C.) This a pleasure to which I have long looked forward. My friend, Rupert, who I regret to say, does not appear to be in the best of spirts this lovely morning, has often talked to me with warmth of the various members of his family.

LADY MONTRESSOR. (*coldly*) Very dutiful of him, no doubt.

FORTESCUE. (*looking round*) But the number is not complete, eh, Rupert? I trust, Lady Montressor, that your niece is well?

LADY MONTRESSOR. Miss Vivian is perfectly robust, I thank you.

FORTESCUE. I am rejoiced to hear it. My young friend, during our travels, has, with all the gush of youth, so often anticipated with joy the happy hour of meeting again his mother, his brother, and his cousin. (*crosses*)

RUPERT. Fortescue, be silent.

FORTESCUE. My dear boy, why should I not allude to an enviable predilection which is patent to others, no doubt, besides myself? A mother's eye sees as quickly as her heart feels.

LADY MONTRESSOR. (*coldly*) I am quite unaware to what predilection you allude.

FORTESCUE. You astonish me.[25]

RUPERT. (*seeing* ISABEL, *impetuously*) Unaware! Is it possible, mother, that you speak the truth? (*turning to* ISABEL) Speak to her, Isabel, tell her that my hopes were not entirely presumptuous. That our mutual preference had been expressed before my fatal absence. (ISABEL *hides her face*) What! silent! are you so completely changed, or I grown so unworthy, that a word is too much to bestow on him who once possessed your heart? Silent still! Mother you cannot really have been blind to my attachment in days gone by.

LADY MONTRESSOR. My dear Rupert, I wish you wouldn't talk so much like a book.

---

25. **V&A** has hand-written annotation '(Isabel returns)' (p. 16).

RUPERT. Have you no reply, but sarcasm? (*to* LORD MONTRESSOR. MONTRESSOR *down* L. *of* C.) You, then, my brother; you at least knew my love. Is it true that you have stepped in between myself and its fruition? Is it indeed true that you seek to purchase with your wealth and title, a love that has been pledged to me?

LADY MONTRESSOR. Oh, I cannot tolerate this language. Be silent, Sir.

RUPERT. You are my *mother*, madam, and I would willingly obey you. But in all candour I appeal to you, my mother. (*crosses to* LADY MONTRESSOR)

LADY MONTRESSOR. Your mother! – you mistake. You are no son of mine!

ARMISHAW. (*aside to* LADY MONTRESSOR) Just so. But let me entreat your ladyship to be cautious.

RUPERT. (*sorrowfully*) In affection, perhaps, you are not my mother. Heaven must judge between us. However much we may wish it, we cannot unmake the facts, and the fact remains that I am your own child.

LADY MONTRESSOR. No fact – a falsehood! I have but one child, and this is he! (*laying her hand upon* MONTRESSOR'S *shoulder*. RUPERT, ISABEL, *and* MONTRESSOR *amazed*, FORTESCUE *looks on curiously*.)

RUPERT. You renounce me then?

LADY MONTRESSOR. You are not mine to renounce. I tell you – I tell all the world, that you *are not my son*. (*Pause*)

RUPERT. (*astounded*) Who am I, then?

LADY MONTRESSOR. A man without a name – a man whose mother's name is stained with shame. A bastard substitute for my dead child!

RUPERT. (*fiercely*) A lie – I'll not believe it.

LADY MONTRESSOR. Mr. Armishaw, the legal documents which prove this *lie* are in your possession. Have the kindness to confirm my statement?

ARMISHAW. Just so. I thought you would ask me to do that. I fear that there's no denying it. The late Earl's papers –

RUPERT. (*staggering*) Oh, is all this a fearful dream?

ISABEL. (*darting forward to him*) Rupert, though all else be false – *I* am not! (*crossing to him*)

RUPERT. (*wildly*) Don't touch me. Remember what I am!

ISABEL. I remember nothing, but that you are my first, my only love.

RUPERT. Your protestations come too late. No power on earth now should make me link my outcast fate with yours.

LADY MONTRESSOR. Nor I permit it, as guardian to my niece. Enough. (MISS CHESTER *appears on steps* L. *Music till curtain*) Go, sir, quit the Castle, and return to it no more.

> MISS CHESTER *sees* FORTESCUE, *who does not observe her. She leans against the wall for support.*

ISABEL. In mercy, speak to me!

RUPERT. Be happy, if you can, and think as little of me as you may. (*To* LADY MONTRESSOR) You shall not find me slow to obey you, madam. Come, Fortescue, you will stand by me, I know.

FORTESCUE. (*cheerily, crosses* C.) With all my heart, my boy. If every friend in this world forsook you, you shall still find one in me. We have been happy enough in our Bohemian life; let us return to it, and see if it cannot provide us sufficient bolts to bar the door against dull care. Nameless, friendless, penniless, what matter! So am I. Bohemians such as I accord the heartiest welcome to those who are driven out, and turn no lingering glances on the false paradise they leave behind them. Come, Rupert, you shall be my son.

> MISS CHESTER *sinks half fainting.* ISABEL *weeps bitterly.*
> LADY MONTRESSOR *puts her arm round* MONTRESSOR'S
> *neck.* FORTESCUE *and* RUPERT *go up* C.
> *Tableau. Curtain quick.*

END OF ACT I.

ACT II.

SCENE. – *The Cascine gardens at Florence.*[26] *A retired spot surrounded with trees and shrubs. At back an opening has been cut through to admit a distant view of mountains. Band is heard playing behind scenes – piano. Sunset. Enter* R. LADY MONTRESSOR *and* ISABEL.

LADY MONTRESSOR. This is truly delightful! Such a charming custom, for people to come out here after dinner instead of sitting in stuffy drawing-rooms! I cannot imagine why Montressor did not seem anxious for us to come. But where can he be? He slipped away quite suddenly.

ISABEL. I think he missed us in the crowd where the band plays. I fancy I caught a glimpse of him afterwards talking to one of those extravagantly dressed ladies, of whom there are so many driving about.[27]

LADY MONTRESSOR. Oh, my dear, you must be mistaken. I cannot for a moment suppose that Montressor can be acquainted with such people. Such extraordinary toilettes, and so very *décolletées.*[28] Oh, impossible! And, of course, Montressor would have mentioned to me any such acquaintance. Ah! here is Miss Chester. (*enter* MISS CHESTER R.) Dear Miss Chester, have you seen Montressor?

MISS CHESTER. Since when?

LADY MONTRESSOR. Since we arrived in the gardens. I have lost him in the crowd, I suppose.

MISS CHESTER. I have seen him nowhere.

LADY MONTRESSOR. Nowhere?

MISS CHESTER. Nowhere. (*she goes up stage*)

---

26. **LCC** setting given as 'Grand fête in the gardens of the Villa Bryano. Music in the distance. Guests pass & re-pass along back of the stage' (f. 38). The removal of the supernumeraries in the published version may have made the play more feasible for small-scale or amateur productions.
27. This mention of 'extravagantly dressed' prostitutes or members of the *demi-monde* further impugns Montressor's character.
28. Revealing of the chest and shoulders, usually spelt *décolleté.*

LADY MONTRESSOR. Oh! dear me, I wish you would not say *Nowhere* in such a provoking voice. It is quite absurd to suppose that he is nowhere; he must be somewhere.

MISS CHESTER. And therefore it seems hardly necessary to worry yourself about his temporary absence.

LADY MONTRESSOR. Oh! you cannot possibly understand a mother's feelings, Miss Chester; how could you? Are you really sure you saw Montressor talking to somebody, Isabel? Good gracious! I hope he has not formed any improper acquaintance. My poor, dear boy! he is so young – scarcely able to take care of himself.

MISS CHESTER. He is older than Rupert.

LADY MONTRESSOR. (*stamping her foot impatiently*) Rupert! I wish to forget that name. I suppose that you and Isabel are always comparing Montressor with Rupert; not at all to the disadvantage of the latter.

ISABEL. Oh aunt! Why should you think so?

LADY MONTRESSOR. Oh, I don't grumble. Of course, I can't expect my taste to be as good as other people's. But I must say that I wish Rupert had not contaminated Montressor.

ISABEL. Aunt, what can you mean?

LADY MONTRESSOR. I know it is Rupert's bad example that has led Montressor astray.

MISS CHESTER. He must be easily influenced then. After Rupert's long absence they only met for an hour, and we have never seen Rupert since.

LADY MONTRESSOR. Oh, of course; I am wrong as usual. Possibly you have not observed how different Montressor has become. He stays out late at night, and evades the questions I put to him in the morning. Looks pale, and can't eat his breakfast. Oh! It's dreadful!

ISABEL. (*timidly*) But we should not forget, Aunt, that my cousin is no longer a boy, but a man, and responsible to no one but himself.

LADY MONTRESSOR. I thank you, Isabel; it is very kind of you to remind me of my son's age, and to teach me my duty. Much obliged to you, my love.

ISABEL. Indeed, I did not mean to offend you.

LADY MONTRESSOR. (*angrily*) But you *do* offend me. Everybody offends me! (*suddenly changing her tone to one of entreaty*) Oh Isabel, if I could but persuade you to return Montressor's love! If you would but fulfil the promise you once half made, you would win him back to be his former self again. It is your cruelty that has brought this sad change in him.

ISABEL. Aunt, dear Aunt, why will you wound me so? You know that I cannot answer as you wish – for it would be more cruel of me to feign an attachment which I cannot feel. I love Montressor dearly, with a sister's love, but he must ask no more.

LADY MONTRESSOR. (*changing her tone again*) You are an ungrateful girl, disobedient too, for I have bade you never think of that wretched boy Rupert again. You can still care for him when he refused your love before us all! For shame! Have you no pride left?

ISABEL. Pride! There is nothing that I cherish so much as the memory of my love for him.

ISABEL goes up to MISS CHESTER.

LADY MONTRESSOR. Oh, this is intolerable![29] It is positively indecent! No, don't cling to Miss Chester. I am sure she would be the last person to encourage such shamelessness.

MISS CHESTER. (*putting* ISABEL *gently from her*) Child, you must learn to bear your sorrows as we all do – alone.

LADY MONTRESSOR. (*looking off* R.) Ah, there is Montressor. Good gracious! He is actually talking to an extremely bold-looking person in pink. Come, Isabel – I desire. This must be put an end to at once. (LADY

---

29. In **LCC**, Montressor and Fortescue enter and converse with Lady Montressor, who tries to persuade her son to stay with her (ff. 41–2). This interchange replaces the conversation in the published version between Rupert and Miss Chester.

MONTRESSOR *and* ISABEL *go out* R. *Band plays louder for a moment or two.*)

MISS CHESTER. And she thinks *I* cannot understand her feelings! What would she do had she to suffer such a woe as mine! She, who cannot bear to be separated from her son an hour—but where is *mine!* I cannot tell if he is alive or dead. I know not whether I may indulge the hope that I shall ever gaze into his eyes again. (*She throws herself into garden seat up* C., *hiding her face in her hands.*)

Enter RUPERT L.

RUPERT. Fortescue cannot have arrived yet. Ah, a lady in distress? That's often the case in Florence, I fancy. (MISS CHESTER *looks up.*) Good Heavens! Miss Chester! (MISS CHESTER *gazes at him wildly for an instant, and seems about to fall back fainting, but with a powerful effort she recovers herself and rises.*) Is it really you, my kind friend? But you seem ill.

MISS CHESTER. Nothing, Rupert, nothing. But you startled me so. I can hardly speak to you.

RUPERT. You cannot be more surprised than I am. I thought you were still living at the Castle. Surely you and – and – Lady Montressor have had no disagreement!

MISS CHESTER. Oh, no – I am still in her company. They are all here.

RUPERT. (*joyfully*) All! What, Montressor and – stay. Miss Chester, tell me the worst at once. What is the meaning of this journey?

MISS CHESTER. I do not understand you.

RUPERT. Has Montressor a Countess?

MISS CHESTER. He has not.

RUPERT. Is he engaged?

MISS CHESTER. No.

RUPERT. Oh, thank Heaven!

MISS CHESTER. Why that thanksgiving? What difference can it make to you? Would you, a penniless, nameless man, link your fate to a girl as penniless as yourself? I thought that absence and reflection would have taught their lessons better.

RUPERT. Who ever learns that lesson perfectly? Miss Chester, you have always seemed to feel for me. Give me some hope that I may yet win Isabel.

MISS CHESTER. I cannot give you that which I do not possess.

RUPERT. But does she still love me?

MISS CHESTER. If I knew I would not say. Take my advice. Forget you ever saw her.

RUPERT. You are cruel and heartless, too! If you are turned against me with the rest, I am indeed friendless! (*Turns away*)

MISS CHESTER. (*starting forward*) Rupert!

RUPERT. Spare your casuistry. It is needless to tell me that I have deceived myself, or that the wound will speedily be healed, and that I shall soon learn to laugh at the love whose agony stings me now. You can have known nothing of all this, and your advice is valueless.

MISS CHESTER. (*aside*) Will he kill me with his bitter words!

RUPERT. I see only too plainly that it is far better that I should avoid the family of Montressor; and yet they might have treated me less harshly. Was I not brought up at Montressor, the Earl my brother, Isabel my first love, the Countess my – No: no mother could, even in thought, have treated a son with such harsh cruelty. Ah! it has no meaning for me that sacred name. I have never known, never can know, a mother's love! Goodbye, Miss Chester. For all your kindness in past years I thank you: and for your advice now tendered I thank you too. I am sure you mean me well. Goodbye, Miss Chester, we shall never meet again. (RUPERT *goes out* L.)

MISS CHESTER. Oh! what has been my sin? Is not my punishment too hard to bear? A mother trembling to fold her child in her arms, and yet kept standing here, helpless, childless, and alone! Oh, Heaven, have mercy upon me, for man has none! (*She goes up* C., *and staggers out among the foliage at the back.* LADY MONTRESSOR, *leaning on* MONTRESSOR's *arm, and followed by* ISABEL, *comes in* R.)

LADY MONTRESSOR. Princess of fiddlestick! If she is a Princess, why does she not behave like one? Or if it is the custom of Princesses to dress like that, why, the less you hear of them the better.

MONTRESSOR. Really, mother, I must be allowed to choose my own acquaintances.

LADY MONTRESSOR. Among men, yes; but you may depend upon it that I understand women better than you do. By-the-bye, you never told me whom it was you dined with last night, and who kept you so late.

MONTRESSOR. Oh! mother, what does it matter? It was an Englishman I met at the club here. You would not recognise his name.

LADY MONTRESSOR. Montressor, I insist.

MONTRESSOR. (*uneasily*) Well, then, Fortescue – Michael Fortescue, Rupert's friend. Do you remember?

LADY MONTRESSOR. Michael Fortescue!

Enter FORTESCUE *on the word*, L. U. E.

FORTESCUE. Surely I heard my name? Lady Montressor! this is most fortunate. Allow me to make my apologies for not having done my duty in calling upon you; but Montressor has always neglected to give me your address.

LADY MONTRESSOR. And he has equally forgotten to mention that you were in Florence.

FORTESCUE. Now that's too bad, it is indeed. But you must forgive us at the club if we have kept him away too much. He is such a boon to us poor cynics. There is nothing so delightful, Lady Montressor, as freshness and youth; the first rekindles our half expired hopes, and contact with the latter seems to renovate our digestions. What we shall do without him when you leave this sweet city, I cannot imagine.

MONTRESSOR. Oh mother! Mr. Fortescue has far too good an opinion of me. You must not believe all his nonsense.

LADY MONTRESSOR. No, I do not.

FORTESCUE. Can Lady Montressor really suspect me of a want of candour when speaking of her son? I never was more serious in my life, except indeed, in those solemn moments when a creditor reminds me of his earthly existence.

LADY MONTRESSOR. Montressor, you will not leave me again this evening? The late hours you keep will ruin your health.

MONTRESSOR. Oh, you exaggerate. (*up* R.)

FORTESCUE. May I venture to remind you Lady Montressor, that in this climate at this season of the year, the safest time to sally forth is when the sun goes down? All the world does so here. And, after all, so long as we take our rest, what matter if it comes to us before or after dawn? A cigarette, a glass of lemonade,[30] and half an hour's chatter with a pretty girl in the moonlight, never seriously injured anybody's virtue yet. And I can stake my reputation that the Earl is one of the most severely virtuous young men I know.

LADY MONTRESSOR. It is very good of you to say so. Montressor, we will return to where the band is playing. It is nearly time to go home. Ah, my dear boy, why do you cause us so much anxiety?

LADY MONTRESSOR, ISABEL, *and* MONTRESSOR *go out* C. *to* R.

FORTESCUE. (*looking after them, smiling sardonically*) Ah, put your arm round his neck, fond mother – coax him as much as you will – he is safe within the toils. (*throws himself upon a garden seat and lights a cigarette. Music in the distance.*) Ha! Ha! does his noble father shudder in his stately coffin in the family mausoleum, I wonder? He well might if he could see the mentor fate has provided for his heir. The spendthrift younger son was no match for the proud Earl's sister, eh? Who has got the worst of that bargain now, Montressor? (*rising*) Don't let me think of it, or I shall grow more wild and reckless than I am. Ah, how is it that Time, with all its

30. Presumably referring to champagne.

boasted power, can put no chains about the Demon Memory! Why must we ever carry about with us this cursed burden of remembrance? (*seats himself again*) And yet the bitter is not unmingled with the sweet. You were wonderfully lovely, Gertrude, in those days, when I won your heart – when I bade you fly with me – when we lived together, believing we were man and wife. Then came the Nemesis of earlier folly, and we were told that the adventuress I had wedded in a fit of pique against my father, and thought dead, still lived to curse me. And then you left me – horror-struck – and the grave closed over your despair. And yet we hear respectable matrons, with marriageable daughters, women who are alive to all the sin that passes in the world, still argue, forsooth, when pleading the cause of an unexception-able *parti*,[31] that young men must sow their wild oats. (*rising*) Miserable cant! I sowed mine in youth, and in my age I gather in the melancholy harvest. Bah! what am I talking about? So long as there is money, and meat and drink, what remains to be desired? Every man for himself, in this world, and the devil take the hindmost. He is the happiest worshipper who carries his idol in his pocket and knows that his religion need never inter-fere with his pleasures. (*stop music*)

Enter RUPERT *from* L. U. E.

Aha! my dear boy, I am delighted to see you back from Rome. You are come in time.

RUPERT. In time for what?

FORTESCUE. The plucking of a fat pigeon. A thorough-bred British Aris-tocrat, whose mind has not outrun his years, and whose unincumbered inheritance is still jingling in his pockets.

RUPERT. (*carelessly*) How does he call himself?

FORTESCUE. By a name not altogether unfamiliar to your ears.

RUPERT. Oh, I know (*he laughs savagely*), I have just heard that he is here. You have got hold of Montressor.

FORTESCUE. In the pleasantest possible grip, yes.

---

31. In this context, *parti* means possible matrimonial match.

RUPERT. Hold him fast, ruin him. If I cannot marry her, he never shall.[32]

FORTESCUE. What, you are there, are you? Take care, my dear Rupert, don't allow yourself to be again deceived by that process of imagination which sentimentalists call love.

RUPERT. I am aware that you have no faith in its existence.

FORTESCUE. Pardon me. I believe that it exists. I know that it never endures. Youth imagines that the profession of the coveted object secures the happiness it seems to promise. Experience has ascertained that the real-ization of desire is not half so sweet as the desire itself.

RUPERT. You cannot persuade me of that.

FORTESCUE. Of course not; but when you have quaffed the cup yourself, you will confess that I am no mean judge of its quality. Who, swimming in the summer tide of life, looks onward to the winter storms that toss him to the sea that lies beyond the stream? Who, in the full flush of health, can realise the torture of disease? Yet there are rocks in the river-bed, storms in the cloudless noon-tide air, cancers lurking beneath apparent health, and – misery in Love!

RUPERT. Your speech is like an eloquent sermon, Fortescue, very nice to listen to, but nothing more. Come, be practical. Tell me is Isabel here this evening?

FORTESCUE. Yes, true son of Adam, she is.

RUPERT. Then preach no more at present. I must see her.

Exit to R.

FORTESCUE. As you please. Run after your will-o'-th'-wisp. You will cry to me to pick you out of the quagmire again before long. (*He seats*

---

32. **LCC** darkens the tone of the dialogue at this point.

> RUPERT. Ha – ha – this is too good. Fortescue, tell me what I can do to aid you to bring him to his destruction.
>
> FORTESCUE. Oh gently – don't use so harsh a term. How I can minister to his amusement, you mean?
>
> RUPERT. Disguise it by what name you wish. (f. 45)

himself, and lights a cigarette.) Would I change places with him? It is hard to say. I feel that I have lived but for myself; and in my age there seems to be nothing strewn across my path but shadows – shadows of a wasted life, say what I will, think what I will, what would I not give to have back some of the hours of the past! Oh, give me back my youth! Let me taste once more, even though it be in dreams, one sip of the cup that once bubbled so brightly to my lips! (*rising*) Bah! I am as great a fool as Rupert. My youth is buried in the grave, without a hope of resurrection. (MISS CHESTER *enters from* R.; *she sees him, recognises him; starts violently, then draws herself up coldly, and stands still* C., *her eyes fixed upon him. He shudders involuntarily.*) How cold the evening has turned! I feel as if I had evoked some phantom that stands by me, and haunts me with reproachful eyes. Stuff! (*looks at his watch*) It is now growing late. I must look for Montressor. (*He turns to go up stage, finds himself face to face with* MISS CHESTER; *he staggers backward, she remains motionless.*) Gertrude! No. What awful mockery is this?

MISS CHESTER. Do you call the uninterrupted pain of two-and-twenty years a mockery? I am no spirit risen to reproach you for your unexpected treachery. I am the wretched remnant of a life your passions wrecked.

FORTESCUE. Oh, my God! the report was false, then, and you did not die?

MISS CHESTER. Die! If every woman who wakes up to the consciousness that she has been betrayed laid down and died, there would be fewer of my sex remaining to endure the torture of a life of shame.

FORTESCUE. To which it was my misfortune, not my fault, to subject you. Gertrude, do me justice!

MISS CHESTER. Justice! Do you call for justice at my hands to whom you showed none?

FORTESCUE. You loved me once!

MISS CHESTER. Ay with a very agony of love, whose trembling touch still – shame upon my weakness – vibrates along the chords of life and wakes at times the more harmonious music of the past. With a love you should have learned to sanctify and not to curse.

FORTESCUE. You were, to all intents and purposes, my wife.

MISS CHESTER. Wife! Do not dare to name the time when you presumed to call me so! I was nothing but your wretched dupe, and I am still your victim. (*cross to* R.)

FORTESCUE. But let me speak. Let me tell you that remorse has helped to make me what I am. Let me declare the strange joy that thrills through me to find that you are still alive whom I thought dead.

MISS CHESTER. To you, I am dead, you killed my heart, and all the hope it cherished. I *was* Lady Gertrude Challinor. I *am* Miss Chester, the humble friend and companion of the Countess of Montressor, and Miss Chester knows no man who bears your name.

FORTESCUE. You are bitter madam.

MISS CHESTER. (*going up stage*) As my life has been. (*Exit C. and* R.)

FORTESCUE. Still alive! The space of years is animated.[33] Time has but ripened all her matchless beauty. She is still a woman to be won! And to think that once she was wholly mine! And I have no power to claim her. Oh wretched fool to gamble away the richest treasure I possessed! (*staggers out C. to* R.)

Enter RUPERT *and* ISABEL.

RUPERT. Isabel it is useless to try and evade the meaning of my words. You *know* what I mean.

ISABEL. But Rupert, as you were ever kind to me, do not press me now.

RUPERT. *Now!* Do you feel weak, and are you afraid that you might yield today, only to repent tomorrow?

ISABEL. Oh, it is not that, and it is ungenerous of you to suggest it. I have no thought for myself now; my one desire is to save Montressor.

RUPERT. Indeed! From what?

ISABEL. From the utter ruin that seems to threaten him.

---

33. **LCC** gives 'annihilated' instead of 'animated' (f. 48).

RUPERT. (*sneering*) Very unfortunate, no doubt. What a pity the young Lord Montressor should forfeit his wealth in such a manner! Sad for him; sad for the lady whom he may choose to honour by asking her to become his wife.

ISABEL. I do not know what you mean. All I ask is that you will help me to save one whom I love as a brother.

RUPERT. (*eagerly*) As a brother! Oh, Isabel, do not trifle with me. Have you indeed given Montressor only a sister's love?

ISABEL. I have nothing more to give him.

RUPERT. Is it so, indeed? Then, Isabel, you love me still. You will let me take your hand. You will not check me when I ask again for hope. (*she gives him her hand and is silent*)[34]

ISABEL. (*passionately*) Rupert! (*checking herself*) But you will promise to do your best to save Montressor from the net in which he is entangled? Think of his mother's anguish.

RUPERT. Do either deserve much generosity from my hands?

ISABEL. Yes, for it gives the opportunity for showing how sweet and grand a thing forgiveness is.

RUPERT. Oh, more than all, I can well afford to be generous to the man who has failed to obtain the priceless blessing of your love. (*voices outside*) Hush! that is Montressor's voice. They come this way.

ISABEL. Then I will leave you. I trust all to you.

RUPERT. You shall not trust in vain. (*Exit* C. *to* L.) Come what may I will keep my word.

---

34. **LCC** gives a longer speech to Rupert here: 'Oh – you have infused new life into my soul, my pulses quicken, my mind grows clear. I have been wild & reckless, Isabel – for, though your image has never left my memory, I did not deem it possible that you could still care for me. But now, a new existence dawns upon me! I will relinquish this Bohemian life, I will return to England, & work honestly & manfully until I can offer you such a home as you shall not be ashamed to enter' (f. 51). The printed version omits this explication of Rupert's epiphany, which also means that Isabel moves from silence to passionate exclamation rather abruptly.

Laughter heard without; then enter FORTESCUE,
MONTRESSOR, *and guests.*

FORTESCUE. And, now, then, what remains to crown the night? What but the warm worship of the fair-faced Goddess Fortune. Come, then, to the cards.

GUESTS. Bravo, bravo.

MONTRESSOR. Ay, the cards! the cards!

RUPERT. (*running forward*) No. Montressor, beware!

FORTESCUE. Idiot! Be silent for your life!

RUPERT. My life. What is it worth? Montressor, I tell you once again, beware.

MONTRESSOR. Of what?

RUPERT. Of robbery! (GUESTS *murmur*, FORTESCUE *fierce*) I say again, of robbery! I know this company; I know there is not a man among them all that would play fairly unless he thought that fair play could win!

GUESTS. (*angrily*) An insult.

RUPERT. As you please, though the truth can never be an insult! Oh, I am not afraid of your black looks.

FORTESCUE. Do you understand what you are saying, maniac?

RUPERT. No man better. I know you all from first to last as a dishonest crew. Take heed to what I say, Montressor.

FORTESCUE. (*savagely*) Be silent.

RUPERT. I will not be silent! I am your accomplice no longer. If you have a grain of sense, Montressor, leave this society and never enter it again.

FORTESCUE. You mean – ?

RUPERT. That he has fallen into a nest of hornets, and that I would rescue him before he is stung to death.

FORTESCUE. Then take the consequence. You lie.

RUPERT. Be this the judge. (*raises his hand to strike* FORTESCUE *who arrests his arm*)

FORTESCUE. (*reproachfully*) Rupert, this to me!

RUPERT. (*passionately*) To you, or any one! Yes, to you first of all. You were the man who brought me down to this shameful depth. You, with your cynicism and miserable sophistry, first hushed the voice of conscience in my heart. You taught me, with a withering smile, that self-respect was only self-deceit, and honour but a vapouring word! You led me on to believe that the language of the cards was the voice that heralded a world of wealth. Above all the rest, I denounce you as a swindler and a cheat.

FORTESCUE. (*furiously*) You shall drink your cup of folly to the dregs. There can be but one answer to such words as yours. Have you forgotten that we are not in England, but in a land where such differences are settled by the duel? Do you understand me?

MONTRESSOR. Oh! this must not be.

RUPERT. Silence! I understand you perfectly. Your weapons, time, and place?[35]

FORTESCUE. Swords! I mean to kill you. Time, now! Place, here! (*turning to the Italian gentlemen*) Gentlemen, this must be arranged at once. I will smoke a cigarette while you fetch the necessary implements. (*The three Italians go off* L. FORTESCUE *is following them slowly. He turns and salutes* RUPERT *with studied politeness.*) For the present, *au revoir* Mr. Rupert – Oh, pardon me, I forgot that you were nameless! (FORTESCUE *goes out* R. RUPERT *goes up to seat* C., *and throws himself upon it.* MONTRESSOR *follows him.*)

---

35. Alternative phrasing in **LCC** makes Fortescue sound more callous: 'Swords! I give him no chance – at twenty paces with pistols we might be equal, I know the sword, & you do not. I will kill you!' (f. 54).

MONTRESSOR. Rupert! Rupert! you shall not sacrifice yourself for me.[36]

RUPERT. It is useless to try and turn me from my purpose. Nothing can change my will.

MONTRESSOR. But this is my quarrel. I dispute your right to meet this man.

RUPERT. No, no, that is impossible. Go, Montressor, your life is a valuable one, dear to your mother, dear to Isabel; while mine is worthless as a grain of sand. Leave me to my fate.

MONTRESSOR. (*coming down*) Weak, irresolute, that I am! What can I do to save him? Who will advise me. Ah, Miss Chester, I will tell her all. Oh, if Rupert falls, I am his murderer!

Re-enter FORTESCUE *and the three* ITALIANS, *one carrying swords.*
VITOZZI *crosses to* RUPERT *and talks earnestly with him,*
hurrying him down stage. Music piano in the distance.

FORTESCUE. (*laughing as he talks to* VICENZI) Yes, he was said to be the best swordsman in the Crimea, but for all that I had the misfortune to send him invalided just before Inkerman.[37]

VICENZI. You have an easier task now.

FORTESCUE. Ah, yes, poor boy. I feel quite sorry for him, but (*seriously to* VICENZI *and the others*) you are my witnesses that I had no alternative. Who could have put up with so gross an insult?

VITOZZI. Impossible.

FORTESCUE. His blood be on his head then. (*Takes sword from* VICENZI *and goes up* C.) What is that something in his face that reminds me so

---

36. **LCC** scene closes in a tableau with Montressor restraining Rupert (f. 54). **LCC** introduces a new scene, in which Montressor joins the female characters at their hotel and tells them Rupert is engaged to duel with Fortescue. Miss Chester rushes off to save him (ff. 54–8). This additional scene slows down the action and makes Montressor appear a much weaker character, having left the scene of the duel in cowardly fashion.
37. The Battle of Inkerman took place on 5 November 1854. It was a major engagement during the Crimean War and was widely reported in the contemporary press as a success for the allied forces.

powerfully of the past? Can it be a dim recollection of what my own features used to be before the world, the flesh, and the devil, had stamped their mark upon them? Pshaw. (*down to* R.)

RUPERT. (*to his second*) No! I have no instructions, except this – Let my grave be nameless as myself.

FORTESCUE. (*to his friends*) Gentlemen, there is no occasion to waste more time.

VITOZZI. There can be no apology then?

FORTESCUE. You shall see. (*to* RUPERT) Will you retract your words? Say you are sorry for your insult. Induce Montressor to return?

RUPERT. No!

FORTESCUE. I give you one more chance. Remember it is life or death that hangs upon your answer.

RUPERT. You have received it.

FORTESCUE. Then take the consequence. (*Music.* RUPERT *mechanically takes a sword that is offered to him. They fight, after a few passes* RUPERT *is wounded and falls fainting to the ground.* FORTESCUE *coolly wipes his sword.*)

RUPERT'S SECOND. (*bending over him*) He is badly wounded. We must take him away at once.

VITOZZI. Have you a carriage?

RUPERT'S SECOND. Yes, we must call it up, it would be dangerous to carry him far – most dangerous.

VITOZZI. Come, then, there is no time to lose (*the others go out,* FORTESCUE *stands gazing upon* RUPERT).

FORTESCUE. I never dreamed that it could come to this! Curse my skilled right-hand! (MISS CHESTER *enters hurriedly* R., *she sees* RUPERT *and stops short aghast*) Butcher that I am!

MISS CHESTER. Yes, butcher!

FORTESCUE. (*seeing her*) Good God, Gertrude, you here!

MISS CHESTER. Where should I be? Man, do you know what you have done?

FORTESCUE. (*regarding* RUPERT) If you mean this, he brought it upon himself.

MISS CHESTER. There was no pity, then, to stay your murderous hand! Ah, your hard heart has never known remorse, you shall learn it now! As surely as we three shall stand before the judgment seat of God, the boy your guilty hand has now struck down, *is your own son!* (*She falls senseless upon the body of* RUPERT, FORTESCUE'S *sword drops from his hands.*)

TABLEAU.

END OF ACT II.

ACT III. – A YEAR LATER.

SCENE. – *Library at Castle Montressor; open French windows giving on to garden terrace* C., LADY MONTRESSOR *writing letters at table* L. C., ISABEL *playing piano* R. C.

LADY MONTRESSOR. There, what one would do without correspondence I can't imagine. (*sealing letter*) Oh my dear Isabel, if you can't play anything but such doleful music, I wish you would leave the piano alone.

ISABEL. (*shutting piano and rising*) I am fond of that piece of music.[38]

LADY MONTRESSOR. The composer must have been very wretched when he wrote it, that's all I can say. What has come to this place I can't imagine. We used to be a very happy party here, and now I see nothing but long faces and cross looks.

ISABEL. We have had a very dreary winter.

---

38. **LCC** specifies: 'I am so fond of that piece of Mendlesohns's [*sic*]' (f. 62). Music is used to heighten atmosphere at key points of the play but this is the only moment at which a specific composer is mentioned.

LADY MONTRESSOR. Dreary indeed! and when we have nothing but clouds inside the house as well as out, the gloom becomes almost intolerable.

ISABEL. It does, indeed.

LADY MONTRESSOR. And whose fault is it, if you please? And why should you think it necessary to intensify the gloom by wearing perpetual mourning!

ISABEL. Oh, aunt!

LADY MONTRESSOR. You are wearing it still I suppose for that wretched boy who was killed in a midnight brawl at Florence; a person who was no relation to you whatever, I call it indecent, Isabel, positively indecent.

ISABEL. What, to mourn for those we love?

LADY MONTRESSOR. Unless they are connections, of course it is. Society, very properly, only allows the display of sorrow under certain well defined regulations. Besides, the time has come for me now to insist upon a change of conduct upon your part, Isabel. You are absolutely demoralising to all of us. There is my dear Montressor in a perpetual state of low spirits, *ennuyé* with everything.[39] Silent and melancholy to the last degree. Miss Chester too, who stayed behind to nurse the boy in such a Quixotic manner, her coldness and reserve are more insufferable than ever; I declare I have no patience with any one of you.

ISABEL. Dear Aunt, I would smile and be light-hearted if I could, but it seems impossible.

LADY MONTRESSOR. What nonsense, when you come to my age, you will find it very easy to forget the past.

ISABEL. Is it wrong then, to hope that I may die young? (*aside. Enter* MONTRESSOR C*., he takes no notice of the others, but throws himself languidly into an arm chair* R. C.)

LADY MONTRESSOR. What are you going to do today, Montressor?

MONTRESSOR. I am sure I don't know, and I care less.

---

39. French word meaning listless or bored in this context.

LADY MONTRESSOR. That is a very childish answer, and I am surprised your making it. Why don't you and Isabel go for a good ride?

MONTRESSOR. I loathe riding.

ISABEL. So do I.

LADY MONTRESSOR. (*starting up*) Really this is unbearable. I am sure I do everything I can to make you all happy and contented. What has come to you? What is the meaning of this miserable change?

MONTRESSOR. Oh mother, how often will you ask that question, and how often will you wring my heart by compelling me to answer? The remembrance of that dreadful affair at Florence haunts me night and day.

LADY MONTRESSOR. This is positively absurd. Mere sentimental affectation. Is this house never to be anything but a house of mourning, just because an unfortunate youth happens to meet his death in consequence of his own headstrong folly?

MONTRESSOR. (*sadly*) Say rather in consequence of your son's headstrong vice.

LADY MONTRESSOR. I shall say no such thing. No words of mine shall encourage your ridiculous scruples. (*enter* SERVANT L.)

SERVANT. Mr. Armishaw desires to see your ladyship.

LADY MONTRESSOR. Show him in at once. (*exit* SERVANT) Anything for a change. (*enter* ARMISHAW L.) How do you do, Mr. Armishaw. This is quite an unexpected pleasure.

ARMISHAW. Just so. I thought you would make that very remark. Hope I see your ladyship well, and my lord, and Miss Vivian? Just so. Not as well as I could wish to see you. You should try change of air. The salubrity of London has a wonderful effect upon constitutions that have suffered from the depressing effects of the country.

LADY MONTRESSOR. I am delighted to see you, Mr. Armishaw, but I do hope you have not come on business. I really do not feel equal to the worry. (*sits on ottoman*)

ARMISHAW. Just so. Very natural. No. I am on business at Ashton Court, and thought I would just step over here.

LADY MONTRESSOR. (*languidly*) Anything happened at Ashton?

ARMISHAW. Nothing very remarkable. You are aware Sir Hugh is dead?

LADY MONTRESSOR. Oh, yes – two months ago – I believe.

ARMISHAW. Just so.

LADY MONTRESSOR. And the place is to be sold, is it not? They say there is no heir.

ARMISHAW. Just so. And when *they* say anything, *they* are always wrong. The title and property have descended to the good-for-nothing second son.

LADY MONTRESSOR. Ah! I thought he was dead.

ARMISHAW. So he was dead – that is, to his relations and the world. But he has thought fit to turn up again, and is now in possession of his estates.

LADY MONTRESSOR. Then I suppose we shall soon have the pleasure of seeing Sir Arthur at the Castle?

ARMISHAW. Just so. Very soon I imagine.

LADY MONTRESSOR. What a comfort. I hope he will enliven us.

ARMISHAW. Shouldn't wonder if he did. Don't think I have anything more to say and haven't time for gossip. Walk through the gardens if you will permit me. Good morning my lady.

Bows to her and to the others, who barely notice him – goes up C. *– meets*
MISS CHESTER, *who just inclines her head to him and comes down*
stage. ARMISHAW *looks after her curiously, and takes snuff.*

(*aside*) Ah! things not straight in Queer Street yet? Humph! Just so.

LADY MONTRESSOR. Oh – here you are, at last.

MISS CHESTER. (*coldly*) Have you required my presence?

LADY MONTRESSOR. Oh, bless me. Certainly not, if you are going to be as doleful as the others. One might as well be in the constant society of melancholy mutes, or misanthropic murderers.

MONTRESSOR. Mother. (*starting up*) Don't say that word.

LADY MONTRESSOR. There again. And I absolutely said nothing. My dear Montressor, I wish you wouldn't jump so. If you have no insuperable objection to showing me the new carriage horses which arrived last night, you would do me no small kindness.

MONTRESSOR. Anything you please, mother. This way.

Exit C. E. R.

LADY MONTRESSOR. Anything I please! It always turns out to be everything I dislike. (*follows* MONTRESSOR C.)

MISS CHESTER. Tears Isabel?

ISABEL. Yes. (*rises*)

MISS CHESTER. Are they never to be dried?

ISABEL. Yes; but they will flow again.

MISS CHESTER. For what purpose? To dim the eyes when the hard life of this world requires that they should ever see sharply in order that they may look keenly into the faces of mankind, that they may learn the motives that prompt soft language, and read on cold lips and in deceitful eyes the falsehood that smooths the tongue! Stay the fountain child, keep your tears till you find something in this world worth weeping for, and you will go through life without another sob.

ISABEL. I do not believe you! How often do you mean to speak to me like this? I have always loved you but you are powerless in your attempts to teach me your harsh creed. You have suffered, I know, though you have never told me how – might not even your sufferings be less – be they what they may if you would but let your proud heart own its trial and seek to be softened in its natural outlet, a flood of woman's tears, which seldom flow in vain? (*sits* R.)

MISS CHESTER. Most vain. If you will not believe me, you must learn the bitter lesson for yourself.

ISABEL. Oh! have you no other comfort for me?

MISS CHESTER. None. I would spare you what I, myself, have suffered. You think me cruel, but my cruelty is kind, I have seen the miserable end of earthly love. I have gauged its depth, and know that it is founded on the shallow mould that hides the hard rock of man's most selfish heart. *We* love and give up all, man smiles and takes the sacrifice, and when he has tasted its sweet savour, he coldly extinguishes the flame; and when it suits his noble fancy, calmly erects another altar for another victim.

ISABEL. (*proudly*) My faith is too strong for your experience.

MISS CHESTER. Then cling to it.

> *Exit* Miss CHESTER. R. *At this moment* RUPERT *appears* C.

ISABEL. But none the less do I believe in love. What proof could I have of its great reality than in his noble death?

RUPERT. (*faintly*) Isabel.

ISABEL. What's that! I seemed to hear his voice. Oh, was it an angel's whisper sent to comfort me?

RUPERT. Isabel!

ISABEL. (*agitated, not daring to look round*) Again! So human, too – Am I mad?

RUPERT. My own – my love!

ISABEL. (*turns and sees him*) Oh, Heaven! Rupert!

RUPERT. Yes – come back at last to claim his love without the shade of shame upon his brow. (*he clasps her to his arms*)

ISABEL. Oh, my own love. I can scarcely believe that this is not all a happy dream, from which I must soon awake. Alive, and well?

RUPERT. What is there strange in that? You did not think me dead?

ISABEL. We did, indeed. We were led to believe that you had died from the effects of the wound you received in the duel at Florence.

RUPERT. Dead – why, where then is Miss Chester?

ISABEL. She is here – as usual.

RUPERT. This is most strange. I have written to her every month since I have been at Turin, and she has answered all my letters.

ISABEL. Impossible! When Miss Chester rejoined us, after having stayed behind to nurse you at Florence – oh, Rupert, how I longed to stay with her – she told us you had died from the effect of your wound.

RUPERT. She told you this! Why she placed me in charge of some friends of hers at Florence, and through them I got a clerkship in an Anglo-Italian house at Turin. A few days since, the partners, expressing themselves well satisfied with my diligence and perseverance, offered me a lucrative appointment in their branch at Calcutta. I accepted it, and came straight home to tell the news to my kind benefactress, and to see my Isabel once more. Ah, Isabel! do you remember your promise to me in the gardens at Florence?

ISABEL. I have never forgotten it for an instant, how could I?

RUPERT. And Montressor was saved?

ISABEL. Yes! at the risk of your precious life –

RUPERT. Is my life so precious to you, dearest?

ISABEL. I never knew how precious till now. (*He folds her in his arms.*) But Rupert is there not something mysterious in Miss Chester's conduct? What *can* it mean?

RUPERT. Leave that to me to discover. (*gaily*) As I must certainly prove a very unexpected visitor, you had better breathe the news of my return to life to your Aunt. Nay, I care not what she says. I am independent now and can claim your heart in safety.

ISABEL. Dear Rupert, I will go and tell her all at once. (ISABEL *goes out*)

RUPERT. What can be the meaning of Miss Chester's conduct? What object could she have had in saying I was dead? (*Enter* MISS CHESTER C. RUPERT's *face is turned from her. She starts, gazes intently at him.*) I will seek her at once and insist upon knowing the reason. (*Turns, sees* MISS CHESTER *with a low moan, she falls into a chair.*) Miss Chester! Forgive me for having come upon you so unexpectedly. I have now so much to thank you for that I long to tell you of my good fortune in person, and would not trust it to a letter. Silent! what is there in my sudden presence that can affect you thus?

MISS CHESTER. (*faintly*) Hush! do not speak to me! (*sitting on ottoman*)

RUPERT. But I must speak. I must ask you why you have wantonly inflicted such pain upon the heart that loves me, as to banish all hope by saying I was dead.

MISS CHESTER. My tongue is tied. It is a question that I cannot answer.

RUPERT. Not answer! The question seems to be a very simple one. Why did you say that I was dead?

MISS CHESTER. Oh spare me! Have you no gratitude? (R. C.)

RUPERT. For your tender care of me, for the thoughtful kindness that has eventually made me independent. Oh yes! But have you been kind to Isabel? Have you not been cruel to her?

MISS CHESTER. I thought it better for both your sakes.

RUPERT. How could that be? You knew we loved each other. (*cross* R.)

MISS CHESTER. Oh yes. I knew it.

RUPERT. And yet you could deliberately cast this shadow of the story of my death across her life! Miss Chester, why did you do so?[40]

MISS CHESTER. (*starting up*) You are determined to have an answer! Be it so. Have you forgotten that you once were told you were a man without a name? That your own mother's name was stained with infamy? That you were a bastard substitute for a dead child! You shall learn the truth from my

---

40. **LCC** has a pencilled stage direction: 'Music' (f. 72).

lips that I thought were sealed for evermore! Unhappy boy, whose questions bring the glaring blush of shame once more upon my brow, which now must be reflected on your own, listen, treat me as you will, spurn me, trample on me, curse me, but I am your mother. (*sinks to the ground*)

RUPERT. Oh heavens, my mother!

MISS CHESTER. Oh be generous, Rupert! Do not ask me to reveal the miserable story of the past. Do not bid me rehearse the bitter tale of early love so wronged, so blighted! Forgive me if you can! You say that good fortune has come to you, be content with that. Pursue your path in life, leave me to mine, nor ever guess the tears and agony that must go with me to the grave. (*cross* L.)

RUPERT. Can this be true?

MISS CHESTER. As true as that God is listening to my confession now.

RUPERT. Then if this be so, my path in life is mingled ever-more with yours. Could I desert you, mother?[41]

MISS CHESTER. Oh say that word again. Let me gaze upon your lips and hear the word my soul so long has hungered.

RUPERT. Mother!

MISS CHESTER. Hush – no more – the echo of that word can never pass away in silence.

LADY MONTRESSOR. (*without* R.) Tell his lordship I wish to speak with him in the library.

RUPERT. What shall you say to her?

MISS CHESTER. Leave that to me.

LADY MONTRESSOR *comes in* R., *followed by* LORD
MONTRESSOR. MISS CHESTER *and* RUPERT *retire up and out* C.

LADY MONTRESSOR. Montressor, I want to speak to you seriously. I really cannot tolerate your gloomy spirit any longer. One might as well be

41. **LCC** gives direction for Rupert to raise Miss Chester from her knees (f. 73).

living in a place where everybody was ill, and nobody ever got well. I insist upon your being more cheerful.

MONTRESSOR. It is only waste of time, mother, insisting upon impossibilities. (*sits* R. *at desk*)

Enter SERVANT, L. H. *Music.*

SERVANT. Sir Arthur Ashton is in the library, my lady, and desires to know if he can be received so early.

LADY MONTRESSOR. Oh, certainly. Show him in here. (*Exit* SERVANT) Now, here's a chance for you. Sir Arthur is sure to prove a lively neighbour. He has led a most romantic life, and I am sure he will be able to cheer us all up. (SERVANT *announces* SIR ARTHUR ASHTON)

Enter MICHAEL FORTESCUE – *his hair is grey, and his whole manner changed – he is quiet and sorrowful.* LADY MONTRESSOR *does not recognise him* – MONTRESSOR *goes up* C.

SIR ARTHUR. Lady Montressor, I owe you thanks for the courtesy which has admitted me at so unusual an hour.

LADY MONTRESSOR. (*cordially*) Pray don't mention it, Sir Arthur. The conventionalities of London need not bind us in the country. I assure you that I am charmed to think that Ashton Court is to be tenanted by someone who is prepared to be sociable. (*takes his hand*)

SIR ARTHUR. I had scarcely anticipated so warm a welcome.

MONTRESSOR *starts at* SIR ARTHUR'S *voice, and turns.*

LADY MONTRESSOR. Did you expect to find us very bearish? Montressor, come and be presented to Sir Arthur Ashton.

MONTRESSOR *and* SIR ARTHUR *meet face to face.*

MONTRESSOR. I thought there could be no mistaking the ring of that voice that has sounded in my ears all these weary months.

LADY MONTRESSOR. Montressor.

MONTRESSOR. See how he hangs his head – he dares not meet my eyes. Ah! how I have longed to meet you, Michael Fortescue.

LADY MONTRESSOR. Fortescue! Sir Arthur Ashton! Why, so it is![42]

MONTRESSOR. (*sternly*) One moment, mother, before we commence our mutual congratulation. Michael Fortescue, Sir Arthur, or whatever you may choose to call yourself – what have you done with Rupert?

SIR ARTHUR. In mercy, spare me.

MONTRESSOR. What! Is it possible that shame and remorse await the new-found owner of Ashton Court? Spare you! Did you spare the boy, who, in a generous desire to save me from the clutches of yourself, and others like you, spoke a few hot words of truth, for which you killed him?

LADY MONTRESSOR. My dear Montressor, if gentlemen will fight duels –

MONTRESSOR. Duel! When a skilled swordsman meets a boy who never handled a sword before, the world may call it a duel, but justice calls it murder.

SIR ARTHUR. (*groaning*) Do I not know it?

MONTRESSOR. You own that? Own one thing more. I have longed to meet you. I have looked for you everywhere, and most, I hoped, to encounter you in the crowded thoroughfare that I might tell the whole world that you are what you know yourself to be – a miserable coward.

SIR ARTHUR. Think what you please – say what you please. No words of yours, however hard, shall provoke me to reply.

MONTRESSOR. (*furiously*) Rupert's pale face is ever haunting me. His spirit will not rest till I have avenged him – life for life!

SIR ARTHUR. If the sacrifice of my life could bring his back I would die in tortures and be thankful for the pain.

MONTRESSOR. Now leave this house.

SIR ARTHUR. One moment. I have come here this morning of a set purpose in the hopes to repair so far as may be, a bitter wrong.

---

42. **LCC** adds: 'Quite like a thing in a novel. And to think that you should turn out to be our nearest neighbour! How very delightful!' (f. 76). Lady Montressor is shown to relax her moral judgement of Fortescue now that he is a wealthy landowner.

MONTRESSOR. Vain words. You cannot restore the dead. (*cross* R.)

SIR ARTHUR. You do not even guess of what I speak. Ah, when you have heard all, yourself shall judge whether Rupert's death will not be terribly avenged through all my wretched future life.

LADY MONTRESSOR. Mystery on mysteries! What can you mean?

MISS CHESTER *appears* C.

SIR ARTHUR. All shall be unravelled soon. Where is Miss Chester?

MISS CHESTER. (*starting at the sound of his voice*) Who asks for me?

SIR ARTHUR. (*turning sharply round*) I, Arthur Ashton!

MISS CHESTER. (*coldly*) What falsehood now?

SIR ARTHUR. No falsehood. Bowed, humbled to the very dust, a broken hearted and repentant man. I come back to speak the solemn truth.

MISS CHESTER. What would you say?

SIR ARTHUR. But one word as I gaze into your eyes, and that one word is – wife.

LADY MONTRESSOR. Is he mad!

SIR ARTHUR. Wife, for so you are. I cannot die till you have spoken pardon to your wretched husband.

MISS CHESTER. Oh Heaven, what am I to believe?

SIR ARTHUR. That we have both been deceived.

MISS CHESTER. Is it possible?

ISABEL *enters* L.

SIR ARTHUR. Listen all. This lady to whom your father's roof has so long given generous shelter, is your aunt, his sister whom you believed to be dead, the Lady Gertrude Challinor.

LADY MONTRESSOR. Gertrude!

SIR ARTHUR. When we were young we loved each other but our attachment was disallowed, and we fled from the Castle and were married.

MISS CHESTER. We thought we were.

SIR ARTHUR. When I stood by Gertrude at the altar, my first wife, who
had deserted me, was dead. But then that woman's wretched friends came
forward for the purpose of extorting money from me to buy their silence,
and falsely swore that at the time of my second wedding she was still alive.
You, Gertrude, believing your good name was lost, fled from me. Then
came the report, that you, the Lady Gertrude Challinor, had died of grief
and shame.

LADY GERTRUDE. Go on. Confess it to the end.

SIR ARTHUR. (*so agitated that he can hardly speak*) We met again at
Florence –

LADY GERTRUDE. To the end, confess!

SIR ARTHUR. The boy Rupert whom I took away from hence, thinking
he might be useful to me for my own selfish schemes, the boy whom I
employed to lead Montressor on to ruin, the boy whose generous warmth
ought to have moved what remained in my hard heart of sympathy – O
God, forgive me! I lifted up my hand against him, and killed – our son! (*he
sinks into a chair*)

ISABEL. (*darting forward*) Oh no, no.

ARMISHAW *and* RUPERT *appear on terrace*, C.

LADY GERTRUDE. (*checking Isabel*) Hush, leave that to me. It is my
right. I never knew till now, how sweet revenge might be.

SIR ARTHUR. Take your vengeance.

LADY GERTRUDE. I do. (*she goes up and seizes* RUPERT's *hand*)

ARMISHAW. (*taking snuff*) Just so, just so. He knows all.

LADY GERTRUDE. (*bringing* RUPERT *down*) Arthur my vengeance
is complete. Hold this warm hand in yours, and you shall learn how

perfectly the future can repay the past, in restoring to our love, Rupert our son. (*puts* RUPERT's *hand in* SIR ARTHUR's *who starts up with an exclamation of joy*)

SIR ARTHUR. Rupert! (*embraces him*) You are saved!

RUPERT. Yes, by my mother's care.[43]

CURTAIN.

43. **LCC** gives the final line to Miss Chester:

> MONTRESSOR. I never felt so happy in my life. Rupert, now indeed my brother. Let me present you with the greatest gift it is in my power to bestow (*giving Rupert Isabel's hand*).
>
> RUPERT. Father, mother, and a wife! I never dreamed that I could be so wealthy!
>
> SIR ARTHUR. All clouds have passed away!
>
> LADY GERTRUDE. And sunshine gilds the future! (f. 81)

Figure 6 Annotated page from *The Missing Witness*, Mary Elizabeth Braddon Collection, Robert Lee Wolff Collection of Nineteenth Century Fiction, The Harry Ransom Center, The University of Texas at Austin.

THE MISSING WITNESS[1,2]

An Original Drama in Four Acts

BY

M. E. BRADDON

Author of "Lady Audley's Secret", etc.

LONDON: JOHN AND ROBERT MAXWELL

1. Variants discussed in the notes are:
   WOLFF: Mary Elizabeth Braddon (1880), *The Missing Witness*, London: John and Robert Maxwell. Mary Elizabeth Braddon Collection, from the Robert Lee Wolff Collection of Nineteenth Century Fiction. Harry Ransom Center, University of Texas at Austin (Box 34, Folder 9).
   This is a copy of the printed John and Robert Maxwell edition of the play with handwritten revisions and annotations made around 1880. The item has been digitised and is available at <https://hrc.contentdm.oclc.org/digital/collection/p15878coll53/id/6076/rec/1> (last accessed 6 Nov. 2018).
   Unusually, the Lord Chamberlain's Collection does not hold a copy of Braddon's play. There is a *The Missing Witness* (LCC Add MS 53234 Q) in the collection but it is attributed to Henry Pettitt and Paul Merritt, and licensed on 14 May 1880 for production at the new Grecian Theatre. It features a sensational plotline but is not related to Braddon's play, except by its title.
2. Contemporary reviewers refer to the play as either *Genevieve* (for example, 'Miss Braddon's melodrama, "*Genevieve*," which was brought out a few weeks ago in Liverpool, is to be produced at the Adelphi'; [no title] (1874) *The Orchestra*, 1 May, p. 72) or as *The Missing Witness* (for example, 'MISS BRADDON has a new drama, entitled "The Missing Witness"'; 'Dramatic Gossip', (1874) *Athenaeum*, 28 Feb., p. 302). We use the title as given in the published version of the script.

Dramatis Personæ:

General de Marsac
Gustave de Beaupré
Raymond Varriere
André Colichot
Pierre Colichot
Horace Bianchon
Pauline de Marsac
Genevieve

Peasants, Goatherds, Servants, &c.[3]
Period, about 1836.[4]

NOTE. *All dialogue enclosed between the parenthetic marks, [ ], and in italic type, may be omitted to shorten piece if the theatre cannot give the time necessary to act the full play as written.*[5]

---

3. Although the printed version does not give a cast list, advertisements for the Liverpool production allow us to piece the original cast together as follows:

> General de Marsac: Mr Constantine
> Gustave de Beaupré: Mr J. F. Stephenson
> Captain Raymond Varriere: Mr E. H. Brooke
> Pierre Colichot: Mr Edward Saker
> André Colichot: Mr F. B. Ward
> Pauline de Marsac: Miss Louise Pereira
> Genevieve: Mrs Edward Saker

Edward Saker was the lessee of the theatre and effectively produced the play. He cast his wife, Emily Saker (known on stage as Marie O'Beirne before her marriage), in the lead role. The Sakers were one of many significant husband and wife partnerships in Victorian theatrical culture. The Royal Alexandra Theatre was a well-appointed and well-esteemed theatre. A clipping from the Mander and Mitchenson collection states that 'all the great stars of the day appeared [at the Royal Alexandra Theatre], Ristori, Sarah Bernhardt, Irving, Nellie Farren, Mr. and Mrs. Boucicault' (Edgar Martlew (1953), 'Playhouses Past and Present', 1 Jan. [location unidentified]. MM/REF/TH/RE/353). The play ran for three weeks up to 18 April 1874. As mentioned in the Introduction, it did not, as had been planned, move to the Adelphi in London after its run in Liverpool. However, at least one mention in the press suggests that the play was restaged in Manchester: '"*Genevieve*" (Miss Braddon) closed its career in Manchester last night. It has not been a success, and yet Miss Braddon, having been an actress (years ago she was a member of the stock company at Hull), might write a good play' (Anon. (1874c), p. 83.)

4. In **WOLFF**, the date is changed to 1780, Horace's name is altered to George and two new characters are added: 'Caspar: an old servant of the General's' and 'Leo: a splendid Mount St Bernard' (p.[3]). Caspar functions as the dog's handler and replaces any unnamed servants who make brief appearances throughout the play. Additional lines added into the opening dialogue between the General and Pauline tell us that Leo is Gustave's dog, left with them while he is in St Petersburg (p.[4]).

ACT I

SCENE:– *A drawing-room in the Chateau de Marsac. Large window and balcony overhanging lake, and commanding exquisite Alpine scenery. Doors, &c.*[6]

GENERAL DE MARSAC *discovered reading paper.* PAULINE *standing in balcony watching eagerly for the approach of someone.*

PAULINE. Papa, papa, hark! This time I am *sure* I hear a carriage.

GENERAL. That is about the fifteenth time you've interrupted me while I have been trying to read the latest news from Paris, and every time it has been a false alarm. What a thing it is to be in love!

PAULINE. Remember how long it is since I have seen him, papa – three years!

GENERAL. Three years; and a very proper delay. You were much too young to marry when my poor sister's orphan son, Gustave de Beaupré, came to visit here, and must needs fall in love with his cousin.[7]

PAULINE. He asked your consent, papa.

GENERAL. He asked my consent to marry you because he was obliged to do so; he never asked my consent to fall in love with you. However, what must be must be. The young man was on the eve of starting for St. Petersburg as Secretary of Legation, and wanted to take you with him. "That's all nonsense," said I. "What does a Secretary of Legation want

---

5. In **WOLFF**, either the dialogue in parentheses has been crossed through or indications are made to integrate it fully into the script. These changes progress the action more quickly, particularly in the later stages of the play. The use of brackets to indicate possible omissions to dialogue was not unusual in nineteenth-century playscripts. Collins uses the device, for example, in his 1873 deposit copy of *The New Magdalen* (British Library, Add MS 53122 R.)

6. See Colley (2010), pp. 57–100, for a discussion of how mountain, particularly Alpine, scenes made their way on to the stage in the 1850s following Albert Smith's *Ascent of Mont Blanc*, which ran for six years at the Egyptian Hall in London. A significant comparison here may be made with Wilkie Collins and Charles Dickens's *No Thoroughfare*, which was first published as a Christmas 1867 issue of *All the Year Round* and then ran at the Adelphi for 150 nights. Both Braddon's play and *No Thoroughfare* feature villains thwarted in their affections, who attempt to kill their rival in the Alps and commit suicide when their evil-doing is revealed.

7. Cousin marriage was not unusual in sensation plots on stage and in fiction: for example, Franklin Blake and Rachel Verinder in Wilkie Collins's *The Moonstone* (1868).

with a wife? Go to St. Petersburg, remain there two or three years, and if, when you come back, you still love my daughter, you shall marry her out of hand."

PAULINE. And at last he has returned, and – and – he still –

GENERAL. And he still loves you?

PAULINE. He says so, in his last dear letter.

GENERAL. His last *dear* letter! As if there were any difference between his letters and other people's.

PAULINE. Hark, papa! (*She runs to window.*) This time it is no false alarm. He is coming. Listen! (*Tinkling of bells heard faintly in the distance.*) You hear, Mr. Sceptic! There are the bells. (*Noise of wheels and postillion's whip.*) And now the carriage-wheels. (*Distant hurrahs.*) And now the peasants are on the road shouting. How good they are, dear simple creatures! They are pleased to see Gustave for *my* sake. (*Shouts renewed nearer; wheels, whip, and coming steps without.*) Hark, he is here. We shall see him once more. It seems too bright to be anything but a dream. (*She rings bell.*)

GENERAL. What is that for?

PAULINE. For Genevieve, Gustave's foster-sister. She loves him so dearly, and will be anxious to be among the first to greet him.

GENERAL. And you are not jealous of her affection?

PAULINE. Jealous of Genevieve! No, papa, I know her too well. She loves Gustave with a sister's devotion, and I firmly believe that she would lay down her life for him.

Enter GENEVIEVE.

PAULINE. He has come, Genevieve. I want you to join me in bidding him welcome to Andermatt.

GENEVIEVE. And you think of me at such a moment! Ah mademoiselle, how good you are! (*Retires and remains in the background.*)

Enter GUSTAVE. *Shakes hands with* GENERAL, *embraces* PAULINE.

GENERAL. Welcome, my boy, welcome!

GUSTAVE. (*To* GENERAL) My friend! My father! (*To* PAULINE) Look up, dearest. Let me see the bright face which has haunted my dreams while I have been away from the home of my heart. What! tears, Pauline? Am I to accept these for my welcome?

PAULINE. Ah, Gustave, you know what these tears mean. And you have returned to me safely at last? And you are well? (*Looking at him anxiously.*)

GENERAL. Safe and well! I should think so, indeed; better than ever, if I may be allowed to form my own judgement on such a subject. [*Why the girl looks at him as if here were something in the way of waxwork, and she expected him to melt before her eyes. Safe and well, forsooth! As safe and well as Hercules when he came home from his encounter with the hydra.*] But where is your friend Bianchon – the young doctor who has been the companion of your diplomatic expedition? I thought you were to have brought him with you?

GUSTAVE. I hoped to have had that pleasure, and the poor fellow looked forward with delight to an introduction to you and Pauline. [*He was my schoolfellow, as you know, and was to have been best man at my wedding.*] But he fell ill of a low fever on the road, and I very reluctantly submitted to the necessity of leaving him at the little inn at Amsteg, fourteen miles from here. The host and hostess seemed kind-hearted people, and I think he will be safe in their hands. The heat on the road today was almost unbearable, and I feared to increase poor Bianchon's fever if I persisted in bringing him on.

PAULINE. And you saw no fashionable beauties in St. Petersburg whose fascinations made you forget me? I have been told that diplomatists are terrible flirts – inconstant as the winds that waft them from shore to shore.

GUSTAVE. In that case I am no diplomatist; for there is only one face in the world which possesses any charm for me, and to the owner of that face I shall be true until death.

PAULINE. Death! Oh, Gustave! do not pronounce that dreadful word. Today it sends an icy chill to my very heart. Tell me only that you will be true through life.

GUSTAVE. Through the nine hundred and ninety years of a new Methuselah's life, dear love, if I were to exist so long.

PAULINE. (*laughing*) Or for the hundred years of a Pierre Colichot?

GUSTAVE. Poor old Pierre! I had forgotten to ask after him. Still in the land of the living, I suppose? Still hale, and hearty, and loquacious?

PAULINE. Yes; and still devotedly attached to his tame goats. [*But you will see him very soon, no doubt; he is to be at our fête tonight.*

[GUSTAVE. *A fête!*

[PAULINE. *Yes; a dance by moonlight in the chateau gardens. Our friends are all invited; but, you know in the heart of Switzerland it is not easy to muster a very large patrician gathering, so papa has consented to admit the plebeian element into our festival. The peasantry are to enjoy their share of the merry-making, and we are to have national dances and national music.*[8] *And all this in honour of your return, Gustave.*

[GUSTAVE. *How proud I ought to be!* (In a lower voice.) *And how happy I am!*]

PAULINE. But there is someone you have forgotten to ask after, Gustave.

GUSTAVE. (*puzzled*) Some one I have forgotten?

GENEVIEVE. (*at the back*) (*Aside*) He is too happy to remember me.

PAULINE. Yes, Gustave, someone who has looked for your return almost, perhaps quite, as anxiously as I have.

GUSTAVE. (*looking round with a half-mystified air, perceives Genevieve*) Genevieve! my foster-sister! Ah, I was ungrateful indeed to forget you.

GENEVIEVE. Brother! (*They embrace. Genevieve is almost overcome by emotion.*) Thank Heaven, I see you again! – well, happy, smiling on me with the old familiar face. [*Oh, Monsieur de Beaupré, you cannot guess how your poor foster-sister has thought of you, and feared for you, while*

---

8. One contemporary advertisement mentions Mr J. H. Loveday as the 'musical director' of the 'new sensation play' ('Public Amusements', (1874) *Liverpool Mail*, 28 Mar., p. 3).

you were away in those distant countries which seem so strange and terrible to the ignorant.] Forgive me, Mademoiselle Pauline; forgive me if I speak too freely. You can never understand how I love him. [*We were nursed in the same arms, mademoiselle; we slept in the same cradle; we climbed the mountains hand in hand, and gathered the wild flowers together.*

[GUSTAVE. *Dear Genevieve!*]

GENEVIEVE. He was but a poor, feeble child, mademoiselle [*tall and strong as he is now*], and I remember the time when I could carry him about in my arms like a baby. [*Ah, then how I used to love him!*] He was so weak and helpless! [*The dear little arms clung so tenderly round my neck! I felt then how sweet a mother's love must be.*] But at last the pure mountain air brought roses to his cheeks and brightness to his eyes. And then [*when he had grown a noble, vigorous boy, strong enough to chase the wild deer from crag to crag*] some grand people came in a carriage, and they thanked me for having been good to him, and offered me money, as if I wanted thanks or money for that! They told me that he was not my brother. I thought my heart would break when they told me that. And then they carried him away! (*With emotion.*)

[PAULINE. *My true-hearted Genevieve!*

[GENEVIEVE. *Ah, Mademoiselle Pauline, that was my first great sorrow. My first great joy was when he came to this house ten years after that bitter day, and I saw him again. But, oh dear! how my tongue does run on! I'm sure I have told mam'selle these things a hundred times at the very least, and here I am telling them all over again.*

[PAULINE. *And you know very well I should never be tired of hearing them, Genevieve.*]

GUSTAVE. I think quite enough has been said about my infantine graces, or disgraces. But how about your own affairs – your own prospects? How is André Colichot, the young farmer?

GENEVIEVE. (*embarrassed*) Oh! he's very well, monsieur.

GUSTAVE. And handsome as ever?

GENEVIEVE. He's just the same as he always was, monsieur – neither better nor worse.

PAULINE. And he is as devoted as ever to Genevieve, though she is ashamed to say so, and ashamed to say that she returns his honest affection.

GENEVIEVE. Well, I suppose I do love him, Mam'selle Pauline, just a little bit.

GUSTAVE. And when is the happy event to take place, Genevieve?

GENEVIEVE. Well, monsieur, André is such an impatient young man, you see; and he does worry and torment me so to fix a day for the wedding, so he – I – that is to say, we were thinking, as Mam'selle Pauline has her new Parisian maid to travel with her, and won't want me any longer, we were thinking –

[GUSTAVE. *What Genevieve?*

[GENEVIEVE. *We were thinking*] that we should like to be married on the same day as you and Mademoiselle Pauline. But, of course, if it would be considered a liberty, we wouldn't think of such a thing.

[PAULINE. *A liberty! You foolish Genevieve! when you know that we have been friends and companions for the last ten years. But how slyly you have managed matters! I had no idea your union was so near at hand.*

[GENEVIEVE. *It was only this morning, mam'selle, that anything was settled. André was in the garden with me, putting up some of the lamps and garlands, and talked me into giving consent, because of your marriage, mam'selle. It would be very convenient, he said; but of course, if you or Monsieur de Beaupré should consider it a liberty –*]

GUSTAVE. We consider it the most convenient arrangement in the world, and I will give you the handsomest gold cross and bracelet that ever delighted the heart of Switzer maiden for my wedding present.

PAULINE. And I will give you a bridal dress.

GENEVIEVE. (*delighted*) Oh, mam'selle! Oh, monsieur!

Noise of goats heard outside

GUSTAVE. What is that?

GENEVIEVE. Old Pierre Colichot's goats. He is in the gardens assisting, or making believe to assist, in the preparations for tonight's fête. [*It pleases the old man to think he is useful, and mademoiselle is so kind, she wishes everybody to be as happy –*

[PAULINE. *As I am myself.*]

GUSTAVE. And André is with his grandfather, I dare say?

GENEVIEVE. (*with assumed indifference*) Very likely he is, monsieur.

GUSTAVE. May they both come here for a few minutes, Pauline? I should like to see the old man; he is quite a curiosity in his way; and I should like still better to congratulate André on his good fortune.

PAULINE. You shall see them immediately. Run and fetch them, Genevieve.

GENEVIEVE. But the goats, mam'selle. Pierre Colichot won't go any-where without his goats, you know. He has left off going to church for years because our good pastor won't let him take his goats with him.

PAULINE. He may bring them here, Genevieve. It will not be the first time they have made their appearance in this drawing-room. They are such tame, gentle creatures that they are almost worthy of his exaggerated affection. Let them come.

Exit GENEVIEVE.

GUSTAVE. And now, Pauline, dearest, tell me something of yourself. You have been happy while I have been away. You –

PAULINE. Happy without you, Gustave! You ought to know the impos-sibility of that. Hush! Here they come.

Re-enter GENEVIEVE, *conducting* PIERRE *and* ANDRÉ. PIERRE *leads two tame goats by a string.*[9]

PAULINE. M. de Beaupré wished to see you and your grandson, Pierre, after his return from abroad.

---

9. Animals were a frequent presence on the Victorian stage. Braddon's own earliest memo-ries of a visit to the St James's Theatre featured performances by dogs and monkeys (Braddon (1894), p. 7).

PIERRE. Your servant, mam'selle – servant, monsieur. Very humble servant, mam'selle. I am only a poor old man, mam'selle, very old, very feeble, very deaf.

GENEVIEVE. (*aside to* PAULINE) They say he's only deaf when he pleases, mam'selle, and I know he can hear sharply enough sometimes.

GUSTAVE. Give me your hand, André Colichot. Genevieve is my foster-sister, and let me congratulate you on your good fortune in having secured the best and truest wife that ever an honest man won for his helpmate.

ANDRÉ. You cannot value her more highly than I do, monsieur. I know that a rough uncultivated fellow like me scarcely deserves to win such a treasure; but I know there isn't a man upon this wide earth, be he gentleman or peasant, who could love her better, or stand by her more faithfully than I shall.

GUSTAVE. Spoken like one of nature's very own gentlemen, my brave André. I hear that you are very well off – likely to be rich some day.

PIERRE. No, no, monsieur, not rich. Where is he to get any money I should like to know? We're a very poor family, monsieur – very poor. We have to pinch – to pinch – and to work uncommonly hard – in order to live. I hope André doesn't cherish any expectations from me. *I've* nothing to leave him.[10] A man who has lived to my age ought not to be an object of charity. The nation ought to support him, for a man of my age is a credit to his country.

GENEVIEVE. (*aside to* PAULINE) You see he's not so very deaf, mam'selle.

GUSTAVE. Rich or poor, my foster-sister shall not come dowerless to her husband. It shall be my pleasant duty to place her little fortune in her hands when she leaves the altar.

GENEVIEVE. Oh, no, no, Monsieur Gustave!

GUSTAVE. That is a point on which I must have my way, Genevieve.

---

10. Braddon's *Aurora Floyd* (1863) also utilises a miser as a key character in Steeve Hargraves.

ANDRÉ. A thousand thanks for your generosity, monsieur, but if you think I want a fortune with such a wife as Genevieve –

PIERRE. (*aside*) Hold your tongue, boy. Are you fool enough to refuse their money? Haven't they more than they know what to do with? And are we not as poor as half-starved mice in an empty barn? (*Aloud.*) My grandson doesn't know how to express himself, monsieur. What he *means* to say is, that he'll be humbly beholden for anything you may please to give him.

ANDRÉ. (*indignantly*) Grandfather! I thank you for your kindly offer, monsieur, with all my soul; but I will take nothing with the woman I love but her own true heart. [*We are a simple people, monsieur, but we are not without our pride. We belong to a canton which has been called the conscience of Swtizerland. We cling to an old faith, and we hold to old customs. I was reared among the wild goats on these mountains yonder, and have fought with the eagles in defence of my herd. It's not much of an education to improve a boy's manners, monsieur, but it makes him very independent.*] As for my grandfather, he's a little bit of a miser, monsieur, and you mustn't take any notice of what he says. He's very old, so I hope you'll excuse him.

PIERRE. Yes, yes, André. Very old – very old – and very poor. How old am I, André, eh? I've almost forgotten myself. I'm a poor, feeble old creature, with very little sense or memory left.

GENEVIEVE. (*aside to* PAULINE) Now it's my opinion that's all pretence, mam'selle, and that there isn't anyone in Andermatt with keener wits or a sharper eye to his own interests than Pierre Colichot.

PIERRE. How old am I, André?

ANDRÉ. Something on the right side of a hundred I believe, grandfather.

PIERRE. What do you call the right side of a hundred, André?

ANDRÉ. Well, say ninety-eight.

PIERRE. Ninety-eight! That's very old, monsieur and mademoiselle! Rich people ought to do a great deal for a man of that age. It must be a great privilege to be able to administer to the wants of a poor old creature of ninety-eight.

GUSTAVE. And do you still live in a cottage under St. Elizabeth's Peak?

PIERRE. Yes, monsieur. I and my goats live there together.

GUSTAVE. It is very lonely, is it not?

PIERRE. Well, yes, monsieur, it is rather lonesome. But then, you see, it's cheap; and a poor old creature of ninety-eight is obliged to consider that. As for company, I'm not without that while I have Punchinella and Dandinette – those are the names of my goats, monsieur. They eat with me, and sleep in the same room with me, and keep me company from morning till night. You've no idea what pleasant company a tame goat is, monsieur, if she has been well brought up, and Punchinella would do credit to a palace.

GENERAL DE MARSAC *has re-entered during this speech.*

GENERAL. I'll tell you what it is, my friend Pierre Colichot. Some harm will come to you before long if you continue to occupy that tumble-down old cottage under the Devil's Bridge. You've been warned more than once that the place is dangerous. [*There is an enormous mass of snow on St. Elizabeth's Peak – that peak which juts out almost immediately above your cottage. That over-hanging mass of snow is an object of terror to every packman and mountaineer who passes beneath its shadow. It hangs there, a very sword of Damocles*[11] *held by a single hair, and at any moment may descend and scatter ruin in its fall. The most trivial cause may precipitate that destruction. A gust of wind, the random sweep of an eagle's wing, the firing of a gun, the blasting of a horn, may loosen its narrow hold on the rock; and in a moment – before you have time to breathe one hurried prayer – in the dead of night it may be that icy shroud will descend to wrap you in its fatal folds forever. Have a care, Pierre Colichot! Men have gone to sleep peacefully, with their children and households gathered round them – happy, prosperous, secure – to wake to find themselves in an eternal night, the inhabitants of a tomb*], and if any harm comes to you, you will deserve your fate, Pierre Colichot, for you could afford to live in a better house.

PIERRE. No, no, Monsieur le Général. That dilapidated old place under the Devil's Bridge is the best shelter I can afford. There are some cantons

11. An ancient Greek reference, here reinforcing the imminent danger of an avalanche.

in which a poor creature of ninety-eight would be cared for at the public's expense, but Uri is a very hard-hearted canton.[12]

GENERAL. Well, well, have your own way; but remember you have been warned.

PIERRE. I am not afraid, Monsieur le Général. When I was a little fellow about *so* high (*putting his hand near the ground*) my father lived in that cottage. Well, monsieur, folks were always warning him. "Have a care, Jean Colichot," said one; "that mass of snow on St. Elizabeth's Peak is a great deal bigger than when I was a boy; and mark my words, it will come sliding down before long." And then another neighbour would come and tell us, "I saw the heap of snow on St. Elizabeth's Peak tremble in the storm last night. I expected every moment to see it come crushing down." My father used to thank them kindly for their good advice. "It'll last my time," he said – "it will last my time." That's about ninety years ago, Monsieur le Général, and the snow keeps its place still, and looks as solid as the rock on which it lodges.

GENERAL. Yes, it looks as solid, but that appearance of solidity may be fatally false. This is the hottest summer we have had for many years; and it is in hot summers that avalanches are most frequent [*I would have you be careful, Pierre Colichot, or your ninety-eight years may be cut short before they blossom into a hundred.*

[PIERRE. *Thank you kindly, monsieur – thank you kindly; But I must take my chance. I'm only a poor old pauper, as my grandson knows.* (Aside to André) *Why don't you say you know I'm a pauper?*] (*Aloud*) So I must take my chance. Good-day, Monsieur le Général. Good-day, mademoiselle. Good-day, Monsieur Gustave.

ANDRÉ. (*aside to Genevieve*) I shall be about the chateau gardens all day, Genevieve; and I shall see you again, shall I not?

GENEVIEVE. (*aside*) Yes – yes – André. There – there – go at once. Mademoiselle would like to be alone with Monsieur de Beaupré.

Exeunt PIERRE *and* ANDRÉ. GENEVIEVE *retires by door leading to* PAULINE'S *apartment.*

---

12. Uri is a mountainous canton in central Switzerland.

GENERAL. Well, Gustave, I suppose you've had a very brief *tête-à-tête* with Pauline, and you're not likely to have a much longer one today, for in an hour's time we dine, and I expect a friend and neighbour, Raymond Varriere, to join us at dinner.

PAULINE. (*displeased*) Monsieur Varriere today, papa.

GENERAL. And why not today, *Mademoiselle Capriceuse?*[13] do you think the world is to come to a standstill because you are going to be married?

GUSTAVE. Who is this Monsieur Varriere?

PAULINE. A French officer who served under papa. He came here in the course of a tour through Switzerland, and was so enraptured with the scenery, and the simplicity of the people, that he [*took up his abode in a little chalet, a few paces from the gates of the chateau, and*] has remained there ever since his first arrival; and he is a great favourite of papa's.

GUSTAVE. And no great favourite of yours, I fancy, Pauline?

PAULINE. You are right. I confess to an instinctive dislike of Raymond Varriere.

GENERAL. Prejudice! – all prejudice! Women are made up of prejudices, and presentiments, and nerves, and hysterics, and all sorts of sentimental folly. Raymond Varriere is a brave fellow, and a good, frank-spoken, honest fellow; but he is the last man in the world to dance attendance upon a fine lady's caprices, and Pauline dislikes him on account of his rough manner.

Re-enter GENEVIEVE.

PAULINE. No, papa: I dislike him because I think he has a bad heart.

GENERAL. (*impatiently*) Bah! prejudice, prejudice, prejudice – all prejudice! Come, Gustave, I want to show you the improvements I have made in the gardens of the chateau during your absence.

13. French for 'Miss Capricious'.

GUSTAVE. And Pauline! You will join us, will you not?

GENERAL. Of course she will. Put on your hat, child, and come. (PAULINE *takes large straw hat from side-table.*) [*I say that Raymond Varriere is as good a fellow as ever breathed – a good, honest, fellow enough – rough, but honest, and brave as a lion. He saved my life when we were in Africa together. But Pauline has been spoiled by the polished graces of a diplomatist, and can't tolerate a brave soldier.*]

[PAULINE. *You know that is not true, papa. There is one brave soldier, and the bravest of soldiers, whom I love with all my heart.*

[GENERAL. *Flatterer! That is the way the women twist us round their fingers, Gustave. It will very soon be your turn to be twisted.*]

Exeunt GENERAL, GUSTAVE, *and* PAULINE.
GENEVIEVE *comes down from back.*

GENEVIEVE. He is coming again today. Ah! Mademoiselle Pauline does well to dislike Raymond Varriere. There is danger in that man. [*There are hidden fires under that frank, soldier-like manner of his. There is the heart of a tiger beneath that broad breast, with its crosses and decorations. Brave? Yes, perhaps. The eagles are brave when they swoop on the helpless lambs feeding in the valley.*] Why does he court and flatter the general? For he does flatter, rough and candid as his manner seems. Why is it that he avails himself of every excuse for his visits to this house?

Enter SERVANT, *ushering in* RAYMOND.

RAYMOND. No one here?

GENEVIEVE. No one, except me, monsieur.

RAYMOND. Ah, you are no one. (GENEVIEVE *is going.*) Stay, where is the General?

GENEVIEVE. In the gardens, monsieur.

RAYMOND. And Pauline?

GENEVIEVE. Mademoiselle de Marsac is in the gardens also, monsieur.

RAYMOND. I heard shouts and huzzas an hour ago. What was that for?

GENEVIEVE. The peasantry were bidding welcome to Monsieur de Beaupré, the betrothed husband of mam'selle.

RAYMOND. Oh, he has returned, has he? – the spoiled darling of Parisian drawing-rooms – the ornament of the Court of St. Petersburg – [*the curled and perfumed fopling. He has come back, has he! And safe and sound, I suppose! I should scarcely have expected so much*]. I should have thought his excellency would have melted like your snows in this sultry weather. (*Laughing savagely.*) Stay, Jeannetton – Madelon – whaever you call yourself; I want to talk to you. You are mam'selle's confidential maid, I believe.

GENEVIEVE. I am, monsieur.

RAYMOND. Then, of course, you know all her secrets?

GENEVIEVE. Mademoiselle de Marsac has no secrets, monsieur.

RAYMOND. Ah! it's your business to pretend that. Come – come, Jeannetton.

GENEVIEVE. I was christened Genevieve, monsieur.

RAYMOND. Oh, very well; if you stand upon trifles, it shall be Genevieve. Now, tell me the honest truth, Genevieve. You *must* know more of Pauline de Marsac's real sentiments than any one else. Does she love this De Beaupré? [*He is rich, high-born, well-placed in the world, and I can understand that.*] It may suit her purpose to marry him; but does she love him? – that is the question.

GENEVIEVE. She does, monsieur. [*Mademoiselle de Marsac is the last woman upon this earth to give her hand to a man she did not consider worthy to be the master of her heart.*] She does love Gustave de Beaupré truly and devotedly, as I love him.

RAYMOND. By Jove! You love him, do you? That's a new side of the question. And how does Pauline de Marsac like that?

GENEVIEVE. Gustave de Beaupré is my foster-brother, monsieur. [*These arms have carried him for miles along the perilous mountain pathways when he was a feeble child*;] and I sometimes think that the love I feel for him is like a mother's love. I know that I would gladly lay down my life for his sake.

RAYMOND. Hadn't you better wait till you're asked? Women are very fond of offering to do that kind of thing; but I never heard of one of the sweet creatures carrying out the idea. A woman always talks as if she carried her life about with her in a paper parcel. Laying it down, indeed! What the deuce would be the use of it, I should like to know, if it were laid down? There, you may go, Mademoiselle Genevieve; you're too sentimental for my comprehension. I'm a plain, rough-spoken soldier, and don't understand such high-flown talk. (*Exit* GENEVIEVE. RAYMOND *walks up and down stage moodily; then, after a pause, soliloquises in bitter snatches.*) He has returned! It's all over; and tomorrow Pauline will be his wife! His wife! Oh, how I hate him! Why did I come here? I was happy – [*my wild existence of alternate riot and danger suited me. Amidst the ruin of an abandoned city, upon the topmost rung of a scaling-ladder, amongst the starving defenders of a surrounded fortress, as the leader of a forlorn hope, I was in my element, and I was happy*;] but, in an evil hour, fate drove me to this place, a wounded wretch, in search of health and strength; and I – to whom women were creatures as strange as the inhabitants of some distant star – I became the daily companion of Pauline de Marsac. [*And yet I did not fall at once into the fatal snare! No; for a long time she was no more to me than that Madonna of Guido's on yonder wall – a beautiful face, smiling on all alike, and smiling on me among the rest. I saw her – I heard that she was the betrothed wife of De Beaupré – and I thought no more of her than I thought of that picture. But all at once, in a moment, I awoke as from some dull stupor into sudden life, and I knew that there was fever and madness in my veins – the fever and madness men call love. So far I have kept my secret.*] Day after day I have resolved that the setting sun should see me from Andermatt, and yet nightfall has found me here – a slave, and the most abject of slaves – a slave who wears his chain without hope of release. [*But if my despair is terrible to myself, it may be terrible to others also. The galley-slave who cannot break his fetters may use them to dash out the brains of his gaoler.*] And so this passionate love, which I cannot pluck out of my heart, may transform itself into revenge. (*Looking off.*) They are here, and *he* is with them. At last I shall see my fortunate rival.

Re-enter GENERAL DE MARSAC, PAULINE, *and* GUSTAVE.

GENERAL. Welcome, my dear Varriere! Why did they not tell me of your arrival? Let me present you to my daughter's affianced husband, Gustave de Beaupré. Beaupré, this is Raymond Varriere, as brave a soldier as ever fought against the foes of France. That muscular right arm yonder was extended between me and the Arab lances at Constantine.[14]

RAYMOND. Pshaw! my dear General, you think too much of a small service. [*This arm would have been extended just as readily to save the humblest soldier in the French army. A battle-field is no place for distinctions, and Raymond Varriere is not the man to observe them anywhere.*] (*Crossing to Pauline.*) Let me congratulate you, mademoiselle, on the safe return of your betrothed. [*He has passed through many perils, no doubt, by land and sea, in the course of his travels, and he has come back to you and this peaceful valley unharmed.*] You have reason to be happy.

PAULINE. I am very happy, Monsieur Varriere – very grateful to Providence for my happiness. (*Aside*) That man's congratulations make me shudder.

[GENEVIEVE *re-enters unperceived during this dialogue,*
and remains up stage.

[GENERAL. (*to* GUSTAVE) *You see what an honest fellow he is, and as brave as a lion; but there's no accounting for the prejudices of a woman.*]

BUTLER *enters, and announces.*

BUTLER. Dinner is served, Monsieur le Général.

GENERAL. And high time for it. I feel like a famished wolfhound. Gustave, offer your arm to your affianced wife. I will lead the way, and our friend Raymond shall bring up the rear.

[*Exeunt* GENERAL, GUSTAVE, *and* PAULINE. RAYMOND
remains standing where they leave him, as if plunged in
abstraction, GENEVIEVE *watching him.*

14. The General refers to the 1836 Battle of Constantine in Algeria, an unsuccessful action for France within the conquest of Algeria (1830–47).

RAYMOND. (*arousing himself suddenly*) Dinner! Yes, the dull, commonplace round of life must go on, whatever fever or whatever madness devours the hearts of men. We hate each other and smile at each other, and chink our glasses gaily together in good fellowship. And I am to eat and drink with *him* – Pauline de Marsac's affianced lover, Gustave de Beaupré. The wandering Arab in the desert refuses to break bread with his enemy, or having broken it suffers his direst foe to go forth unharmed. Civilisation teaches us better manners.

GENERAL. (*without*) Varriere, we are waiting for you.

RAYMOND. (*calling*) I am coming, General. Yes, civilisation teaches us better manners, so I go to eat and drink with Gustave de Beaupré.

[*Exit* RAYMOND.

GENEVIEVE. (*watching him*) There is murder in that man's face. But I will watch – I will watch!

END OF ACT I

ACT II

SCENE:– *The gardens of the Chateau, illuminated with coloured lamps, which are reflected in the lake.*

Stage crowded with peasantry in gala dresses. Ballet.

GENEVIEVE *advances to front of stage, followed closely by* ANDRÉ.

ANDRÉ. Genevieve, there is something amiss with you tonight. You avoid me at every turn – tonight above all other nights, when I thought we should be partners in every dance.

GENEVIEVE. I have not danced at all tonight, André.

ANDRÉ. I know that.

GENEVIEVE. Oh, you have been watching me then, André Colichot?

ANDRÉ. What should I do but watch you, Genevieve? You stand apart from the rest – you creep stealthily here and there, following someone, or searching for someone. I don't know which. Something has changed you, Genevieve.

GENEVIEVE. Why, what would change me you foolish André?

ANDRÉ. The return of that man.

GENEVIEVE. What man?

ANDRÉ. Gustave de Beaupré.

GENEVIEVE. My foster-brother?

ANDRÉ. Yes, the foster-brother whom you love so dearly.

GENEVIEVE. (*After looking at him earnestly.*) Why I do believe the man is jealous!

ANDRÉ. Oh, it's very easy to make it a laughing matter.

GENEVIEVE. No, André, it is not so easy to make it a laughing matter. I am much more inclined to be sorrowful than merry. I did not think you were capable of such a meanness as to be jealous of me.

ANDRÉ. Oh, that's what every woman says.

[GENEVIEVE. *Indeed, André Colichot, then you have been jealous of other women, have you?*

[ANDRÉ. *No, Genevieve; but I know what women are.*

[GENEVIEVE. *Then you have no business to know what women are. If you were really as devoted to me as you have pretended to be for the last three years, you would know nothing of the ideas and sentiments of other women. Suppose I were inclined to be jealous, Monsieur André? But I should despise myself if I were weak enough to cherish any such contemptible feeling.*

[ANDRÉ. *Ah, it's all very well to say that, Genevieve. I haven't got a foster-sister!*

[GENEVIEVE. (taking his arm coquettishly) *André!*

[ANDRÉ. *Genevieve!*

[GENEVIEVE. *Can you look at me and be jealous of me?*

[ANDRÉ. *The more I look at you the more I am inclined to be jealous. If you were old and ugly I might rise superior to any such meanness.*] But I will trust you, darling. You shall have a whole regiment of handsome foster-brothers if you like. And now come, dearest, you must be my partner in the next dance.

GENEVIEVE. I shall not dance tonight, André.

ANDRÉ. But why not, Genevieve?

GENEVIEVE. I want to be near mademoiselle.

ANDRÉ. Mademoiselle does not want you. She is engaged with M. de Beaupré. It's very strange you can't dance with me tonight, Genevieve. I must say I think it's very strange. However, I see what it means.

GENEVIEVE. (*indignantly*) Yes, André Colichot; and *I* see what it means. It means that you can trust me with all your heart and soul just so far as you can see me. It means that you would take me for your wife. You would do this, and yet you would be base enough to suspect me, and watch me, and follow me, and persecute me at every turn, simply because there is some slight change in my manner which you cannot understand.

ANDRÉ. It is not a slight change, Genevieve. It is a change that has come about since Monsieur de Beaupré's arrival. I am not quite blind, Genevieve.

GENEVIEVE. (*passionately*) What! You dare to doubt the truest and deepest feelings of my heart? Then I have done with you, André Colichot. From tonight all is over between us. The man who pretends to love me, and yet cannot trust me, is no husband for me, so you had better go and seek a mistress for the farm. (*She goes up stage, and disappears amongst the crowd.*)

ANDRÉ. (*following her*) But, Genevieve – Genevieve!

RAYMOND *and* PIERRE COLICHOT *advance as others retire.*

RAYMOND. And so you live in that little tumble-down cottage under the old stone bridge, do you, Maître Colichot?

PIERRE. Yes, Captain.

RAYMOND. The Devil's Bridge, I think they call it hereabouts?

PIERRE. They do, Captain.

RAYMOND. How came it by such a name?

PIERRE. Well, you see, Captain, there was a time when there was no bridge whatever across the gulf that yawns between Uri and Ursern[15]; and it was said that no mortal builders were capable of building such a bridge. So folks were obliged to do without one, till one day the devil offered to build it with his own hands.

RAYMOND. Very obliging of his Satanic majesty; but I suppose he expected some recompense for his trouble?

PIERRE. Yes, Captain. The price he demanded for his work was the soul of the first creature that passed over the bridge.

RAYMOND. And a very moderate price too, considering what very bad souls there are to be found in the world, and that the devil gets a great many for nothing.

PIERRE. (*chuckling*) But the people of Uri were too clever for him, Captain; they managed to cheat him after all.

RAYMOND. What! His Satanic majesty got the worse of the bargain for once in a way, did he?

PIERRE. He did, Captain. The people of Uri sent a he-goat across to Ursern, and got the best of the black gentleman.

RAYMOND. And did he take that quietly?

PIERRE. No, Captain. He was in a furious rage when he found how he had been swindled. He seized hold of an enormous rock, and just as he was about to hurl it at the bridge, which it would have smashed to a thousand atoms, Saint Elizabeth appeared to him in a flame of fire, on the peak just above his head, whereupon he vanished in a blue smoke. That is the last the

15. The neighbouring canton to Uri.

people of Uri ever saw of the devil, monsieur; but the stone may be seen in the valley to this day, with the mark of his claws upon it.

RAYMOND. A wonderful story, Monsieur Colichot! And you live in that old hovel under the bridge, do you?

PIERRE. Yes, Captain. It's a poor place, but I'm a poor man, Captain.

[RAYMOND. *Are you, Maître Colichot? In that case report belies you, for I've heard you spoken of as a very rich one.*

[PIERRE. *Me, monsieur? – me? Ah! that's just the way with those country people. If they see an old man dressed in rags – living on bread and water – "Oh ho!" they say – "he's a miser!" That's just the way with them.*

[RAYMOND. *Then you are not rich, Maître Colichot?*

[PIERRE. *What is that to you, Captain Varriere?*]

RAYMOND. Oh, you know my name, do you?

PIERRE. Yes, Captain. I've my faculties pretty well yet for ninety-eight.

RAYMOND. Would you like to earn some money, Pierre Colichot?

PIERRE. I would, Captain – I would. I'm a very poor old man, and people of Uri do very little for me; but I should like to eke out my miserable existence a little longer if I can. It's a hard thing to die of want, Captain Varriere, at ninety-eight.

RAYMOND. Well, I think I can put you into the way of earning a little money, and very easily, Maître Colichot, before long.

PIERRE. Couldn't you put me in the way of it at once, my noble captain? Life is very precarious with a man at ninety-eight.

RAYMOND. Wait about here until I speak to you again, and before night-fall tomorrow you shall have earned a handful of gold. (*Turns away.*)

PIERRE. A handful of gold! (*Rubbing his hands.*) Another handful to add to the great heap. It swells – it swells – it swells! They tell me the pile of snow upon St. Elizabeth's Peak grows larger and larger every day, and I know of a bright, glittering, yellow pile that gets larger and larger too – yes, larger every day. How I have pinched and scraped for the sake of adding a coin now and then till the silver pieces could be changed into gold, glittering gold! Other men spend their money on eating and drinking, and fine clothes and comfortable houses. I love my gold – heaps of gold! I count my gold pieces, and they are sweeter to me than meat or drink. They give me more comfort than good clothes, or a cottage that would keep out the wind and weather. And by pretending to be poor I contrive to live upon foolish folk's charity. I should get nothing from other people if I were to spend my own money. No, I'm not so simple as that. I'm a very old man, but I've got my faculties, and I make other people contribute to my support. What's the use of having lived so long if one isn't a little wiser than one's neighbours? (*Retires up stage.* GENERAL DE MARSAC *advances between* PAULINE *and* GUSTAVE.)

GENERAL. Don't you see, Pauline, that poor Varriere feels himself quite neglected? As the daughter of his host you are bound to pay him some attention. Will you dance with him presently?

GUSTAVE. I was about to ask for the happiness of Pauline's hand for the next dance, General.

GENERAL. Nonsense! You have been dancing with her all the evening. You'll dance with Varriere, won't you Pauline, to oblige me?

PAULINE. You know I would do anything in the world to oblige you.

GENERAL. Spoken like my own darling girl. Varriere – (RAYMOND *advances*) – if you are not otherwise engaged my daughter would like to be your partner for the next waltz.

RAYMOND. (*enraptured*) Engaged with Pauline – when Mademoiselle de Marsac – offers to dance with me! (*Recovering himself.*) Ah, I understand. I owe this to the General's compassion. Mademoiselle gives me her hand for a waltz as she would fling a sou to me if I were a beggar – out of charity.

> *Waltz. After a few turns the music ceases, the couples scatter*
> *right and left.* PAULINE *and* RAYMOND *advance.*

PAULINE. I will go back to my father now, Captain Varriere, if you please.[16]

---

16. In **WOLFF**, a manuscript page is inserted at this point (facing p. 20), bringing in a shortened version of the second conversation between Genevieve and André.

RAYMOND. Stay, Pauline – pardon a soldier's rudeness – Mademoiselle de Marsac; this is the last night of my residence in Andermatt. Surely you will not grudge me a few moments of your society?

PAULINE. The last night of your residence here! Your departure is very abrupt, is it not?

RAYMOND. It is, and it is not. Every day for the last six months I have endeavoured to tear myself away from this place, but in vain; I could not – I could not. The charm which held me here was stronger than myself – stronger than the heart of him whom rugged warriors have called Varriere the Tiger. Ah, Pauline, you do not know what it is to suffer as I have suffered. You do not know what it is to fight against destiny as I have fought.

PAULINE. I do not understand you, Captain Varriere.

RAYMOND. No, you do not understand. You are colder than the snow on yonder mountains, or you would have guessed my fatal secret ere this. You would have known that I love you, and that it is my love alone that has retained me here.

PAULINE. And you dare to talk to me thus, Captain Varriere, on the eve of my wedding day? Your insolence deserves that I should appeal to my father for protection, and I will do so if you presume to assail me again. (*Going.*)

RAYMOND. (*laying his hand upon her wrist to detain her*) Stay, Pauline de Marsac. [*You think that a man who loves as I love should choose his time for speaking. He should await the fitting moment, conform to the rules of etiquette, subdue his voice to the most approved softness of tone – like that of your courtier and diplomatist yonder, Gustave de Beaupré – and then declare his love as thousands of other men have done before him, with the same conventional formalities, in the same stereotyped phrases. That is all very well for a man of the world, but I am not a man of the world: I am a soldier, a wanderer, a dweller in tents, wild as the Arab who lies down under the stars with the shoulder of his horse for a pillow. A man of my stamp speaks when he must, when the passion that he has held enchained bursts its bonds all at once and overmasters him.*]

PAULINE. There is one fact you appear to forget, Captain Varriere – I am the plighted wife of Gustave de Beaupré.

RAYMOND. His plighted wife, perhaps; but that plight shall never be kept.

PAULINE. Is that a threat, Captain Varriere?

RAYMOND. No, Mademoiselle de Marsac; it is a warning.

PAULINE. What is it that I have to fear?

RAYMOND. Your lover's falsehood. What! cannot you see that there is something more than brotherly and sisterly affection between him and Genevieve? Watch, Pauline, watch! and let your own senses confirm my warning. And when you have discovered that Gustave de Beaupré can be faithless, you may better value a rough soldier's honest passion.

PAULINE. You might have spared yourself the trouble of these insinuations, monsieur. I am not so weak as to be influenced by them.

RAYMOND. What if I can offer you proof? (*She turns away from him to go up stage.*) Nay, you shall hear me. (*Seizing her hand.*)

PAULINE. Release my hand, monsieur.

RAYMOND. Not till you have heard me out.

PAULINE. Release my hand, or I will call for help!

RAYMOND. I say you shall hear me!

PAULINE. Father! Gustave! – help!

> GENERAL, GUSTAVE, *and* GUESTS *rush forward.*

GUSTAVE. (*in a threatening tone*) Captain Varriere! Pauline! What has happened?

PAULINE. (*recovering herself with an effort*) It is nothing – only an adder in the grass at my feet. Monsieur Varriere has killed it. I was very foolish to give such alarm.

RAYMOND. If Monsieur de Beaupré thinks that I am responsible for the adder, I am quite ready to answer for the reptile's inopportune appearance.

GENERAL. My dear Varriere, there is no occasion to be warlike.

GUSTAVE. Not the least. I am the last to fear a snake in the grass. Come, Pauline.

*Curtains before two large windows of Chateau are suddenly drawn
aside, revealing supper tables brilliantly illuminated.*

GENERAL. Come, friends, the lamps are waning, so with your leave we will adjourn to the chateau. [*The salon on the right has been made ready for my friends, the villagers; and I hope they will drink to my daughter's happiness in brimming bumpers of our native wine. The salon on the left has been reserved for our own small party.*] Gentlemen, escort the ladies to the supper-table. Come, Pauline! Why, you look pale, child! That adder has frightened you more than you care to confess. Come, Varriere!

General movement towards supper-room. Exeunt all but RAYMOND,
*who remains behind unobserved. Crimson curtains fall over the
windows. The light is seen shining through them. Occasional
sounds of huzzas as the scene continues.*

RAYMOND. She has defied me. Be it so – I accept the challenge. Here, you – Jean, Gaspar, Guillaume – whatever your name may be – bring me a bottle of brandy and a couple of glasses to yonder table, under those trees. I can't stand the heat of your supper-rooms, and will take my refreshment under the open sky.

SERVANT. Shall I bring you some supper, Captain?

RAYMOND. No; you need bring nothing but the brandy. I shall eat no supper tonight. (*Exit* SERVANT.) Eat! – (*laughing bitterly*) – Eat! – with my lips dry – hot as iron at a white heat; with a fever in my veins which is so near akin madness that I begin to wonder whether I am not really mad. (*After a pause.*) [*Am I not mad? Is there any difference between the disease which men call madness, and this desperate passion which carries me along in spite of myself, as that mountain stream yonder carries a log of pine-wood, sweeping it across every obstacle, bruising and grinding it against every crag? The lifeless log could scarcely be more powerless than I am to resist the force of the torrent. It bears me on in spite of myself, I know not whither.*] (*Re-enter* SERVANT. *He draws table from under the trees to C., places brandy and glasses, sets chair, and exit.* RAYMOND *paces stage in profound thought, then seats himself, pours out brandy, and drinks meditatively.*) Yes, De Beaupré must fall into the snare. Friendship's fetters are as firm as those of love or hate. (*Looking round.*) What can have become of that old man, Colichot? (*Calling.*) Colichot! (*Looking round.*) Pierre! – Pierre Colichot! (GENEVIEVE *disappears.*) No; it is no one. (*Enter* PIERRE.) Ah! you have returned at last. Where have you been, man? I have been waiting for you.

PIERRE. I ask your pardon, Captain. I have been at supper, honoured Captain. At ninety-eight years of age a poor old creature must make the best of the few festivities that remain to him. I have been at supper, and I have made so bold as to bring away a few fragments which may serve to eke out my frugal repast tomorrow. (*Ties up bundle, in which a large silver spoon is plainly visible among broken victuals and sundries.*) A few poor fragments, Captain Varriere, such as the wealthy are wont to fling to their dogs, but good enough for me – good enough for me. (*In his hurry and eagerness spills contents of bundle on stage.*)

RAYMOND. (*pointing to spoon*) Is that one of your poor fragments, my friend Colichot?

PIERRE. Which, monsieur? (*Business. ad lib.*)

RAYMOND. This. It looks very like a silver table-spoon.

PIERRE. Does it, Captain? My poor old eyes are not so good as they used to be. It may look like a silver spoon, but it can't be one. (*Secures bundle.*)

RAYMOND. I'll tell you what it is Maître Colichot. I begin to think you are a little bit of a thief, as well as a miser.

PIERRE. Thief! Miser! Well, well, it is the privilege of the rich to abuse and trample upon the poor. And what is a helpless old creature of ninety-eight but a door-mat for other men to wipe their feet upon?

RAYMOND. However, that's no business of mine; and I am not going to play the spy for the benefit of General de Marsac. Put up your treasures, Pierre Colichot, and drink a glass of that brandy; it will restore the equilibrium of your nerves. (*Business.*) And now, as I think by this time we thoroughly understand each other, we'll come to business at once. You know the village of Amsteg?

PIERRE. I have known it these ninety years.

RAYMOND. And you know the landlord of the "White Cross"?

PIERRE. As well as if he were my own son.

RAYMOND. I told you just now that I could put you into the way of earning a pocketful of money, and I'll show you that I can keep my word. You are free to come and go as you please to this house, are you not?

PIERRE. Yes, Captain – free to come and go. The General is very kind to me as far as that goes, but his kindness goes very little beyond that. It pleases him to call me a miser – that's a cheap way of satisfying his conscience. The people of Uri do very little to reward a man for his perseverance in living to be ninety-eight. They don't give him much encouragement to push on to a hundred, in order to be a credit to his native place.

RAYMOND. They treat you very badly, I dare say, friend Colichot; but if you'll listen quietly to me I'll put you into the way of making, say, a hundred francs without any more trouble than you are taking this moment.

PIERRE. My brave Captain, I am all attention.

RAYMOND. I suppose you know the nature of a practical joke?

PIERRE. Well, I believe I do, Captain. Something that is very amusing for the joker, but very unpleasant for the subject of the joke.

RAYMOND. Precisely. Now I'm very fond of jokes, especially of practical jokes.

PIERRE. You are, are you, Captain? I should scarcely have thought it. You haven't got it in your looks.

[RAYMOND. *Oh, yes. I am one of the funniest fellows in existence, I assure you.*

[PIERRE. *You don't say so, Captain.*]
  [*During this scene both men drink considerably.* GENEVIEVE *watches and listens, appearing and disappearing ad lib.*

[RAYMOND. *Yes, I am. You may not believe it, but I am. Now it has struck me, Maître Colichot, that at such a time of festivity as this, a practical joke – a good one, you know – would be highly appropriate. The General would be delighted with it, I know, for he's just the man for that sort of thing, and I have no doubt it would amuse Mademoiselle de Marsac, to say nothing of everybody else in the village, to whom it would, of course, afford considerable entertainment.*

[PIERRE. *Always excepting the object of the joke.*]

RAYMOND. [*Excepting him. Of course he must suffer a little inconvenience for the general good.*] Now, I think I have hit upon a capital joke, and a perfectly harmless one, but in order to carry it out successfully I must have your help.

PIERRE. (*reflectively*) My help! Ah, to be sure, my help.

RAYMOND. For which you shall be handsomely rewarded.

PIERRE. Oh, if it comes to that, I can enjoy a practical joke. I've a strong sense of humour left in me yet, though I am ninety-eight. How much did you say the reward was to be, Captain?

RAYMOND. A hundred francs.

PIERRE. (*holding out his hand*) I'm your man, Captain. I'll enter into your joke with all my heart and soul. What do you want me to do?

RAYMOND. My idea is that it would be a capital bit of fun to get him out of the way tonight, on the eve of his wedding-day.

PIERRE. A capital bit of fun for everybody except M. de Beaupré himself.

[RAYMOND. *Oh! he would come to no harm, you know. He'd come back in time for the wedding next morning. But in the meantime everybody would be frightened out of their wits by his absence.*

[PIERRE. *Oh! they're to be frightened out of their wits first, and very much amused afterwards.*

[RAYMOND. *To be sure they are. That's the essence of a practical joke.*][17]

PIERRE. And how are you to get M. de Beaupré out of the way?

RAYMOND. Well, Maître Colichot, it is for that I want your assistance.

PIERRE. I'm all attention, my brave Captain.

RAYMOND. Gustave de Beaupré has a friend called Bianchon – a friend who accompanied him on his travels, and was to have come here with him. That friend is now lying ill at the "White Cross" at Amsteg. Now, if a message were to come from the "White Cross" to say that M. Bianchon was dangerously ill, and implored his dear friend Gustave de Beaupré to hasten to him immediately, Gustave would be sure to go; and if we contrived to lock the stables of the chateau, and hide the keys, de Beaupré would be able to get no mule to carry him, and would be obliged to go by the path across the mountain, which would be very tiresome for him.

PIERRE. And intensely funny; I see, I see.

RAYMOND. What I shall want you to do is, first to lock the stables and hide the keys. You are very friendly with all the men about this place, and can manage that easily enough presently, while the servants are at supper.

PIERRE. Ay, ay, I think I might manage that; but it will be very troublesome, and dangerous into the bargain, and I must have more than a hundred francs.

RAYMOND. Pshaw, man, you shall have double what I promised if you only serve me faithfully.

PIERRE. I will, Captain, I will. What next?

17. **WOLFF** gives hand-written annotation adding dialogue:

> Pierre: I'm afraid I can't see it, I'm too old.
>
> Raymond: Well I suppose it was like your little joke with the spoon (*pointing to bundle*), you can see the fun of it, the General couldn't.
>
> Pierre: Oh ah. Yes. I understand – But . . . . (p. 26)

These additional lines strengthen the sense that Pierre is blackmailed into his part in the conspiracy rather than doing it only for the promised monetary reward.

RAYMOND. Next you will present yourself at the chateau an hour hence. Hark, it is now midnight. (*Clock strikes.*) At one o'clock you will come, as if returned from the valley where you live, and tell M. de Beaupré that the messenger from the "White Cross," having walked across the mountain, and having broken down from sheer exhaustion near the foot of the Devil's Bridge, entrusted you with his message, and you have come to deliver it.

PIERRE. They will give me a trifle for that, I dare say.

RAYMOND. You will inform M. de Beaupré of his friend's danger, take any reward that is offered to you, and depart. Leave all the rest to me. There will be nothing more for you to do, and I think that your share in the joke is easy enough.

[PIERRE. *Tolerably easy, perhaps, Captain, but excessively dangerous. If my share in the business should be found out I should forfeit the General's esteem forever, and though he does little for me in a pecuniary way, I should be very sorry to lose his esteem, for it's a nice house to come to, you see, Captain – a very nice house to come to.*

[RAYMOND. *Play your part with only a common prudence, and there is no possibility of discovery.*]

PIERRE. I'll do my best, Captain, but I must have something in the way of earnest money, just to make a beginning. Time is short at ninety-eight. (RAYMOND *tosses him a gold piece.* PIERRE *picks it up, and contemplates it with the air of a discontented cabman.*) You must contrive to make it a little more than this, Captain.

RAYMOND. (*impatiently*) Pitiless scoundrel! There, take all I have. (*Tosses him a purse.*)

PIERRE. Thank you kindly, Captain. But if this is *all* you have, how are you to pay me the balance when the business is done?

RAYMOND. Unconscionable miser! you shall have your due if I must needs spill my heart's blood to satisfy you.

PIERRE. Oh! I don't want *that*, Captain; that wouldn't be of the slightest use.

RAYMOND. You need have no fear that you will be cheated out of one coin of your promised reward. (*Passionately.*) You shall have your money. If nothing less than Eldorado would satisfy you, you should have your claim. Yes, if the gold of an empire were demanded of me I should find it – I would obtain it to buy revenge!

PIERRE. (*starting up*) Revenge! I thought we were talking of a practical joke?

RAYMOND. (*recovering himself*) Yes, yes, of course, a practical joke, a playful sort of revenge. De Beaupré offended me tonight, and I am resolved to indulge myself in a harmless little bit of revenge.

GENERAL, *lifting curtain of salon, and calling.*

GENERAL. Varriere, Varriere! Where the deuce has the man hidden himself? Varriere!

RAYMOND. I am coming, General. (*To* PIERRE.) You can remember your lesson?

PIERRE. To the very letter, Captain; but how about the balance?

RAYMOND. Come to my chalet two hours after you have delivered your message, and you shall have the uttermost farthing due to you.

GENERAL. (*calling*) Varriere!

RAYMOND. At your service, General. (*Goes to salon.*)

PIERRE. That man is either mad or a fool. The idea of anyone paying solid gold for such impalpable trumpery as revenge.

[GENEVIEVE *springs forward from her hiding-place, and swoops upon* PIERRE.

GENEVIEVE. You wicked old man! I have heard every word of the vile scheme in which you have engaged yourself. I know all the details of the hideous plot, for it is a plot, and you know it. You know it, Pierre Colichot. Down upon your knees – down upon your knees at my feet, old man, and swear by the heaven above you that you will have neither act nor part in the delivery of that lying message! Swear! swear it, Pierre Colichot, unless you want me to strangle you with my own hands!

PIERRE. Don't be violent, Genevieve. I don't want you to strangle me, and I will swear anything you like.

GENEVIEVE. Swear that you will not deliver that message!

PIERRE. I swear! I swear! What a very violent young woman you are, Genevieve!

[GENEVIEVE. *So help you Heaven!*

[PIERRE. *So help me Heaven!*]

GENEVIEVE. And now the money.

PIERRE. What money, my dear Genevieve? (*still on his knees*)

GENEVIEVE. The money you took from that man. Give it to me this instant.

PIERRE. Good gracious me, Genevieve! Give it to you – my money, my honest earnings?

GENEVIEVE. Give it me, I say, Pierre Colichot.

PIERRE. No, Genevieve, don't be cruel. Don't take my money away. It's the one thing I love. People call me a miser. Granted, perhaps I am a miser. But think of the long years of toil and deprivation I've gone through for the sake of saving a little money – such a little, Genevieve. It has come so slowly, it has been so hard to earn, I feel as if every coin were a drop of my heart's blood. Don't take it from me, Genevieve. I'll do whatever you like, but don't rob me of this bright gold piece. It isn't dull, cold dross to me. I love it as if it were a living thing. Don't take it from me, Genevieve. (*Business. A struggle.* PIERRE *shrieks aloud for help, but after resisting, he gives up the money.* GENEVIEVE *flings the purse into the lake.*)

GENEVIEVE. Let that ill-gotten gold lie buried amongst the foul weeds and slime, a fouler thing than they. And now go, Pierre Colichot, go and repent your infamy. I despise and abhor you, and it is a shame and bitterness to know that you are akin to the man I love. (*She flings him from her, and retires to the background.*)

PIERRE. (*alone*) You're a nice young woman, Mademoiselle Genevieve, to rob a poor old man of his hard-won earnings. But I'll be revenged on you, my young lady, and whatever mischief there may be in Monsieur Varriere's jest, I'll stand by him, and help him carry it out. I might have changed my mind, perhaps, if Genevieve had been civil; but she's taken my money, touched me in my tenderest point, and I'll make her pay for it. An hour hence, said the Captain. That's nearly half an hour ago. As the clock strikes one I'll be here with my message. Genevieve has robbed me of the earnest money, but it shall go hard with me if I don't get the balance. The moon is rising. A fine night for Monsieur de Beaupré's walk.

[*Exit* PIERRE.

Enter GENEVIEVE, *followed by* PAULINE.

PAULINE. Stay, Genevieve, I must and will speak to you. (*She takes her hand.*) There is something wrong. I can see it in your face. What is it that makes you sad, Genevieve? On this night – of all others – the eve of your wedding.

[GENEVIEVE. *It is not the eve of my wedding, mademoiselle.*

[PAULINE. *Not? Have you and André quarrelled, Genevieve?*

[GENEVIEVE. *Our wedding is to be deferred, mademoiselle.*

PAULINE. [*That is no answer to my question, Genevieve.*] Is there anything amiss between you and André? He loves you so dearly.

GENEVIEVE. I am not so sure of that, mademoiselle.

PAULINE. Oh, I see, it is some jealous fancy of yours, arising out of the fête tonight, perhaps. My foolish Genevieve, why should you be jealous? In all cantons there is not a fairer maiden than Gustave de Beaupré's foster-sister.

GUSTAVE. (*who has entered while* PAULINE *was speaking*) A fact which the gentleman in question is ready to attest at the point of the sword if need be. What is the matter with my foster-sister?

[GENEVIEVE *has retired.*

PAULINE. She has quarrelled with André, and the intended wedding is to be deferred.

GUSTAVE. Ah, I can never consent to that. We must prevent it somehow. [*These lovers' quarrels are the easiest things in the world to adjust. I'll send for André, and bring him to book immediately.*

[PAULINE. *But do you think he will come?*

[GUSTAVE. *It shall be my business to make sure of that.*] (*Seats himself at table and writes.*) Genevieve!

GENEVIEVE. Monsieur.

GUSTAVE. Is André anywhere within call? I saw him just before supper. Has he left, do you think?

GENEVIEVE. I believe he has, monsieur.

GUSTAVE. That is provoking. I wanted particularly to see him tonight, and without delay. [(He waits, as if expecting GENEVIEVE to speak, but she remains silent.) *Does he live very far from here?*

[GENEVIEVE. *Not more than half a mile, monsieur.*

[GUSTAVE. *And you are familiar with the way, I suppose?*

[GENEVIEVE. *With every inch of it, monsieur.*]

GUSTAVE. Would it be asking too much if I were to beg you to go in search of André? I know you mountain maidens do not fear to be abroad after dark, and the moonlight is almost as bright as day. I want to see André on imperative business, which must be settled tonight. Will you fetch him for me?

GENEVIEVE. (*painfully embarrassed*) Oh, pray pardon me, monsieur. You and mademoiselle are so good to me, and it seems so ungrateful to refuse you anything, but I had rather not go in search of André tonight. (*Aside*) If Pierre Colichot should break his oath! And if he should bring that lying message, and lure Gustave to his death! I dare not warn him, for in order to do that I must tell the whole story, and then there would be hot words, bloodshed perhaps, between him and Captain Varriere. And then to warn him against Pierre would be to bring disgrace upon André. Heaven must help and guide me, I know not what to do. (*During this speech* GUSTAVE *and* PAULINE *have been talking by the table.*)

GUSTAVE. (*aside to* PAULINE) She is proud, you see. But I shall not allow her pride to stand in the way of her happiness. (*Aloud*) Genevieve, you will be doing me a real service by carrying this note to André Colichot.

GENEVIEVE. I *cannot* go, monsieur. I am not ungrateful; I would give my heart's blood to serve you. But I have a reason for wishing to stay in this house tonight, and I cannot carry your letter.

PAULINE. (*pleadingly*) Genevieve, to oblige me – your friend, your sister.

GUSTAVE. By the memory of our childhood, I entreat you.

GENEVIEVE. Mademoiselle, Gustave – M. de Beaupré, you know I cannot refuse you when you ask me thus. But – you do not know what it is you are asking. Give me your letter, monsieur; I will do what you wish, and may Heaven guard us all this night!

[*Exit*

PAULINE. Her manner alarms me, Gustave. What does it mean?

GUSTAVE. (*carelessly*) I strongly suspect it means jealousy, a madness which takes every form.

Enter GENERAL DE MARSAC *and* RAYMOND VARRIERE

GENERAL. (*seeing* GUSTAVE) Aha! Monsieur de Beaupré, I see why you stole away from the supper table just now. [*You insult my hospitality for the sake of a tête-à-tête with my daughter. A man who is going to be married is the most unsocial creature in the universe. Is he not, Varriere?*

[RAYMOND. (with a feverish gaiety of manner) *A man who does not appreciate such Burgundy as yours, General, is an idiot or a milksop. That Chambertin was exquisite – liquid rubies, perfumed with all the violets of the drowsy South – nectar, which Hebe*[18] *might have poured into the golden goblet of Jupiter.*

[GENERAL. *Why, Varriere, you have blossomed into a poet all at once. I never saw you so excited, so gay –*

[RAYMOND. *When should we be gay if not tonight, on the eve of a bridal? It is in your happiness I rejoice, Mademoiselle Pauline* (approaching her, she shrinks from him) *Ah! do not fear me, I offended you an hour ago, but it was in a moment of madness. Let the memory of that moment pass as the madness itself has passed.*] (*Aloud*) Monsieur de Beaupré, it is to your happiness I have been drinking. Your friend the doctor has not arrived from Amsteg, by the way?

GUSTAVE. No, he has not yet arrived.

RAYMOND. In that case he is not likely to come tonight. But if a rough soldier will serve you I am ready to be your groomsman.

PIERRE. (*speaking without*) Stand out of the way, everybody! It's a matter of life and death I come about, and I must see Monsieur de Beaupré.

GUSTAVE. (*alarmed*) A matter of life and death! What can he mean? (*Enter* PIERRE.) What is it that brings you tonight Maître Colichot?

PIERRE. Pardon, monsieur, pardon, General, pardon, mademoiselle, if I intrude, but it is a matter of life and death, the good man tells me.

GUSTAVE. What man?

PIERRE. The messenger, monsieur – the messenger from the "White Cross" at Amsteg.

GUSTAVE. Great Heaven – then Bianchon is worse! Where is the messenger from the "White Cross"? Let me see him.

PIERRE. He is at my chalet, monsieur: the poor fellow had walked across the mountains, and had not strength to come a step further. I had only just got home, and was going to bed, when he was attracted by the glimmer of

---

18. In ancient Greek mythology, Hebe was the goddess of youth and cupbearer to the gods. Raymond is likening his host's wine to ambrosia. Jupiter was the king of the gods, according to ancient Roman myth.

my poor little morsel of candle, and knocked at my door to ask the way on here. I told him the nearest way, but seeing that he was scarcely able to crawl, and knowing that it was a matter not to be delayed, I offered to bring the message myself, for I am very active upon my legs, monsieur, considering my age, and I thought I might be doing you a service.

GUSTAVE. You have done me a service, Maître Colichot – a service for which you shall be amply rewarded.

PIERRE. Shall be, monsieur? Could you conveniently put it in the present tense? At my age a man can hardly afford to give credit.

GUSTAVE. You're a sharp practitioner, friend Pierre. There's my purse, and you may help yourself out of it. But the message! Ah! I can guess its nature. My friend is worse?

PIERRE. He is, monsieur – very much worse, the messenger from the "White Cross" tells me. Jean Groguard, the landlord – I dare say you remember old Groguard – a little man with a red nose – drinks too much of his own wine, and it comes out of him in the shape of pimples – old Groguard feared that the poor gentleman could scarcely outlive the night, and he thought you might wish to see him before –

GUSTAVE. He thought I might wish! – I must see him at any cost! Ah, yes, Pauline! I must see this friend, who has been almost a brother to me, even if the event of tomorrow must needs be postponed. Dying! Horace – my old companion, my faithful friend! How can I soonest reach Amsteg?

GENERAL. There is a mule path – rather a round-about route, but safe; and there is the footway, by which goat-boys and mountain herdsmen only travel – a perilous path.

GUSTAVE. I do not fear danger. The first seven years of my existence were spent amongst Alpine passes, and I have not quite lost the mountaineer's instinct. The footpath is the shorter way, I suppose?

GENERAL. Shorter by two or three miles; but you must not dream of it!

PAULINE. Oh, no, no, Gustave!

GENERAL. Pierre! Go tell one of the men to saddle two mules – the surest footed in the stable – for a journey of fourteen miles; and he must get himself ready to accompany M. de Beaupré without a moment's delay.

PIERRE. Yes, General.

[*Exit.*

PAULINE. *Must* you go, Gustave?

GUSTAVE. Ah! dearest one, can you ask that question? It is very hard to leave you thus, but I must go. He is dying! – remember that my friend and comrade is dying amongst strangers, with no loving hand to grasp his own, with no familiar face beside his bed – dying in a roadside inn!

GENERAL. Never fear, Pauline; the journey by the mule-path is a difficult one, but by no means perilous. That broad moonlight is the next best thing to day. Gustave will reach Amsteg safely enough in two or three hours, see and cheer his sick friend, and return hither at daybreak in time to make you his wife. Come, Gustave, there is no need for such a sorrowful face. Your friend may be in no imminent danger. Ignorance takes alarm so easily.

GUSTAVE. My dear General, bless you for your ready help and cheering words. Has there been time for the saddling of the mules yet, do you think?

GENERAL. There has, if those fellows in the stable are as quick as I should be under the circumstances. Varriere, will you go and hurry them? Do, there's a good fellow! Ah, here is Colichot, with a face of ominous meaning. Well, Pierre, are the mules ready?

PIERRE. No, monsieur; nor likely to be tonight, as far as I can see. There's a fine to-do down yonder – one running here and another running there, and everything in confusion.

GENERAL. Why! what is amiss?

PIERRE. The grooms are not as sober as they might be. The stable door is locked, and the key is nowhere to be found.

GENERAL. Let them break open the door then – fools that they are to have locked it!

PIERRE. That's no easy matter, monsieur. The door is barred with iron; the stables are part of the ancient chateau, and that door has stood against iron-clad hands, with murderous hatchets in them, in the days when there was war in the forest cantons.

GUSTAVE. (*with despair*) And all this time has been lost!

GENERAL. Run to the village in search of other mules, Pierre; or despatch some of the men.

GUSTAVE. But more time will be lost. I will go on foot. The mountaineer braves the hazards of that journey in pursuit of his daily bread; shall I hesitate, when my friend calls me from his bed of death?

RAYMOND. Bravely spoken, Monsieur de Beaupré! I know that mountain path well enough, and know that it has no dangers which a brave man need fear.

[PAULINE. *M. Varriere! It is but a narrow cornice on the side of a rock.*

[RAYMOND. *For a little way past the Devil's Bridge the path may be a trifle hazardous, but the goat-boys tread it fearlessly every day. After that it is a journey which a child might travel.*]

GUSTAVE. Whether it is hazardous or not, I will go.

GENERAL. Pshaw, man! wait for the mules from the village.

GUSTAVE. I have waited too long already, and I will wait no more. Death does not wait. Come what may I will grasp my friend's hand before he dies[19] – farewell, Pauline – fear no harm, dearest. Heaven will protect my steps yonder amongst the stars and eagles. I go to perform a duty.

[*Exit.*

19. **WOLFF** gives an additional note and dialogue: 'Enter dog from the back followed by Caspar'.

> Pauline: Then take Leo with you, he would protect you from any attack.

> Gustave: No one will attack me my darling. I will leave Leo to protect you and warn you if anything evil comes near your house this night. (*look at Varriere*) (p. 33)

The stage direction here suggests Gustave's suspicion of Raymond, while the printed version presents him as a more trusting character.

[RAYMOND. *You have reason to be proud of your lover tonight, mademoiselle. I hope you may have cause to be proud of him tomorrow.*]

PAULINE. (*looking up*) Gustave – Gustave!

GENERAL. Come, dearest, and trust in Providence. Your lover has acted nobly. Better to see him dead upon the craggy bank of the Reusse than to know him a coward. (*He leads her off gently, she still looking towards the door by which* GUSTAVE *has gone.*)

RAYMOND. (*with a mocking laugh*) Very fine philosophy for the General, but rather a poor consolation for the lady. So my plan has succeeded. The diabolical engineer who spanned the Reusse smiles on my schemes. If one's patron saint will have nothing to do with one's affairs, it is as well to have the evil one for a coadjutor; you and I will meet at the Devil's Bridge, M. Gustave de Beaupré.

Turning to go up stage, PIERRE *meets him.*

PIERRE. Captain, I'll trouble you for the balance.

RAYMOND. Didn't I tell you to meet me at my chalet in two hours? I haven't the money about me, and I've something to do before I go home.

PIERRE. I don't much like giving credit, but I suppose there's no help for it. Remember, Captain, two hours hence I shall expect the balance.

RAYMOND. (*turning upon him savagely*) Do you want me to strangle you, or fling you into yonder lake?

PIERRE. (*frightened, but still persistent*) No, Captain, but I should like you to settle with me at once.

RAYMOND. Take care I don't settle *for* you.

Business and curtain.

END OF ACT II

ACT III[20]

SCENE:– *Moonlight – A magnificent panorama. View of Alpine scenery. On the right, and midway between stage and flies, the Devil's Bridge – a rough stone bridge crossing broad and impetuous torrent, and uniting two mountainous districts. On the left a jutting pinnacle supporting gigantic mass of snow. A winding path leads from the front of the stage to ridge of mountain near the flies. In a rocky gorge in foreground the dilapidated chalet occupied by* PIERRE COLICHOT, *cattle-shed, &c., &c. Above the Devil's Bridge a buttress of rock, against which there hangs a wooden plank suspended by chains, wide enough for two men to stand or walk on.*

As the curtain rises the Rang des Vaches[21] is heard amongst the mountains. The last notes of each phrase repeated by distant echoes. The sound of the bells worn by the cattle mingles with accompaniment of this Alpine chorus.

Chorus.

After the chorus the peasantry are seen winding across the pathway in foreground. Then suddenly they are arrested by the sound of chapel bells. All kneel in reverent silence for some moments, while the bells sound at intervals, and are repeated by mountain echoes.

The peasants disperse.

Enter PIERRE COLICHOT, *leading two goats.*

PIERRE. Come along, Punchinella, come, Dandinette; I'll see you two safe at home and to bed, at any rate, before I go back to the chateau. A purse of golden napoleons tossed into the lake! as if it had been a handful of mountain hay. Oh! it was infamous, it was abominable, it was execrable! That young woman must be mad, or she would never have

---

20. A drawing of the opening scene of Act III is pasted into **WOLFF** at this point (facing p. 34). See Fig. 6 on p. 308. The three layers of gauze mentioned would have given an illusion of depth and the mountain path is created by the use of practicables. No evidence has been found to elaborate exactly how the staging worked for the original Liverpool performance, but it is likely to have been staged similarly.
21. Regional variant of *ranz-des-vaches*, a traditional Swiss melody sung to call cows from the mountains.

thrown away the money. But that young man Varriere must also be mad, or he never would have given me the money. People who don't know the value of money can be nothing *but* lunatics. And after she had robbed me – yes, robbed me in the most audacious manner, I was to keep my oath, was I, and not deliver Captain Varriere's message, and not assist in the playful practical joke, and not earn the balance due to me? What an unreasonable young woman she must be to think I'm such a fool as to keep an oath that was extorted from me by physical violence! Oh, no, no, no, Mademoiselle Genevieve, we're a very simple people, we children of the forest cantons, but we're not quite so simple as all that comes to. Now then, Dandinette, now then Punchinella, your comfort and your supper shall be my first consideration, and after I have seen to that I shall be under the necessity of leaving you to yourselves for an hour or two. (*He opens door of stable, lights lantern inside, and leads in the goats. He is seen attending to them as he continues his soliloquy.*) And so the General is afraid I shall be buried in the snow some day, is he? Why doesn't he give me an apartment in the chateau then? But I'm not going to turn out of my comfortable little place to please a French General who doesn't give me anything. Oh, no, no, I've lived in this place rent-free for the last eighty years, and I'm not going to fall into such a bad habit as paying rent at my age. As for the avalanches, they come and they go, and sometimes they kill a few people more or less, and sometimes they destroy a hundred or so of cattle more or less. An old man at my time of life has quite enough to do in looking after his own comforts – which reminds me that it's a long time since I had my supper, and the night air has made me hungry again. (*By this time he has finished with the goats, and is seen preparing his own meal.*) I'll indulge in a basin of goat's milk and a lump of black bread; that's as much luxury as I can afford myself. Father Ridesard is always preaching against the vice of gluttony. That's not my failing, at any rate. If I had only the money which Genevieve threw into the water, I should feel myself beyond the reach of want. It must be delightful to feel one's self beyond the reach of want. (*He eats by fits and starts, looking about him and talking.*) Ever since that young woman's atrocious conduct tonight, I have felt myself actually surrounded by thieves. It's quite awful even to think of it. I'll just see if my poor little hoard is safe. (*Climbs upon table and takes down earthenware pipkin full of gold. He examines the contents.*) Yes, it's all safe – all safe; and the General's spoon goes to increase the hoard. He told us at the supper table that we were to make ourselves happy and take whatever we fancied, and if the General did *not* mean that he ought to have been more precise in his language.

[*Replaces pipkin, and comes out of chalet. Sounds of a mountaineer's horn without.* PIERRE *closes shutters of one large window and bolts them. The goats are seen over the edge of stable door feeding.*

PIERRE. (*as he closes shutters*) Not safe, indeed! I should like to know which of their chalets is safe if mine isn't? Why, the stable is a natural hollow in the breast of the rock. Walls of granite – what could be stronger than that?

ANDRÉ. (*who has entered in time to hear the last words – he carries an Alpine horn*) You would find them only too strong, grandfather, if you were walled up in them.

PIERRE. (*startled*) André, what brings you here at this time of night! – two o'clock in the morning?

ANDRÉ. I don't know, grandfather; I don't know what brings me any-where. I don't know what to do with myself.

[PIERRE. *Don't you? It's a great pity you can't find something better to do than to prowl about my neighbourhood.* (Very suspiciously.) *You haven't been watching me, have you?*

[ANDRÉ. *Watching! What?*

[PIERRE. *Me.*

[ANDRÉ. *Why should I watch you?*

[PIERRE. *No, to be sure, there's no reason why you should watch me. Nobody takes any interest in the proceedings of a pauper; nobody cares what becomes of a poor, penniless wretch – I repeat, a penniless wretch – not even his own relations; but still I thought you might possibly have been watching me just now, just to see what I'd got for supper. Young men are so suspicious.*

[ANDRÉ. *I have no suspicions, grandfather – of you* (very depressed in tone).

PIERRE. [(Aside) *Not of me; that means he has suspicions of somebody else. Who is that, I wonder?*] (*Aloud*) You seem rather melancholy tonight, André. Is there anything amiss with you? Have you lost any money?

ANDRÉ. (*passionately*) Money! you think of nothing but money! No, grandfather, it is not the loss of money which affects me; I – I – my heart is breaking.

PIERRE. (*compassionately*) Poor lad – poor, foolish lad, I know the sort of feeling you mean. I had it about eighty years ago, when I fell in love with a beautiful girl, the only daughter of a rich herdsman. A very comfortable match it would have been, André, but she wouldn't have me, and I used to feel sometimes as if my heart would break, especially when I saw the thriving condition of her father's cattle. However, I got over it, and married your grandmother, who was poor, but saving – very saving, so I don't know but what I had the best bargain after all. The other would have been extravagant – (*recollecting himself*) but what's the matter with you, André? Your heart needn't break; things go smoothly enough with you; you're going to marry Genevieve tomorrow, and that foster-brother of hers is sure to give her something handsome by way of dowry.

ANDRÉ. (*with intense but suppressed passion*) Her foster-brother? Yes, yes, her old companion, the elegant young Frenchman, whom she loves so well. Grandfather, there will be no marriage tomorrow in which I shall take a part. Genevieve and I are strangers now.

PIERRE. (*with animation*) I'm glad of it. I'm very glad of it. And now that she is not to be a Colichot I may speak plainly. I don't like her; I never had any opinion of her.

ANDRÉ. Grandfather!

PIERRE. Don't pounce, André, I detest pouncers. Where is the respect due to advanced age if a man at my time of life is to be pounced upon? As Genevieve is not to be a Colichot I ought to be able to speak plainly without laying myself open to pouncing. I do not like her, and I congratulate you upon your escape from her fangs. A young woman who could take a purse of gold from a man – (*stops suddenly*).

ANDRÉ. As she took what? – from whom?

PIERRE. (*with affected imbecility*) Took what – from whom? What were we talking about? The goats, wasn't it? Yes, yes, the goats. I was telling you how Punchinella was improved lately – she gives me a good half-pint of milk a day beyond her usual quality, and I hope to get more out of her yet.

ANDRÉ. (*impatiently*) Pshaw, grandfather! Do you think to deceive me by this affectation of folly? It was of Genevieve you were talking, of Genevieve alone, and you know it. She took a purse of gold from a man! From what man could she take it but one? She took a purse of gold, a purse of gold from *him*, and without my knowledge. Oh, the heartless deceiver! after she had smiled in my face, after she had told me to trust her, after she had indignantly denied my right to question her truth, she accepted his gold. Oh, cruel, cruel! (*Walking up and down the stage.*)

PIERRE. Another case of madness. It's very late, André. In point of fact, it's tomorrow morning; I think I'll go to bed. (*Aside.*) I must get rid of him somehow. (ANDRÉ *is walking up and down lost in abstraction.*) Good night, André. If you don't hurry home I know you'll be caught in that storm. Good night. (*He enters chalet, and closes door, but peeps out furtively every now and then.*)

ANDRÉ. (*looking up suddenly*) What was that you said, grandfather? Gone! What is to become of me? I wander here and there like the spectral goatherd who haunts our forests, forbidden to rest in death, and doomed to wander forever. (*Cry of some bird.*) Hark, was that his cry? Pshaw! It was only the note of the cuckoo. She is false to me. She is false; no wedding for me tomorrow, no maidens and mountaineers in their gay holiday dress will bring my bride to me. Alone I may wander up and down the narrow paths. Her heart is harder than the granite of our rocks, colder for me than the eternal ice of our glaciers. What am I to do? (*With simulated lightness.*) Why, forget her, go back to my herdsman's life amongst the mountains; go back to my goats, and do battle with the eagles once more. Let them pluck the heart out of my breast if they will; it is but a weary burden to me.

[*Goes up stage slowly; as he retires, climbing a precipitous path, sounds a few plaintive notes every now and then upon the Alpine horn.*

PIERRE. (*emerges cautiously as* ANDRÉ *disappears*) He is gone! I shall just have time to meet Captain Varriere, and get back again before the storm comes on. I got my key hampered in the lock last night, and haven't been able to lock my door since, but I think it's all tolerably safe. They must have sharp eyes who would find anything where I have hidden it, and I'll hurry back, I'll hurry back, directly I've received my balance from Captain Varriere. He told me to meet him at the door of his chalet, where he would be ready for me with the balance. And if Genevieve gets hold of *that* money, I'll forgive her.

[*Exit.*

[A full moon, cloudy sky, which darkens gradually as the storm proceeds during the ensuing scene.

Enter GENEVIEVE *hurriedly. She is breathless, as if from running.*

GENEVIEVE. André was not at his own chalet, had not been seen there since the evening. He must be wandering about somewhere, poor fellow. And all for jealousy – jealousy of Gustave. My poor foolish André! There is but one place where I can look for him, and that is his grandfather's chalet. If he is not there he is doubtless wandering amongst the mountains, and in that case I have no chance of finding him. (*She goes to door of chalet and knocks gently.*) Maître Colichot, Maître Colichot, it is I, Genevieve. They have sent me in search of André. He is wanted at the chateau. Maître Colichot! No answer! He has gone to bed, no doubt. (*Tries door.*) The door is not bolted. That is very strange; the old man is usually so cautious. (*Goes into chalet, and presently returns.*) No one there! What takes him away from home at such an hour? (*Suddenly.*) The plot, the vile plot concocted between him and Raymond Varriere! The old man has broken his oath, the solemn vow which I extorted from him. He has gone to deliver that false message – gone to assist in that hideous treachery. Oh, why did I think it possible that he would keep any promise, however sacred – he who will do anything for money? But I will run back to the chateau; I may yet be in time.[22]

[She is going hurriedly, but suddenly recoils as GUSTAVE *and* RAYMOND *enter. She withdraws to background, watching them, and following them stealthily step by step. They are winding up a narrow pathway leading towards the Devil's Bridge.*

GUSTAVE. I thank you for the friendly feeling which prompted you to follow me, Captain Varriere, but believe me, I do not need your help. I know every inch of the way; I trod it frequently when I was at Andermatt, three years ago.

RAYMOND. You have not trodden it so lately as I have.

[GUSTAVE. *Perhaps not, but the mountains do not change.*

22. **WOLFF** has an inserted folio with additional dialogue between Genevieve and André. It is an emotional passage where André expresses his violent jealousy of Gustave. When Genevieve passes André the written message expressing Gustave's wish for the couple to be married and reinforcing his offer of a dowry, André's reaction is jealous rage. 'And you would have me soil my hands with his money. No that's not my way. If he pays me, it shall be with blood. Do you hear me, with blood?' (facing p. 40).

[RAYMOND. *The mountain pathways do. Let me be your guide, M. de Beaupré; I am a more practised pedestrian than you. Let me be your companion in this midnight journey. I offer you my services in the name of my General's daughter, Mademoiselle de Marsac, and of my friendship for you.*

[GUSTAVE. *Then I cannot be so churlish as to refuse them. Did Pauline ask you to follow me?*

[RAYMOND. *No, but I saw she was alarmed, and her terror suggested the idea that I might be of some use to you.*]

GUSTAVE. You must have walked very rapidly in order to overtake me just now. (*They are now crossing the Devil's Bridge.*)

RAYMOND. I am used to rapid walking.

[GUSTAVE. *The roar of the torrent almost drowns our voices.*

[RAYMOND. *Yes, that hoarse roar of the Reusse has drowned many a cry for help.*

[GUSTAVE. *But of late years Switzerland has been a peaceful country.*

[RAYMOND. *The heart has the same passions everywhere. In peace or in war they are unchanged – despair and hate, jealousy and revenge. See Gustave de Beaupré, that buttress of rock above us with a ledge of wood against its jutted face, a narrow plank you will have to pass before you come to the easy part of your journey. The spray of the torrent almost hides it from us. See, now the spray clears away.*

[GUSTAVE. *Yes, I had forgotten that hanging plank.*

[RAYMOND. *There is still time to withdraw if you have any fear.*

[GUSTAVE. *Fear! I am going to perform a sacred duty.*] (*A distant sound of thunder nearer and louder as the scene advances. The bridge shakes with the concussion.*)

RAYMOND. There is a storm at hand. We can do no better than hasten our upward way. On those mountain tops yonder we may be above the storm and look down upon the lightning in the valley from a serene and tranquil atmosphere. This frail arch seems to tremble beneath our feet.

[*They leave the bridge, ascending a precipitous pathway, followed closely by* GENEVIEVE, *who clings to the crags. The two men step upon the hanging plank above the torrent.*

GUSTAVE. You spoke truly when you said there was danger here, Captain Varriere.

RAYMOND. Yes, Gustave de Beaupré, there is danger. (*With passionate vehemence.*) There is more than common danger. When two sworn foes meet on such ground as this, there is certain death for one, or it may be for both.

GUSTAVE. Are you mad, Captain Varriere?

RAYMOND. No, I am not mad – I am only desperate. (*Seizing him.*) Do you know *why* I have lured you to this mountain pass, Gustave de Beaupré? That I might kill you! I have brought you here to kill you. Here, above the boiling foam of the mountain torrent, where your death will seem accident, and not murder. Here, where there is no witness but the sky above us, where the hoarse roar of the torrent drowns every cry for help, and where no human help could reach you, did men know your deadly peril. Your last hour has come – your presence here is my work. When you thought you were obeying the call of duty, you were my dupe. The message which brought you here was a lie, prompted by my lips, and paid for with my gold. Now do you begin to understand me better Gustave de Beaupré?

GUSTAVE. I understand only that you are a traitor and a villain.

RAYMOND. (*laughing wildly*) Blind fool! you cannot even guess why I hate you. I hate you because I love Pauline de Marsac, [*your promised bride, who may weep over the mutilated corpse of her lover tomorrow, bruised and beaten out of all human semblance upon the stony bed of the Reusse. Poor girl – poor girl!*].

GUSTAVE. For her sake I shall know how to fight for my life, villain!

[*There is a desperate hand-to-hand struggle, which ends in the defeat of* GUSTAVE, RAYMOND *hurls him from the ledge into the torrent. During the struggle* GENEVIEVE *screams for help. The storm rages, with frequent lightnings. The sky inky black. After the fall of* GUSTAVE, RAYMOND *turns to descend the crags, and finds himself face to face with* GEN-EVIEVE. *Then ensues a terrific struggle, as the two descend the crags to*

the Devil's Bridge, which they cross, and then descend the winding pathway
to the chalet, GENEVIEVE *grappling with* RAYMOND, *until at the last*
overpowered by him at the door of the chalet. This business takes place
while the ensuing dialogue is spoken. The storm continues.

GENEVIEVE. Murderer! – foul, treacherous assassin, who thought there
was no witness – no witness but the open sky. But there was a witness – a
witness who saw your murderous deed, and who will drag you to justice!

[RAYMOND. *Release your hold!*

[GENEVIEVE. *Never, until I have dragged you to those who shall secure*
you in the iron chains of the assassin. The hold of death itself is not a firmer
grip than mine, weak woman though I am. Ah! you do not know the unnatu-
ral strength of despair.]

RAYMOND. Woman, are you mad? Let go, I say, or I will hurl you into the
torrent where he has met his doom!

GENEVIEVE. I can brave death, but I will not live unavenged. He was my
foster-brother. Oh! perhaps you have forgotten that? I suspected you, and
I have watched you from first to last. From first to last I knew there was
danger, but I did not know that you would murder him – I might have saved
him if I had only spoken.

RAYMOND. Let me go!

GENEVIEVE. Not while I have power to hold you.

RAYMOND. Loose your grasp, I say!

GENEVIEVE. Never, with life.

RAYMOND. Let me go! What can I do with this wild cat? (*Seeing the*
chalet.) Ah, the chalet!

[*He drags her to the door of the chalet, thrusts her in, and stands*
for some moments breathless, with his back against the door.
Then, after recovering himself, he examines door.

RAYMOND. No key in the lock; there are staples, but no bolt. Ah! my dag-
ger, that will serve as a bolt. Her strength must be well-nigh exhausted by
this time. What am I to do? How silence this woman except as I silenced

him! But I cannot do that; I do not hate her as I hated him; she has not come between me and the only creature I ever loved. (*Storm increases.*) What a night! The lightning almost blinds me. What is that? (*A rumbling noise, then a sound of bells, peasants, and goat-herds rush and cross fore- ground of stage shrieking, "The Avalanche!" "The Avalanche!" "The Avalanche!"*[23] RAYMOND *has only time to reach higher ground, when the mass of snow descends from the peak and buries the chalet. He pauses on a crag to look back.*) Buried alive! The one witness of my crime is locked in that icy tomb. [*Surely some diabolical power abets my guilty purpose when even Nature lends herself to my service.*]

[*More snow falls, he climbs the crag and hangs on to the Devil's Bridge, as the avalanche continues. Presently the storm abates, the thick darkness clears,*[24] *and reveals a sky of deep purple, illuminated by a moon and studded with innumerable stars. RAYMOND climbs onto Bridge and departs. Below all is ruin. All trace of the chalet and winding pathways has disappeared beneath a smooth plain of snow. After a pause, the plaintive notes of the Alpine horn are heard, and ANDRÉ appears on the topmost ridge. A pistol shot is fired below; a pause, and then another. ANDRÉ is seen listening and looking down. Then suddenly he perceives something or some one below.*[25] *He unwinds a rope from his waist, attaches it to a* point d'appui,[26] *and lets himself slowly down into the gorge. He is seen emerging from the spray of the torrent, and supporting* GUSTAVE *in his arms on a ledge of rock as the*

Curtain falls.

END OF ACT III

---

23. Braddon was not the first playwright to use an avalanche for a sensation scene. Dion Boucicault's *Pauvrette* staged a similar scene in New York in 1858 (see Booth (1981), p. 63). The Drury Lane melodrama *Hearts are Trumps* (1899) would later use an avalanche as a *deus ex machina* to sweep the villain to his death. Ibsen also used an avalanche in the final scene of his *When We Dead Awaken* (1899).
24. Additional instruction, '(lift gauzes)', added in **WOLFF** (p. 43).
25. In **WOLFF**, the rescue is staged differently. Leo finds Gustave, André watches from the bridge and narrates the action as Leo (off stage) digs Gustave out. André then descends into the gorge, then 'climbs up steps from sink carrying Gustave and – followed by the dog – lays him down centre' (p. 43).
26. A support or brace.

ACT IV

SCENE I. *An apartment in the Chateau*

PAULINE *and* GENERAL *discovered.* PAULINE *dressed in black.*

The GENERAL *is standing at the window.*

PAULINE. Do you see Captain Varriere, papa?

GENERAL. Not yet, my poor girl; but he will be back soon, rely upon it.

PAULINE. And the result of his inquiries and researches today will be the same as yesterday's. [*No tidings – no tidings of the lost! Oh! why do I watch and wait for his coming? Why do I still cherish a faint glimmer of hope, which only serves to make the darkness of despair more terrible?*

[GENERAL. *Nay, dear child, we are indeed lost when hope abandons us.*

[PAULINE. *Better to despair entirely than to endure all the horrible fluctuations between hope and despair. I did hope – I did hope while the peasantry were still digging in the snow – but what can I think? How can I hope any longer, when they who are so resolute, so patient, and enduring have abandoned all efforts as useless?*]

GENERAL. (*with an involuntary sigh*) After an interval of three weeks there can be little hope –

PAULINE. [*That any living creature can ever emerge from that icy tomb.*] Yes, father, I understand you but too well. There can be no hope – none!

GENERAL. My hope is that Gustave was not amongst the victims of the avalanche.

PAULINE. And the alternative! That he lost his footing on the narrow path above the Reusse, and was dashed to atoms upon the crags. Oh, father, why do you talk to me of comfort and hope? There is no hope, no comfort – none. (*Enter* RAYMOND.) Ah, Captain Varriere! your tidings!

RAYMOND. (*gravely*) They are no better tidings that I had to give you yesterday, mademoiselle; nothing has been heard of Gustave de Beaupré.

[PAULINE. (with despair) *Nothing! And the peasants, the diggers in the snow, they have not resumed their labours?*

[RAYMOND. *Why should they recommence a task which had become useless long before they abandoned it?*

[PAULINE. (thoughtfully) *And yet people have been known to be rescued from an icy prison-house after a weary interval.*

[RAYMOND. (with a smile) *Not after one and twenty days, and one and twenty nights.*

[PAULINE. (looking at him earnestly) *You keep a close account of the time, Captain Varriere. One would think there were some one buried beneath that impenetrable shroud whom you do not wish to rise.*

[RAYMOND. *When the buried Abbots of bygone centuries arise from their graves in the Abbey of St. Gall, and not till then, will those arise who lie buried under the avalanche.*

[PAULINE. *There are times when in spite of all better reasons I fancy that Gustave was not in the gorge when the avalanche fell.*[27] *There are times when I think he met his death in a more terrible manner, and that, lured by that lying message, he was assassinated by the hand of a traitor, amidst those desolate pathways.*

[GENERAL. *What could have induced Pierre Colichot to deliver that false message?*

[RAYMOND. *That is a secret that you will never know. The loss of his hoarded possessions has completely unsettled the poor miser's mind, already feeble with extreme age. He does nothing but wander about in an imbecile manner, talking about his goats and his buried treasures. Strange that he who could never be brought to speak of his hoarded wealth cannot now be induced to talk of anything else.*]

PAULINE. And Genevieve. There are no tidings of Genevieve?

---

27. **WOLFF** inserts extra dialogue here in which Pauline states, 'Twice since her disappearance I have seen Genevieve in a dream' (p. 45). It is Pauline, not André, who experiences the third vision in the annotated version.

RAYMOND. None. Have you never thought it strange, mademoiselle, that those two, M. de Beaupré and Genevieve, should have disappeared on the same night?

[PAULINE. *It can be in no manner strange, if both were buried beneath the avalanche.*

[RAYMOND. *If. But it would be still a strange coincidence that those two should be in the gorge beneath the Devil's Bridge at that one fatal moment. Pardon me, Mademoiselle de Marsac, if I distress you, and you also, General, forgive me if I breathe one word against the honour of the man who was to have been your son-in-law, but it has struck me that there is a deeper mystery in this business than we have yet sought to penetrate.*

[PAULINE. (eagerly) *What mystery?*

RAYMOND. [*Will you*] pardon me if I wound you, mademoiselle?

[PAULINE. *I will pardon anything in the world if you can give me the faintest hope that the man I love is still living.*

[RAYMOND. *Have you any reason to suppose that Genevieve was in the neighbourhood of the Devil's Bridge that night?*

[PAULINE. (with some hesitation) *No. I can imagine no reason.*

[RAYMOND. *She did not leave the chateau with the intention of going there?*

[PAULINE. *She left the chateau to go into the village in search of André.*

[RAYMOND. *Then we have no reason to suppose that she fell a victim to the accident of that night.*

[PAULINE. *In that case where is she?*

[RAYMOND. *May she not have had some motive for leaving mademoiselle, altogether?*

[PAULINE. *What motive could she possible have?*

[RAYMOND. *Oh, Mademoiselle de Marsac, pardon me, I implore you! To speak plainly I must needs give you pain, and yet it is my duty to speak plainly.*

[PAULINE. (with mingled hauteur and passion) *Then speak quickly, monsieur, and without further preface.*]

RAYMOND. In plain words, then, it seems to me that the mystery of the disappearance of Gustave de Beaupré and Genevieve at the same time may be explained in one short sentence – they fled together.

PAULINE. Captain Varriere!

[RAYMOND. *You asked me to speak plainly, mademoiselle, and I have spoken. Your generous nature is above jealousy, but almost any living woman except you would have suspected the attachment between M. de Beaupré and his foster-sister.*

[PAULINE. *Go on, Captain Varriere.*

[RAYMOND. *That pretty sentiment about the days of childhood, in which the peasant girl and the young patrician had wandered side by side, would have been charming enough in a poem, but in real life the boundary between sentiment and passion is very narrow, and it is difficult to believe that Genevieve's sisterly affection for her foster-brother was not something more than sisterly. He may have returned that affection.*

[PAULINE. *He – Gustave – my true-hearted lover!*]

RAYMOND. Your lover of three years ago. It is just possible that his feelings may have undergone some alteration during that lengthened separation. It is just possible that on returning to you he found his heart changed, and a new affection awakened by the enthusiastic regard of Genevieve. Men are very weak, Mademoiselle de Marsac, and it is not from the Court of Catherine of Russia that you should expect the classic virtues of constancy and truth.

PAULINE. Your argument is very forcible, Captain Varriere. Go on.

RAYMOND. I have little more to say, mademoiselle. A hasty flight was the only plan open to M. de Beaupré if he found his feelings changed on the eve of his wedding day. You will remember Genevieve's strange conduct throughout that day – the melancholy which may have been remorse, the agitation inseparable from the contemplation of such a guilty step. The flight agreed upon between those two, nothing remained but to give a colour to their departure. The message delivered by Pierre Colichot afforded the required excuse. What was more likely than that the lying message was prompted by Gustave de Beaupré, who knew better than anyone the name of the inn where his friend was staying, and the particulars of that friend's illness?

PAULINE. I cannot believe it. No, a thousand times no! If Gustave had changed towards me he would have told me so frankly. [*He would not have stooped to the infamy of an acted lie. But I will wring the truth from one who has the power to tell it, and who shall be made to speak.*

[RAYMOND. *How, mademoiselle?*

[PAULINE. *From the lips of imbecility itself I will confound you. Pierre Colichot, who carried that message, shall be made to tell who prompted it.*

[RAYMOND. *You would employ violence against the old man?*

[PAULINE. *No, monsieur; I will employ a woman's wit. Ah! you cannot imagine of what a woman is capable when she hears the man she loves traduced, and knows that his voice cannot confound the slanderer.*

[GENERAL. *Bravely said, Pauline! We will go at once to that old man. He is to be found at his grandson's cottage.*

[RAYMOND. *Would it not be better to wait until –*]

GENERAL. [*No, it is no case for delay.*] Varriere, you have aroused a doubt in my poor girl's breast which must be more painful to her even than the thought of her lover's untimely death. That doubt must be made into a certainty, or set at rest forever. There is but one way – we must extort the truth from Pierre Colichot. Come with us if you like, Varriere, but do not attempt to hinder us. Come, Pauline.

[*Exeunt.*

SCENE II.[28]

The chalet inhabited by ANDRÉ COLICHOT *in the village of Andermatt. A picturesque interior. Rough bed in corner. Door opening upon landscape. Door leading to inner apartment.*

ANDRÉ. (*seated, speaking in depressed tones*) The mystery still remains unsettled. Does Genevieve lie beneath the ruins of the buried chalet, or did she fly from Andermatt on that night to meet Gustave de Beaupré, and is she now hiding in some distant village, ashamed to return to those whom she has wronged? I had rather think her dead than believe that she was guilty. I had rather weep for her in her grave of snow than blush for her falsehood and infamy. But it is so difficult to believe her innocent – every incident of that fatal day points to her guilt. Her strange and fitful manner – the watchfulness of Gustave de Beaupré, which was observed by every one in the chateau – that lying message, which could be prompted by no one but Monsieur de Beaupré himself – all alike point to that one conclusion which Captain Varriere suggested to me on the day after the fall of the avalanche. An elopement had been planned between the two – an elopement which accident alone prevented. I have tried in vain to extort the truth from my unhappy old grandfather; but there is one yonder (*with a gesture indicating the inner chamber*) who *shall* speak when the time comes.

HORACE BIANCHON *enters from inner room.*

ANDRÉ. (*eagerly*) Well, Monsieur Bianchon, your patient?

BIANCHON. The progress is still favourable, but it is slow.

[ANDRÉ. (with an impatient sigh) *It is indeed slow. He has not spoken yet?*

[BIANCHON. *Not yet; and I dare not hasten the hour at which he shall speak. In his case repose is all-important.*

28. In **WOLFF** scene II is deleted. Pierre is brought to the chateau rather than sought in André's home. This, along with changes to Scene 4, mean that all of Act 4 takes place within one setting, allowing the action to flow more smoothly towards the finale. Two hand-written pages are inserted at this point in which Varriere insists that Gustave will never be found and Pauline tells him she could never love another. In her desperation, Pauline says, 'I would question Leo even if I could find him. Dumb though he is!' (facing p. 48).

[ANDRÉ. *I must wait your time; but it seems very long.*]

BIANCHON. Why are you so anxious for my poor friend's recovery?

ANDRÉ. Because I await that recovery to ask him a question – a question which he must and shall answer, and on the issue of which my future happiness depends.

BIANCHON. Gustave de Beaupré can refuse nothing to you, to whom he owes his life.

ANDRÉ. Gustave de Beaupré owes me no gratitude, Monsieur Bianchon. It pleased Providence that I should preserve his life. When I heard that pistol shot in the ravine below the Devil's Bridge, I knew that it must be the signal of some unhappy creature in deadly peril. What I did to save that human being I have done many a time in my boyhood to preserve the life of a goat. It was no new thing for me to hang 'mid earth and sky, with the knowledge that my life depended on the strength of the rope by which I hung, and that one crack in those twisted fibres might hurl me to destruction. I did that for your friend which I should have done for a stranger. I wish that the life I saved *had* been the life of a stranger!

BIANCHON. Why do you speak with such bitterness?

ANDRÉ. I have good reason to be bitter, monsieur. But we will not talk of that. Happily for Monsieur de Beaupré the ledge on which he fell was so laden with snow as to form a natural bed on which he lay comparatively unharmed. [*It is something like a miracle to escape with a few broken bones from such a fall as that.*]

BIANCHON. It was his brain that suffered most from that terrible accident. But the clouds are beginning to clear away. It is to you he owes his preservation. It was your happy idea to come to Amsteg in search of me, his old friend and companion, than whom there could be no one better fitted to watch him through a slow and fatiguing illness.

ANDRÉ. And in return I have asked you but one favour – secrecy – silence on the subject of M. de Beaupré's preservation.

BIANCHON. That shall be strictly kept.

ANDRÉ. I thank you, monsieur. Believe me I do not act without a strong motive. Our silence may inflict pain on Mademoiselle de Marsac as long as it lasts, but it will serve a good purpose. (*Bells heard without.*) [*Hark, my poor demented old grandfather is coming this way. Retire to that room, monsieur, I beg. He must not see you here.* (Exit BIANCHON. ANDRÉ goes to outer door and opens it.) *Poor old man! His mind is quite gone. He wanders about hopelessly, ringing those bells by which he has been accustomed to summon his goats.* (Enter PIERRE COLICHOT, ringing bells, and looking around him with a vacant gaze. He has all the appearance of imbecility.) *He does not see me. He wanders here and there, unable to rest even for a few minutes. He comes here, and I feed him, and he seeks this place instinctively when the pangs of hunger assail him; but his instincts are less keen than those of a dog, and I doubt if he knows the hand that ministers to him.*]

SCENE III.

PIERRE. Punchinella, Dandinette, come home, naughty children, come home, it is supper time, a very frugal supper, because we are poor, and goats have such large appetites, and the mountain hay costs a great deal of money. (*Starting.*) Money! Who was it spoke of money? Where is my money? (*with a sudden cry of despair*) I was the richest man in Andermatt, though they didn't know it. No, no, I was too wise for that. They never knew how rich I was or they would have robbed me, the avaricious wretches. They would have murdered me for the sake of the gold. I kept my secret. I kept my secret well. But I was rich, very rich. Oh! What a hoard it was. But it is all gone – it is all gone. The cruel snow came down, and buried all – the gold, the silver, Punchinella, Dandinette – gone, gone, gone! (*He seats himself by table in an attitude of despair, and continues muttering to himself.*)

Enter GENERAL, PAULINE, *and* RAYMOND VARRIERE

PAULINE. Ah, he is here – that is fortunate – Pierre Colichot. [*I have come hither to seek that old man.*] I have come if possible to learn the truth about that message. The false message from the "White Cross" at Amsteg.

[ANDRÉ. *You will never learn it from his lips, mademoiselle. I have questioned him not once only, but a hundred times. It is quite useless. His mind is gone.*

[RAYMOND. *You hear, mademoiselle. Your woman's wit may work wonders, but it cannot restore the light of reason when that subtle flame has been extinguished.*]

[GENERAL. *Question him, Pauline. His memory may be awakened by your pleading.*]

PAULINE. (*approaching* PIERRE) You remember me, do you not, Pierre?

PIERRE. Remember you. Ah! yes, yes, I remember *you.* (*A pause.*) You're Dandinette. You usen't to talk though, but then you did all but talk, so I don't wonder you've come to that. No one knows how sensible goats are except those who have lived with them. (*He lays his hand upon* PAULINE'S *head and smoothes her hair gently.*) Yes, you're Dandinette. Such lovely soft hair, like the finest silk, and valuable too, worth ever so much to sell. They make shawls of it for the English market. Bless you, Dandinette!

GENERAL. I fear it is quite useless.

PAULINE. Pierre – Pierre Colichot. Look at me. I am Pauline de Marsac, she who was to have wedded Gustave de Beaupré. Do you not remember coming to the chateau that night with a false message? Oh! For pity's sake tell me who bade you to deliver that false message. Speak! Pierre, speak! On my knees I implore you.

PIERRE. Go away. (*Pushing her aside.*) Go away. You come between me and my gold. See, see, it is there before me – a shining heap, brighter than the summer sun yonder – within reach of my outstretched arm, and yet I cannot grasp it. When I stretch out my hand to seize it, it moves slowly away, and I follow it. I follow that bright heap of gold all through the day, all through the dark, dreary night. Ah! how it shines in the darkness, upon the mountains, in the valleys – and still I cannot grasp it.

[*Exit as if following some object. Business. ad lib.*

[GENERAL. *We will follow him. If one glimmer of reason remains he shall be made to speak.*]

[RAYMOND. *When the dead find a voice then perhaps he will answer your questions as you would have them answered.*]

PAULINE. Come, father. Let us follow him.

[*Exeunt* PAULINE *and* GENERAL, RAYMOND *following slowly.*

RAYMOND. (*as he goes off*) He will never speak, he will never speak.[29]

ANDRÉ. He will not. But there is one who will. (*Barring the outer door.*) I am weary to death. My wasted toil among the diggers in the snow. My hopeless wanderings to neighbouring villages in search of her who was to have been my wife have well nigh worn me out. Last night, and the night before last, I slept soundly for the first time since the disappearance of Genevieve, and on both nights I dreamt the same dream. I fancied I saw her; that I heard her voice; that she was living beneath that fallen snow, and that she called to me to save her. Each time the dream was strangely vivid. But what of that. Such dreams have no meaning. They are but the embodiment of our waking thoughts, and take their colour from the hopes we still cherish, even when reason has bidden us despair. (*As he lies down on the rough couch.*) Will the dream come again to me tonight, I wonder?

> *Music. A vision of* GENEVIEVE, *in a crouching attitude between two goats, surrounded by broken wood-work and snow. She stretches out her arms to* ANDRÉ *in an appealing attitude. The vision vanishes.*[30]

ANDRÉ. (*springing up from his couch in a state of wild excitement*) Again! again! For the third time – the same dream! The same in every detail. (*He snatches up the lanthorn*[31] *and spade, and goes out into the village street, where he is heard calling.*) Jean! Philippe! Justin! Theodore! friends, neighbours to the rescue! Genevieve lives. Three times I have seen her in a dream! Come, friends, to the Devil's Bridge. Come![32]

----

29. **WOLFF** cuts from this point (p. 50) to the end of play and inserts rewritten material in extra folios (ff. 50a–b, 51a–h). Genevieve's dream vision appears to Pauline, who then tells André to dig out Pierre's hovel to save her. Genevieve is brought to the chateau to denounce Varriere, who then shoots himself. André also reunites Pierre with his hoarded money, which prompts the return of his senses, the realisation of his wrongdoing and the announcement that he will use his money as a dowry for the young couple.
30. The appearance and sudden disappearance of the vision may have been effected by back-lighting Genevieve from behind a gauze and then rapidly plunging that section of the stage into darkness. Pepper's Ghost, a stage trick using reflection to create a ghostly image, had been used from the early 1860s, and some form of reflective stage trick may also have been used to create this 'vision'.
31. 'Lanthorn' is an archaic spelling of 'lantern'.
32. The sensation scene reportedly caused a standing ovation at early performances. The audience was reported to have called for the author at the end of the third act, as well as at the end of the play (Anon. (1874g), *Daily Courier* [Liverpool], 7 Apr., p. 5).

SCENE IV.

The Devil's Bridge. Twilight.

Enter ANDRÉ *and* PEASANTS.

ANDRÉ. Come, friends, come! Shoulder to shoulder, side by side.

PEASANT. 'Tis but a useless labour, I fear, André; but for friendship's sake – (*All begin to dig in the snow with energy, piercing now here, now there, and throwing up large quantities of snow.*)

ANDRÉ. It is no useless labour. I feel that the dream which has been repeated three times has more than common meaning. (*The work proceeds throughout the dialogue.*) [*It is an inspiration of Heaven. It came once, and I disbelieved it. It came twice, and still I fancied it no more than the reflection of my own thoughts. It came a third time, and it brought conviction with it. I know that it is true. The hands of the woman I love are stretched out for me to help as they were in that dream.*] She lives! She has not fled to Andermatt. She is locked up in a prison of ice and snow.

PEASANT. There is something more solid than snow here. Hark! do you hear, friends, the dull thud of the pickaxe? It strikes upon wood. We have found the right spot at last! We are close to the roof of the old chalet. Come, lads, this way. Come! (*The diggers all gather round one spot. They dig with renewed energy for a few moments. Then there is a cry of triumph from all.*)

ANDRÉ. The dream was true! She lives – she is saved! Great Heaven be praised! (*He falls on his knees as the peasants lift* GENEVIEVE *from out of the snow. The goats are seen by her side among loose straw and broken woodwork. An empty manger and a few shreds of hay scattered around.*)

ANDRÉ. Genevieve! Genevieve! my beloved girl.

GENEVIEVE. (*very pale, very faint and feeble*) They have come in time, André. We must all have died very soon. If it had not been for these poor creatures I should have perished long ere this, but their milk supported me in that living tomb. They were my companions too, poor faithful animals, and that dark silent vault was less terrible because of their companionship. Oh, André, it has been a time of bitter anguish. The darkness, the silence, the loneliness. The one eternal night I have been in a living grave, André!

ANDRÉ. Ah! thank Heaven, you are rescued at last. It was a dream, Genevieve, a dream which brought me here, when hope had been abandoned by all. [*Fetch a litter, friends, she cannot walk.*]

Enter GENERAL, PAULINE, RAYMOND *and* BIANCHON.

ANDRÉ. She lives Mademoiselle Pauline! She is saved!

PAULINE. (*rushing to her*) Genevieve!

RAYMOND. (*confoundedly*) Genevieve! The dead arisen from the grave!

GENEVIEVE. (*standing up with a sudden convulsive effort and supporting herself by* ANDRÉ's *help*) Yes! Raymond Varriere, she whom you thought dead has risen from a living grave. When you murdered Gustave de Beaupré, you thought there was no eye but that of Heaven to behold your guilty deed, but there was a witness, who watched you step by step, and who [*would have denounced you. The avalanche came, and you thought that one witness lay buried forever in an icy tomb. But the ways of Heaven are not to be reckoned by the thoughts of men. That witness*] still lives to declare you the assassin of Gustave de Beaupré.

GENERAL. An assassin! Seize that man! He would escape us.

RAYMOND. I would escape you, and you shall not hinder my escape. I will be judged by no tribunal but one, and that the highest. (*Business to be decided on at rehearsal.*)

GENERAL. Secure him, I say. (PEASANTS *make a rush at him, he draws pistols and presents – they recoil.*)

RAYMOND. Ha! ha! ha! These are your brave mountaineers! Pauline de Marsac, tell them that Raymond Varriere died like a soldier, and you heard the volley over his grave. Listen. (*He shoots himself; raises himself on his hands.*) Adieu. (*Dies.*)

BIANCHON. (*stoops over* RAYMOND) He is dead. (PEASANTS *bear him out.*) Mademoiselle de Marsac, your lover was true to you, he still lives to declare his truth.

[*Exit.*

GENEVIEVE. He still lives! I saw him flung from yonder pinnacle into the boiling cataract. I saw him perish by the hand of that man – that man who bribed Pierre Colichot to lure him to the fatal spot by a false message.

ANDRÉ. The assassin did his work badly, clever as he was. The falling man lodged on a broad shelf of rock laden with snow. Behold!

Enter GUSTAVE *carried on a litter, supported by* PEASANTS.

PAULINE. (*running eagerly to* GUSTAVE) Gustave! Alive!

GUSTAVE. Yes, dearest, thanks to my noble preserver, André.

GENERAL. Then there may yet be a wedding at the little chapel of Andermatt.

GENEVIEVE. (*giving her hand to* ANDRÉ) Two weddings, Monsieur le Général, if you'll not consider it a liberty. Ah, mademoiselle, in that living grave, through the endless, changeless night and the awful silence, but one hope sustained me. I thought of that Power which rules the elements and protects the helpless. Heaven has heard my prayers, and I come back to the glad, bright world of the living, come back to find Monsieur Gustave alive and happy with his true-hearted bride, come back to tell André that I never was false to him by so much as a thought. And thus through every peril honesty and truth pass unscathed, while Providence permits the guilty a brief triumph, only to make the hour of retribution more bitter.[33]

TABLEAU AND CURTAIN.

---

33. The final inserted folio in **WOLFF** gives alternative final lines:

> Gustave: Thank God the shadows of doubt have all passed away with that man's death.

> Pauline: Yes, and the mystery of his crime has been cleared up by "The Missing Witness." (f. 51h)

A small diagram also gives the stage positioning for the characters in a final tableau. Pauline and Gustave are front centre, with Genevieve, André and Pierre stage right and the General stage left. The peasants form two lines, flanking the other actors.

Bibliography

Cited archival sources

Austin, Texas, Harry Ransom Center, Mary Elizabeth Braddon Collection, Robert Lee Wolff Collection of Nineteenth Century Fiction
Box 34, Folder 9. Braddon, Mary Elizabeth [1880], *The Missing Witness*, London: John and Robert Maxwell, digitised printed copy with annotations and 15 ff. inserted.

Bristol, UK, University of Bristol Library, Mander and Mitchenson Collection
MM/REF/TH/GR/HLT. Material relating to Holborn Theatre, London.
MM/REF/TH/RE/353. Material relating to Empire Theatre, Liverpool [formerly known as Royal Alexandra Theatre], containing Martlew, Edgar (1953) 'Playhouses Past and Present', 1 Jan. [magazine clipping, unidentified location].

Cambridge, MA, Houghton Library, Theatre Collection
2016T-469. Daly, Augustin (1867), *Under the Gaslight: A Totally Original and Picturesque Drama of Life and Love in These Times*, Author's edition, New York: W. C. Wemyss, printed playscript.
23498.1.29.77. Hazlewood, C. H. ([185–?]), *Never Too Late to Mend; A Drama of Real Life in Four Acts, Founded on Charles Reade's novel*, London: T. H. Lacy, printed playscript.
DAL 966.1.17. Boucicault, Dion ([1860?]), *The Colleen Bawn, or The Brides of Garryowen: A Domestic Drama, in Three Acts*, London: T. H. Lacy, printed playscript.
MS Thr 1265. Boucicault, Dion (probably 1860), *Colleen Bawn: By Dion Boucicault*, hand-written playscript, 36 ff.

Canterbury, Kent, UK, Templeman Library Special Collections, Boucicault Collection
UKC-BOUC-LET.0648355. Carew, George (1864), 'Letter from George Carew/Dion B – dispute over Colleen Bawn', 10 Nov., letter.
Colleen Bawn Box.
UKC-CALB-BIO.F205506. Material relating to law suits/infringement of copyright in which Boucicault was involved.

UKC-CALB-BIO-F205507. Material relating to Dion Boucicault's relationship with Benjamin Webster.
UKC-BOU-CUT.0648421. Series of photocopied/original reviews of Boucicault plays.

Canterbury, Kent, UK, Templeman Library Special Collections, Melville Collection
UKC-MEL-PLA-ASGr10600078/60007814P. (1874), 'Play assignments – letters from Colin Hazlewood'.

Canterbury, Kent, UK, Templeman Library Special Collections, Pettingell Collection
PETT B.186. Boucicault, Dion ([1860?]), *The Colleen Bawn*, London: T. H. Lacy, ex libris pgs added by Arthur Williams.
PETT BND.125(5). Daly, Augustin (n.d.), *Under the Gaslight: or Life and Love in These Times. An Original Drama, of American Life. In Four Acts*, London and New York: Samuel French, printed script.
PETT D.9. Daly, Augustin (n.d.), *Under the Gaslight: or Life and Love in These Times. An Original Drama, of American Life. In Four Acts. [Version of this called "Rail River + Road" played at East London and Pavilion]*, London: Thomas Hailes Lacy, ex libris prompt copy of printed script.

Canterbury, Kent, UK, Templeman Library Special Collections, Playbill Collection
UKC/POS/LYN R: 0595608. (1859), *It Is Never Too Late to Mend*, Theatre Royal King's Lynn, 1 Apr., playbill.

Leeds, Leeds City Council, Leeds Playbills <leodis.net>
200399_17570132. (1860), 'The Hole in the Wall', 'Colleen Bawn!' (or, 'The Brides of Garryowen'), 'Love Conquers All!', Princess Theatre, Leeds, digitised playbill.

London, UK, British Library, Lord Chamberlain's Collection
Add MS 52973 P. Anon. (1858), 'Never Too Late to Mend. A Drama in Four Acts', Apr., 59 ff., hand-written playscript.
Add MS 52975 A. Conquest, George (1858), 'Never too late to mend. A Drama in Four Acts', Jun., 46 ff., hand-written playscript.
Add MS 52980 K. Hazlewood, C. H. (1859), 'Never to [*sic*] late to Mend. A Drama of Womans [*sic*] faith + Mans [*sic*] Treachery in Two Acts [altered from 'Never to [*sic*] late to Mend. The Golden Secret or Life in the New World' (f. 1 (a))]', Mar., 45 ff., hand-written play script.
Add MS 52995 B. Boucicault, Dion (1860), 'The Colleen Bawn or The Brides of Garry Owen. A Drama in Three Acts', Aug., 107 ff., hand-written playscript.

Add MS 52995 T. Hazlewood, C. H. (1860), 'Eily O Connor. A Drama In Two Acts', Oct., 17 ff., hand-written playscript.

Add MS 53002 M. Young, Henry (1861), 'The Bride of Garryowen or The Colleen Bawn. A Drama in Two Acts', Mar., 48 ff., hand-written playscript.

Add MS 53009 I. [Byron, H. J.] (1861), 'Miss Eily O'Connor. A Burlesque in One Act', Nov., 50 ff., hand-written playscript.

Add MS 53014 Z. Brough, William, and Halliday, Andrew (1862), 'The Colleen Bawn Settled at Last. An Original Farce', Jul., 13 ff., hand-written playscript.

Add MS 53044 D. Reade, Charles ([1865]), *It's Never Too Late to Mend. A Drama, in Four Acts*, London: Clowes and Sons, 95 pp, printed playscript.

Add MS 53070 T. Anon. (1868), 'Rail, River and Road', Sep., 52 ff., folios 14–19 are printed (n.d.) and headed 'Under the gaslight', otherwise hand-written playscript.

Add MS 53112 C. Marryat, F. and Young, Sir Charles (1872), 'Miss Chester. A Drama in Three Acts', Oct., 45 ff., hand-written playscript.

London, UK, Victoria & Albert Museum, Theatre and Performance Archive
Photo File: (1865) *It's Never Too Late to Mend*, Princess's.
THM|LON|ADE|1861. (1860) Colleen Bawn Production File, New Adelphi.
THM|LON|HRA. Holborn Theatre file

Primary sources

Anon. (1862), 'The Philosophy of "Sensation"', *St. James's Magazine*, 5, Oct., pp. 340–6.

Anon. (1863), 'An Old Sensation Drama', *London Review*, 6: 132, 10 Jan., pp. 38–9.

Anon. (1865), 'A New Sensation Drama', *Reynold's Miscellany*, 36: 916, 30 Dec., p. 21.

Anon. (1866a), 'A Gossip about Scenery and Scene-Painters', *Era*, 4 Feb., p. 4.

Anon. (1866b), 'Sensation Harpies', *London Review*, 12: 294, 17 Feb., pp. 190–1.

Anon. (1868), 'Holiday Theatricals', *St. James's Magazine*, n.s., 2, Oct., pp. 752–62.

Anon. (1872a), *Bell's Life in London and Sporting Chronical*, 19 Oct., p. 2.

Anon. (1872b), 'Holborn Theatre', *Athenaeum*, 12 Oct., p. 476.

Anon. (1872c), *Punch*, 2 Nov., p. 185.

Anon. (1874a), 'Lost in London', *Era*, 11 Oct., p. 11.

Anon. (1874b), *The Scotsman*, 13 Apr., p. 5.

Anon. (1874c), 'Provincial', *Orchestra*, 2 Apr., p. 3.

Anon. (1874d), [no title], *The Orchestra*, 1 May, p. 72.

Anon. (1874e), 'Dramatic Gossip', *Athenaeum*, 28 Feb., p. 302.

Anon. (1874f), 'Public Amusements', *Liverpool Mail*, 28 Mar., p. 3.

Anon. (1874g), [no title], *Daily Courier* [Liverpool], 7 Apr., p. 5.

Anon. (1891), 'Provincial Productions', *Stage*, 9 Apr., p. 13.

'B' (1865), 'Sensational Literature', *The Christian Observer*, 6, Nov., pp. 809–13.

Black, Helen C. (1893), *Notable Women Authors of the Day*, Glasgow: David Bryce and Son.

Boucicault, Dion (1862), '"Sensation" Dramas', *Musical World*, 40: 13, 29 Mar., pp. 203–4.

Braddon, Mary Elizabeth (1880), *The Missing Witness*, London: John and Robert Maxwell.

— (1894), 'In the Days of My Youth', *Theatre*, 24 Sep., p. 7

— (1998 [1863]), *Aurora Floyd*, ed. Richard Nemesvari and Lisa Surridge, Toronto: Broadview.

— (2012 [1862]), *Lady Audley's Secret*, ed. Lyn Pykett, Oxford: Oxford University Press.

Byron, Henry J. (1864), *Sensation Dramas for the Back-Drawing Room*, London: Thomas Hailes Lacy.

Collins, Wilkie (1990 [1852]), 'Letter of Dedication', in *Basil*, Oxford: Oxford University Press.

— (1999), *The Letters of Wilkie Collins, 1866–1889*, 2 vols, ed. William Baker and William M. Clarke, New York: St Martin's.

Daly, Joseph Francis (1917), *The Life of Augustin Daly*, New York: Macmillan.

Dickens, Charles (1999), *The Letters of Charles Dickens, The British Academy Pilgrim Edition, Volume Eleven 1865–1867*, ed. Graham Storey, Oxford: Clarendon.

Farmer, John S., and W. E. Henley (1905), *A Dictionary of Slang and Colloquial English*, London: George Routledge & Sons.

Jerome, Jerome K. (1891), *On the Stage – And Off: The Brief Career of a Would-be Actor*, New York: Henry Holt.

Lewes, G. H. (1863), 'Our Survey of Literature and Science', *Cornhill Magazine*, 7, Jan., pp. 132–44.

McCarthy, Justin (1864), 'Novels with a Purpose', *Westminster Review*, 46, Jul., pp. 24–49.

Mansel, H. L. (1863), 'Sensation Novels', *Quarterly Review*, 113, Apr., pp. 481–514.

Marryat, Florence, and Charles Young [1875], *Miss Chester*, London and New York: Samuel French.

Mayhew, Henry (1850), 'Interview between Henry Mayhew and William West, Monday, February 25, 1850', *Hugo's Toy Theatre*, <toytheatre.net/JKGFrame.htm> (last accessed 29 Nov. 2016).

Morley, Henry (1866), *The Journal of a London Playgoer from 1851–1866*, London: George Routledge & Sons.

Oliphant, Margaret (1862), 'Sensation Novels', *Blackwood's Magazine*, 91, May, pp. 574–80.

Palmer, T. A. (1874), *East Lynne: A Domestic Drama in a Prologue and Four Acts*, London: Samuel French.

Reade, Charles (1872 [1856]), *It Is Never Too Late to Mend: A Matter of Fact Romance*, Boston: James R. Osgood.

Sala, George Augustus (1867), 'The Cant of Modern Criticism', *Belgravia*, 4, Nov., pp. 45–55.

Sala, George Augustus (1868), 'On the Sensational in Literature and Art', *Belgravia*, 4, Feb., pp. 449–58.

Taylor, Tom (1863), *The Ticket of Leave Man* <http://victorian.nuigalway.ie/modx/assets/docs/pdf/Vol59iTicket.pdf> (last accessed 27 Nov. 2017).

Wood, Ellen, *East Lynne* (2000 [1861]), ed. Andrew Maunder, Peterborough, Ontario: Broadview.

Young, Charles (1873), 'The Woman About Town', *The Sporting Times*, 12 Oct., p. 320.

Secondary sources

Bailey, Peter (1998), *Popular Culture and Performance in the Victorian City*, Cambridge: Cambridge University Press.

Banerjee, S. (2014), 'Troubling Conjugal Loyalties: The First Indian Novel in English and the Transimperial Framework of Sensation', *Victorian Literature and Culture*, 42: 3, Sep., pp. 475–89.

Baugh, Christopher (2005), *Theatre, Performance and Technology: The Development of Scenography in the Twentieth Century*, London: Palgrave Macmillan.

Beller, Anne-Marie (2017), '"Fashions of the Current Season": Recent Critical Work on Sensation Fiction', *Victorian Literature and Culture*, 45: 2, Jun., pp. 461–73.

Beller, Anne-Marie, and Tara MacDonald (eds) (2013), 'Beyond Braddon: Reassessing Female Sensationalists', Special issue of *Women's Writing*, 20: 2, May.

— (eds) (2014), *Rediscovering Victorian Women Sensation Writers*, London: Routledge.

Bisla, Sundeep (2013), *Wilkie Collins and Copyright: Artistic Ownership in the Age of the Borderless World*, Athens: Ohio State University Press.

Booth, Michael R. (1981), *Victorian Spectacular Theatre 1850–1910*, Boston, London and Henley: Routledge and Kegan Paul.

— (1991), *Theatre in the Victorian Age*, Cambridge: Cambridge University Press.

Brantlinger, Patrick (1982), 'What is Sensational About the Sensation Novel?', *Nineteenth-Century Fiction*, 37: 1, Jun., pp. 1–28.

Bratton, Jacky (2003), *New Readings in Theatre History*, Cambridge: Cambridge University Press.

Brewster, Ben, and Lea Jacobs (1997), *Theatre to Cinema: Stage Pictorialism and the Early Feature Film*, Oxford: Oxford University Press.

Brodie, Marc (2004), *The Politics of the Poor: The East End of London 1885–1914*, Oxford: Clarendon Press.

Brooks, Peter (1995 [1976]), *The Melodramatic Imagination: Balzac, Henry James, Melodrama and the Mode of Excess*, New Haven, CT, and London: Yale University Press.

Burridge Lindemann, Ruth (1997), 'Dramatic Disappearances: Mary Elizabeth Braddon and the Staging of Theatrical Character', *Victorian Literature and Culture*, 25: 2, Fall, pp. 279–91.

Carnell, Jennifer (2000), *The Literary Lives of Mary Elizabeth Braddon: A Study of Her Life and Work*, Hastings: Sensation Press.

— (2008), 'Introduction', in William Suter, *Lady Audley's Secret*, Hastings: Sensation Press, pp. 7–12.

— (2016), *Mary Elizabeth Braddon and the Victorian Theatre*, Hastings: Sensation Press.

Cattell, Tracy (2015), 'Transmitting the Thinking: The Nineteenth-Century Stage Manager and the Adaptation of Text for Performance', *Nineteenth Century Theatre & Film*, May, 42: 1, pp. 39–49.

Chiles, Katy L. (2004), 'Blackened Irish and Brownfaced Amerindians: Constructions of American Whiteness in Dion Boucicault's *The Octoroon*', *Nineteenth Century Theatre & Film*, 31: 2, Nov., pp. 28–50.

Choudhury, Suchitra (2016), 'Fashion and the "Indian Mutiny": The "Red Paisley Shawl" in Wilkie Collins's *Armadale*', *Victorian Literature and Culture*, 44: 4, Dec., pp. 817–32.

Colley, Ann C. (2010), *Victorians in the Mountains: Sinking in the Sublime*, Abingdon and New York: Routledge.

Cook, Jim, and Christine Gledhill (eds) (1994), *Melodrama: Stage, Picture, Screen*, London: British Film Institute.

Costantini, Mariaconcetta (2015), *Sensation and Professionalism in the Victorian Novel*, Bern: Peter Lang.

Cox, Jessica (ed.) (2012), *New Perspectives on Mary Elizabeth Braddon*, Amsterdam: Rodopi.

Cox, Philip (2000), *Reading Adaptations: Novels and Verse Narratives on the Stage, 1790–1840*, Manchester: Manchester University Press.

Cvetkovich, Ann (1992), *Mixed Feelings: Feminism, Mass Culture, and Victorian Sensationalism*, New Brunswick, NJ: Rutgers University Press.

Daly, Nicholas (1999), 'Railway Novels: Sensation Fiction and the Modernization of the Senses', *ELH*, 66: 2, Summer, pp. 461–87.

— (2004), *Literature, Technology, and Modernity, 1860–2000*, Cambridge: Cambridge University Press.

— (2009), *Sensation and Modernity in the 1860s*, Cambridge: Cambridge University Press.

— (2015), *The Demographic Imagination and the Nineteenth-Century City: Paris, London, New York*, Cambridge: Cambridge University Press.

— (2017), 'Fire on Stage', *19: Interdisciplinary Studies in the Long Nineteenth Century*, 25.

Davis, Jim (1991), 'The Gospel of Rags: Melodrama at the Britannia 1863–74', *New Theatre Quarterly*, 7: 28, Nov., pp. 369–89.

— (ed.) (1992), *The Britannia Diaries 1863–1875: Selections from the Diaries of Frederick C. Wilton*, London: Society for Theatre Research.

— (1999), 'Sarah Lane: Questions of Authorship', in Tracy C. Davis and Ellen Donkin (eds), *Women and Playwriting in Nineteenth-Century Britain*, Cambridge: Cambridge University Press, pp. 125–47.

— (2006), 'Collins and the Theatre', in Jenny Bourne Taylor (ed.), *The Cambridge Companion to Wilkie Collins*, Cambridge: Cambridge University Press, pp. 168–80.

Davis, Jim, and Victor Emeljanow (2001), *Reflecting the Audience: London Theatregoing, 1840–1880*, Iowa City: University of Iowa Press.

Davis, Tracy (ed.) (2012), *The Broadview Anthology of Nineteenth-Century British Performance*, London and Toronto: Broadview.

Davis, Tracy C., and Peter Hollands (eds) (2007), *The Performing Century: Nineteenth-Century Theatre's History*, Basingstoke: Palgrave Macmillan.

Diamond, Michael (2003), *Victorian Sensation: Or, the Spectacular, the Shocking and the Scandalous in Nineteenth-Century Britain*, London: Anthem Press.

Dolan, Terence Patrick (2004), *A Dictionary of Hiberno-English*, 2nd edn, Dublin: Gill & Macmillan.

Donohue, Joseph (ed.) (2004), *The Cambridge History of British Theatre, Vol. 2 1660–1895*, Cambridge: Cambridge University Press.

Eltis, Sos (2013), *Acts of Desire: Women and Sex on Stage, 1800–1930*, Oxford: Oxford University Press.

Fantina, Richard (2010), *Victorian Sensational Fiction: The Daring Work of Charles Reade*, London: Palgrave Macmillan.

Fantina, Richard, and Kimberley Harrison (eds) (2006), *Victorian Sensations: Essays on a Scandalous Genre*, Columbus: Ohio State University Press.

Fawkes, Richard (2011 [1979]), *Dion Boucicault: A Biography*, London: Quartet.

Featherstone, Ann (2000), 'Shopping and Looking: Trade Advertisements in the *Era* and Performance History Research', *Nineteenth-Century Theatre & Film*, 28: 1, Jun., pp. 26–61.

Feldman, David (1994), *Englishmen and Jews: Social Relations and Political Culture, 1840–1914*, New Haven, CT, and London: Yale University Press.

Garrison, Laurie (2011), *Science, Sexuality and Sensation Novels: Pleasures of the Senses*, Basingstoke: Palgrave Macmillan.

Gilam, Abraham (1983), 'The Burial Grounds Controversy between Anglo-Jewry and the Victorian Board of Health, 1850', *Jewish Social Studies*, 45: 2, Spring, pp. 147–56.

Gilbert, Pamela K. (ed.) (2011), *A Companion to Sensation Fiction*, Malden: Wiley-Blackwell.

Gould, Marty (2011), *Nineteenth-Century Theatre and the Imperial Encounter*, New York and London: Routledge.

Hadley, Elaine (1995), *Melodramatic Tactics: Theatricalized Dissent in the English Marketplace, 1800–1885*, Stanford: Stanford University Press.

Hammett, Michael (ed.) (1986), *Plays by Charles Reade*, Cambridge: Cambridge University Press.

Hays, Michael (1995), *Melodramatic Formations*, Cambridge: Cambridge University Press.

Hays, Michael, and Anastasia Nikolopoulou (eds) (1999 [1996]), *Melodrama: The Cultural Emergence of a Genre*, New York: St Martin's Press.

Henderson, Ian (2004), 'Jacky-Kalingaloonga: Aboriginality, Audience Reception and Charles Reade's *It is Never Too Late To Mend* (1865)', *Theatre Research International*, 29: 2, Jul., pp. 95–110.

— (2006), 'Looking at Lady Audley: Symbolism, the Stage and the Antipodes', *Nineteenth Century Theatre & Film*, 33: 1, May, pp. 3–26.

Hofer-Robinson, Joanna (2018), *Dickens and Demolition: Literary Afterlives and Mid-Nineteenth-Century Urban Development*, Edinburgh: Edinburgh University Press.

Holder, Heidi J. (2000), 'Misalliance: M. E. Braddon's Writing for the Stage', in Marlene Tromp, Pamela Gilbert and Aeron Haynie (eds),

Beyond Sensation: Mary Elizabeth Braddon in Context, Albany: State University of New York Press, pp. 165–79.

— (2007), 'Nation and Neighbourhood, Jews and Englishmen: Location and Theatrical Ideology in Victorian London', in Tracy C. Davis and Peter Holland (eds), *The Performing Century: Nineteenth-century Theatre's History*, Basingstoke and New York: Palgrave Macmillan, pp. 105–20.

Howard, Diana (1970), *London Theatres and Music Halls*, London: Library Association.

Hughes, Winifred (1980), *The Maniac in the Cellar: Sensation Novels of the 1860s*, Princeton: Princeton University Press.

Johnson, Kathryn (2009), 'Gems from the Lord Chamberlain's Coal Cellars? An Informal Account of the Genesis, Progress and Results of the Buried Treasures Project', *Nineteenth Century Theatre & Film*, 36: 2, Nov., pp. 2–5.

Jones, Anna Maria (2007), *Problem Novels: Victorian Fiction Theorizes the Sensational Self*, Columbus: Ohio State University Press.

Kaplan, E. Ann (1992), *Motherhood and Representation: The Mother in Popular Culture and Melodrama*, London: Routledge.

Knight, Mark (2009), 'Figuring out the Fascination: Recent Trends in Criticism on Victorian Sensation and Crime Fiction', *Victorian Literature and Culture*, 37: 1, Mar., pp. 323–33.

Krause, David (ed.) (1964), *The Dolmen Boucicault*, Dublin: Dolmen Press.

McAleavey, Maia (2015), *The Bigamy Plot: Sensation and Convention in the Victorian Novel*, New York: Cambridge University Press.

McFeely, Deirdre (2012), *Dion Boucicault: Irish Identity on Stage*, Cambridge: Cambridge University Press.

Mangham, Andrew (ed.) (2007), *Wilkie Collins: Interdisciplinary Essays*, Newcastle upon Tyne: Cambridge Scholars.

— (ed.) (2013), *The Cambridge Companion to Sensation Fiction*, Cambridge: Cambridge University Press.

Mattacks, Kate (2015), '(Per)forming the Adaptive: Watts Phillips's The Woman in Mauve (1864/65) and the Sensation Genre as Commodity', *Nineteenth Century Theatre & Film*, 42: 1, May, pp. 66–79.

— (2016), 'Reading Theatre Writing: T. H. Lacy and the Sensation Drama', in Paul Raphael Rooney and Anna Gasperini (eds), *Media and Print Culture Consumption in Nineteenth Century Britain: The Victorian Reading Experience*, London: Palgrave Macmillan, pp. 183–97.

Maunder, Andrew (2013), 'Sensation Fiction on Stage', in Andrew Mangham (ed.), *The Cambridge Companion to Sensation Fiction*, Cambridge: Cambridge University Press, pp. 52–69.

Maunder, Andrew, and Grace Moore (eds) (2004), *Victorian Crime, Madness, and Sensation*, Aldershot: Ashgate.

Mayer, David (1980), *Henry Irving and The Bells*, Manchester: Manchester University Press.

— (1996), 'Changing Horses in Mid-Ocean: *The Whip* in Britain and America', in Michael Booth and Joel Kaplan (eds), *The Edwardian Theatre: Essays on Performance and the Stage*, Cambridge: Cambridge University Press, pp. 220–35.

— (2009), *Stagestruck Filmmaker: D.W. Griffiths and the American Theater*, Iowa City: University of Iowa Press.

Meer, Sarah (2009), 'Boucicault's Misdirections: Race, Transatlantic Theatre and Social Position in *The Octoroon*', *Atlantic Studies*, 6: 1, May, pp. 81–95.

— (2015), 'Adaptation, Originality and Law: Dion Boucicault and Charles Reade', *Nineteenth Century Theatre & Film*, 42: 1, May, pp. 22–38.

Meisel, Martin (1983), *Realizations: Narrative, Pictorial, and Theatrical Arts in Nineteenth-Century England*, Princeton: Princeton University Press.

Moody, Jane (2007), *Illegitimate Theatre in London, 1770–1840*, Cambridge: Cambridge University Press.

Nemesvari, Richard (2011), *Thomas Hardy, Sensationalism, and the Melodramatic Mode*, New York: Palgrave Macmillan.

Newey, Katherine (1997), 'Melodrama and Metatheatre: Theatricality in the Nineteenth-Century Theatre', *Journal of Dramatic Theory and Criticism*, 11: 2, Spring, pp. 85–100.

— (2005), *Women's Theatre Writing in Victorian Britain*, Basingstoke: Palgrave Macmillan.

Nicoll, Allardyce (2009), *A History of English Drama, 1660–1900, Vol. V, Part 2*, Cambridge: Cambridge University Press.

Norwood, Janice (2007), 'Sensation Drama? Collins's Stage Adaptation of The Woman in White', in Andrew Mangham (ed.), *Wilkie Collins: Interdisciplinary Essays*, Newcastle upon Tyne: Cambridge Scholars, pp. 222–36.

— (2009), 'The Britannia Theatre: Visual Culture and the Repertoire of a Popular Theatre', in Heinrich Anselm, Katherine Newey and Jeffrey Richards (eds), *Ruskin, the Theatre and Victorian Visual Culture*, Basingstoke: Palgrave Macmillan, pp. 135–53.

— (2014), 'Documents of Performance: The Assignments Book of the Britannia Theatre, Hoxton', *Nineteenth Century Theatre & Film*, 41: 1, May, pp. 85–95.

— (2015), 'Adaptation and the Stage in the Nineteenth Century', *Nineteenth-Century Theatre & Film*, 42: 1, May, pp. 3–8.

Palmer, Beth (2011), *Women's Authorship and Editorship in Victorian Culture*, Oxford: Oxford University Press.

Parkin, Andrew (ed.) (1987), *Selected Plays of Dion Boucicault*, Gerrards Cross: Colin Smythe/Washington, DC: The Catholic University of America Press.

Pate, George (2014), 'Daly, Boucicault, and Commercial Art in Late Nineteenth-Century Drama', *Theatre Symposium*, 22: 4, pp. 9–21.

Pearson, Richard (2007), '"Twin-Sisters" and "Theatrical Thieves": Wilkie Collins and the Dramatic Adaptation of *The Moonstone*', in Andrew Mangham (ed.), *Wilkie Collins: Interdisciplinary Essays*, Newcastle upon Tyne: Cambridge Scholars, pp. 208–21.

Phegley, Jennifer, John Cyril Barton and Kristin N. Huston (eds) (2012), *Transatlantic Sensations*, Farnham: Ashgate.

Pisani, Michael V. (2014), *Music for the Melodramatic Theatre in Nineteenth-Century London and New York*, Iowa City: University of Iowa Press.

Powell, Kerry (ed.) (2004), *The Cambridge Companion to Victorian and Edwardian Theatre*, Cambridge: Cambridge University Press.

Pykett, Lyn (1992), *The 'Improper' Feminine: The Women's Sensation Novel and New Woman Writing*, London: Routledge.

— (1994), *Sensation Fiction: From The Woman in White to The Moonstone*, Plymouth: Northcote Press.

Radcliffe, Caroline (2009), 'Remediation and Immediacy in the Theatre of Sensation', *Nineteenth Century Theatre & Film*, 36: 2, Oct., pp. 38–53.

— (2015), 'Behind Closed Doors: The Theatrical Uncanny and the Panoptical Viewer in the Dramas of Wilkie Collins', *Nineteenth-Century Theatre & Film*, 42: 1, May, pp. 80–98.

Radcliffe, Caroline, and Kate Mattacks (2009), 'From Analogues to Digital: New Resources in Nineteenth-Century Theatre', *19: Interdisciplinary Studies in the Long Nineteenth Century*, 8.

Ragussis, Michael (2010), *Theatrical Nation: Jews and Other Outlandish Englishmen in Georgian Britain*, Philadelphia: University of Pennsylvania Press.

Redmond, J. (ed) (1992), *Melodrama*, Cambridge: Cambridge University Press.

Richards, Jeffrey H. (ed.) (1997), *Early American Drama*, Harmondsworth: Penguin Books.

Rowell, George (1988), 'Glossary of Stage Terms', in George Rowell (ed.), *Nineteenth-Century Plays*, Oxford and New York: Oxford University Press, p. xiii.

Schwartz, Vanessa R. (1998), *Spectacular Realities: Early Mass Culture in Fin de Siècle Paris*, Berkeley and London: University of California Press.

Singer, Ben (2001), *Melodrama and Modernity: Early Sensational Cinema and its Contexts*, New York: Columbia University Press.

Smith, James L. (1973), *Melodrama*, London: Methuen.

— (1976), *Victorian Melodramas: Seven English, French and American Melodramas*, London: J. M. Dent.

Stephens, John Russell (1992), *The Profession of the Playwright: British Theatre 1800 – 1900*, Cambridge: Cambridge University Press.

Taylor, George (1989), *Players and Performances in the Victorian Theatre*, Manchester: Manchester University Press.

Thomson, Peter (ed.) (1984), *Plays by Dion Boucicault*, Cambridge: Cambridge University Press.

Tomaiuolo, Saverio (2010), *In Lady Audley's Shadow: Mary Elizabeth Braddon and Victorian Literary Genres*, Edinburgh: Edinburgh University Press.

Tromp, Marlene, Pamela Gilbert and Aeron Haynie (eds), *Mary Elizabeth Braddon in Context*, Albany, NY: State University of New York Press.

Voskuil, Lynn M. (2002), 'Feeling Public: Sensation Theater, Commodity Culture, and the Victorian Public Sphere', *Victorian Studies*, 44: 2, Winter, pp. 245–74.

— (2004), *Acting Naturally: Victorian Theatricality and Authenticity*, Charlottesville, VA: University of Virginia Press.

Waters, Hazel (2007), *Racism on the Victorian Stage: Representation of Slavery and the Black Character*, Cambridge: Cambridge University Press.

Watt-Smith, Tiffany (2010), 'Darwin's Flinch: Sensation Theatre and Scientific Looking in 1872' (Graduate Prize Essay Competition Winner, 2009), *Journal of Victorian Culture*, 15: 1, Apr., pp. 101–18.

Weig, Heidi (2017), 'Amateur Theatricals and the Dramatic Marketplace: Lacy's and French's Acting Editions of Plays', *Nineteenth-Century Theatre & Film*, 44: 2, Dec., pp. 1–19.

Wolff, Robert Lee (1979), *Sensational Victorian: Life and Fiction of Mary Elizabeth Braddon*, New York: Garland.

Ziter, Edward (2003), *The Orient on the Victorian Stage*, Cambridge: Cambridge University Press.

Web resources

(All last accessed 29 November 2018, unless otherwise indicated.)

British Newspaper Archive <https://www.britishnewspaperarchive.co.uk>

British Periodicals I and II <https://www.proquest.com/products-services/british_periodicals.html>

Cross, Gilbert and Joseph Donahue (eds), *The Adelphi Calendar: A Record of Dramatic Performances at a Leading Victorian Theatre* <https://www.umass.edu/AdelphiTheatreCalendar/pref.htm>

The Dion Boucicault Collection (USF Libraries) <https://www.lib.usf.edu/boucicault/>

The East London Theatre Archive (V&A) <http://www.elta-project.org/home.html> (last accessed 1 June 2018)

Gale Cengage Nineteenth Century Collections Online <https://www.gale.com/intl/primary-sources/nineteenth-century-collections-online>

Leeds Playbills (Leeds City Council) <http://www.leodis.net/playbills/>

The Mander and Mitchenson Collection <https://www.bristol.ac.uk/theatre-collection/>

National Fairground and Circus Archive (University of Sheffield) <https://www.sheffield.ac.uk/nfca/researchandarticles/sideshowexhibition-sacts>

National Library of Australia <https://www.nla.gov.au>

The Plays of Wilkie Collins: A Digital Archive <http://www.wilkiecollins-plays.net/>

Templeman Library Special Collections (University of Kent) <https://www.kent.ac.uk/library/specialcollections/>

The Victorian Plays Project <http://victorian.nuigalway.ie/modx/>

The Victorian Web <http://www.victorianweb.org>